T0367401

The
TransBeingness
of Man

GOD AND ULTIMATE REALITY

THOMAS MARTIN NEWALD

BALBOA.
PRESS
A DIVISION OF HAY HOUSE

Balboa Press books may be ordered through booksellers or by contacting:

Balboa Press
A Division of Hay House
1663 Liberty Drive
Bloomington, IN 47403
www.balboapress.com.au
1 (877) 407-4847

Because of the dynamic nature of the Internet, any web addresses or links contained in this book may have changed since publication and may no longer be valid. The views expressed in this work are solely those of the author and do not necessarily reflect the views of the publisher, and the publisher hereby disclaims any responsibility for them.

The author of this book does not dispense medical advice or prescribe the use of any technique as a form of treatment for physical, emotional, or medical problems without the advice of a physician, either directly or indirectly. The intent of the author is only to offer information of a general nature to help you in your quest for emotional and spiritual well-being. In the event you use any of the information in this book for yourself, which is your constitutional right, the author and the publisher assume no responsibility for your actions.

Print information available on the last page.

ISBN: 978-1-5043-0403-0 (sc)
ISBN: 978-1-5043-0404-7 (e)

Balboa Press rev. date: 08/22/2016

Dedicated
to my beloved grandson
Mitchell

Let us be like a bird for a moment perched
On a frail branch when he sings;
Though he feels it bend, yet he sings his song,
Knowing that he has wings.

Victor Hugo

Contents

Preface

I am not bound to win, but I am bound to be true.
I am not bound to succeed, but I am bound to live
up to what light I have.

Abraham Lincoln

In this book, I discuss and answer the following questions. What is the purpose and origin of life? What is our divine destiny? What is the ultimate and objective reality? What is Heaven? What is Hell? What are the formless, physical, purgatorial, and spiritual realms? What is the genesis of the universe? What is core reality? What is the nature of God? What is the difference between a personal and non-impersonal God? What is the nature of Man? What is the transbeingness of Man? What is the power behind our infinite self-conscious existence? What is the significance of alternative lives lived? What is the source of self-conscious thought? What is the origin and penalty for the committing of sin and evil?

The purpose of life is to experience our self-aware existence. Do not be misled by the seeming simplicity of this answer. The understanding of what it means to experience our lives as existence requires a new understanding of God, Man, and ultimate reality. This book consists of describing and discussing these new concepts and understandings.

Herein, I describe new understandings and interpretations of things spiritual, to serve as a thinking-tool to encourage the readers to seek, accept, obey, and honor the God-reality of their individual divine understanding. To ponder upon things spiritual is to self-identify with the purpose of our existence. I describe the contents of my book as philosophical spiritualism unattached to any specific religion.

Several years ago, I began to write down these new ideas and concepts which had somehow found entry into my self-consciousness. At the beginning of this writing process, I had not fully developed a mastery of these new understandings. However, as I wrote, re-wrote, and edited my material, my understandings of these new ideas continually increased.

I have not the slightest interest in whether or not anyone agrees or disagrees with the ideas I present. My sole desire is to share my thoughts so readers may find spiritual or philosophical things of interest to encourage the inner process of thought-pondering. In my opinion, one of the most significant components of our self-aware existence is the ability to ponder upon the forever unknowable.

In this manner, each of us discovers our individual, unique, and infinitely divine path of spiritual unfoldment, as we share together in the self-experiencing of our God-unified and individualized existence. I am always grateful for all the ideas, new or old, which encourages me to opine upon the significance of our forever united and individual self-beingness.

The vast majority of ideas in this book are original, or at least unique in their presentation. In the writing of this book, I learned where ideas came from, and so will you as you read its contents; however, I have no understanding, whatsoever, why these new ideas and concepts came to me. I found these new ideas interesting, and I thought others might also find them interesting; hence, my authorship of this work.

I have no in-depth training, credentials, or accomplishments in the fields of philosophy, theology, or science. As I wrote this book, in my six times twelve, plus two years of my present life span, all of my previous attempts to understand, accept, and demonstrate things spiritual have been woefully inadequate. Thus, the purpose and understanding of existence and ultimate reality have been a life-long mystery. Writing this book has not particularly made me a better person, but it has pointed me in the direction to become a better person.

It behooves each one of us to discover for ourselves, the God of our understanding. In my life travels, I have encountered numerous religions; studied a few. However, I never encountered any religion that provided me with satisfactory answers, for my spiritual searching inquiries.

Virtually, all religions profess to have the one true understanding of God, and the true relationship of God to man. My life-long nature has been to reject such claims of pontifical nonsense, but I always listened to anyone's spiritual ideas in the hope of finding something spiritually meaningful even though discovering new spiritual insights rarely happens. Thus, I am not now a follower, member, adherent, practitioner, or exponent of any religion, organized or unorganized. I choose to be my teacher, thinker, and guide.

However, even as I recognize the spiritual frailty of all religious faiths, I have often pondered to myself, what a wonderful blessing it is for individuals who have found and accepted religious teachings, which provided them with divine happiness, comfort, and serenity. They have discovered the spiritual pathways to their true understanding of divinity, realized, and experienced. For these divine fortunates, the blessings of this life, both here and hereafter are theirs' to enjoy.

My only counsel to them would be to continue to follow their accepted spiritual beliefs and progress in their spiritual understandings and continue to evolve spiritually, to be the very best that they can be. Thus, each day their spiritual understandings increase beyond the day previous. In this manner, individuals resonate with the religious beliefs compatible to their self-conscious yearnings, for the discovering of things divine, in their continuing allegiance to the God of their understanding.

It is my belief that anyone's understanding of God is the manifesting of universal spirituality if that understanding encourages respect for all life, in combination with expressions of kindness to all, and a self-fulfilling love of God. Thus, there is only one God and that one God is forever identified, understood, and individually accepted by all of us.

In the writing of this work, I have absolutely no desire whatsoever to criticize anyone's sacred tenets; I am merely expressing my understandings of God, Man, and ultimate reality. I never understood why some individuals get so worked-up by the spiritual understandings of others when it comes to the nature of God. Religion is like ice cream, it comes in many flavors, with everyone believing his or her divine flavor preference is superior to others. This book is going to give some individuals spiritual heartburn, but hopefully, it is going to make them think of how to answer many of my observations. To me, that is what makes the world go around.

No one, possessing self-conscious awareness was ever given the Shakespearean option: "To be or not to be." This book represents my understandings of our infinite individualized existence, God's infinite individualized existence, and the substance of ultimate reality itself. If we cannot understand the purpose for why we exist, our infinite existence seems to be self-consciously meaningless.

Our individual self-aware existence as live our lives is a forever process, corresponding to the continuous revealing of our self-identity to ourselves. As honest, sincere seekers of truth, we acknowledge the things we understand, confirm the things we desire, and accept the things we cherish.

To recognize and accept ideas, without an understanding meaningful to ourselves, represents a stumbling and faltering faith which embraces concepts and ideas that often appear non-comprehensible. Our ability to self-consciously understand our existence and existence itself gives us the power, purpose, and potentiality for experiencing the foreverness of ultimate reality.

Our infinite existence is one of spiritual discovery forever expressed incrementally, with failure always dangling doggedly as an ever-present, persistent, and consistent companion. Thus, in the realm of things spiritual, we are often incapable of attaining and maintaining a sense of spiritual relevance or certitude.

All seeming spiritual failures represent our non-spiritual understandings, as we continually experience our existence. The mere process of experiencing our foreverness commands and demands the encountering of failures, because if we never experienced failures, our spiritual wings would remain untested, unused, and without the divine strength needed to discover our individual self-identities.

Thus, we could never interpret our infinite existence, and thereby never experience the joys infinite beingness affords. Therefore, no matter how we choose to experience our forever beingness, our infinite existence involves the spiritual overcoming of failures. The overcoming of failures enables each one of us to evolve spiritually as we forever interpret our self-emerging divinity.

Our individualized mind is God's mind expressing through each one of us individually. Within our individualized mind, we are always in possession of a free will controlling, determining, and streaming through our forever spiritual and non-spiritual self-evolving journeys. Our free will provides us the divine transmuting ability to change failures into spiritual successes. Any failure is merely an unknown spiritual success self-conscious being experience, at the evolving spiritual level of our divine understanding. Sometimes we use our free will to cede control of our self-evolving spiritual destiny to the illusionary and mesmerizing effects of unreality.

All spiritual awakenings or reawakenings begin with our desire to uncover and reveal to ourselves, our true divine identity. Our forever spiritual awakenings and reawakenings result in our infinite urge to self-understand and divinely realize our predestined destiny etched into our forever beingness, which is to experience the infinite realms of objective reality in combination and coordination, with the infinite inner realms of God's Self-Beingness.

The substance of this book consists of describing the various aspects of ultimate reality and their relationship to our infinite existence. Each one of us is one component of ultimate reality and ultimate reality never changes in its infinite identity. Therefore, our infinite divine nature and our infinite divine destiny can never be permanently abridged, altered, changed, or affected by anything possessing real infinite existence.

The only way for each of us to find the true God of our understanding and acceptance is through our continuing and self-conscious desire to discover, uncover, and recover things spiritual, combined with our desired willingness to practice kindness, tolerance, and forgiveness in harmony with a reverence for all of life. There is no other way.

Spiritual understanding is the delivering source for all salvation. As we seek and find God in a kind and loving manner, we become the self-conscious originators for all of our forever ongoing need of salvation. Thus, all things needed for our continuing spiritual advancement, understanding, and growth become available to us, as we progress along pathways divine, where our individual spiritual destiny is forever present, forever assured, and permanently secured.

A key concept in this book is the realization that our self-understanding and self-interpretation of all things occurs within the confines of our uniquely individualized self-conscious minds. Thus, each of us possesses the ability to understand, interpret, and experience our infinite self-existence. Our collective understanding of ultimate reality barely chafes the facade of infinity.

Ultimate reality is uniquely and infinitely realized and explained by each one of us individually. Imagine how dull and colorless our infinite self-aware existence would be, if we were void of the capability of grasping and understanding the nature of ultimate reality, with all its wonderments, diversities, mysteries, and enchantments.

Our continuing capability for comprehending reality is a forever self-functioning process of our objective existence. Each of us is innately designed to understand all phases of our infinite existence. These understandings impel us towards things spiritual, which then become the source of our ongoing blessings. However, no understanding of ourselves ever results in a final apprehension of our infinite self-aware foreverness.

The things we cherish in our thoughts are the things we attract to ourselves. If we love the goodness of truth, our forever self-existence is a blessing. When it comes to the things non-provable, there is no definitive commonality of answers, because, in the course of our understandings in the living of life itself, those understandings are the things we cherish in our thoughts are the things we attract to ourselves. If we love the goodness of truth, our forever self-existence is a blessing infinite.

A careful reader of this work will notice that I, at times, change the emphasis on the worthiness of our infinite existence. I could have edited out any waverings in my evolving understanding, but I have no reason not to be forthright, other than to look foolish.

We are infinite spiritual beings, inheriting a forever and spiritual kingdom, for each of us to discover, interpret, and make meaningful and relevant to ourselves. I wrote this book, in part, for those who revere the desire to seek, find, understand, and accept things spiritual because things spiritual represent the only true value there is in the experiencing of our infinite existence.

To enhance my book's originality, I now and then created new words, or I used unusual words rarely found in printed text. The context surrounding these words easily shows their intended meanings. Whenever I created new words or used rare words, I placed them in italics to emphasize their uniqueness.

Throughout my writing, I quoted many notable luminaries to augment the newness of my thoughts. I placed my favorite quotation, written by Victor Hugo, at the very beginning. His words are simple yet deeply profound, and this book is in part, an interpretation of those words.

I searched a long time for a suitable title. I required a title to complement my book's originality. I came with numerous title options only to discover those titles had been previously appropriated. Then the word *transbeingness* came to me. To my astonishment, when I entered it into a google search, it did not register a single hit.

In these writings, I have strived to be consistently logical within the framework of these newly acquired ideas. However, due to the poverty of language, I discovered that to be a daunting task, because things I consider logical or illogical are often dependent upon a subjective understanding and interpretation of the material.

Thus, the things I recognize as logical, others may not. However, I know what I have written: I understand what I have written, and I believe what I have written. Therefore, I assert, as the authoring scribe, that there are no contradictions in the content of this work when viewed and understood in the entirety of its presentations.

Until I felt compelled to write this book, I had no desire to be an author; in fact, I never thought myself capable of writing a book of this nature. I am not a person predisposed to be long in the narrative of expression, whether verbal or written. This book is a major exception to my innate nature.

The vast majority of the ideas in this book came to my self-consciousness, shortly before I set pen to them. When I started writing, I felt I had two choices: write what I was inspired to write without question, or question the ideas I was inspired to write. I chose the former. Hopefully, my new concepts and ideas were inspired rather than mentally forced, but who knows?

In my objective understanding of my capabilities and the books length and contents, I anticipate that it will have few readers. However, that realization gave me the freedom to express my unvarnished thoughts. Basically, what difference does it make what I write if it is only destined to have few readers? Still, I always tried to be faithful to my inspirations.

Also, I ask the reader to bear with me. In the writing of this book, I encountered what I thought to be random bouts of inspiration. I knew from previous experiences, in the scribbling down of my thoughts, that if I did not put them down quickly, they would vanish forever from my self-consciousness. Thus, at times, you will find that I temporarily break off from the topic under discussion, to drop in a quick inspiration.

The writing of a book of this nature has been challenging and arduous. Often, I was consumed with self-doubt. This book has taken me years to write and edit, especially edit. Even now, just before it goes to print, I believe I have foolishly wasted my time. To continuingly doubt any value in new understanding is assuredly an unwelcome, unneeded, and unwanted burden.

If I thought this book was destined for a wide readership, I most likely would have, in many instances, used different phraseology or terminology. However, my authorship *scribings* honor the wandering ideas and inspirations that somehow found their way into my self-conscious awareness, for better or worse.

I repeat, for our individual and shared divine destiny to be spiritualized realized, divine truth must be desired, sought, acknowledged, accepted, and combined with the expression of kindness, in combination with a love of God, and a reverence for all life. This self-conscious process for discovering the truth of our infinite existence is the sacred distinguishing feature of our forever divine nature.

To evolve in our understanding and interpretation of ideas is our forever preordained divine destiny of forever beingness, implanted into all aspects of our infinite existence. Why or how I do not know. It is simply the infinite nature of our infinite existence. However, once again, the purpose of our forever beingness is to experience our forever beingness.

Thus, we exist to know, understand, and experience the reality of whom and what we infinitely are, so that we can realize the infinity of our unfolding self-divine identity of ourselves, to ourselves. This book is my contribution to a new and meaningful understanding of God, Man, and ultimate reality.

I realize my book is lengthy, and thus many individuals will be discouraged from reading it. I could have written an abridged version, but I choose to put forth these insights as given to me. Thus, you will find that I repeat myself, once and again, as new tinges of insight inspired me.

I have a recommendation for anyone who may choose to read my book. First, read the introduction. In the introduction, I discuss the main ideas described throughout this work. After reading the introduction, read the first chapter, in which I discuss critique, and expand upon my evolving understanding of the nature of God. After that, read the book in any order.

My ideas are presented in such a manner as to be read, in virtually any sequence or non-sequence of presentation. I found it interesting that the same or similar ideas can be understood and interpreted, with slightly different nuances, giving slightly different meanings. That realization made writing my book a somewhat enjoyable experience, albeit complicated, challenging, and time-consuming.

Finally, if you are an individual who's not religiously orientated, not a member of any religion; yet, possess a spiritual sense about the nature of life and existence, and intuitively know that there is an infinite God, you may find my book interesting. However, if you are an individual who belongs to a religion that meets your spiritual needs, which assuredly is a good thing; you would most likely be wasting your time reading my thoughts, ideas, and concepts on God, life, and existence.

T. M. N.

Introduction

If all mankind minus one were of one opinion, and only one person were of the contrary opinion, mankind would be no more justified in silencing that one person, then he, if he had the power, would be justified in silencing mankind.

John Stewart Mill

Following is a summary of the new ideas contained in this work, to familiarize the reader with them before being discussed in detail. In this introduction, I am only describing my book's main new ideas. There are subsets to these new ideas revealed and reviewed throughout this material.

Ultimate Reality

There is no reality outside of ultimate reality. Thus, ultimate reality is all-inclusive and consists of the following components: God; Man; the Idea Realm; objective reality; the formless, physical, purgatorial, and spiritual realms; core reality; matter; real and non-real experiences; and infinite void. Ultimate reality expands infinitely, but within itself and infinite void.

Objective Reality

For the purpose of clarity, I use the term objective reality, instead of ultimate reality, when discussing our individual and collective experiencing, of our actual physical realm existence. Objective reality is the portion of ultimate reality giving each of us, the capability of experiencing existence.

Specifically, objective reality includes the following components of ultimate reality: the formless, physical, purgatorial, and spiritual worlds; matter, real and non-real experiences; the idea realm; and a portion of the infinite void. Non-real experiences are claims to real existence, but they have no infinite real substance, lives, or identities of their own. However, the objective realm unknowingly provides an environment for the expression of non-reality, through the self-conscious thinking process of each one of us.

In the objective realm, each of us is the Self-consciousness of God understanding and realizing our destiny, as we infinitely experience our objective existence. God does not experience His forever Infinite Beingness; hence, He has no knowledge, understanding, or awareness of objective reality, other than the realizing of His Self-infinite existence, as a portion of ultimate reality, of which He has no Self-awareness.

However, due to God's ever-presence within each one of us, He is present in objective reality, whenever we are individually and collectively present. It is our spiritual destiny to interpret objective and ultimate reality, through our infinitely progressing spiritual understandings of ourselves, and our forever self-identities in God.

To objective reality, nothing is new, and nothing is old. Objective reality is the realm where universes explode into evolving and unique physical existences, which includes the type of world we are presently experiencing. Eventually, all created cosmoi or infinities implode out of their identifiable realities, returning them to their pre-created formless state of existence.

This compressed state of matter in flux now becomes the base substance-force for the creation of the next new universe. Thus, the imploding energy from the old universe provides the required new energy for the next new Big Bang explosion, to create the next new universe, new world, new eternity, new cosmos, or new infinity, whatever term is preferred.

The exploding or the Big-Bang creation of a new universe, into objective existence, evolves through the infinite and unpredictable contrivances of chance, opportunity, randomness, and general unpredictability which function in a symbiotic relationship with idea realm ideas. Each new physical world is created for each of us to experience, as the infinite, individualized, and indestructible self-conscious in and of God.

Our understandings and interpretations of objective reality decree the sifting-shifting understanding of all things self-consciously experienced. Thus, objective reality exists for our understanding and interpretation to realize and comprehend our existence, God's existence, and existence itself.

Therefore, the external environmental world allows for the expressions of the actual realities and false realities impacting our ever evolving self-understandings, as determined by our self-actuating self-conscious choices. Thus, in the objective realm, real and unreal experiences seemingly intermix and comingle, as we individually, collectively, and infinitely understand and interpret our existence.

Correctly understood, all functionings within objective reality exist simultaneously, meaning no actual happenings have any beginnings or endings. Thus, all processes, within objective reality, represent the infinite expressions of objective reality's encapsulated and infinite wholeness.

Without our individualized self-conscious ability to interpret physical existence, there would be no interpretations of any appearances, in objective reality, which from our perspectives have seeming beginnings or endings. There would only be the wholeness of infinite objective reality, not understood, not interpreted, and not self-consciously experienced.

If that were the case, objective reality would be infinite real existence, existing for no purpose; thus, it would be infinite meaningless existence. Therefore, any form of expression, without an infinite identifiable utility, would be an infinite meaningless reality. It is not comprehensible to me that there could be such a thing as infinite real existence having no purpose, for existing infinitely.

Core Reality

Core reality consists of God and God's expression, individualized-Man. God's expression of Man comprises the totality of God's individualized self-aware family. In core reality, God and individualized-Man are only self-consciously aware of their infinite existence, in the forever harmony of divine blissfulness. Thus, in core reality, individualized-Man is self-aware of his infinite beingness forever embedded in God. However, God has no Self-awareness of the collective or individual existence of the man of this world.

Neither individualized-Man nor God self-consciously experiences core reality; thus, core reality is not self-consciously understood or interpreted. Therefore, in core reality, the self-thinking capability of self-conscious thought is not known to God or us. In core reality, there is only the self-realization of our individualized-Man's infinite, blissful self-knowingness and the infinite, blissful forever existence of God's Self-knowingness.

In core reality, our self-realizing of our continuing existence and God's Self-realizing of His continuing existence is pure divinity Self-absorbing Itself. Here, each of us, as individualized-Man, is entirely self-unified with God; hence, there is no separation between the individualized-Us and the totality of God. Here, we are the individualized b of God knowing Himself, to Himself, as Himself.

In core reality, God's is forever unfolding in His Self-divine Beingness. God's infinite unfolding Beingness belongs to Him alone; therefore, His perpetual spiritual unfolding is not an aspect of our individualized-Man self-identity. We only possess the capability of understanding God's unfolding nature, but that capability is only available in objective reality.

As individualized core-Man, we are only capable of self-consciously absorbing God's unfolding nature. In our self-conscious core reality existence, we do not spiritually unfold within ourselves. Outside of our core reality beingness, each one of us has an individual, unique, and special destiny to discover, follow, obey, and self-realize.

Core reality consists of the purity of joy and harmony Self-known by God and self-known by each of us. However, the experiencing of our infinite existence necessitates our exiting from core reality and descending into the formless realm of objective reality. For each of us, core reality is self-known and objective reality is self-experienced.

In core reality, we have no destiny to discover, understand, or interpret; we only exist in the joyful blissfulness of our self-aware forever God-derived existence. Thus, in core reality, we have no self-determining destiny to be self-realized; we are only participants in a core-divine ongoing divine destiny, forever structured into our infinite individualized existence.

When we leave core reality for objective reality, we are consigned and resigned to an individual and collectively shared objective existence and destiny. At that time, our individually unfolding future becomes the self-conscious understanding, interpreting, and experiencing of our divinely infinite indestructible self-conscious objective beingness.

Each time, we are propelled from core reality into objective reality; we enter into a reality which involves the infinite production of eternities. In core reality, we only know the wholeness of our divinity. In the objective realm, we only understand our divinity in finite-infinite bonds of our encapsulated spirituality.

Repeating, for any infinite real existence to be meaningful, its existence must have a definite purpose. If we were to remain infinitely in core reality, objective reality would remain forever meaningless. The sole purpose of objective reality is for each of us to understand, interpret, and experience our self-aware presence, as an infinite individualized reality within ultimate reality.

The mechanics involved in exiting core reality and entering objective reality are not known. However, our descent from core reality into objective reality is triggered when we become self-consciously bored with our blissfully-idyllic core reality self-aware existence. When that happens, we are involuntarily propelled from core reality into objective reality to experience our existence.

Core reality is intolerant of any individualized self-knowingness of boredom. If our infinite self-aware existence were ever to become infinitely boring, our infinite self-existence would become infinite excruciating torment. Did you ever consider the realization that an infinite self-awareness of blissful existence could ever become a self-aware existence of infinite boringness, which would then become an infinite self-aware existence of endless self-suffering?

Therefore, if we never truly experienced our forever existence, we would self-consciously remain in core reality, without purpose, motivation, or desire to understand the who, the what, and the why of our forever beingness. We would remain self-aware of an infinite, blissful existence, and nothing more. You have heard it said: "Too much of a good thing is a bad thing."

Thus, our non-motivated infinite divine self-aware core-existence, although blissful, cannot be infinitely understood, but it can be and does become spiritually mind-numbing. Our self-existence, to be meaningful, must be experienced. Thus, the self-experiencing understanding of our infinite individualized existence is a forever categorical imperative.

However, this concept of the self-understanding of our self-existence is not applicable to God because God's nature is forever and endlessly unfolding within Himself. Thus, within God's infinite nature, there is no need or requirement for Him to experience existence. To God, His existence is the only existence, and His existence is the infinite unfolding of forever newness. Thus, He Self-consciously experiences His existence, if one chooses to apply the idea of experience to God, as the forever Self-knowingness of forever divine newness.

God's existence is the fulfillment and the fulfilling of infinite wholeness, wholiness, and harmony beyond anything any of us are capable of apprehending. One of the primary differences between God and each of us, as the individualized expression of God, is that God never becomes Self-consciously bored, in His infinite unchallenged existence.

In core reality, we know the forever harmonious blissfulness without any self-seeking effort. However, in the experiencing of our objective existence, the realizing of harmony and blissfulness must be earned and obtained, through our continuous self-progressing efforts to understand things spiritual. Thus, in the objective realm, the understanding of our forever divinity requires our self-conscious mentally directed efforts to be the self-conscious expression of our forever divinity.

In core reality, the knowingness of our forever blissfulness is infinitely attained and requires no continuous self-initiating effort whatsoever. It is interesting that our infinitely unchanging self-aware existence of God-filled blissfulness is not necessarily a desirable forever unchanging self-realization, considering that it is the idea of harmonious bliss that we seek to experience in the objective realm.

There is an old philosophical conundrum asking: "Would you rather be an unhappy Socrates or a happy pig"? I believe most individuals would choose to be an unhappy Socrates self-aware of existence including the experiencing of life which combines happiness with unhappiness, rather than a non-self-aware of life, consisting solely of the realization of bliss-filled happiness.

It is hard for me to see the desirability of an infinite existence of blissfulness self-consciously realized. It seems evident that such self-awareness would inevitably become infinitely tedious. If an individual enjoyed keeping busy, then in a forever blissfully pleasant heavenly environment all that he or she could ever do, would be to keep busy being blissful.

We could never become infinitely bored, in the objective realm, because we are finite-infinitely self-choosing our self-desired experiences, as each of us is encountering the process of infinite self-conscious existence. Thus, in the objective realm, we always have the option of choosing boredom or non-boredom. In core reality, we do not have that option.

Our spiritual blissfulness in core reality is, in a sense, both unearned and earned. Our infinite core blissful existence is spiritually unearned because our forever indestructible divine beingness is unearned. Thus, in core reality, we are infinitely self-consciously being our infinite self-conscious beingness of total divine perfection. However, core reality is also earned through our infinite self-conscious spiritual progression and evolvement through the objective realm. When we become totally spiritually victorious, in the objective realm, we return to core reality. Still, in core reality, we are totally self-consciously realizing our perfect spirituality, not experiencing it.

The objective realm is different. Here, we evolve from the non-understanding of God to the understanding and knowingness of God. As we objectively evolve, we learn about God, ourselves, our relationship to God, and ultimate reality. In this process of self-evolving spiritual learning, we come to understand the reason for our forever existence, and our spiritual purpose for self-realizing our existence. For our objectively successful evolvement of spiritual awareness, we are spiritually rewarded by being permitted to abide self-consciously in the spiritual realm, or Heaven, until the end of the eternity we are occupying.

In core reality, the experiencing existence as life or even the capability to experience existence as life is not possible. Struggles, pains, heartaches, and sorrows, ever-present in the objective physical realm, are entirely non-existent in the core realm of our self-awareness. In core reality, our existence is the forever self-realization of Godliness without opposition of any real or non-real forces of beingness.

In core reality, there is only the infinite harmony of wholeness forever self-realized, as we infinitely self-consciously ingest the knowingness of our forever self-divinity. Thankfully, in the objective realm, there are continuous finite-infinite interruptions and experiences, not self-known in core reality.

In the objective realm, we forever determine our eternal destiny, but the forever ingrained direction of our existing self-foreverness is never permanently altered. We are forever destined to express our built-in divine nature. In the objective realm, each one of us becomes the self-understood divinity of our infinity. Still, in that realization, not one of us ever asked for the infinite self-aware existence we infinitely possess.

Thus, we are infinitely and intermittently destined to experience objective existence. What greater gift does infinity provide for us, than the gift of being capable of understanding and experiencing our forever existence? We forever exist to self-realize and self-be our infinite existence.

Inside core reality, we forever self-know our infinite divinely-enthralled existence. Outside of core reality, we forever self-understand, self-interpret, and self-experience our infinitely ordained destiny. Thus, we infinitely exist in two aspects of our infinite beingness. We are forever individualized core-Man, and we are forever individualized objective-Man.

Inside of core reality, we only know the blissfulness of our God-filled destiny as wholeness and wholiness. Outside of core reality, we experience the infinite wonders of objective reality as we understand and interpret our individualized self-identities, through the non-real realm of experiencing our existence.

Each one of us is an infinite, individual, and indestructible part of God. We have infinitely existed, we exist now, and we will infinitely exist. We did not ask for everlasting life as self-aware existence. Our infinite self-aware existence is a part of ultimate reality. In core reality, we exist without a free will. In objective reality, we exist with a free will. Our free will allows each of us to determine the expression, the direction, destiny of the self-realizing of our divinity.

Idea Realm

The idea realm is the forever objective domain source for all ideas. All ideas exist for us to gain the forever acquisition of knowledge and comprehension which enables us to self-establish ongoing understandings of God, current understandings of ourselves, and constant self-understandings of existence itself.

The idea realm, in infinite association and collaboration with our self-awareness, gives each of us the capability for self-conscious thought. Core reality has no relationship with the idea realm. Thus, we do not self-consciously think in core reality. Ideas are only self-accepted in their infinite interdependence with the objective realm.

Our individualized free will is an independent function designed into our infinite existence. Ideas give us the ability to understand and experience the power of our free will. It is our designed nature to divinely self-harness our free will to seek and find the understanding and purpose of our forever existence.

Our free will functions independently of our self-understood Godliness, or non-Godliness. Our free will, combined with our ability to understand, gives each one of us the capability for interpreting ultimate and objective reality. However, it is our self-determined proclivities, in the living of life that shape, color, authorize, and explain the directions of our desired intentions.

Thus, without the desire to follow the divine spark, within each of us, to seek, find, understand, and unite in the accepting of our relationship to God, our interpretations of the objective realm remain in an echoless abyss of self-realized, self-accepted, and self-cherished frigid godlessness.

When we accept the wickedness of godlessness, we have unabashedly dishonored the gift of our self-aware divinely-based existence. Thus, we must come to the understanding that the realizing of our divine spirituality, must begin with our desire to embrace the ever-presence of divine goodness, forever within ourselves and forever outside of ourselves.

The desire for things spiritual results from our self-evaluations, in the experiencing of our existence. It is the self-reviewing of our experiencing of objective reality as life, which leads us to the self-awareness and self-acceptance of our forever spiritual identity in eternal progression. This subject is discussed more thoroughly, in the purgatorial-Man section of this work.

In the objective realm, chance often is instrumental in determining the footpaths of the desired destiny we take, in the realizing of our ongoing existence. However, it is possible to mitigate the influence of unpredictability, by spiritually attracting the wholeness of ideas, for the self-realizing of our divine destiny. The greater we allow the forces of unpredictability to grind on us; the greater is our drift from our God-centered self-awareness.

Ideas provide us with understanding the meaning, purpose, and experiencing of our forever existence. The expression of ideas in any aspect of objective reality fulfills their purpose for existence. Ideas are forever circling and interjecting themselves into the objective realm, but they know nothing of how they are being incorporated, utilized, or assimilated.

Thus, all ideas are omnipresent and are continuously seeking a means and opportunity for objective acceptance and expression. Some ideas are designed and established for the creative evolving of universes. Some ideas are specifically assigned and designated for incorporation, into our experiencing of existence, through our individualized self-awareness.

Ideas permeate objective reality devoid of any self-consciously directed volition. Within themselves, ideas provide the power impetus for the forming and evolving processes, in the seeming creation of universes. The functionings of the ever-presence of ideas are like the assembling of infinite puzzles. Thus, objective reality is an infinite mosaic of ideas forever building upon themselves to ever new expressions of reality. Ideas exist to find harmonious acceptance in the objective realm. Ideas are the inner and outer understandings of all things real. Without ideas, objective reality would be non-comprehensible and thus meaningless.

Ideas interact with us corresponding to the intensity of our desires. Thus, in the objective realm, ideas continually bombard our individualized self-awareness for our acceptance and confirmation. However, we only objectively confirm self-conscious understanding and interpretation to those endlessly wandering ideas which are compatible to our evolving self-receptive self-conscious awareness.

Each one of us possesses the ability to understand or misunderstand the real true meanings of all ideas. There is an infinite ever-presence of ideas awaiting our recognition, understanding, acceptance, and confirmation. The forever flowing fount of ideas prevents our objective existence from ever becoming continuously self-consciously boring and stale.

All ideas are infinite in their capability of being incorporated into the functionings of objective reality. The symbiotic relationship between physical realm universes and idea realm ideas rests on the forever catalysts of chance, opportunity, randomness, and general unpredictability. Thus, it is randomness alone that often provides the means for wondering ideas to fulfill their purposes for existence.

In all evolving created physical worlds, varying combinations of ideas are made manifest, through incremental building blocks of sub-set ideas. Ideas provide each new physical world, in a newly created universe, its unique identity, and history. All creation forming ideas are uniquely whole, complete, perfect, and harmonious.

Free Will

I did a little research on the subject of free will, and it seems somewhat mentally sticky, obtuse, and confusing. Thus, I will just present my understanding of our forever self-existing free will, as the individualized indestructible Man of infinity. It seems self-evident, that if we, as self-conscious beings did not possess a free will, the self-realizing of our existence would be meaningless. We would be mere animals with no self-choosing destiny to understand, fulfill, or experience.

I see two issues to deal with in discussing the subject of free will. First, there is understanding of free will from the standpoint of the existence of an all-knowing God. Second, how do the factors of chance, opportunity, randomness, and general unpredictability, in our experiencing of life as reality, affect our free will choices?

If an all-knowing God exists, He would know all of our life choices before we made them. Therefore, we would seemingly have no free will because, as we live our lives, our choices would always be in agreement with the knowledge of an all-knowing God. However, just because an all-knowing God knows what choices we will make in any situation does not mean that our choices are not free will choices.

As we live our lives, the reality of unpredictability is always impacting and assaulting us. There is no question that the unpredictabilities of life limit our free will choices. For example, in an unforeseen emergency, it seems that the only free will choices we have are to attempt to survive or not survive.

However, disregarding the unpredictable events relating to our physical survival, all the unpredictable things we encounter in the experiencing of life, limit to some degree our free will choices. That is because we almost always make our free will decisions, on what is most advantageously desirable to us. Thus, all of our free will choices are predictable, to a significant extent.

Each one of us is an immortal, infinite being. We possess infinite self-awareness, a spiritually non-self-judgmental free will, and the capacity to understand all aspects of infinite reality. Now, from my present understanding of free will, our free will is completely unrestrained, in the dealing with any factors outside of our individual self-awareness.

Therefore, our infinite free will along with our unlimited capability to understand all aspects of reality, combined with the realization that God, makes each one of us potentially all-powerful. The potential power of our free will gives each of us the potentiality of changing any experience, predictable or unpredictable, into the manifestation of God's nature expressing visibly.

Thus, each of us has the free will understanding capability of eliminating any adverse effects of predictability or unpredictability, and we also have the forever capability of overriding all the so-called universal laws operating in ultimate reality. However, the exercising of this all-powerful ability is dependent upon the infinite depth of our spiritual understanding and development self-realized. Our free will gives us forever control in our self-determining experiencing of our infinite existence.

Our forever self-discovering of our all-powerfulness is the continuing potentiality of our forever objective existence. Of course, not one of us is presently all-powerful. We have existed infinitely, but we are still at a fledgling state in our developing spirituality. We can only use our free will to determine self-knowingly our existence based on the depth of our acceptance of God. Still, we will always have infinity to discover the all-powerfulness of our forever true divine selves.

Physical/Purgatorial/Spiritual Worlds

The physical, purgatorial, and spiritual worlds represent a portion of objective reality, and they exist for each of us to objectively experience our existence. The origin of all universes consists of infinite matter in formless flux. Each contiguous evolving infinite-like universe begins with a Big Bang and continues through ever-evolving forms of ongoing progressions. These evolutionary processes require continuous interactions with idea realm ideas.

All components of objective reality exist without prescribed beginnings or endings. However, the eternities appearing in objective reality do seem to have beginnings and endings; but the creative and de-creative progressions of physical worlds are part of an infinite seemingly creative continuum. From the overview of objective existence, all things apparently created are reality's components in an endless progression.

Thus, all appearances of objective reality, including universes, and the world we self-consciously inhabit, appear as having seeming beginnings and endings, but are merely endless baseless arcs, in the wholeness of forever existence. One present expression of infinity is but one of an ongoing string of infinities.

Each universe expands until it eventually ceases expansion. Then it collapses in upon itself and returns to its original primordial state of formlessness. This single process I understand, describe, and interpret as one eternity. The objective physical world we are now self-consciously occupying is made up of the forming, and deforming of one physical world, which is a portion of one eternity.

When a physical infinity-like eternity returns to its formless state, a new Big Bang occurs impelling and propelling a new universe into existence, which includes our physical world. Each new physical world appears as creation, but its appearance is, in reality, the progressively increasing functionings of the objective realm.

When a new physical world comes into evolving reality, its counterpart worlds also come into their evolving existence. These coexisting counterpart worlds, derived from a physical world, I describe as the purgatorial and spiritual worlds or realms. They occupy the non-physical vibrational realms of objective existence. Purgatorial worlds are lower vibrational duplicates of physical worlds and consist of two sections, the physical and the non-physical.

The physical purgatorial section ceases its replication of a physical world before the advent of any life forms. Eventually, this physically dense, murky, and opaque portion of purgatory becomes the eternal repository, for all the divine unfortunates who self-consciously and steadfastly choose to deny and reject God.

These godlessly-based family members understand their relationship to God, but still they choose to reject Him. It is here that they find their eternal abode where the presence of God, which remains forever within them, is self-willed and chilled into eternal self-conscious oblivion.

In this physical section of purgatory, there is no self-conscious self-actuating experiencing of existence. Here, there is no growth, evolvement, or any expressions of life. Here, self-conscious existence is self-awareness without the recognition or desire for God-awareness or life-awareness.

Here, there are only the ongoing real experiences of erosion and corrosion. Here is the habitat of utter and complete barrenness. Here, individualizations of purgatorial-Man spend the remainder of their eternity, with their godless self-awareness as their only comfort. Here, existence is known as the darkness of deadness.

The non-physical section of the purgatorial realm is where all punishment occurs. Here, our past self-conscious experiencing of existence as our self-conscious living of lives is relived and reviewed mentally and punished accordingly. Here is the realm where our eternal destiny is determined, for the remainder of the eternity occupied.

The spiritual world is a higher vibration counterpart of the physical world. The spiritual world consists of the same idea realm ideas, which had found receptivity in the physical realm. In the spiritual world, these physical realm ideas appear in their wholeness.

Thus, in the spiritual world, ideas are only incorporated in the complete realization of their intended purpose for existence. Here, there are no processes of growth, evolvement, or development, and there are no self-consciously self-created experiences. Here, there is only the realization or the expression of idea-completeness. For example, physical world trees begin with seeds that develop and evolve into fully blossoming trees. In the spiritual world, trees appear fully grown, to the extent of their forever design.

Formless Realm

The formless realm is the portion of objective reality concerning our formless mental existence. We first enter the formless realm of objective reality, as we are compelled to descend from core reality into objective reality. In the objective formless realm, we have self-conscious awareness and access to the realm of ideas. In core reality, we have no self-conscious access to the idea realm.

The formless realm provides the environment for the objective and non-objective understanding of real and non-real existence. Also, the formless realm is our mental home between the *journeyings* of our souls through objective eternities continuous. In other words, as each physical world or eternity ends, we return to the totally mental formless realm, of our objective existence.

Here, in the formless realm, we become capable of self-conscious thought enabling us, to self-consciously experience our physical realm lives. Thus, in the formless realm, experiencing our existence consists of our self-awareness stimulated by the realm of ideas. Therefore, the thinking of thoughts becomes the non-physical experience of our forever presence, in the objective non-physical formless realm.

In the formless realm, there are ideas compatible to our arrival from core reality, enabling us to develop an evolving self-conscious receptivity to ideas. In the formless realm, our capability for self-conscious thought requires the ability to understand, interpret, and integrate ideas for our organized self-aware comprehension. Thus, our acceptance and understanding of ideas necessitate our self-aware embodiment of languages to provide the means for our individualized self-expression.

Thus, in the formless realm, our self-awareness in conjunction with the ideas generates and evolves languages, within our individualized self-awareness. Thinking in a language provides the self-conscious foundational process for our understanding, interpreting, and experiencing all aspects of our infinite existence which includes all components of ultimate reality.

Our ability to language-think highlights a significant difference between objective reality and non-objective reality, or core reality. In core reality, we have no association with idea realm ideas. Therefore, we are incapable of self-conscious thought; thus, there is no self-capability to understand our self-existence. In core reality, there is no self-thinking, there is only self-being.

In core reality, our self-awareness is self-conscious existence beyond language. Languages enable us to self-understand our existence as a self-realizing evolving infinite destiny. However, in core reality, our absolute existence only evolves in our non-comprehensible self-knowingness.

In core reality, our blissful self-known reality is infinitely unlimited. In objective reality, the process of understanding is self-limiting to our self-interpretation of our expression of existence as life. God, in the totality of His reality, is beyond any Self-conscious ability to understand, interpret, or experience His forever Beingness. However, God is infinitely unrestrained in the Self-knowingness of His forever unfolding Self-existence.

Our self-conscious ability to think independently results from our self-conscious awareness, functioning in combination and cooperation with idea realm ideas. As individual formless-Man, we are thought-consciously aware of all aspects of ultimate reality, but we are unaware of any specific physical, purgatorial, or spiritual objective realm happenings.

Divine Family

All expressions of individualized-Man make up the entire membership of the divinity of God's family is forever unified destiny, in the self-realizing their divinity. All of God's family is equal in their relationship to one another and equal also in their relationship to God.

It is the forever future of all God's family members to seek, find, accept, and obey the God of their understanding.

Every individualized member of God's family has a common destiny, with all other divine family members and also each God family member has an individually unique destiny to seek, find, and to fulfill. No member of God's family has the same understanding of existence as any other member of the God's perfect family. That is the marvel of our individualized reality; we each possess a unique self-conscious awareness of our forever divinity in and through all of ultimate infinity.

Infinity withholds no gifts from any member of God's family. However, our spiritual self-awareness must evolve to the place where infinity's gifts become perceivable, to our evolving spiritual self-awareness. Thus, our realizing and acceptance of God is the divine source for all of our receptivity to infinity's gifts. For the non-spiritual expressing members of God's family, self-aware existence is fundamentally the only gift of infinity they are self-consciously capable of receiving.

Infinity's bestowing gifts, resulting from acquired spiritual understandings must be desired, sought and earned, to be self-consciously accepted. Also, it must be understood that each one of us, as a divine family member, has the forever capability of rejecting our divinity; thereby, rejecting our receptivity to the gift-blessings, ultimate reality forever proffers.

Although all of God's family members are equal, each member of His family is unique in the understanding, interpretation, and the experiencing of their forever self-aware existence. Concerning our combined infinite reality, all divine family members share the same method for objectively experiencing their lives as existence.

All divine family members share the same mind of God, forever realized, in their experiencing of reality, albeit that one same mind of God is individualized, by each member of God's family. Also, all God's family members share the same abilities and capabilities, in their physical realm experiences of life.

Throughout this work, I define the purpose of our forever existence is to experience our self-realizing beingness. Often, it has been said that all the things that happen to us, come to us for a purpose. That claim is completely false. We exist infinitely and we self-choose how we self-interpret meaning into all things coming to us.

Nothing that ever happens to any of us, in the experiencing of our lives, has a purpose, other than that embedded into the infinite structuring of our self-conscious beingness. Simply, there is no purpose for welcomed or non-welcomed occurrences, imposed upon us, as we experience our infinite existence unless we self-translate those occurrences, into spiritual learning lessons. We provide the purpose in the happenings of the unpredictable.

If there were such a thing as randomly imposed occurrences specifically designed to affect our lives that would presuppose a self-directing infinitely existing intelligence or power, separate from our forever enduring lives. That cannot be. We, alone and individually, express the only self-directing power there is in all of absolute and ultimate reality.

Since the mind within each one of us is the individualized mind of God, each of us understands and interprets God individually. Thus, our understanding of God is infinite and unique. Since our interpretations of God are infinitely individual and unique, no one's self-attained knowledge of God should be considered more spiritually noteworthy than another's.

However, all real spiritual understandings of God must be based on the universal expression of kindness. Any understandings of God lacking the requiring manifestations of kindness are incorrect interpretations of God's nature. However, even those who do not believe in any God, but still enthrone kindness in their self-chosen actions are expressing their divinity.

We can only understand God by self-consciously understanding, expressing, and experiencing His qualities. The knowledge of the one true God is the interpretation of God that spiritually enhances our experiencing of life. Thus, the realization of God which uplifts, sustains, and maintains a self-conscious realization of the human condition is the understanding of the one true God.

God's infinite divine family consists of all individualizations of Man in both objective reality and core reality. Imagine what our collective objective experience of existence would be like if all divine family members were self-consciously aware, of their unbroken lineage to their forever divinity? However, this total and complete self-knowingness of God, forever desired in objective reality, is only self-consciously known in core reality.

Every member of God's family forever understands God individually. Our destiny is to see ourselves as the understanding of God, manifesting in the realm of experience, to harmoniously partake in the infinite rewards, resulting from our self-acceptance, of our foreverness in and with God.

Thus, our infinite objective free will choice is forever-present, either we self-consciously choose to accept God or decide not to accept Him. Unfortunately, to a large number of God's family, that option remains a non-choice. When we self-consciously choose to accept God, we are at the beginning of self-conscious spiritual evolvement.

For divine family members who choose not to accept God, their self-understood existence mandates that their experiencing of living life increasingly devolves into all manners of self-accepted fears, sins, and evils, forever crouching godlessly upon their self-awareness. Thus, their experiencing of self-beingness is sorrowfully laden, aimless, pain-ridden, and dependent upon the uncontrollable factors of objective reality.

Woefully sad is the realization that so many members of God's family remain lost, for the lack of desire to find, accept, and obey His Divine Beingness. Without the humble acceptance of God, the transparent transient fire-breathing dragons of godless unreality are free to godlessly romp, stomp, and tromp, as they thrust their falsity, into our objectively unreal realm of experiencing existence.

No member of God's family is ever permanently lost to perdition, but it is unnatural for any divine family member to experience objective reality without God. We are part of God. Why would anyone ever choose to deny that forever present holy truth? Each one of us is the substance of God in self-conscious realization.

Neither God nor anyone of us has a choice concerning our infinite existence. However, each of us, as a divine family member, has the forever capability of understanding and interpreting our spiritual forever lives, into the physical experience of reality. God in His allness is forever void of that capability.

Evil and Sin

So-called evil and sin represent the unreality of existence mirroring our false interpretations. The seeming reality of evil and sin results from our individualized self-consciousness providing them with a pretended claim to the experiencing of life, by accepting their false appearances, due to our self-conscious spiritual insecurities, in the evolving of our understandings, of our forever divinity.

Therefore, without our individualized self-consciousness, evil and sin have no power or capability to self-proclaim their non-real identities, upon our objectively lived self-existence. So-called evil and sin are truth-void constructs of our infinite spiritually bankrupt and deprived self-awareness. Evil and sin result from our forever choice to dethrone our divinity from the top-reaches of our infinite existence.

Evil and sin have no real identifiable infinite existence. They are only falsely interpreted into the realm of objective reality, by providing them with an assumed identity of their own. Our experiencing of objective reality necessitates our exposure to the pretended clutches of evil and sin. However, each of us has the forever ability to return evil and sin to the nothingness of their non-real existence.

In ultimate reality, all forms of independent appearances of evil and sin have no real self-identities. However, the infinite potentiality for their appearances resides within the free will chambers of our forever self-beingness. In my chapter on evil and sin, I discuss how evil, and sin originate, and why they seemingly have a persistence of existence, in the realm of experience.

God

God is one of the independent components of ultimate reality. God is not all-powerful; in fact, He possesses no Self-power whatsoever, except through each one of us, as individualized-Man. Also, He is not all-knowing and not all-present. God's Infinite Beingness is Self-contained within His Infinite Self-knowingness.

God is Self-consciously aware of His infinitely unfolding divine nature, and nothing else. To God, the only existence He is aware of is His Self-existence. In short, God has no Self-originating power. His divine presence is limited to the Self-awareness of Himself. He does not Self-knowingly understand anything expressing as the reality of existence. He is only Self-aware of His Infinite Beingness.

God knows nothing of our existence, our circumstances, or our experiences. From His perspective, He is totally impersonal to our collective and individual self-aware lives. Still, each of us remains His infinite expression. Therefore, each one of us is part of God, and His presence is within us as our forever soul. Now, the question becomes: How is God not personal if He permanently resides within each of us?

If God has no Self-awareness of our existence, He cannot be a personal God. However, His nature is our nature. Thus, His nature or essence is at the center of each one of us. Understood in this manner, God is indeed personal. Therefore, in our continuing and evolving understanding of God, He is forever personal, but He remains forever personal from our individualized-Man perspective, as the expression of God.

God infinitely and patiently awaits our recognition, acceptance, and obedience. In this understanding of God, He is the ever-present source of divine love. Each of us forever seeks His love and His embrace. In the objective realm, there is no greater achievement than our self-conscious awareness being consistently inspired, with an active self-acknowledgement of God's loving presence.

Thus, God's love is always understood, interpreted, and desired by each one of us individually. As we understand the sacredness of ourselves, we transmute God's love, residing peacefully within each of us, into the realm of appearance. Thus, God's love is made objectively visible, and we become the self-proponents of our forever divinity.

God's nature and our nature, as the individualizations of collective-Man, are identical. From God's infinite perspective, He is one hundred percent non-personal. From our individualized perspective, He is one hundred percent personal. He is our ever-filling Soul, and thus He is the spiritual substance of our foreverness.

The infinite reality of God's existence is common to us all, and our acceptance of God's nature divinely empowers us. The forever spiritual destiny of all of sinners and doers of things evil is to realize and willfully obey the forever changing-changeless goodness of God. God is unaware of anything outside of His Self-knowingness; therefore, He has no awareness of evil and sin or no knowledge of the concept of evil and sin.

When we self-consciously resurrect, our unbroken unity with God, within our individualized self-awareness, God becomes our infinite Guide, Comforter, Protector, and Deliverer from all the snares of spiritual ignorance forever attempting to engulf us. Thus, by way of God's ever-presence, we become our self-evolving saviors, in our self-acceptance of God. God never accepts us or saves us.

Individually spiritual-based understandings of God are not unimportant. It is spiritually debilitating to criticize the sacred beliefs of fellow God-seekers, who are discovering for themselves, a meaningful sense of divine certitude. How arrogant is it for anyone to believe that his or her spiritually based understandings of God are superior to others? Our self-process of knowledge of things divine is infinite, and there is no finality to our forever divinely expanding self-understanding.

The only thing of lasting divine relevance is to discover a spiritual path of understanding which encourages the continuous development of kindness and love for another and respect for all life. In the forever fulfilling of our unity, within the presence of God, the realizing of the one true God, meaningful to each of us, is our divine destiny in revealment.

Man

All of God's Man is the forever expression of God, whether in objective reality or core reality. God's Man is infinitely composed of individual and unique divine identities. Thus, for each of us, our nature is God's nature individualized. The totality of all the unique individualities of Man, emanating from God, comprises the one perfect divine family. To God, each one of us remains forever Self-unknown and not understood. To each one of us, as objectified Man, God is to be forever known and to be forever realized.

If God knew of our forever objective existence, He would be weeping infinitely. We are God's Self-aware divinity in infinite vibration. Our present experiencing of life, resulting from our feeble-weak understandings of His Divine Beingness, is an abomination to His ever presence within us. Since our understandings of God are infinite, and our misunderstandings of God are infinite. We are presently in a spiritually infantile understanding of His Beingness.

In the objective realm, as individualizations of expressing-Man, we possess a self-actuating self-consciousness, in combination with a free will, giving us the ability to create physical world appearances, interpreted in our individualized minds, as experiences. This ability to create experiences enables each of us to understand and explain our existence, God's existence, and the existence of all other aspects of ultimate reality.

As individualized-Man, our self-aware lives were never created. Our singular reality is objectively self-realized finite-infinitely. Our self-conscious ability to interpret our existence separates us from all other aspects of ultimate reality. Thus, one of the fundamental understandings of this work is that we have always existed, and we have always existed in and with God.

Each of us possesses the ability to understand and self-consciously experience our environment along with our capability of using our free will to choose the direction of our finite-infinite destinies. We understand and interpret infinity in incremental snippets of beginnings and endings, as we forever trod our self-determined spiritual pathways.

Each one of us forever and individually exists as the self-conscious center of infinity. In the objective realm, we are always moving from one center point of infinity to the next. Therefore, each of us interprets our existence from both, a localized perspective, and an infinite viewpoint.

The battle in the understanding our self-conscious spiritual existence is won or lost in the objective physical realm. Overcoming the spiritual amnesia of our previous physical presences, through our continuing experiencing existence as life provides the spiritually-driven means, to understand ourselves forever divinely anew.

Individually, we possess an infinite free will; but, our free only manifests in objective reality. Our individualized free will gives each of us the ability to interpret and misinterpret our expressing existence. If we did not have a divine destiny to fulfill, our misinterpretations of objective reality would infinitely imprison us in a non-controllable reality of forever reacting existence, to a constant stream of external realm stimuli, in the same manner as non-self-aware animals.

As we misinterpret actual existence, we misinterpret idea realm ideas. Our individual capability for misinterpreting ideas is the wellspring for all appearances of all so-called evils and sins, existing and persisting in the self-experiencing of our existence. Thus, it is each one of us that bring evil and sin into the realm experience.

Through each of us, the process of creating experiences becomes a real function of our objective nature, but the experiences we create are not eternally or infinitely real and have no objective basis, for any independent existence, in reality. Thus, through our ability to freely make choices, we determine the direction of our destiny, as we experience the unreal-real realms of objective reality.

Throughout each ensuing eternity, we must rediscover, re-interpret, and re-experience God's love anew. Thus, God's ever-presence as love, within each of us, is meaningful to us as a forever reality. The understanding of that truth consecrates our objective existence. Our primary divine purpose, in the experiencing of our individualized physical lives, is to experience our apprehensions of God.

Our receptivity to God and all things divinely real determines our understanding and acceptance of the one true God. All realizations of God promoting God-based kindly behaviors lead to and exalt the God of our understanding and acceptance. The one true God is the God we self-consciously embrace, the God that encourages us to be the expressions of the ever increasing understandings of our divinity.

Thus, there are not Gods many; there is only one God infinitely understood and interpreted by each of us individually and independently, through the ever unfolding distinctive uniqueness, of our ever evolving self-understanding, of our non-evolving divinity. Our self-understood oneness with God is our forever divine destiny in continuing self-realization.

I coined the word transbeingness for describing the cyclical progression of our individualized objective existence. In this understanding, each of us interprets, accepts and experiences object reality from four spiritual perspectives. Following are the four phases of our immortal-Man transbeingness: formless-Man, physical-Man, purgatorial-Man, and spiritual-Man.

Often, I use the term individualized-Man or immortal-Man as a non-specific identity of the individual universal-Us, the individual universal-We, or each of us as individualized universal-Man. Thus, our transbeingness is a function of our objective nature and only occurs in objective reality; therefore, our transbeingness is an unknown function of our infinite self-aware beingness, in core reality.

Our objective transbeingness is the process enabling each of us to understand the purpose of our infinite existence. Thus, our self-conscious awareness is manifested in the above four phases of our progressive objective expression. Our transbeingness is the finite-infinite process for the cycling and recycling of our self-conscious awareness, through seemingly eternities endless.

Each cycle of our transbeingness is separate from ones previous. However, the ever increasing spiritual depth-awareness of our progressive apprehensions of divine truth continues into our future *transbeing* self-conscious existences, as receptivity to things spiritual. We eternally become the self-realized evolving of our self-directed evolving.

Our continuing objective destiny is to seek an understanding of our place in reality. However, if we totally comprehended our existence, our thought-evolving existence would lose its incentive to be meaningfully understood. Thus, our objective self-conscious beingness would have no impetus to identify, understand, interpret, or experience itself.

We are spiritually empowered when our self-conscious unity with the presence of God remains unaffected by anything denying God's wholeness. Our realizing of divine success in our never changing divine destiny requires the experiencing objective reality, as God's essence made visible.

However, in this present progression of eternities, we must continuously spiritually conquer and make non-relevant the infinitely flaying claws of chance, opportunity, randomness, and general unpredictability. Thus, we are eternal prisoners of unpredictability until unleashed by the power of our self-God understanding, expressing without any constraints of seeming opposition.

In our experiencing of existence, each new eternity we enter seems to be the only eternity there is to understand, interpret, and experience. We guide ourselves ever onwards to the fulfilling of our infinite unfulfillable divine destiny. Our understanding of existence is forever limited because the infinite realizations of our beingness are forever increasing.

Thus, we begin to experience a new existence in each new eternity we inhabit, to rediscover and re-experience the foreverness of our objective destiny, as we infinitely continue to rediscover our changeless divinity. We forever exist to experience our forever existence at the level of our ever amassing understanding, of thing spiritual.

I describe our transbeingness as Man, as our individualized objective existence interacting with all of objective reality's components. As required, I use the distinct appearances of our individual transbeingness, in the designations of formless-Man, physical-Man, purgatorial-Man, and spiritual-Man, as the context dictates.

When I use the word Man with a capital "M", I am referring to my definition of Man, as God's unknown divine expression of Himself. When I use the word man, with a small "m" I am referring, to the presently accepted understanding of man, as indicative of humanity.

If by defining humanity as consisting of infinitely conjoined divine beings, that understanding of humanity becomes comparable to my understanding of the individualizations of Man, comprising the whole of God's family. Regardless of how we interpret our collective existence, we are all spiritual beings, and we all belong to God's infinitely divine family.

Each one of us, as immortal-Man, has a designed destiny to fulfill. The fulfilling of our divine destiny is our divine destiny, in the realization of being forever fulfilled. Our divine destiny is to understand ourselves as a forever part of God and a forever non-part of God simultaneously. The non-part of our God-beingness self-consciously experiences existence. The God part of our beingness knows its divine destiny in core reality.

Life

We are the only component of ultimate reality self-consciously capable of apprehending the purpose life. The experiencing of existence is life. Regarding our self-conscious experiencing of objective reality, we have no choice. We only have the option of how we choose to understand and interpret the experiencing of existence.

Further, life includes all things having the capability of acting, reacting, or interacting with their physical environments. Thus, besides each of us expressing life, the expression of life includes animals, insects, vegetation, microorganisms, et cetera. Their experiencing of life is a real direct function of objective reality.

All real things that experience life possess infinitely unfolding identities. These unfolding identities seem to have beginnings and endings, but they are only our interpretations of objective reality. The idea realm provides the means for interpreting and understanding all aspects of objective reality.

Non-self-aware forms of life lack the creative capability of self-conscious self-actualization. The primary difference between our individualized self-aware experiencing of life and individualized non-self-aware experiencing of life is that our self-conscious awareness can create experiences. Non-self-aware expressions of individualized life have no self-conscious self-actuating ability, to self-consciously create anything.

In the objective realm of the forever continuing of evolving eternities, each one of us eventually triumphs and overcomes the challenges, obstacles, and imprints of all seeming unreality having pressed mightily upon each of us, to cajole us into repudiating and disavowing our forever divinity.

When we become final spiritual victors, in our pathfinding *souljourns* through objective reality, we return to core reality. We remain in core reality until our infinite existence becomes once again that of yawning blissfulness, then we are re-impelled once again into objective reality, to begin afresh the experiencing of our forever physical objective existence.

Our finitely-final spiritual victory takes countless eternities for our collective and individual spiritual success to be objectified triumphantly. The seeming foreverness of our spiritual journeys must be correct because it is patently self-evident that each of us, as individualized-Man is presently at an individual and collective primitive state of spiritual deprivation.

It may take some of us a hundred, a thousand, or more eternities before our present trek-travels through the objective realm of endless and continuous eternities becomes an unshakeable spiritual knowingness, to each one of us. Regardless of any opinions about our infinite existence, this is the infinitely mandated and imposed process, for the understanding of ourselves as infinitely divine.

Real and Unreal Experiences

One of the primary understandings in this book is that there are two types of experiences, real and non-real. Infinite real experiences are based on the interacting functions and processes, within the foreverness of objective reality, and pertain primarily to physical worlds.

Seemingly real created experiences result from the symbiotic relationships between idea realm ideas and the physicality of matter driven by the non-controllable forces of chance, opportunity, randomness, and general unpredictability. However, the unpredictability of happenstance can be transmuted into harmony, through our evolving spiritual understandings.

All self-consciously created experiences are the creative activities of our self-conscious objective experiencing of existence. These self-created experiences have no real infinite identities of their own. The concept of creation itself is meaningless to ultimate reality. Thus, appearances of seeming creations result solely from our individualized self-conscious awareness.

Also, all self-created experiences have prescribed beginnings and endings. In other words, our self-conscious thoughts create experiences containing prescribed beginnings and endings. In contrast, all seemingly generated real experiences in objective reality are finite-infinitely whole, in their segmented expressions.

Thus, to infinite reality, the beginnings, and endings of experiences are interpreted segments of the infinite whole, and therefore part of the finite-infinite continuum, of their forever processing existence. A circle represents infinity infinitely expanding within itself. To infinity, all seemingly created experiences, identified as arcs within the whole, are part of an infinite expanse of infinite wholeness.

Our self-consciously created experiences are independent of the realness of objective reality's components. Thus, the beginnings and endings of our self-created thought-experiences have no realness attached to them. Thus, they are not part of infinite objective real existence.

Real experiences include the interactions of the infinitely various non-self-conscious forms of life, such as animals, insects, and vegetation. In short, real experiences result from the never-ending mechanical functions, within and without the forever evolving physicality of the endless processions, of evolving universes.

All real experiences are devoid of any self-conscious thought-directed power. Real experiences forever result from the infinitely elected laws of chance, opportunity, randomness, and general unpredictability bombarding the wholeness of objective reality. To objective reality, unpredictability is a built-in function of real existence.

In physical worlds and universes, these unpredictable laws operate automatically, without any designed purpose of self-aware directed thought. Only through our individualized objective presence are the laws of chance, opportunity, randomness, and general unpredictability meaningfully measured, understood, interpreted, and transmuted into experiences reflecting the forever real.

Self-conscious self-activating created non-real experiences are unknown in the infinite nature of worldly appearance. These created thought-derived experiences are unreal because they have no infinite sustaining identity or self-creating driving power, of their own. Real experiences belong to a continuum of everlastingness. Non-real experiences are not part of any everlasting continuum.

The realness of objective reality is forever independent of our self-conscious thoughts. The objective realm is the infinitely changing-changeless. We alone self-consciously mold and interpret objective reality, into the realm of experience. The infinitely present aspects of objective reality do not have forever identities.

Objective reality is the infinite stage where each one of us, as actors, creates stories of presumed existence to experience, in the physical world. All of our self-created stories of our self-willed expressions are infinitely non-tethered to any real aspect of objective reality, except through our self-conscious confirmations of the forever actual and genuine.

All experiences self-consciously created never become a real part of objective reality. If experiences were real, in the absolute sense, which would mean new creations added to ultimate reality's changelessness and infinite wholeness. There is nothing newly born into ultimate reality because ultimate reality is singularly and infinitely whole.

Therefore, objective reality, including all physical worlds is all-inclusive. To objective reality, nothing is added; nothing removed. Objective reality exists solely for each of us to experience, but its infinite existence is entirely independent of our infinite existence except for the realization that if we did not exist, objective reality could not be interpreted into a meaningful living reality.

Thus, there is no such thing as creation, if defined as something new coming into infinite existence, with an infinite uniqueness of its own. Creation, if one chooses to use that term, applies to the externalization of a matrix of ideas, whose manifestations as experience, have assumed beginning-starts and assumed ending-stops.

The understanding, interpreting and realizing of objective reality only occurs within our individualized mind. Therefore, all experiences self-consciously created have no real objective existence. Thus, things made manifest in the realm of objective reality, by our self-conscious creative volition, occur as created experiences, and all self-consciously designed experiences are devoid of any reality-infused identities.

The spiritual purpose of our objective existence is to understand ourselves and then experience that understanding, as God's nature manifesting. Our non-spiritual interpretations of objective reality result in the experiencing of limited realizations of ourselves. Thus, we infinitely experience the acceptances of our infinite ongoing understandings.

Our forever self-aware existence is divine, but not necessarily recognized as divine. Hence, that is the forever paradox of our infinite self-aware lives. We are forever self-expressing and thus self-experiencing the depthless-tinges of our divinity. We have infinity to never-reach the bottom depth of our divinity.

Following are two examples demonstrating the creative power and process of our self-actuating self-consciousness as related to the creating of experiences.

First, everyone has heard the age-old adage asserting that the existence of a watch presumes the existence of a watchmaker. Thus, it is assumed, there must be an originating process for presenting seeming creation. Therefore, there must be a Creator God. This book is in part, a refutation to that seemingly logical conclusion.

The existence of a watch merely demonstrates the original, inventive function of our self-actuating self-consciousness, operating in the arena of objective reality, as experience. Our self-conscious self-actuating creations are experiences and have no real substance or identity of their own, and are independent of objective reality's functionings.

If we could not self-consciously interpret and comingle the real components of objective existence, a watch could not be made to manifest objectively, in the realm of appearance. It is our ability to self-create our desires that bring unreality into seeming material existence. Our self-conscious creations of unreality are composed of created experiences.

Giving seeming real existence to something without a forever identity requires a self-consciously directed free will, a desire to create the appearance of ideas, and a self-coordinating self-conscious effort. Thus, each one of us is a creator, a creator-interpreter, or a self-willing conduit for all things expressing unreality. Objective reality cannot create real existence; objective reality is forever part of absolute and unchanging ultimate reality.

The appearance-experience of a watch affirms the interlacing components of objective reality, including idea realm ideas, matter, and a directing and organizing self-conscious self-activating free will, driven by the effort of concentrated desired thought. Thus, as individualized-Man, we create the appearance of a watch as experience composed of interpretations of reality, as an expression of our free will.

All self-consciously designed experiences are segments in time unattached to the wholeness of objective reality, and self-perceived in our individualized-mind. Time has no self-real existence in objective reality. Each of us interprets time into existence. The concept of time makes objective reality meaningful, for our ability to understand reality.

Everything comprising the seeming physicality of a watch possesses its own absolute independent and real identity. Therefore, the manifestation of a watch is the temporarily coordinated appearance, of the forever unchanging components of objective reality, manifesting in the non-real real realm of experience.

Simply, the physical appearance of a watch is a created appearance as experience and has no infinite reality to proclaim, identify, or absorb into ultimate reality. To ultimate reality, the appearance of a manifested watch is not known and meaningless. Only the components comprising the expression of the watch are real and infinite elements of objective reality.

Second, suppose someone chooses to create a sandcastle. Ideas are selected, for the sandcastle's design, from the idea realm. The sandcastle comes into a physical appearance by combining and coordinating our real infinite self-consciousness, with infinitely real ideas and infinitely real matter.

The sandcastle appears in the realm of appearance-experience as an aesthetically pleasing structure. Presently, tides rise, and it becomes engulfed in water, and washes away returning to its pre-thought created state of formless matter. Throughout this process, objective reality has remained unchanged, unmoved, untouched, and indifferent.

What portions of the above illustration is representative of objective reality? First, there is our self-actuating self-conscious awareness desiring to create and erect a sandcastle. Note, all things we experience in the realm of worldly physical existence, begin with self-conscious desire. It is our destiny that our self-conscious desires be divinely grounded.

Second, ideas are selected for its design and construction. Third, malleable matter, existing as real water and real sand, are fashioned to form its structure. Finally, the completed sandcastle's aesthetically pleasing appearance reflects two of God's infinite attributes, harmony, and beauty.

Based on the above discussion, the final appearing of the sandcastle, in the realm of worldly physical experience, has no independent identity-attachment to reality. Therefore, it is devoid of any real existence. Thus, so-called self-consciously created experiences belong to the non-real realm and are eternally and infinitely the gossamer rustlings of unreality.

We self-realize our infinite objective existence through the realm of experience. The significance of real and unreal experience relates to our infinite and indestructible spiritual nature. No experience of any kind ever impacts our forever beingness. We only experience ourselves as we interpret ourselves. Each of us possesses real existence, but our experiencing of physical worldliness has no objective or ultimate reality.

Unreality

Unreality is the infinite existence of non-reality or pretended reality. Unreality is the experience of reality by our self-desired creations. The forever appearance of unreality is only displayed in the objective physical world and is completely unknown to the functioning of ultimate reality.

Unreal existence is a derivative of our individual and collective self-conscious awareness. Our understanding of reality requires the semblances of non-reality to facilitate our understandings and interpretations of genuine reality. Simply, it is not possible for us to understand reality if we do not understand the non-reality of non-reality.

In the formless realm, we may become aware of unreality, through the misinterpretations of ideas, but in the formless realm unreality cannot be experienced; therefore, unreality's infinite non-existence is without meaning. The physical realm is the only realm where we self-consciously create the unreal appearing existence and then experience those creations.

In the purgatorial realm, we re-experience the unrealities we created in the physical realm. In the spiritual realm, we are aware of unreality, but there we have spiritually progressed to the correct understanding of our individualized spirituality, to the point where it is not possible to use our free will to create experiences of unreality.

The only power of unreality is the power we self-consciously bestow upon it. We self-consciously entrust unreality with power through our self-though misinterpretations of idea realm ideas. If objective reality existed and there was no self-conscious awareness to interpret it, unreality would have no infinite non-real existence.

In the final divine analysis of our infinite existence, we are never able to shed ourselves of our forever self-reality, but we may ask ourselves once again this nagging spiritual question: Is our infinite individual indestructible self-conscious existence an infinitely desirable self-living realty? After all, our infinite existence will always include the experiencing of sorrow, heartache, and pain interspersed with interludes of experiencing joy, harmony, and happiness.

We are the forever shapers of our forever existence. We possess the infinite ability to reshape and remold appearances of evil and sin, into divine truth realized. When we experience the pains of a wrongfully-lived existence, we self-consciously deny our real identities. When we experience the joys of beingness, we are self-consciously affirming our spiritually complete identities.

Thus, it seems that we are infinitely rejecting and infinitely accepting the foreverness of our self-existence. If we always objectively identified ourselves with God, we would always be self-understanding our real existence. However, for our infinite existence to be meaningful, we forever possess the free will option, to deny our forever divine existence.

Thus, we infinitely have the capability for understanding our forever beingness, and we infinitely have the capacity for misunderstanding our forever beingness, by accepting the ever enticing, shining, dancing, dangling bobbles, babbles, and bangles of unreality's infinite expressions, as self-accepted by us. Unreality is a foreverness of self-consciously assumed existence.

The All-powerfulness of Understanding

When I began writing this book, I did not have an awareness of this topic, in my consciousness. My understanding of this subject evolved, as I wrote and re-wrote the contents of this book. The all-powerfulness of understanding makes each one of us all-powerful because, in all ultimate forever reality, we are the only components capable of self-conscious thought.

Here is my understanding. Each one of us infinitely self-consciously exists. The idea realm, which contains all knowledge and all perceptions and interpretations, exists infinitely. Each one of us has the equal potential capability of uniting our self-consciousness with idea realm ideas. Thus, each one of us is capable of understanding and determining all that occurs, in ultimate reality.

God also has Self-awareness, but God has no relationship or association, with the idea realm, whatsoever. Hence, the infinite God of infinite existence is powerless because He does not Self-think. The wielding of power understanding only ensues from the self-awareness of existence, the self-awareness of ideas, the self-awareness of desire, and the self-awareness of knowledge. The idea realm is the source, for all power ever exerted, in ultimate reality.

The idea realm contains the awareness of all thoughts and ideas of understanding, which enables ideas to manifest their purpose for existence. Some ideas only exist as thought recognitions, of assumed realities; however, these ideas cannot manifest in reality. For example, I am thinking of the concept of a square circle. A square circle cannot exist in the realness of reality except as an idea-thought.

However, for the most part, anything we desire to do or to understand, there is an idea or series of ideas allowing desires to manifest into reality. However, here's the most important thing. All manifestations of the things we crave, through the understanding of ideas, are directly related to our spiritual or non-spiritual evolvement.

If each one of us had a self-conscious unbridled willy-nilly all-powerfulness, without any self-spiritualized development of understanding, infinite existence would be a sham of unregulated immoral experiences. Then, our infinite self-realized existence would be the unbroken self-realization of non-stop self-aware torment.

Thus, it is that our developing spiritual understanding that gives each of us the capability of self-actuating our desires into harmonious fruition. The interesting thing concerning our individual potentialities, for the exerting of the all-powerfulness of our understandings, is that each one of us has the possibility for exhibiting all-powerfulness, without depriving any others of doing the same.

Also, the greater the depth of our spiritual understanding, the commanding all-powerfulness of our self-conscious wielding of knowledge is filled with divine goodness. Thus, even though each of us possesses a free will direct our infinite potential all-powerfulness, the free will directing of our self-understood all-powerfulness, can be self-consciously directed for the expression of goodness.

Infinite Void

Infinite Void is simply the infinite vastness of ultimate reality enabling each new universe to expand to its limit. Metaphorically speaking, the endless void is the womb for the birth and expansion of each new universe. Also, within its infinite void domain, all the other components of ultimate reality find their abode.

Concluding Introduction

Heavenly desires demand spiritual preparation. Divine truth can only be self-realized if divinely sought. In the present condition of our collective self-awareness, humanity is spiritually weak and the God, of our individual understandings, is mocked. Our individual and group, spiritual experiences of existence, remain a far-off vision, a far-off understanding, and a far-off gift to the foreverness of our self-evolving self-realization, of our forever divinity.

Religions have their place in our acquisitions of things spiritual and are often helpful in guiding us along pathways divine. However, God and each one of us have coexisted together, before any religion ever proclaimed its certitudes of truth. To me, the only divinely authentic faith is the understanding of ourselves, as the divine breath of God, breathing and exhaling the purity of God's wholiness, into all aspects of our living of life.

For the self-consciously spiritually possessed, they attract to themselves the spiritual understandings enabling them to become self-active participants in the realizing of things forever divinely pure. Thus, we attract to ourselves the religiosity of things divine that promote within us, an understanding of God that is spiritually self-acceptable, to the forever evolving of our infinite divinity.

Regardless of the strength of our individual desires for spiritual knowledge, the wholiness of truth is forever presenting itself, sometimes in rags, sometimes in riches. Try as we may, we will never escape from the realization that we are divine beings, experiencing our self-existence, at the level of our spiritual or non-spiritual understandings.

The destiny of our forever existence is realized and actualized through our choices, and our choices are always divinely and non-divinely personal. However, for each of us to self-actualize our infinite existence as a blessing, our free will choice to identify ourselves with God, is universally decreed by way of the gift of our forever non-quenchable divine self-understanding reality.

However, we always retain a free will option to reject our inherited divinity, and then self-consciously choose to exist without the self-awareness or self-acceptance of God. Still, we are infinitely preordained to understand our innate divinity and inculcate our self-consciousness with the presence of God, dwelling divinely and serenely within each of us, forever unmolested, by the pantheon of unrealities.

The actual realization of our infinite destiny is our self-conscious process of kindling and rekindling the forever spark of our inner divinity. As that occurs, it is always from our individualized perspective, never from God's perspective, or from the vantage point of ultimate reality.

We forever realize our divine destiny in spiritual spurts. Still, each of us has the free will choice to reject our divinely ingrained heritage, as we continually follow our designated infinite fate, in the realizing of our infinite existence. Thus, we are forever destined to experience non-divinity in the fulfilling of our divine destiny.

The expounding of spiritual truths encouraging each of us to practice kindness, in consonance with the love of God is pure, unvarnished divinity in expression; no other requirement is necessary. All religious teachings encompassing the divine exaltation of that understanding belong to the one true and forever changeless God.

Permanently residing within each one of us is an infinitely endowed desire to discover, rediscover, know, and re-know the essence of infinite goodness, as our individual destiny in continuous fulfillment. The simplicity of spiritual truth realized is the practice of kindness combined with a self-acknowledgement, acceptance, and love of God.

Thus, our ceaselessly divine commission is to reveal to ourselves our divinely mandated destiny in the experiencing of existence. In the realizing of truth, we are infinite divine beings in infinite spiritual expression, throughout infinitely progressing eternities. Even so, we will never experience the wholeness of our infinite divinity because that is a never possible realization, designed into the foreverness of our forever existence.

Each of us represents the outpourings of God, discovering, realizing, and experiencing the infinity of our divinity. In the quiet sanctuary of our self-awareness, each of us is the infinite individualized-Man of God understanding ourselves, to ourselves, as ourselves.

Unfortunately, many so-called followers of the forever divine are devoid of spiritual qualities, such as the genteelness of kindness, understanding, compassion, and tolerance. Some of God's family become finitely-infinitely lost in their desire to continuing cling to unworthy spiritual self-conscious wrongdoings, but our collective spiritual destiny forever remains unchanged.

The army of the godless is showing their false of graspings and raspings of reality in the disclosing of their self-created displays of disharmony. Their experiencing of disharmony is godlessness in appearance. Wherever disharmony is purposely scratched, scorched, and etched into the experiencing of existence, God is self-consciously scorned and dishonored.

Spiritual truth is described, in multiple ways. The correct understandings of spiritual truth result from our sincere self-actuating desire to objectively dwell in an acquired self-consciousness, driven to understand things forever divinely pure. Our greatest demonstration of divine truth is experiencing our existence infused with a continuing self-conscious awareness of the presence of God.

Our peaceful recognition of the spiritual expressions of others is our acceptance of their understandings of divine truth, interacting with meaningful truth-realizations of themselves. In the realm of expressing spirituality, the only thing of supreme religious importance is to find the understanding and acceptance of God that provides the divine meaning, understanding, and thankfulness for our infinite existence.

Thus, all spiritual celebrations based on sincere interpretations of God bind all spiritually minded members, in their engravings of spiritual unity, throughout the family of God's different recognitions and assimilations of His Divine Beingness, His love, and His foreverness.

God must be understood and interpreted individually because our self-understood existence is forever individually realized. Everyone objectively reveals their individualized love of God through their expressions of God, and therefore everyone's genuine and sincere understandings of God are equal, provided those understandings are immersed in peaceful expressions of harmony and comforting kindness.

Manifestations of kindness provide a spiritual barometer enabling each of us to validate self-consciously to ourselves that the one eternal, infinite, everlasting God that we all are divinely and faithfully seeking is the one universal God that we are self-consciously realizing and accepting. Thus, the one true God, of anyone's understanding, must promote kindness and respect for all life, or it is not the authentic God of forever existence.

Our forever divinity is self-realized by acknowledging and accepting the presence of God. The pathway to our inner self-conscious awareness of God is infinitely illumined, infinitely patient, infinitely available, and forever prompts us to the divine realization, that we are forever inheritors, of our divine existence.

Our individualized free will determines how we understand and interpret the infinity of our divinity. Regardless of appearances, true or untrue, our infinite spiritual procession through unknown realms of undiscovered divinity is ceaselessly accelerating. In this respect, material reality is to be forever interpreted through our ever-evolving self-conscious unity, with the presence of God.

Since each of us is infinitely and divinely bound to God, salvation from the godless and gnarled talons of unreality is forever within our grasp. Each one of us possesses an everlastingly active free will. Thus, our individual salvation is forever and willfully self-consciously obtained. Still, we are enslaved, by our free will; we are saved, by our free will.

Salvation is mandated whenever we deviate from infinity's divinely understood designed plan forever embedded within each one of us. However, our salvation remains foolishly unredeemed, if not self-consciously desired. Still, many individuals, who seek salvation, remain trapped and snared, in the mesmerism of their uncontrollable existences.

The power of spiritual truth is independent of our self-conscious self-actualizing will to express the living of life. As the power of truth reveals itself to us, our God-identity is prepared to be objectively experienced. Thus, divine truth spiritually understood is revealed and externalized into the realm of physical experience. This light of divine revelation forever brightens our emerging spirituality.

Although our trudge through the physical realm is finite-infinite and forever, our self-aware emerging destiny is forever understood and interpreted by each of us individually, at the level of our individualized spiritual understanding. In the objective realm, what we are in thought, we are in expression.

Thus, in the light of spiritual truth, the self-awareness of our divinity is our destiny self-realized, through expressions of divine demonstrations. In our non-divine objective travels, our divine fate is forever realized, in the broken shadows of godlessness. Spiritual truth not desired is non-existent to self-conscious awareness.

Spiritual progress is experienced but never measured. God is at the center of our self-aware beingness, and each one of us is at the center of infinity. In the timelessness of existence, from our individualized perspective, our spiritual progress is in a constant state of stationary progression, because as we increase in divinely spiritual understandings, we are continuingly testifying to the continuing expanding of forever reality.

The purpose for our forever individualized beingness is to interpret our existence. The difference between the lowliest of sinners and the loftiest of saints is their self-center view of the interpreting of themselves. Each one of us exists at one of the infinite centers of infinity, where there are no shadows of darkness, or even darkness itself. Thus, if we do not understand ourselves as the center of infinity, never interpret existence accurately.

From our self-present perspective of our self-awareness, we are unable to see beyond the eternity we are occupying. Thus, we are obliged to accept this seemingly reasonable conclusion that the eternity we self-consciously inhabit is the only eternity, in infinite forever existence. Thus, if we feel hopelessly lost now, we feel hopelessly lost forever.

We are non-stopping in our objectively evolving understanding of our existence. Etched into the foreverness of our spiritual unfolding is the endless and depthless realm of our infinite identities. Our objective destiny is realized, through the transbeingness, of our divine nature self-understood through our self-understandings of the creative realm of experience.

Our forever divine future rightly understood keeps us on the sacred path, keeps us engulfed in spiritual wisdom, and keeps us sanctified through are ever increasing apprehensions of reality. The pathways of our forever evolving divinity are revealed to us, as we acknowledge and accept the infinity of our self-beingness. Each one of us, saint or sinner, is the divinity of our self-aware existence, in dynamic expression.

How each one of us chooses to find God is uniquely personal, because the God we seek is forever dwelling within us. No self-evolving perceptions of God are wrong if those thoughts fulfill our spiritual need to discover and rediscover the God of our apprehension, which impels within each one of us, the blessing of goodness to all things experiencing life.

Goodness in the demonstration that God's love is actively expressing through our self-willed actions. The God we acknowledge in our acts of unbridled goodness is the one everlasting and universal God, forever encircling and forever enriching our sense of divine existence. Our divine birthright is to know and to experience the forever goodness of God.

The experiencing of existence challenges each of us to understand our infinite existence. Only when our free will choices become completely subjugated, by our steadfast resolve and adherence to divine understanding, do the temptations of unreality, lose their power to hold, control, and bind us, to the bondage of illusions.

Let us always seek truth in an atmosphere of harmony and joy-filled expectations. Let us always encourage one another to desire a continuing and self-conscious awareness of God's presence, forever abiding harmoniously within us. Let it forever reign brightly in our unfolding individualized self-conscious awareness, that each one of us is forever part of God's infinite divine family,

CHAPTER I

God

God is the name people give to the reason we are here. But I think that reason is the laws of physics rather than someone with whom one can have a personal relationship. An impersonal God.

Stephen Hawking

Our forever ongoing self-developing spirituality requires a consistent desire for a divine certainty of understanding. Some religions are helpful in molding, and directing the progressing goodliness of our individualized desires, to evolve spiritually. Our self-aware developing of spirituality reflects the culmination of our forever ingrained willingness to understand and experience the goodness of our God-beingness.

Religions of the world often aid us in opening our mired sense-clogged self-consciousness, to find and walk upon the divine stepping-stone pathways of truth, leading to ever increasing spiritual renderings, and understandings of this infinite thing called life we share, in the commonality of our divinity.

However, to become successfully and spiritually directed by any worldly religion requires our self-conscious receptivity to all things, which are forever divinely real. Our responsiveness to things spiritual is our genuinely truthful self-identity accepting itself, understanding itself, and experiencing itself.

Our infinite existence demands infinite understanding. It is not reasonable to assume that our forever process of learning things spiritual is to be infinitely consistent and ongoing. Thus, all of our apprehensions of truth are consistently appropriate to our developing of our ongoing spirituality.

We forever infinitely and partially understanding God, but we will never wholly appreciate God. We can only recognize and acknowledge God in incremental grasps of divine truth. However, all of our ongoing understandings of God are equal, in the expressing of our existence, but not the same, in the experiencing of our progressing self-existence.

Thus, our self-sought understandings of things spiritual evolve and progresses through a series of never-ending self-ascensions of divine truth realized. Since God exists throughout all infinity, our understandings of God are increasingly changing in our mentally marbled sanctums of spiritual receptivity.

God's Self-knowingness is His forever Self-realizing of His infinite divinely unfolding nature, as the purity of infinite harmonious goodness. Thus, our forever destiny is to interpret God in the truthfulness of being, and then experience that understanding, at the evolving spiritual level of our progressed divinity.

We realize the purpose for our existence as we individually express and experience the God-nature of our forever identity. We exist to understand and know ourselves as infinitely divine. We only exist because God exists. The purpose of our infinite existence is to interpret God.

The problem in the understanding and knowingness our infinite existence is that we must determine those realizations for ourselves. In other words, each of us, alone and individually, determines our forever destiny to be realized. The only assistance we ever realize is our forever evolving self-acquired understandings of reality.

In our self-aware experiencing of existence, we must become increasingly aware of the wholiness of God. We externalize our understandings of God, in our expressions of kind acts of goodness, towards all things experiencing the living of life. Our ability to self-consciously evolve spiritually demands that we accept the divine mantle of responsibility, for all life expressing their existence.

Our active expression of kindness towards all life is the flowing of God's love, funneling through our individualized self-proclamations of existence. Through our behavior of loving-kindness, we are self-experiencing the forever soul of God, which is the eternally lasting source of our infinite divine self-identity.

Our active expressions of kindness represent the flowing of God's love, funneling through our individualized self-proclamations of existence. Through our behavior of loving-kindness, we are self-experiencing the forever soul of God, which is the eternally lasting source of our infinite divine self-identity.

In our sincere and self-conscious desires to apprehend God, we attract religious or philosophical systems of thought, push-pulling us ever onward, towards the increasing realization that our self-divinity is our self-identity. Thus, in our forever knee-bending trekking and sloughing through objective reality, we are driven to understand God, as the substance of our forever ingrained divinity.

Often, spiritual opportunities go unnoticed because we have not prepared ourselves, to assimilate the sacred truths we are seeking. Our infinite and indestructible beingness is the wholiness of God individualized. We must continuingly pursue the recognition that without the self-acceptance of God, the experiencing of existence becomes a fatally damning curse, rather than a divine exultation.

The forever purpose of our self-aware lives, both individually and collectively, is to express the essence of God. Unfortunately, in this physical world of objectivity, our inner divinity is self-denied, until we self-willingly cherish the desire to embrace the foreverness of God's Beingness.

We are destiny's strangers stranded, in the foreverness of our divinity. We cannot realize our divine destiny until we reveal our true nature, to our self-evolving understanding of our identity. In truth, we are the infinite and continuous unfulfillment of God's Beingness forever being Self-realized.

Our understanding of God demands that our existence provide meaning and purpose for o God's existence. There was never a timeless speck of reality when our individualized existence and God's existence were separate realities. The individualized-Us and God are inseparably linked as we navigate ourselves through objective reality's timeless time-filled eternities.

Each of us is individually responsible for finding, understanding, and obeying God. Our preordained destiny inhabits each of us with a divine urge to seek, understand, accept, and acknowledge our everlasting universality in and with God. Infinity's installed deep-rooted urge which permeates our infinite existence leads to our continuous self-conscious reconnection to God, as we forever seek to embrace a self-acknowledging acceptance of Him.

Even though each one of us is forever part of God, our understandings of God always result from our self-conscious interacting relationship, with idea realm ideas. From our individualized perspectives, God consists of the highest apprehension of divine truth, infinitely bringing the source of meaning and happiness, to our objective self-conscious awareness.

Thus, our destiny is a fate of continuous divine realization of God's infinitely divine completeness, through our self-incorporation of idea realm ideas. God's Self-evolving existence is infinite and the self-evolving of ideas, into their manifesting purpose, is infinite. However, the foreverness of God and the foreverness of ideas function separately in ultimate reality.

God is only aware of the infinite progressiveness of His Self-existing foreverness. In His Infinite Self-realizing of Himself, His Infinite Self-awareness is His infinite forever divinity realized. He is infinitely unaware of all things having real existence. God is forever a sole and separate component of ultimate reality's infinite composition.

God's Self-aware existence is forever limited, by His Infinite Self-encapsulated Beingness. No happenings in this world, or in any aspect of ultimate reality, are ever caused or directly influenced by God. God is eternally and infinitely isolated in the endlessness of His Divine Self-being Self-knowingness.

God is understood as His nature is acknowledged, understood and demonstrated, by each of us individually. In the understanding of God, there are infinite realms of depth-filled reaches, awaiting our acknowledgment, accessibility, and understanding. However, the total realization of God, although infinitely desired, cherished, and sought is never to be fully self-realized.

All meaningful understandings of God result from our infinite ongoing, unbroken cord of divine assimilations of truth endlessly accrued, in the infinite progressions of our infinite existence. If our understanding of God were not an endless succession of spiritual knowingness, the purpose for our self-aware existence, as the living of life, would lose divine meaning.

One of the great misinterpretations in the spiritual journeying of humanity is the belief God has a specifically designed, purpose, or plan for each person in this world. However, the purpose for individualized-Man's existence is not, has not, and cannot be Self-willfully determined, by the God of anyone's understanding. God's existence and our existence have a separate expression and a different purpose.

To God's Self-realization, His existence is the only existence. Our individualized divine self-awareness necessitates an understanding of God. However, God's Self-existence requires no Self-awareness or Self-understanding, of our individualized-Us reality, by Him. We forever exist as a part of God's Self-aware unknowingness.

Thus, we are the infinite offspring of God's unknowingness, forever seeking the divine understanding of our God-identity. We are the divinely infinite part of God that is never to be self-consciously fulfilled, through our self-acting awareness of Him. However, it is the self-conscious fulfilling of our inner communion with God; that makes our existence a desirable self-aware forever divine treasure.

There is no Self-aware God who leads or guides any member of His spiritual family. Success in the self-realizing our desired embracing of our spirituality is determined individually, through our interpretations of objective reality, as we forever traverse the earthly realms of physical experience.

God remains supremely Self-consciously unaware of our spiritual or non-spiritual travels, experiences, challenges, and sorrows that we encounter, as we unceasingly venture onward into the foreverness of the finitely-infinite. Our forever destiny is to experience an existence of which God has no Self-awareness.

Our destiny is to experience objective reality, from the viewpoint of our divinely unique specialness. Thus, objective reality exists for us to understand, interpret, experience and celebrate our self-activating uniqueness, distinctness, and individuality. Our self-aware existence is the celebration of ultimate reality understanding itself.

Our unified togetherness and our uniquely self-realized existences have an assigned destiny forever designed into our wholiness of our God-nature. The design aspect of our infinite existence is forever unfolding in the expression of our infinite existence. Through our self-aware capability of understanding all the components of reality, we are the forever designers of our fate.

Thus, since each one of us possesses infinite existence; each one of us is the design-interpreter of our destiny and the design-interpreter of our unfolding divinity. The designed purpose for our lives is to understand ourselves as divine beings, uniquely expressing our Godliness individually, divinely, and uniquely.

The primary objective for God's existence is to know His forever unfolding Self-beingness, as the forever ongoing fulfilling of His infinite divine nature. Thus, the only portion of ultimate reality God knows is His Self-divine Self-identity. If it were not for each one of us part of God, ultimate reality's existence would be completely impervious to God's existence.

Thus, God exists to forever Self-Be, Self-know, and Self-absorb His unlimited and unobstructed divine nature. However, each of us has a real existence to discover forever, to understand forever, to realize forever, to interpret forever, to experience forever, and to know God's forever Beingness. We exist to understand and know ourselves in God.

Although, God's nature and our nature are identical in substance; it is only God's nature forever unfolding within Himself. God's nature is the total evolving wholeness of His Infinite Self-identity. Our individualized divine nature is the wholeness and wholiness of God's infinite divinity, self-understood by us, uniquely and individually.

Each one of us is the only component of ultimate reality capable of understanding, using, and experiencing God's nature, including God's love. Since God has no Self-conscious knowledge or awareness of any other self-conscious existence in ultimate reality, other than His own, He does not Self-consciously love us, or Self-consciously love anything possessing infinite existence.

God existence is beyond any capability of Self-willing influence upon anything. Thus, He cannot impact, determine, control, or recognize any reality, other than His own. The sole purpose for God's Self-realizing of His existence is to give meaning to our existence. Without the existence of God, we would have no divinity to inherit, and our self-individualized existences would consist of infinite godless meanderings through realms of meaninglessness.

The understanding that God does not Self-consciously love us or Self-consciously love anything possessing infinite existence should not distract us from the truth of His ever-presence. God is at the center of our individualized beingness. His forever-presence stretches forth within us, urging and encouraging us, to experience the far-reaching rims of the objective realm.

Our evolving understandings forever take root in our self-acceptance of our divinity. God is forever within each of us, from the darkest depths of our painful realizations of godless unreality to the highest reaches of the truth-drenched summits of divinity realized. God within each one of us is our forever source of salvation. Where there is no understanding of God, there is no salvation.

We are the purposeful fulfilling of God's existence forever providing meaningful justification, for the existence of all reality. If God did not exist, there would be no ultimate reality to interpret divinely. All of existing reality must contain a spiritual meaning for its infinite beingness. Thus, God's infinite existing reality gives ultimate beingness a purpose for existence. Each one of us is the portion of God that interprets divinity into all of the unchanging foreverness.

We have always existed, we exist now, and we will always exist. Nothing ever permanently alters or impinges upon the indestructibility of our foreverness. Since God is always at the center of the self-revealment of ourselves, He must ceaselessly be sought and self-consciously understood and experienced, throughout the entirety of our ongoing objective existence. We are the individualization of God forever surveying His Kingdom.

If we are not the individualized God-kings of reality, our self-existence would be entirely controlled, determined, and empowered by the gods of unreality. Even though the God of actual reality exists forever, the potential existing god of unreality is also ever-present, in our commonly shared individualized self-conscious awareness. The self-claiming non-real god over unreality prevents our recognition of the true God forever blessing our self-beingness, with His divine presence.

When our self-conscious choices displayed by our actions, turn us from God, we are self-consciously choosing to misinterpret the reality of idea realm ideas. These misinterpretations result in the birth-apparitions for all so-called godless evils and sins, appearing as warped truths, wrapped in the audacity of pretended existence.

Where our misinterpreted evil and sin-laden ideas are accepted and acted upon, punishment is unavoidable, lest we lose the cleansing power of our infinite existence that enables us, to eternally redeem ourselves to the self-awareness of our divinity, forever expressing in divine perpetuity. The self-accounting for our depraved godless acts of sin and evil is our forever eternal punishment realized infinitely.

However, our ever increasing spiritual understanding of divine awareness enables us to self-consciously, reunify ourselves with God. Thus, in our forever divinely unfolding understanding, we only accept the one true God as our eternal and infinite Comforter, our eternal and infinite Guide, and our eternal and infinite Protector. The divinity of God is the divinity we see in all things.

As we self-consciously identify ourselves with God's ever-presence, we become His self-appointed emissaries, to all of forever reality. Thus, God is forever bestowing His infinite blessings to each one of us, and thus throughout all of the objective realms, through our individualized self-acquiring understandings of our spiritual existence, forever in Him.

The one true God is forever non-personal in His relationship to each one of us, as individualizations of Man. However, as we become self-consciously obedient to His divine nature, we are continuingly guided through the discovering and rediscovering of our forever spiritual identity.

Therefore, there is a sense in which an impersonal God is forever in consonance with each of us as individualize-Man. However, the one true God only speaks to us, through His infinitely divine nature, ongoingly extending forth into the foreverness of our collective and individualized self-realizing spiritual identities.

God's forever Beingness, within each of us, is the sanctum of our beingness. God's Voice is our spiritual communion with His ever-present divine essence. His inner divine nature becomes His Voice reaching out to us, for our cognition, receptivity, acceptance, and obedience. Thus, the outpouring of the sacredness is His divine nature is forever calling to us for our recognition and acceptance.

Self-consciously experiencing the reality of God must be earned, by expressing the goodness of God understood, in the realm of appearance. The calling Voice of God is blessed within each of us. However, one of our greatest of spiritual sins is the desire to experience God calling essence, without the required divine effort of demonstrating His nature, in the realm of experience.

The understanding of divine truth and the experiencing of divine truth are not the same. Divine realization must always precede spiritual expression. Delays, in interpretations of truth, understood, are due to the enticing ambrosia of godless unreality clinging steadfastly to our evolving self-spiritual awareness.

Our capability to self-consciously return to God is God's infinite grace bestowed upon the individualized objective-Us, who are infinitely unworthy of His inner-spiritual divine presence. God's grace is forever manifesting through His divine essence. Correctly interpreted, God's grace is His infinite ever active Divine Beingness forever enriching our self-understanding of ourselves.

Thus, the grace of God is obtained by each of us through our self-conscious acceptance God's nature expressing objectively through us. As we self-consciously accept God, we automatically repudiate the taunting drums of godlessness, continuingly beating upon the self-awareness of our forever divinity.

The grace of God is our saving grace from all things unreal. Without the inner grace of God, we could never realize our divine destiny. God's grace is His forever indwelling divine presence, understood by each of us, adhered to by each of us, and cherished by each of us, as the expression of our divinity in self-conscious action.

Our understandings of God are always from our individualized perspectives. In the understanding of God, there is no such thing as the Word of God, if that means there are words attributable to a Self-thinking, Self-acting, and Self-producing Deity. God resides in a state of perpetually permanent blissfulness. He is incapable of Self-consciously imparting any understanding of Himself, to us as individualized-Man.

Thus, there is no such thing as the infallible Word of God. God is always understood by each of us individually, and it is always our understandings of God's divine nature that are meaningfully considered the Word of God. God's Word is His forever silent beingness speaking to each of us, as the supreme authority over all of the existence of reality. However, it is our receptivity to God's Word that makes God's Word, the Word of God.

God is the source-understanding for all things exhibiting the reality of all Isness. Still, there is no Self-conscious God, who knowingly and directly expresses His Voice, His Word, or authors a Sacred Book containing His infinite divine wisdom. All sacred books represent the man of this world's limited spiritual understandings and interpretations of God's existence, essence, purpose, and desires.

The closest concept regarding the Word of God is when we self-consciously identify, accept, and demonstrate the qualities or attributes of God, in our self-conscious experiencing of existence. Thus, the divine inspiration of God is identifiable and realized by each one of us, individually and independently.

The Self-conscious knowingness of God is forever spiritually mute, in the timelessness of ultimate reality. Our forever understanding of God is God's Self-consciousness recognition of Himself, through our objective receptivity to His divinity. Thus, each one of us, individually, is the sacred book of God, in forever active expression.

The entirety of God is infinitely whole. The entirety of each one of us is the forever evolving individual wholeness. Thus, in our true divinity realized, we are the nature of God, understanding the essence of God, expressing the essence of God, as the spirit of God. Each one of us is the forever allness of God, forever understanding the allness of God, and forever expressing the allness of God, individually.

We cannot understand ourselves until we see the expression of ourselves. We only spiritually receive the things we are spiritually prepared to receive through our acceptance, understanding, and connection with our inner divinity. We are always divine beingness, we have always been divine beingness, and we will always be the forever beingness of our divinity.

We are infinite beings, and our understanding of ourselves is infinite. We exist to understand ourselves as divine. Our understandings of ourselves are infinitely individual. The only measure for understanding the progression of our self-evolving spirituality is the depth of our desire to express the love of God, in our expressions of kindness.

The Kingdom of God pertains to a divine principality where God's Self-authority reigns supreme. However, God does not Self-rule over or control realm housed in reality. Simply, the Kingdom of God is our inherited and forever ingrained divinity. Our divine identities are forever unknown to God, but we forever know God.

Thus, the Kingdom of God is God's forever unfolding nature, which becomes available to our ever increasing spiritual self-awareness of God's presence, closeted within our self-awareness. When the self-ruling control over ourselves is consistently divinely-minded, we experience existence as the knowingness of God.

The Kingdom of God is the forever presence of deistic truth understood, accepted, and applied by each one of us. Thus, the Kingdom of God is God's indwelling presence, including all of His ever forever expanding attributes, and qualities. Understanding His Kingdom, within each of us, allows us to interpret our physical world existence, and divinely explain all aspects of objective reality.

Often, new-God insights replace old-God insights. In the progressiveness of our infinite existence, all understandings of God are finite-infinite and incremental, equal and divinely necessary. It is forever mandatory that in the objective realm, we express our divinity at receptivity level, to the acceptance of things that are forever divinely real. Therefore, all of our expressions of divinity are incremental.

Thus, the realness of truth is only understood incrementally. All incremental spiritual understandings of truth are on equal footing to all progressions of our comprehensions of divinity. Therefore, on the infinite linear range, of our spiritual unfoldment, our self-conscious awarenesses of forever reality are equal, in our infinite spiritual progressions.

Thus, there is no superiority in the process of spiritual truth self-consciously assimilated. Increasing understandings of ever-real truth represent the highest evolving understandings of divine truth. Therefore, our infinite divine existence is a continuum of the highest at-the-time spiritual truths understood.

Our experiencing of existence is to be forever unveiled and realized, as a finitely infinite reality, unknown to ultimate reality. Our understanding of God is the forever source of our continuing salvation as we finitely and infinitely experience and re-experience our individual existence.

However, our salvation is always eternally experienced finitely in the endlessly moving streams of spirituality understood and demonstrated. Since our experiences are forever finite, our punishments are forever finitely limited, and the finalizing of our salvations is forever finite. Our forever ongoing salvation is the forever realizing of our divinity. All salvation comes from God, but only through our understanding of God, and our oneness with God.

To the evolving man of this world, God grants pardoned salvation, for his sins. Thus, there seems to be a collective self-conscious need instilling into this world's man, a yearning desire to believe in a personal anthropomorphic God, who answers prayers, heals the sick, comforts the suffering, protects the needy, and forgives the sinner.

This humanization of God has distorted and prevented a clearer understanding of Him, in relationship to the man of this world's existence, and to the forever reality of ultimate reality. The man of this world, in his spiritual isolation, has chosen to cede his power of self-conscious understanding to a personal God, whom he is incapable of understanding.

The man of this world cannot understand God because he cannot understand himself. To understand himself, he must understand his existence. Since the man of this world attributes his beingness to God, he has no inherent driven desire to comprehend the why and wherefore of his physical world self-realized existence. He exists because his God gave him life, so he believes, so accepts, and un-questions.

Thus, the man of this world has chosen to find comfort in believing in a God as Someone whom to talk with, Someone who listens, Someone who cares, and Someone who removes the pains, heartaches, and sorrows continuously crowding into his life. The man of this world accepts a watchful God, a guiding God, a protecting God, and especially a personal God who loves him unconditionally.

The instilling understanding, interpretation, and acceptance of a personal God has contributed mightily to the misunderstanding of God's true nature. The God presently understood by the man of this world has molded his understanding of God, in relationship to the image of himself he accepts, the image he acknowledges and interprets himself to be.

The man of this world chooses to believe in a personal God because he has failed to recognize and understand that the infinite self-regenerating power of existence resides forever within him. The man of this world feels so impotent that he seeks an all-powerful personal God to sustain, maintain, and comfort his forever existence.

As the evolving worldly-man, of objective existence, contemplated God's nature, he grasped ever hopefully, onto the concept that the God of his understanding was a higher divine crystallization of himself. He attempted to identify himself with God's qualities such as love, harmony, peace, joy, contentment, et cetera. Then, he endeavored to accept those divine qualities into his self-awareness and projects them onto a Deity that he understands, and self-actively creates.

God is not personal because He is completely and wholly unaware of the individual existence of worldly man. God did not create the man of this world, and He did not create this world. God has never created anything or anyone. However, the man of this world whom I identify as the physical-Man of this world, which is the immortal-Man of God, came from God as the expression of God.

The present existing man of this physical world, whom I now understand and identify as individualizations of God's infinite family of Man, has infinitely existed and infinitely existed as part of God. Thus, as individualizations of physical-Man, we accept God as the source-substance of our infinite wholiness, as we forever know and experience our infinite existence.

God's nature possesses the quality of Self-conscious Self-awareness. Since God's nature includes Self-conscious Self-awareness, our divine nature as the individualized extension of God, must also contain the reality of self-conscious self-awareness. God's Self-awareness only encompasses the infinite realizing of Himself only. Our self-awareness, as individualized-Man, includes the forever realization of all aspects of ultimate reality.

If God knows nothing of our existence, what is the significance of His reality to us? God's existence is our existence. Thus, as individualized-Man, God's nature is our nature individualized. God does not depend on us, but each one of us is entirely dependent upon Him. Since God is the substance of our individual and collective beingness, all the power of infinite self-aware beingness, resides within each of us.

God does not possess the power of Self-conscious understanding because His Self-consciousness is only aware of the reality of Himself. God has no realization of anything, except the forever evolving of harmonious perfection. Only each one of us possesses the self-conscious power of understanding. This innate power of self-attained understanding knowledge is the only self-conscious directing power, in all aspects of ultimate reality.

In this sense, each one of us, as individualized-Man, is more authoritatively powerful than God, who has no power. The infinite impersonal God has no Self-power, knows no Self-power, and wields no Self-power. It is each one of us who understands, interprets and utilizes, the non-matched power of truth realized.

To amplify my contention that God is not anthropomorphic, I begin this section by discussing the three universally accepted beliefs concerning the man of this world's present understanding of God's nature. I give these three assumptions for the purpose of discussion, even though I reject them, as containing any real spiritual validity or actual divine understanding.

God as All-powerful

For God to be God, it is assumed that He must possess all power. Thus, there cannot be any power or anything superior to Him, or capable of opposing Him. An all-powerful God knows nothing of failure. Since He cannot fail, He is never fearful, insecure, uncertain or anxious. He never lacks Self-confidence for He can achieve anything He chooses or desires to achieve.

An all-powerful God is never disappointed. He only knows success. Nothing or no one ever challenges Him. He never loses at anything because of His all-powerfulness. He is infinitely indestructible. Thus, as being all-powerful God, He is infinitely Self-confident in His forever nature.

If God is all-powerful, He has no worries, of any kind, for His powerfulness is unchallenged and unchanging. He is forever undaunted, and His power exists throughout the forever always of the forever always. He has no enemies. There is nothing in existence capable of opposing, influencing, or impacting Him, in any way.

God as All-knowing

For God to be God, it is assumed He must be all-knowing. Thus, there cannot be anything anywhere He does not understand. God, at all times, Self-understands all the forever things of existence. In God's forever all-knowing understanding of reality, He is the divine King over all of forever infinity.

God is never uncertain about anything for He comprehends the nature, substance, and outcomes of all things. He possesses no curiosity because there is nothing outside of His Self-awareness to understand. He never contemplates "what-if" possibilities, because He forever knows the outcome of all things, situations, circumstances, and conditions for of forever existence.

There would never be anything new for an all-knowing God to learn, enjoy, or anticipate. He would never know the excitement of expectation, in the discovering of the newness of things because there would never be anything new or unknown, to Him. An all-powerful, all-knowing, all-present God cannot experience existence because that would presuppose that something exists that He would have a desire to experience.

He would never attempt to understand anything, for He is forever Self-aware of all things. Finally, if God is all-knowing, He would never change His mind, for He would always know the most beneficial and perfect outcome or solution to all circumstance, and all situations. An all-powerful, all-knowing, all-present God would be simultaneously aware of all things real.

God as All-present

For God to be God it is assumed that He must be all-present, in all places, at all times. Thus, He is self-continuously present everywhere, from the furthest star to the nearest tree. If God is all-present, nothing is ever new for Him to discover, unearth, or experience. To Him, there are no new worlds, or new realms of any kind, to be unearthed or discovered.

Thus, an all-present God never knows the child-like anticipation of venturing into the mysterious vistas of the unknown. An all-present God would know nothing of the alluring mysteries and veiled enticements, of undiscovered realms. If God is present everywhere, He would entirely lack curiosity concerning any locale, throughout the entirety of all realities.

It seems self-evident that an all-powerful, all-present God, having an infinite understanding and an infinite awareness of all things, would have anything in common with the presently self-aware disgracefulness we collectively identify ourselves to be, as individualized worldly-man.

If an all-powerful, all-knowing, all-present God created the man of this world, with the potentiality of committing the most ungodliness of actions; He most assuredly demonstrated a poor decision-making process. How could the God of anyone's understanding create an environment, such as our, which fosters the antithesis of the forever glory of divinity?

Why would any infinite, all-knowing, all-powerful, and all-present God, be the author of the man of this world, if He pre-knew His creations would become overwhelmed with sorrow-wrenching actions and torments, of ungodly awfulness? Such a God, who would choose do such a thing, could never be the God of my acknowledgment, understanding, or acceptance.

If a personal God created worldly-man, He created the potential for the expression of ungodliness. However, no all-powerful God ever created the man of this world or has ever created anything into existence, for even in the all-powerfulness of God, if such a God existed, He would not be capable of creating infinite reality, into infinite reality.

However, as the individualized infinite-Us, forever individually and uniquely expressing God, we are ultimate reality's gods of creation. We express ourselves as creative gods because we are the only infinite self-conscious awareness capable of knowing, understanding, and interpreting existence into experiences. Thus, our creations are the interpretations of our living reality, through the experiencing of our forever beingness.

Thus, we are the only the creators of experiences, and experiences have no reality in ultimate reality. Hence, we are not creators of anything that is to possess infinite existence. Real forever permanence exists as infinite non-changeability. Thus, in our forever existence, we cannot alter, change, impact, or affect anything containing infinitely real continuity.

There is no God, no one, or no thing capable of creating reality. The foreverness of ultimate reality is the changing-changeless. All that comprises ultimate reality has existed in past foreverness, present foreverness, and in the perpetuity of continuing timeless foreverness.

Following is a further discussion on this subject containing what I understand to be some main difficulties in the believing of a personal all-knowing, all-powerful, and all-present-God, whom Self-knowingly comforts us, protects us, serves us and saves us. The God of my understanding is the God of my self-forever beingness.

Is humanity's belief in a personal God a necessary belief?

The answer is both "Yes" and "No". The spiritually interpretative answer depends on understanding the divine perspective of existence. The answer also involves understanding the purpose of our lives, which is to experience the forever reality of our self-awareness. The fundamental question to be asked: Was man of this world created by a personal God, or has he infinitely existed?

If a personal God created the man of this world, the divinely conceived man of this world must be and is awe-struck by his self-conscious awareness, of his existence. Assuming a personal God did create the man of this world, would he have had a pre-created existence? Yes, because the man of this world would have always existed in the all-knowing mind, of a personal God. Incidentally, if a personal all-knowing God knows the infinite-us, how could any us be anything other than what He knows us to be?

So the created man of this world comes into this world ignorant, confused, and bewildered. He soon becomes tormented by his inability to understand and control the factors impacting his physical beingness and his environment. "Surely," he thinks to himself, "there must be someone or something that can me save from the wretchedness of this world and also from my wretchedness?"

Thus, created–man feels completely helpless in meeting the challenges engulfing his physical existence. Often, he knows he is doing wrong, but he cannot help himself. Thus, he needs something outside of himself to save him from his uncontrollable self-actions. Hence, due to his needs, as created man, he created a personal God to save him, to understand him, to guide him, to protect him, to love him, and to free him from the torments of physical existence.

However, when the so-called created man of this world, realizes he is the physical-Man of a non-personal God, he understands that he has self-knowingly and infinitely existed and that he is forever the indestructible wholiness of perfection. Now, he understands that the only accountability for all of the occurrences, in the experiencing of his existence, is to himself, never to a personal God, or anyone's understanding of God.

Also, physical-Man realizes that he needs no saving grace from a personal God because he has never sinned in the eyes of God. Thus, if he has never sinned in God's eyes, why would he need God's salvation, personal or non-personal? Thus, for him, the existence of God has no meaning that would require His Divine Self-conscious intervention into his life.

The purpose of life is to experience our self-aware reality. However, why do we have an infinite, never created self-aware reality, to experience? I have no answer. However, the forever process of experiencing existence brings its blessings, its punishments, and its salvation. We exist to know God; He does not exist to know us.

Is it necessary to believe in a personal God? It only matters if that belief is the present state of someone's spiritual apprehension and acceptance. Our ongoing spiritual understandings are the forever stepping-stones, in the evolving of our forever divinity. Since all understandings of God are infinite, all realizations of God express the realizations truth, self-accepted, and self-understood.

The only things of real lasting spiritual import are the displays of kindness, in the expressions of our divinity, respect for all life including vegetation, insects, microorganisms, animals, and especially the unborn, and to sincerely seek the God of our understanding.

Anyone who believes in a personal God and is sincere in their spirituality will find their finite-infinite salvation. These individuals eventually arrive in one of the seven Heavens of this eternity. I will discuss the Heavens of eternity in the portion of this book where I describe the eternal spiritual worlds.

Thus, how each one of us sincerely and lovingly understands God is forever irrelevant. How we express our understanding of God is forever relevant. How can anyone's belief in God be judged, if their realization of divine truth brings them happiness, and encourages them to be loving ambassadors to all of life? It is our destiny to experience life, and the experiencing of life includes forever and innumerable understandings, interpretations, and divine obedience.

Did a personal God create man the universe?

For discussion, let's assume that a personal God exists, and He created the man of this world and the infinite universe. Presently, the man of this world, supposedly created by a personal God, suffers in varying degrees of pain, heartache, sorrow, and misery. If a personal God created worldly man, He created an earthly mess.

Thus, does it not follow that if a personal God created the man of this world, did He not also create the potentiality for countless worldly bouts of miseries and unpleasantness, which came into existence due to the existence of created man? No matter how the preverbal pie, is divinely sliced, the so-called personal God, of all creation, is the first cause of all misery that ever was, ever is, and ever will be.

In other words, if the man of this world were never created, by a personal God, the various forms of suffering, sorrow, and pain would never have come into existence. Thus, a personal God created the physical environment stage for the appearances of all evils. It takes twisted logic not to blame a personal God for being the first cause for all of the ensuing actions of His created man.

I understand many will be those who reject the above conclusion. Believers in a personal God would maintain that a personal God did not create the evil sufferings of this world, because when He created man, He endowed His creation with a free will. Therefore, the created man, of this world, was given the free will capability not to seek, understand, or accept his Creator. He could reject his Creator, or ignore his Creator; thus, the created man of this world earned the godless consequences of his godlessly lived existence.

Therefore, in the exercising of created worldly man's free will, all the resultant pain, heartache, sorrow, and unhappiness, he self-willingly brought down upon himself. Therefore, his Creator God is absolved of the responsibility for his pain filled existence including heartaches, sorrows, and unhappiness, due to his sovereign free will.

Still, if a personal God created man and the universe did He not also create the conditions giving rise to the POTENTIALITY for the experiencing of pain, heartache, sorrow, and unhappiness? If a personal God had not created man, the world, and the universe, experiences of pain, hurt, anguish, grief, et cetera, would never have existence.

Further, why would a personal God choose this time-speck of infinity, to create the present universe, the world, and man? Think of it, if a personal God exists, He existed before He created man and the universe. Perhaps, this personal God has created, and will create infinite varieties of man, and countless families of worlds? This observation has a similarity to my understanding of ultimate reality.

If a personal God created anything that never before had real infinite permanence, would not He be adding something new to His forever unchanging understanding of Himself? How could a God, of anyone's understanding, create something new, and that newly created something, is then added to the reality of ultimate reality, or to Himself? That is illogical.

Also, an all-knowing personal God would have the infinite Self-awareness of everyone who has never existed, exists now, or will ever exist. Thus, as I said earlier, no individual man has ever actually been created into existence, because the entire reality of created man has existed, in the foreverness of His infinite, all-knowing mind. Thus, a personal God did not create the man of this world. Rather, He pictured forth the man of this world, from the infinite chambers of His infinite mind.

Thus, a personal God is the infinite repository for all of the individualizations of man, to be created or not to be created, into existence. The individualizations of man, forever residing within His Self-conscious knowingness, were impelled into the outer created world of appearances. Hence, the man of this world was never created into existence, by a personal God. Thus, all individualities of created man have no beginnings or endings, only the infinite reality, within His Infinite Self-knowingness.

The man of this world was never a creation of a personal God. Thus, he has no reason to be grateful to a Creator God's existence, for his self-aware existence. It is logically not possible to create infinite self-aware existence. Self-conscious awareness is an infinite reality of beingness, without antecedent.

The real individualize-Man of this world, along with all of forever reality possesses forever existence, devoid of any concept of creation. The individualized-Man of *Godness* has always existed devoid of a beginning or an ending, throughout the timelessness of God's forever niche in ultimate reality.

Still, the concept of self-aware existence is interesting to contemplate. Some individuals believe that our presently lived lives in this world are the only lives we will ever live. Thus, when we cease to exist in this world, we forever self-consciously cease to exist in all reality, itself.

If that was true, what would be the meaning of a one-time self-aware existence? It seems illogical that there could be such a thing, as a single self-aware being, having only one beginning and only one ending. It is inconceivable, to me, that self-conscious beingness could ever permanently cease to exist, in foreverness of reality.

On the other hand, some individuals believe that after we experience our presently earthly lives, we will continue to experience self-conscious existence. The dilemma with that possibly is: What will be doing, if we self-consciously continue to exist? If we are to do something infinitely, there must be a forever designed-in plan for each of us. In this book, I say there is, and there is not a forever guiding plan, for our forever existence.

If there is an infinite design for our infinite existence, how did it originate? Some would say the plan, for our infinite beingness came from a personal God. However, what if there is no personal God? More pointedly, what if there is no God at all, of anyone's understanding, anywhere in the foreverness of ultimate reality?

To me, it is self-evident that our self-aware existence must have a purpose. Are we to believe that we have only one short lifespan of self-consciousness, and that is it? If we only existed for one life, there would be no accountability for our wrongful actions. If we only lived for one life, our self-aware existence would be significantly influenced by the forces of unpredictability, and there would further opportunities for adjusting to self-aware existence.

If we only lived one self-conscious life, the luck-factors of existence would be the primary determiners, for experiencing or not experiencing happiness, in anyone's briefly lived self-aware life. Thus, self-evident self-conscious existence must have a purpose, beyond a one-time existence, or the experiencing of life is nothing by a self-aware rumbling, rambling, ringing reality of meaninglessness.

Further, if we only had a one-time self-awareness of existence, we could never acquire an understanding of why we exist to live life. Therefore, we would have self-aware existence having no knowledge of the how or the why we are self-consciously experiencing life. How ridiculous is that? To me, meaningless existence in a functioning reality is incomprehensible.

The only thing that makes logical sense, to me, is that each one of us has self-consciously existed forever. If we have not self-consciously existed forever, how did our self-consciousness originate? Are we to believe inanimate matter evolves and suddenly becomes self-conscious of itself? Still, our infinite existence does not necessary mean that God exists. So, why believe in the existence of God?

God exists because there must be an infinite source of harmonious reality that we can rely upon, to joyfully experience our infinite existence. Without the forever reality of goodness, embedded into a forever God for each of us to understand and experience, the unpredictable factors of reality would render our infinite self-aware existence as immortal beings reigning over godlessness.

This book describes the aspects of ultimate reality that enable us to understand why we exist, to understand the plan for our existence, to comprehend the existence of God, and to understand our relationship to and with God. Most importantly, this book provides the realization that each one of us is all-powerful through the infinite realizing process of understanding. In the foreverness of divine truth, I accept the realization that each one of us self-consciously exists in the forever reality of harmony, wholeness, wholiness, and joy.

What does it mean to say that each of us is all-powerful? It means, through our ability of self-comprehending infinite reality, we can potentially accomplish anything. We can understand our existence. We can understand and assimilate God. We can make our forever beingness infinitely joyous. We can control the infinite functions of chance, opportunity, randomness, and general unpredictability. We can override the physical laws of the universe. We can understand and rejoice that we are infinitely and individually part of God.

Still, consider this. If a personal all-knowing, all-power God exists, why could not He, in the fairness of His divine Infinite Beingness, have had a pre-creation talk with every individual He planned to create into existence? In that talk, He would explain the consequences of an individual's designed-into-existence self-conscious life.

He would explain to them what the self-conscious actions of their creatively established self-aware existence would be like, with its profusion of troubles, heartaches, and sorrows. He would also explain the joys involved in successfully experiencing a temporal worldly reality. He would explain to them that if they followed His Divine Plan, they would forever exist in infinite self-aware joyfulness.

After discussing, with all individuals, the options that created self-aware existence involve, He would then ask them if they desired a self-aware living existence as life. If they said "Yes" they would be formed and molded into infinite existence, which includes the self-conscious living of life. Thus, they would truly be responsible for their future life decisions because they chose to accept the self-conscious responsibility to exist infinitely.

If they said "No" they would remain uncreated. Of course, in the all-knowingness of a personal God, He would pre-know the choice each would make, but still, there's a sense of infinite fairness in giving each non-existent entity a choice regarding the creative implementation of their infinite objective existence.

Did a personal God create Hell?

Surely an all-knowing, all-powerful free will wielding personal-God, could if He chose to do so, create an infinite environment for endless torment. Think of the irrationality, in believing in an infinitely loving personal God, who would Self-consciously choose to establish a place of everlasting torment, for His wayward subjects that have forever existed in His Infinite Self-knowingness?

However, I do not believe that it is possible for an infinite God, of anyone's understanding, to create a torture place of endless punishment; for creatures that never self-consciously asked to be created, into infinite existence. That is divine self-evident unfairness. How could an infinite God, who had no responsibility for His infinite existent reality, make others responsible for their non-asked-for self-aware reality of existence?

A personal God did not create Himself; thus, a personal God did not create His infinite nature, which even He cannot change. Now, it is evident that each of us, as a perpetual self-aware being, is gifted with the capability to imagine. Now, imagine yourself existing as an infinite non-created personal-God.

Ask yourself this question: Would I, if I was the infinite, all-knowing, all-powerful personal-God of the foreverness of ultimate reality, create a place of infinite and everlasting torment and punishment, for my divinely created but spiritually recalcitrant and rebellious children, a place I knew each would eventually inhabit?

I do not believe anyone who answers the above question honestly, would admit to a willingness to create such an infinite place of tortuous punishment, for created creatures destined to exist infinitely. However, say you: "An infinite personal all-knowing, all-powerful personal God can do whatever He so chooses." True, but if a personal God does create a place of forever punishment, He is choosing to be infinitely unforgiving.

Still, even an infinite personal God cannot do anything contrary to His nature. If a personal God is capable of creating an infinite abode for the infinite torment of His rebellious recalcitrants, understanding of the nature of a personal God, would have to be altered. That type of a personal God, who creates a place for infinite torture, cannot be a personal God consumed by love.

The bottom line is this, if you as a created creature of a personal God would not create a place of such infinite torment and punishment, for the spiritually unworthy of the one sacred family, how could the one true infinite personal God create such a place? It appears to me that a created being of a personal God, who would not create such a horrid tortured destination, is spiritually superior to His so-called Creator.

Does a personal God forgive His self-aware creations and then discipline them?

The answer to this question involves a quagmire of uncertainties. If sincere followers of their personal God believe He forgives them of their sins, He most assuredly must forgive them. However, what if His spiritually loyal subjects continue to commit the same transgressions repeatedly, while they continually and sincerely seek and beseech His forgiveness? Does a personal continue in His forgiving of their same sins?

If the answer is "Yes;" then, how many times does a personal God forgive someone for repeating the same sins? There are many sincere followers and believers, in a personal God, who have no intention of ever changing their sinful ways. Should these individuals expect a personal God's ongoing, perpetual, and non-ceasing forgiveness?

Now, let's suppose a personal God chooses to discipline those individuals who habitually commit recurring sins. In His omniscience, He would pre-know how successful or unsuccessful His imposed discipline would be. Thus, would God only choose to punish those individuals whom He pre-knew would spiritually benefit from His punishment? Would He still continue to punish His children whom He pre-knew would not spiritually benefit?

What about non-believers? Does a personal God discipline them, if so, why? Does He punish non-believers whom He knows will eventually choose to become believers? Does He punish non-believers and believers in the same manner? More importantly, does not any form of imposed punishment; go against the concept of an individual's infinite free will?

If a personal God disciplines His faithful followers, He would know the required punishment needed to correct of their unwanted sinful behaviors; therefore, all of His divinely dispensed punishment would be spiritually fruitful. If a personal God's discipline were not successful, that would denote incompetence attributed to an all-knowing personal God. How could that be?

Still, would a personal God discipline His subjects while at the same time knowing His discipline would not be successful? Consider this, for a personal God to give His created man a free will and then punish His creations, to alter their free will choices, seems as though He is Self-contradicting Himself.

Finally, how would a true believer or a true non-believer, in a personal God, ever understand that their received punishment, came from their personal God? Imagine someone saying on the Day of Judgment: Lord, if You had disciplined me appropriate to my sinful behavior, I would have become Your obedient servant, rather than the despicable creature You created me to be."

Also, is it not possible that the divinely applied punishment, administered by a personal God, may prompt some individuals, to turn away from their Creator? Thus, would a personal God punish some people if He pre-knew His Self-imposed discipline would result, in their final rejection of Him?

Does a personal God have a plan for each of His created subjects?

What might be some of the general purposes a personal God might choose for His creations? First, it could be assumed that His divine plans would include the successful achieving of common life goals, such as obtaining a productive profession. Second, it could be expected that His divine plans would include, believing, trusting, loving, and obeying His forever Creator. Third, it could be assumed that all His divine plans would include the realizing of happiness, in their expressions of life.

What might a personal God design, in general, for His creations? First, it could be assumed that His divine plans would include the achieving general life goals. Second, it could be expected that His divine plans would include, believing, trusting, loving, and obeying His Creator. Third, it could be assumed that all His divine plans would include the realizing of happiness, in His created subjects experiences of life.

Now, what might some designed purposes of a personal God be, for His creations? For example, are some members of His divine family destined to become famous, to become wealthy, to be uniquely talented, to have high intelligence, to be beautiful, or perhaps predetermined to be liked by all, et cetera?

If the above represents specific plans for some of a personal God's creations, there seems to be an apparent unevenness, in His distribution of individually designed plans, especially considering that few of us, would be successful, in realizing or achieving of many of the above outcomes. Why should not all individual goals, established by a personal God, in the creation of worldly man, result in the same amount of potential happiness realized? It appears that there is no fairness, in the realizing of satisfaction, in a personal God's creations of man.

To me, it seems unfair, that if a personal God provides His creations with individual talents and abilities, for the realizing of happiness in earthly lived lives, the amount of self-happiness to be experienced seems to vary individually. In other words, the happiness involved in possessing the talent to paint beautiful pictures seems more satisfying than the joy involved in other creative type endeavors. There are degrees of difference in the self-experiencing of joy.

However, it would seem reasonable that a just personal God would establish individual divine goals or plans with equal potential opportunities, for the realization of happiness and fulfillment. Also, consider that all individually created man has supposedly one life to achieve the goal or goals that a personal God has preordained for His creations to achieve.

Observing our present environment, how many individuals do we see or believe is following a divine plan? How many of God's family are enjoying life with consistent happiness? How many people are even seeking an awareness and understanding of God? So, it may be assumed that few, if any, individuals are consciously following a divine plan.

An all-knowing personal God, before creating man would know who of His creations would follow His divine plans, and who would not. Does it not seem illogical, that an all-knowing, all-powerful God would waste His forever timeless-time, devising plans that His creations would never follow?

I understand the significance of an individual's self-conscious ability to make free will choices. However, there is still this gnawing unanswerable question: Why would an all-knowing and all-powerful personal God create individuals, to follow His individualized divine plans for them, while at the same time, He pre-knew they would never follow their divine plans?

A personal God never created the so-called man, of this physical world. These so-called created individualizations of man are, in truth, the appearances of individual immortal-Man, whom I identify in the physical realm, as individualized physical-Man. When individualized formless-Man comes into this physical realm and becomes individualized physical-Man, he becomes eternally set upon by the unpredictable intrusions of chance, opportunity, randomness, and general unpredictability.

Besides experiencing existence, indestructible-infinite-individualized-Man has a purpose for experiencing life. This infinitely ingrained purpose is to understand himself as himself, as the self-conscious expression of God. If God did not infinitely exist, but each one of us did, there would be no substance of divine truth to guide us forever, for us to seek and identify with the reality of our divinity.

Thus, we as all self-aware representatives of God exist to experience existence as life through our ever increasing ability to understand ourselves, and our relationship to ultimate reality. It is that forever ineradicable plan which drives our self-conscious beingness, we have no choice, no say, and no option but to obey our destiny that forever is.

Does a personal God have a sense of humor?

Suppose an all-knowing personal God created the man of this world and the universe. Would He ever see any humor as a result of His creations? Unquestionably, His creations led to incalculable experiences of misery, heartache, pain, including all manners of debauchery, unimaginable awfulness, and the continually manifesting horrors of evilness, et cetera. Thus, is there any humor to be found in any of that?

I understand the free will argument. However, if God created the man of this world and the universe, and He pre-knew the resulting outcome of His creations, He must bear some responsibility for the awfulness, resulting from His creations of man, He empowered with a self-conscious free will.

Modern technology is advancing at a rapid pace. In the not too distant future, humanity will create robots capable of performing all the functions, we as human beings presently accomplish, and these robots will fulfill those duties far more effectively and efficiently. In fact, there will come a time when there is going to be only one way to do something, the most robotically efficient way.

Eventually, robots will be created and infused with a free will-driven self-awareness. Now, if any of these manmade built robots were to use their free will to harm and destroy, which bears the responsibility for the caused damage and destruction, the created self-aware robots, or the creators of those created self-aware robots?

Excluding humor, is there anything occurring is this world that could make a personal God smile, or for that matter cry? If such happenings were possible, a personal God would be infinitely laughing, infinitely smiling, infinitely crying, and infinitely sad, for all things ever happening in the world of created man are ever-present, in a personal God's all-knowing Self-awareness.

Does a personal God predestine His creations?

One of the main themes of this work is that God has not or cannot create anything, including individuals. For the sake of discussion, let's assume a personal all-knowing God exists, and this personal all-knowing God created all individualizations of worldly man. Now, let's also suppose that when He created or creates individualized human man, He endowed His creations with a free will.

I am certainly not a theological scholar, but I do like things to be logical and sensible. Thus, an all-knowing personal God would know, whom of His created children, would use their free will to find and obey their divine identity in Him. Therefore, a personal all-knowing personal God would know the free will destiny for all of His created self-conscious subjects.

My first question: If the above is true, why is there any need for any means of salvation? In a personal God's all-knowingness, the spiritually loyal individuals have used their free will to be faithful to their Creator, as their Creator pre-knew they would. Thus, by their free will, they have saved themselves, in the Self-awareness of His forever timelessness of Being. Thus, His created subjects require no divine saving grace or no saving intervention of any kind.

Now, the individualizations of created man who use their free will to reject their Creator and to reject all things divine are sent to everlasting punishment, as their personal Creator pre-knew their final destination. For these unfortunates, no form of salvation or saving divine grace is now possible. They were destined, by their free will choices, not to seek, find, follow, or know their personal God. From that perspective, it is assumed that they deserve their forever punishment.

Now, let's look at the logic of the above scenario. A personal God creates His individualizations of man. He gives His creations a free will. He asks His creations to obey and follow divine dictates. If they follow His dictates, they are spiritually rewarded infinity. If they do not follow His dictates, they are punished for infinity.

Now, it is true that if a personal all-knowing, all-powerful God exists, He can do whatever He chooses to do. If a personal God created the man of this world, with a free will, whom He pre-knew would abuse their created self-aware existence and reject Him, and thereby to receive infinite punishment, that personal God is tragically, blatantly, and horrifyingly unfair.

Created man did not ask to be created by a personal God. In fact, no one has ever requested to be created and given a free will, with all the self-responsibility that a free will entails. No one ever asked to be part of a divine creative plan. Imposed self-conscious existence is not a gift if it involves a self-awareness of infinitely inflicted and ongoing punishment.

Now, conceding the above, some individuals are destined to suffer endlessly for their free will actions taken, in their self-aware existence, an existence never self-consciously sought and never self-consciously chosen. That result, of an imposed created self-aware life, is unquestionably and entirely unfair, unwarranted, and absurd.

Still, there is underlying truth to the above discussion; it is a new understanding of ultimate reality describing our objective and non-objective existence, which I present throughout this work. Each one of us, as the individualization of Man, was never created, but we infinitely exist to create our understandings of infinite existence. As individualized-Man, we exist infinitely and follow a forever-lasting divine plan which requires us to know, understand, and endlessly interpret our forever reality.

The non-created Man, of infinite reality, is infinitely punished and infinitely rewarded, but not by any personal God. Individualized-Man, alone and singly, punishes himself. The infinite-Man of infinite existence, and the created individual man of a personal God, both follow a divine plan, and both are punished and rewarded infinitely.

The primary difference between the infinite-Man, of infinite existence, and the individually created man, of a personal God, is that infinite-Man is endlessly saving and rewarding himself. Also, for us as infinite-Man, there is no Self-aware thinking God that interdicts Himself into our existence in any way, especially in the manner of punishment.

For the individual man created by a personal God, self-aware physical life is a one-time challenge. However, the infinite-Man, identified in this work, was never created, into reality by God. For infinite-Man, self-aware existence is a continuing problem, in his continuous self-realizing of an ongoing and real life, unknown and uncaused by God. Infinite-Man is the only infinite portion of reality; that can understand and realize the foreverness of himself and God.

Thus, infinite-Man is punished infinitely because infinite-Man experiences existence infinitely. The countless experiencing of objective reality demands punishment because, in the foreverness of individual-Man existence, individual-Man possesses an infinite free will, which allows him to interpret and misinterpret objective reality, infinitely.

No endless punishment ever results from the understanding of the one true God. The administering of forever punishment is not consecutively ongoing; rather, it is interwoven into the infinite attaining of our forever spiritual victories, permanently required, as we self-consciously experience our existence.

Does a personal God know the possibility of alternative lives lived?

The created man, of this world, is severely handicapped by the *whimfulness* of unpredictability. Even by accepting the understanding of a personal God, much of created man's lives are based on chance, opportunity, randomness, and general unpredictability. In other words, created man's existence is a crapshoot of uncontrollable possibilities, with a severely limited functioning free will.

Due to the possibilities of unpredictability, all individualizations of created man have the potentiality of living many alternative lives. An all-knowing personal God must have of awareness of each and every one of those potentially lived lives. This concept is similar to the one I discuss, in the purgatorial-Man section of this work, dealing with punishment.

Thus, due to these unpredictable factors of existence, there are many potential outcomes for created man, in the experiencing of life as existence. Therefore, the accountability for each created man's individualized life often rests upon the interdictions, of the unexpected unpredictable.

Thus, does an all-knowing personal God know the virtually endless possibilities that the law of unpredictability brings into everyone's experiences of life? For example, suppose a young man is killed, in an automobile accident. Does an all-knowing personal God know the life that young many may have lived, had his life not been cut short?

Now, if a personal God does know the life that young man would have lived, is that young man's alternative life also subject to the whims of unpredictability? If that is true, would an all-knowing personal God know the seemingly endless possibilities of potential lives lived, for all of the created man of this world, which have previously existed, exist now, or are to exist?

Assuming the possibility of potential lives lived, would a personal God only judge the first life of a created man's worldly appearance, or would He also assess potentially lived lives. If He only ruled on the first life lived, I can imagine someone saying to his personal God, on the Day of Divine Reconciliation "What about the good I did in alternative lives I lived?

Perhaps, in some potential lives lived, I would have lived as a spiritually evolved person, and earned my way into Heaven. Also, the converse, to the preceding, is possible: "Thank goodness I died young in my first life, or I may have lost my salvation, in a potentially lived life. This discussion establishes, for me, that no one's unique and individual self-aware existence should be the determiner, for someone's infinite destiny.

The question is: If a personal God judges created man's life individually, does He account for the randomness of unpredictability, resulting in the self-conscious realization of alternative lives? How could a personal God possibly judge any created man's singular life experience, when so much of his life experience is subject to the unpredictable whims of chance?

Due to the law of unpredictability, some created individualizations of created man may be spiritually lucky while others may be worldly unlucky. If it is true, that created individual man's destiny is based, to a large extent upon the luck involved in the experiencing of existence, how much of a person's spiritual migration heavenward, includes his relationship to worldly success?

Think of it, due to the ever-presence of unpredictability, a personal God's individualized created man has the potentiality to live a wide-range of potential lives. In some of these potential lives, created man may find and accept God, while in other possibly lived lives, God may have been unsought, unheeded, and rejected.

In the determining anyone's ultimately deserved destiny, which possible alternative lives would a personal God choose to judge? What happens to a created man who did not find God in his beginning worldly life existence, but due to the randomness of unpredictability, he found God in an alternative life lived? How would a personal God judge such an individual?

If a personal God takes into consideration the randomness of unpredictability, would He judge some possible lived lives but not others, or would He judge all potentially lived lives in the same manner? Would He punish all individualizations of created man, for all their sins in possibly lived lives He knew they would have lived, had it not for the uncertainties of unpredictability?

All lives lived, either actual or potential, were self-consciously lived. If a personal God does punish everyone, on the Day of Divine Reconciliation, for actual and potential lives lived, many will be those who receive punishment for potentially lived lives, lives for which they have no self-awareness.

Imagine individualizations of created man being infinitely punished, for the living of alternative lives, lives for which they had no self-conscious remembrance? The seeming existence of alternative lives varies widely, based on the frequency of life's unpredictable occurrences.

However, it does seem that numerous possible lives lived would eventually establish a pattern for or against created man's receptivity to things divinely real, including the acceptance of God. Thus, a personal God objectively would know the innate spiritual essence for all individualized created man's self-aware existences, by knowing their choices in their potentially lived lives.

The idea of possibly lived lives due to the influences of unpredictability is complicated. For example, due to unpredictability, some individuals may have more opportunities to experience the living of life. Thus, some persons would have more opportunities to seek, find, and accept God than others. That alone seems unfair? Everyone should have the same potential opportunities to find the God of his or her self-understanding and acceptance?

However, this subject is even much more complicated than the above discussion infers. In the above, I interpret unpredictability of 'life-forking' existences, into new potentially lied lives. Thus, in the overall considering of the living of forking-lives, we are experiencing the same life differently, based on the life-forks of unpredictability continuing to occur in virtually endless of possibly lived lives.

Now, I will discuss a similar understanding of the above. Let me illustrate with the following example of a male-female couple. Let's assume this couple produces a child. If the child is a male, he creates billions of sperm in his lifetime. If the child is a female, she produces hundreds of eggs in her life. Thus, for the above couple, one sperm united with one egg to produce one child.

The chances of any individual, coming into physical existence are trillions upon trillions upon trillions to one. These odds do not include the random odds of any couple meeting, and then that meeting turning into a relationship. Those odds are also trillions to one. Thus, individual human life, appearing in physical reality, based upon those above odds alone, should be cherished as sacred existence, with ongoing thankfulness.

However, if it is correct that a personal God chose to create individual man, then our physical existence did not come about by chance. If that is true, why would a personal God establish such a complex human procreating system, based on the incalculable whims of chance?

Still, it seems reasonable, that if a personal God exists, He would be the Creator of our individual existences, thereby eliminating the odds of chance, and providing each of us with a living human identity. However, no one was ever created by God. Each of us has forever existed with our infinite individual identities. We infinitely experience an interpretation of creation, but to all things of infinite existence, there is no such thing as creation.

What about the trillions upon trillions of possibilities of individual human existence, which could have been produced by a couple? Would an all-knowing personal God know those potentially lived lives, based on the trillions upon trillions of possible combinations? These would be lives that never existed, except in the all-knowingness of an all-knowing God. From the standpoint of an all-knowing God, what is the difference between an actual lived physical life and a potentially lived physical life? All things existing in the mind of God are infinitely real.

It is even much more complicated than the above possibilities indicate. Let's assume that there is a final number of sperm generated by all males who have ever existed, exist now, or are ever to exist. Also, let us assume that there are a final number of eggs generated by all females who have ever existed, exist now, or are ever to exist.

Now, does an all-knowing personal God know the potential existences for all the possible combinations of sperm and eggs, for the entirety of human physical life? The number of possibilities for potential lives lived would be so vast; it is most likely that such a figure is not calculable.

Let's suppose that a personal God knows how each one of those potential lives, which might have been lived, based on the infinite possibilities of chance. This knowingness would have to occur within His Self-consciousness. Now, the individuals living these potential lives, within a personal God's Self-consciousness, must have self-awareness, and must possess a free will.

If all of the above is true, what difference does it make, to all all-knowing God, if any individual self-realizes his or her existence as potentially living life, or living a real life? Individuals self-experiencing self-conscious life think and believe that their personal self-recognized life is real? Again I ask: Would a personal God punish and reward self-aware beings who only experienced potential existence?

Imagine individuals, who never had real existence living potential lives, and are punished infinitely, for their ungodly conduct, in those potentially lived lives? If that reality occurs, there is no difference between actual lives lived and potential lives lived. This hypothesis gives new meaning and understanding to the experiencing of self-conscious existence.

Based on the above discussion, not one of us could ever be sure, with metaphysical certitude, whether we were living a real, or a potentially real life. Thus, each of us may be living the self-conscious experiencing of an illusion. Still, if our lives are illusions, our lives would be real, in the Self-knowingness of a personal God.

Perhaps none of us ever actually existed, except in the mind of an all-knowing personal God? If a personal God exists, and we infinitely exist in His forever Mind, it could be assumed that we forever exist in total harmony. Still, an all-knowing personal God would know the choices we made in non-physical reality existences. These pretended lives were never directly created by God; they are the byproduct of creatively established lives. In the mind of God can there be any difference between the two?

Does a personal God place burdens upon His followers?

It has often been stated: "God never places burdens upon anyone they cannot handle." If the purpose of these burdens placed on our physical existence is to promote spiritual understanding, I am in sympathy with that realization. However, in my understanding of divine truth, there is no God, personal or non-personal, who places burdens upon anyone.

However, our individual spiritual progression ensues from the overcoming the burdens and obstacles, involved in our objective existence. If burdening troubles are understood, as spiritual lessons and opportunities, the individual fate of forever-Man is eternally secured because it demonstrates the realization that individualized-Man is in a forever spiritual battle to discover and rediscover his true relationship with his soul, God.

Assuming there is a personal God, who burdens individuals. The purpose for those burdens would be to promote spiritual awareness, and progress. That concept is similar to the one I present, concerning the attracting of circumstances to ourselves, urging, encouraging, and abetting us spiritually onward, along our individualized pathways of forever divine unfoldment.

However, here's the problem with believing in a personal God who places burdens on His divine subjects. A personal God in His all-knowingness would know how successful or unsuccessful His imposed weights on self-conscious existence would be. Thus, would He only place burdens upon individuals whom He pre-knew would benefit spiritually?

If the above is true, would not a personal God be showing some form of divine favoritism? Why should some individualizations of created man be spiritually benefited, by the spiritually cleansing power of divinely imposed burdens, and not others? An all-knowing personal God would know how to place the correct burdens upon everyone, to make everyone spiritually mindful.

Thus, if a personal God selectively chose who to burden, how could He possibly be considered a benevolent God? The mere process of creation favors some and not others. Excluding interdiction from a personal God; how is it fair that the obstacles involved in created man's existence are harsher for some and not so harsh for others? If there is unfairness in the living of life, how is anyone fairly judged?

It seems that much of created man's impetus for self-thinking is constantly being tangled, mangled, and strangled by the conditions, prohibitions, and restrictions involved is the experiencing of existence.

In short, the free will of created man is constrained in a self-conscious muddy quicksand, of chance-driven circumstances.

If a personal God only placed burdens on individuals, He pre-knew would be spiritually benefited, is He not interfering with created man's free will choices? Why would a personal God create individuals, give them a free will, and then manipulate their free will, to make them conform to His divine authority?

Also, would a personal God place burdens on individuals whom He pre-knew would never change their evil and sinful ways. If a personal God was ever to place such burdens, then the only difference between saved corrupt and non-saved corrupt, evildoers is whom He chooses to weigh down with life's difficulties.

It is challenging for the created man of this world to understand that all burdens, seen from a spiritual perspective are blessings. Thus, it is most often difficult for anyone to see the shining goodness that rests peacefully behind all the pains and sufferings of self-consciously experiencing existence.

Regardless of how anyone would ever recognize that burdens may, or may not come from a personal God, burdens are a necessity for our spiritual advancement. However, to believe any load of heartache, placed on self-conscious existence, came from a personal God is a misinterpretation of immortal-Man's divine destiny? All burdens ensue from the mere process of experiencing life.

A butterfly requires effort to break itself free, of its chrysalis, for the purpose of experiencing its existence. So it is with each of us. Our individual spiritual efforts determine our spiritual progressions. The effort required for possession, compression, and expression of our spiritual understanding is entirely self-determined, through our self-effort. There is no personal God that self-consciously interferes or impacts our divine progression of understanding.

In the eyes of a personal God, are all sins equal?

Are all the sins of created man equal in the eyes of his personal God? In other words, is a personal God's forgiveness, for someone who steals a loaf of bread, the same forgiveness He gives someone for abusing a child? If it is assumed sin is sin and all sins are equal, then a personal God should look upon everyone, with the same amount of divinely loving forgiveness

However, it seems self-evident that the spiritual liability for someone who abuses a child is far greater than the spiritual debt required for stealing a loaf of bread. An individual who abuses a child, and then sincerely asks forgiveness from his personal Creator God, must have a much harsher spiritual liability, as compared to someone who steals a loaf of bread, and also honestly asks his Creator God for forgiveness. If that is not true, then the committing of sins is meaningless concerning punishment.

If a personal God recognizes differences in the wrongdoings of created sinners, but He forgives all equally, He may love all of His world man creations equally, but He may not like them all equally. If a personal God created human man with a free will, why should He like all of His creations equally? It seems reasonable that if a personal God exists, He would have favorites. Although, when He created someone, He would pre-know is that person was destined to be one of His favorite.

Thus, it seems possible that a personal God could love all of His creations equally, and at the same time favor some individual creations over others. Thus, it appears likely that a personal God could say to some of His Offspring: I love you, but I do not like you, because you used your free will to live such a horrid and debauched life, before turning to Me. The things you did, I forgive, but I cannot eject their awfulness from my mind."

Under the above scenario, a personal all-powerful, all-knowing God would pre-know that He would dislike some of His individual creations of man for infinity. How would it feel to be loved by a personal God, but at the same time, be disliked by Him? How is it possible that a child abuser, an animal abuser, or a callous murderer, even though forgiven of their evils, could be divinely and infinitely liked by anyone, including a personal God?

Our individual and personal spiritual evolving are earned, through the spiritual self-conquering of ourselves; it is attained by the simple unmerited forgiveness of the God, of anyone's understanding. Each one of us, alone and individually are the only ones, in all realms of ultimate reality that can erase the forever stinging horridness of our actions, from the self-realization of ourselves. We are all equal in the purity of our beingness. Eventually, we will become equals in the purity of our thoughts.

Only the understanding of actual reality makes the expressions of the awfulness of sinfulness bearable to the self-consciousness of our thoughts. In the purity of ultimate truth, no one has ever truly suffered; no one has ever truly caused suffering, and no one has ever lost his or her forever self-realized individual existence. All experiences of awfulness we self-consciously create are illusions wrapped in experiences.

Thus, each one of us is an infinite indestructible being whose infinite reality is forever untouched, by any self-conscious or non-self-conscious created experience. Therefore, as we see others as the purity of divinity in expression, all things seemingly requiring our forgiveness are washed away, into the foreverness of unknowingness.

After we have received total and complete punishment for our sinful-evil acts, we all self-consciously remain in God's family, equally understood, equally accepted, and equally loved. No matter the depth or degree of our commissions of awfulness, the sins we have committed, are committing now, or will commit, cannot deter from the realization that we are all equally spiritual, equally divine, and equal members of God's forever family.

Does a personal God think?

If a personal God was capable of Self-conscious thought; what could He possibly be Self-thinking? After all, He knows all things, the outcomes of all things, and the "what ifs" of all things. If a personal

Self-thinking God exists, that would presuppose that there would be something, in existence, motivating Him to Self-conscious thought. However, is it possible for an all-knowing personal God to be motivated?

If there is something for a personal God to think about, would not that infer that He is not all-knowing? If a personal God is All-in-all, where would ideas come from to motivate Him to think self-consciously? Interestingly, if an all-knowing personal God existed, it would not be possible for Him to think creatively because that would presuppose newness of thought in His all-knowingness. That seems illogical.

Still, if an all-knowing, all-powerful, all-present personal God is assumed to be able to think Self-consciously, what would be the purpose of His Self-conscious thinking thoughts? If He had a purpose for His Self-conscious thoughts, that presupposes there is something for Him to understand, accomplish, realize, or take action.

However, if by definition, a personal God has a purpose or objective involved in the Self-thinking of His infinite existence that would contradict His infinite divine nature as being all-powerful, all-knowing, and all-present. Imagine the possibility of an infinite personal God having Self-conscious thoughts. Even if true, even an infinite God must eventually become bored. However, I repeat that the one God existing throughout infinity does not Self-consciously think.

Any ideas or thoughts that a personal God could conceivably think about, in relationship to the definition of His forever existence, would have to come from within the Self-knowingness of Himself. Any thought-producing impulses or ideas could not from outside of Him because anything that would exist outside of God presupposes an existence, separate from His existence.

Thus, if by definition, a personal God is all-knowing, all-powerful, and all-present Being, anything existing outside of His Self-knowingness is not possible. Thus, if an all-knowing personal God Self-consciously thought, the source of His Self-conscious thinking would have to be part of His infinite nature.

Even if that is true, it remains to be asked: What possibly could be the subjects, for any thoughts, an all-knowing personal God would contemplate? If a personal God thought and ideas were part of His nature, would He prefer some ideas over others? Still, what could be the subject or focus of His Self-active mind content?

Also, an all-knowing personal God would have no need for memorization because all things would simultaneously exist, in His forever self-knowingness. Since a personal God requires no memory, His self-conscious awareness contains includes, all of His Self-active awareness of all infinite happenings, simultaneously.

I cannot imagine that if a personal God is experiencing such an infinite existence. How could that possibly be an infinite Self-conscious desirable reality for Him to experience infinitely? Imagine, in a personal God's Self-aware mind exists forever, all the horridness of things past, things present, and things to come. That is not an infinite self-conscious existence I would never choose for myself. Imagine believing such a God capable of such an infinite reality?

The real understanding of God is that God Is. God is Self-consciously aware of only one thing, His infinite divinely unfolding nature, forever revealing Himself to Himself. In His Infinite Self-knowingness, He is void of the capability of Self-conscious thinking, Self-conscious understandings, Self-conscious interpretations, and the Self-conscious experiencing of anything.

God does not understand His Self-knowingness; He is the infinite Self-knowingness of His changing-changeless perfection. He only knows and is only aware of His infinitely unfolding Divine Beingness. His existence is the pure reality of forever blissfulness. Thus, His realization of Himself is the everlastingness of changing harmony, joy, and bliss, et cetera, within His Infinite Self-realizing, Self-knowing, and Self-consciousness.

His existence and His Self-consciousness are one and the same. Thus, God does not Self-consciously understand Himself, Self-consciously express Himself or Self-consciously control Himself. God forever Self-consciously knows Himself and thus, His existence is the only Self-awareness of reality He forever realizes.

In contrast, as individualized-Man, our infinitely uniquely designed independent in-God self-aware existence, gives each one of us the ability to think independently. Thus, each of us as God's infinite unknowingness of Himself is that part of God capable of independent, self-aware thinking.

Because God, in the totality of His Self-beingness is not capable of Self-conscious Self-aware thought, He does not possess the power of understanding, the power of interpretation, the power of expression, or the power involved in the experiencing of existence. God is never capable of experiencing the Self-knowingness of His Infinite unfolding Beingness.

The forever revealing of God's Self-conscious awareness is the total of His infinite divine attributes. The idea of God's infinite unfolding attributes is analogous to random numbers combining, without any repetition, into endless harmonious arrays and matrixes, of inner-designed divine expressions.

There is nothing for God to discover or know outside of His existence. God never realizes anything new, except the newness of His infinite unfolding inner divinity. In contrast, each one of us, as individualized-Man, is in the forever process of self-consciously discovering and rediscovering the foreverness of our inner divinity. God is not capable of any such Self-understanding effort.

Here is an interesting question: Would an all-knowing personal God know the how and the why of His infinite existence? If He does know the how and the why of His existence, does He know what gives power to His infinite reality? If God does not know how or why He exists, He cannot be interpreted as an all-knowing God. An infinite existing God would be infinitely captive, to the nature of His Infinite Beingness. God can only be what He forever Is.

Recapping: God and Man share the quality of self-awareness, but each of us as individualized-Man, possess the quality of self-actuating self-conscious, self-aware thought. We can create a seeming reality through our ability to create experiences; God does not possess that capability, except through each one of us.

Thus, each one of us, as individualized-Man, is the only component of ultimate reality capable of self-conscious self-actualizing thought, manifesting in the realm of objective reality, as experience. God is pure divine infinite existence forever, blissfully unaffected by anything having or claiming real existence.

Is a personal God all-powerful and all-knowing?

If a personal God is all-power, could He create other all-powerful, all-knowing, and all-present Gods? Thus, if God could create other Gods, similar in capability to Himself, why would He not? One might think that an infinite, all-powerful God would create other Gods for sheer companionship, if for nothing else. One would think that a personal God could create infinitely divine companions, more spiritually worthy than His creations of the man, of this world.

If man's personal God is not able to create other all-powerful Gods, He is by definition be not all-powerful. However, there can be only one supreme, omnipotent, all-infinite God because if an all-power forever God created other all-power never-ending Gods, those Gods could not be forever infinite, except to themselves because they were creatively into a new forever existence.

Theoretically, if an infinite, all-powerful Gods created other Gods, ultimate reality could be composed of infinite, all-powerful, all-knowing, all-present God's creating their divine individual niches, in the foreverness vastness of ultimate reality. Such is the ridiculousness of attempting to apply "what if" possibilities to an infinite, all-powerful, all-knowing, all-present personal God.

How does a language or languages affect a personal God and man?

If a personal God is capable of Self-conscious thought would He think in a language? If He thinks in a language, how and where did the His language of words originate? If God's nature is unchanging, and if He thinks in a language, the language He thinks in must be part of His infinite divine nature.

Still, if a personal God thinks in a language, the concept of language itself presupposes a process of organized understanding. However, for an all-knowing personal God, there should be no such thing as a process of organized understanding, for Him to follow or for Him to understand.

An all-knowing, all-powerful God could not be constrained to obey any seeming language rules for the Self-knowingness of His infinite existence.

The idea that a personal God would think in a language limits the understanding of God as being all-knowing because He would be dependent upon the words of a language to express to Himself, His Self-thinking thoughts. The mere concept of a Self-consciously aware God, whom Self-consciously thinks thoughts, is not logical.

For a personal God to think in a language requires ideas. Ideas come from the idea realm. The one and only God of reality, cannot and does not, interact with the realm of ideas; therefore, He cannot and does think in a language. The concept of thinking in a language is only applicable to our self-conscious individualized-Man experiencing of existence.

Created man's evolving objective existence is determined, to a great extent, by chance, opportunity, randomness, and general unpredictability. Thus, all individualizations of created man have the same opportunity to be born into any world culture, with its unique language. Spiritually speaking: Do the various established languages, vary in their facility, for the understanding of God, whether He is personal or non-personal?

In other words, do some languages, due to their natural structure, cadence, and volume of words enable the attaining of deeper understandings of God than other languages? Thus, is the nature of God understood equally, by created worldly man, in languages such as English, German, Russian, French, Swahili, Bantu, Navajo, et cetera? It does not seem reasonable that all languages are equal, in their facility, to impart the same depths of spirituality, in the understanding of God.

Therefore, depending on the language an individual is born into, through the aegis of chance, the ability to comprehend God may be easier or more difficult. Thus, even language itself is an impediment to created man's ultimate salvation. Thus, when the judgment for created man occurs, does a personal God take into account the language used in the seeking, finding, understanding, and accepting of His forever Beingness?

In all languages, words have varying nuances of meanings. It is not reasonable that the nature of God could be understood equally in all languages.

Does a personal God possess a free will?

Let's assume a personal God possess a free will. Could an all-knowing, all-powerful, all-present personal God use His free will to change His mind? Alternatively, could He decide to do evil instead of good? Alternatively, could He choose not to exist? The answer to those questions must be "No." or a personal God's existence would be meaningless. Thus, even if an infinite personal God has a free will; His free will is infinitely limited.

Spiritually minded individuals, who believe in a personal God, believe He does have a free will. They maintain, even though He possesses a free will, He could never do anything contradictory to His divine nature. The divine nature of God must be inviolate, or the concept of an infinite God loses meaning.

For a personal God to do something contrary to His divine nature would presuppose He has an understanding of things contradictory to His divine nature. Anything that a personal God would be aware of, contrary to His divine beingness, would have to be something having infinite reality. However, nothing contrary to the nature of God could have any infinite reality.

A personal God is infinitely constrained to obey His infinite nature. Thus, regarding the functioning of His divine beingness, He does not possess a free will, if He cannot do anything contrary to His divine nature. God must be limited to the Self-conscious obeying of His divine nature. This understanding is consistent with my contention that each of us is also limited, by our infinite divine free will expression, of our infinite existence, due to our ever evolving spiritual understandings.

In other words, when the time comes when each of us, as individualized-Man, actually understands and accepts our forever divinity, it would be impossible for anyone of the individualized-Us to do anything in contradistinction to our divine beingness. Spiritual truth self-confidently realized and accepted, limits each of us, as infinite divine-Man of God, to only express spiritual truth, as we understand spiritual truth. Our evolving spirituality cannot contradict itself.

Since I assert God does not Self-consciously think thoughts, it follows He does not Self-consciously have a free will. God's nature is the completeness of His divine perfection, along with the completeness of all the other aspects of His infinite divine nature that provides the meaningfulness to His existence.

God does not have a free will which would allow Him to interpret His divine nature, in any way other than in the total, unconditional, and uncontaminated harmony and wholeliness. God has no infinite choice other than to be the recipient of His is infinitely endowed divine nature. God is not capable of making any assumptions about Himself. God cannot choose to know anything about Himself.

Does a personal God punish His sincere followers to correct wayward behavior?

There two primary situations requiring punishment. First, there is the required punishment for the sinful things created man does to himself. For example, the self-imposed punishments for sins of excess, such as drinking, smoking, use of drugs, and overeating, et cetera. Thus, the consequences of the excesses of sinful wrongdoings become the deserved punishment. Thus, a personal God's interdiction, in such matters, is not required or necessary.

However, the question to be asked is: Would a personal God still punish His sincere followers for the consequences of their self-imposed sinful actions? If He does choose to punish these sinners, whom does He choose to punish, and who does He choose not punish? Still, God's additional punishment to sinners who harmed only themselves through their self-imposed actions seems unnecessary.

It seems evident that a personal God does not punish all of His sincere followers. Does He have a divine preference in which of His followers He chooses to punish, in order to correct their sinful ways? If there is a preference in how He administers punishment, where is the fairness in that? It would seem reasonable that a benevolent personal God would punish all of His world man creations equally, according to the depth of their sins.

If a personal God had a choice on which of His followers He punishes, to save them from their evilness that would presuppose He favors some of His sincere follows over others. Would a personal God still punish someone even though He pre-knew His punishment would not be spiritually advantageous?

Second, punishment is required for the evil and sinful acts perpetrated upon others. Mandatory imposed penalties, for all wrongdoings, are unequivocally deserved, and there is, and there should be no escape from all deserved punishment. Let's assume a personal God forgives His sincere followers of their evil and sinful wrongdoings perpetrated on others; the question is: Will He still punish those whom He has forgiven of their sinful wrongdoings?

However, the real issue is: Should forgiveness from a personal God, for sinful and evil acts, be a substitute for deserved punishment? My contention is that there must be no escape from all deserved punishment, or our self-conscious existence loses motivation to discover our everlasting and infinite divine identity.

If a personal God faithfully punished His followers, to make them receptive to divine understanding, then the truly remorseful doers of evil and sinful things should pray earnestly, for all spiritually regenerative punishment deserved. We would never be capable of understanding the consequences of accepting and acting upon the thought-power, we self-willingly cede to unreality, if our sinful-evil actions are to go unpunished, instead of forgiveness.

Thus, even if a personal God exists, He should never wash away anyone's evil and sinful wrongdoings with simple forgiveness. All deserved punishment must be self-consciously accepted and endured, to understand the divine compassion residing in our infinite self-aware existence. However, no punishment is ever given by any God, personal or non-personal, for self-consciously living life.

How could mere simple pardon, in the form of divine forgiveness, be spiritually beneficial? Our spiritual growth demands punishment. A punishing storm purifies, with its punishing expression, because it provides vegetation with new means to grow, evolve, and adapt to their environments. Punishment for all wrongdoing is mandatory, for any understanding of worldly man, to spiritually advance in divine knowledge.

How would anyone ever understand that their punishment comes from a personal God? Again, should anyone be infinitely punished for exercising the use of his or her free will, divinely bestowed to them? Punishment is mandatory, but it never comes from God. No forgiveness of any kind should ever replace deserved punishment, for all wrongdoing knowingly committed or unknowingly committed. Without punishment our forever ability to increase in spiritual understanding is not possible.

Everyone is responsible for his or her actions. However, if an all-powerful creative personal God exists, He is responsible for everyone's existence. If no one existed, no one would be doers of evil and sinful things. However, individualized-Man lives and has a free will, and there is no escape from all deserved punishment, for all his wrongdoings.

All punishment results from our self-conscious departure, from an awareness of the presence of God. Our self-conscious suffering punishment for our wrongdoings is determined by each of us, without the self-interdiction or self-aware accounting of any God, personal or non-personal.

If a personal God exists and he forgives all sincere followers of their sinful wrongdoings, there must be a difference in His degree of forgiveness, between remorsefully genuine evildoers, compared to sincerely repentant sinners. The amount and depth of pain caused by spiritually challenged wrongdoers must equal or exceed their punishment, or where is there fairness in the living of life.

If there are no differences in the degrees of punishment given for various sinful and evil wrongdoings, created man's relationship with his personal God remains forever muddled. If a personal God punishes someone for the taking another's life, in the same manner, that He punishes someone for stealing a loaf of bread, created man's existence lacks any real divine accountability.

In truth of the experiencing of our self-existence, no God of any person's understanding is capable of any Self-willed punishment, for any member of His forever perfect family. If a personal God exists, a personal God would infinitely be responsible for all of the unraveling of truth, in the experiencing of existence, by all individualization of man, in all the things that the living of life entails. In that realization, a personal God should be the forever punisher of Himself.

Thus, punishment by a personal God is divinely illogical, if a personal God created man, with the pre-knowledge that His creations would require punishment. When created man experiences his created existence and is punished finitely and infinitely by a personal God, who of us would ever desire to be God-created with an infinite self-aware existence? I would say to God: "Do not create me and hold me responsible for an existence I never self-consciously desired! "Who makes You responsible for Your never-asked-for infinite Self-aware existence?"

However, there is no escape from all deserved punishment. Only after all punishment, has been given to us, is forgiveness applicable. Punishment for all of our wrongdoings is self-imposed, self-accepted, and self-suffered by each of us, individually. All punishment is the experiencing of the pain we have caused to ourselves and others. Who is more qualified to punish ourselves, other than ourselves?

All the evil and sinful wrongdoings result from our individualized self-consciousness becoming temporarily devoid of God-awareness, and our self-acceptance of the presence of God. It is not possible to commit evil and sin while being self-consciously wrapped and enveloped in the self-acceptance of the forever present God, within us.

The successful experiencing of our infinite existence demands that our self-conscious desires be directed, to the understanding that our self-acknowledgement of the presence of God, as our inner forever substance is the forever truth concerning the foreverness of our infinite divine selves. Thus, we forever exist to self-accept and realize that understanding.

Built into our infinite existence is a designed plan for our forever continuing self-conscious discovery and rediscovery of God. This purpose is embedded in ultimate reality and comprises the forever realizing of our infinite individual and collective destinies. According to forever plan, all of our spiritual lapses, in the forms of ungodliness, while discovering our infinite divine destinies, must be punished, to keep our divine destiny a reality to our self-aware existence.

Does a personal God punish non-believers after death?

The forever destiny of non-believers in a personal God is an interesting question on several levels. For example, why would a personal God punish non-believers for abusing the existence He gave them? What would motivate a personal God to punish non-believers infinitely, these same non-believers who were never given a choice to participate in self-conscious life? Okay, they did wrong, perhaps they did very wrong, but so what, what would their infinite punishment accomplish?

Why would not a personal God choose to redeem His divine sin-evil vagabonds instead of punishing them forever? Again I ask: What would be the purpose of infinite punishment for non-believers? To me, that is imposed cruelty beyond belief. Endless punishment without the possibility of redemption is a sign of unlovingness which is inconceivably harsh, especially as applied to the concept of a loving Deity.

The concept that a personal God would punish someone infinitely is divine foolishness. In other words, a person God creates an individual, who did not ask to be created, and gives that individual a one-time life to live. If that individual turns lives his one-time life and turns out to be a godless rogue, he is infinitely punished, for a one-time existence he barely understood.

Incidentally, this godless rogue was predisposed to be a godless because he was brutalized, in his childhood. Punish him "Yes," but punish him infinitely "No." Is anyone to believe that a personal God creates someone into existence, who did not ask for creation, and whom

He pre-knew would be a doer of evil things, to suffer infinitely? I could never believe in a God capable of such cruelty.

What about individuals who committed sins and evils, but thought they were doing good? Would a personal God also infinitely punish them? Does it seem logical or fair, for individuals to be endlessly punished, for actions they believed to be the doings of things good? Would not it be more Godlike to provide those wrongdoers with the understanding of their wrongdoings, allow them to repent and self-consciously exist anew?

Is a personal God required to tell individuals why they deserve infinite punishment? If not, individuals could be punished infinitely, while at the same time, not understanding why they deserve endless punishment. It is a realization buried deep within our self-aware existence that sinful-evil things can be accepted, as divine truths. Thus, spiritual ignorance is a forever aspect of our infinite divinely unfolding nature, for which we suffer endless punishment until infinitely redeemed.

Our deserved de facto punishment is the result of self-conscious abusing of the gift of infinite life. This punishing penalty is forever self-imposed and consists of experiencing the pain, heartache, and violence we caused to ourselves and others. Without our self-imposed punishment, we could never understand ourselves as the forever expression of divinity.

Thus, each one of us, as individualized-Man, justly determines our deserved punishment. No one escapes the penalty of punishment. All the wrongdoings of collective individualized-Man require the sentence of punishment, whether or not the perpetrators of those wrongdoings, realized their actions were wrong.

Thus, the punishment for all of our wrongdoings, whether intended or unintended, is the only form of punishment which provides universal fairness when accounting for all the expressions of evil and sin-filled wrongdoings, as each of us is forever self-consciously experiencing our existence.

Does a personal God save us from our evils and sins?

Salvation in a theological sense refers to our deliverance from the consequences of our wrongdoings. Many believe that only a personal God can grant such salvation. However, the God of my understanding knows nothing of our evil and sinful ways. Thus, there is no God, according to my understanding that saves us from the abusing actions of our forever self-realized existence.

Thus, a personal God's Self-conscious commutation for our sinful-evil wrongdoings is not possible. All the evils and sins ever committed upon ourselves and others are only accounted for, by each one of us, as individualized-Man, never by any God, whether understood as personal or non-personal.

If a personal God exists, He saves whom He chooses to save; therefore, infinite salvation is divinely arbitrary. However, through the infinite nature of a non-personal God, our salvation is assured because our universal salvation resides in the foreverness, of our God-based existence, as unlimited and forever expressions of God's Beingness. Our infinite salvation rests on the understanding of that divine truth.

In objective reality, eternities wait for our appearance which includes God's divine presence, which forever abides within each one of us. Thus, the timelessness of our existence combined with the timelessness of objective reality, assures our individual and collective spiritual salvation.

Eternal and infinite self-suffering is the deserved penalty individualized-Man must pay for his forever incrementally evolving divine existence. Without self-suffering, there is no infinitely divine salvation. Without self-forgiveness, there is no infinitely divine salvation. Without our self-acceptance of God, there is no infinitely divine salvation.

Salvation from all our evils and sins is achieved, by removing the stains of their awfulness from our self-conscious awareness. Thus, our salvation is determined by accepting all deserved punishment until the futility of our non-spiritual actions is self-understood, self-accepted, and self-forgiven as the wrongness of our experiencing of existence.

Since all created experiences are unreal, salvation after punishment becomes the acquiring of a self-conscious realization that rejects the spiritually harmful imagined into the realm of experience, and choose only to accept the divinely pure which is the divine forever real. Thus, our acceptance of the desire for spiritual self-awareness is the forever source of our forever salvation.

Thus, when we self-consciously exist as God's divine nature in our understanding of self-beingness, no wrongdoings we ever committed, in the experiencing of our lives, have any authority over the spirituality of our infinite wellbeing. Thus, to the reality of our active self-awareness, we are the presence of God in dynamic expression; nothing ever alters that truth of our divine beingness.

Implications of praying to a personal God

If a personal God exists, He cannot be pleased with our present individual opaque and personal spiritual journeys. As the individualized-Man of forever existence, we are discovering, for ourselves, the God of our understanding. Following are some of the difficulties I have in praying to a personal God.

How long should individuals pray to their personal God before they can assume the answers to their prayers are not to be forthcoming? They could petition their personal God ceaselessly, seeking the same outcome, never realizing that their personal God has no intention of answering their divine requests.

A personal God gives existence to created man and then requires His created man to rely upon Him. Why should sincere followers of their personal God, ever have to ask Him more than once, for their prayed-for outcomes? Alternatively: Why should any genuine believer in a personal God ever have to beseech Him prayerfully for anything?

An all-knowing personal God must know all the needs of His children, even before His children realize their required needs. Loving parents do not inquire as to the needs of their children; they automatically fulfill those needs. Should a personal God do less for HIs individualizations of created man, He brought into physical existence?

The recognition that a personal God presumably created the individualizations of mortal man requires that He infinitely provide for their comfort, their wellbeing, and their ongoing and forever needs, without the necessary task-effort of prayer requesting? A personal God is forever all-knowing; however, His creations of individual physical man needs divine comfort.

An all-knowing personal God would always know what is best for the physical and spiritual wellbeing, of His children. To continually petition Him for a definite answer seems like an attempt to cajole the actions of a personal God through the strength and persistence, of the human power of will.

Does a personal God respond to begging? I understand some individuals are often in such dire circumstances that they beg and bargain with their personal God, for His divine intervention. They may pledge all forms of pacts and agreements, for the acquiring of their supposed needs. However, the idea of begging or bargaining, for a personal God's intervention, represents a sad and tearful form of their God's divine intervention.

Thus, the overwhelming pains of experiencing existence often prompt many individuals to bargain with their personal God. When prayers and bargaining efforts continue to go unanswered, the result is often great sadness. Sometimes, this great sadness of disappointment turns to anger, against their personal God. Surely, no God, of anyone's understanding, would create an environment for such a frustrating spiritual existence?

A personal God in the exercising His free will is a forever source of spiritual uncertainty. Thus, the forever ways of a personal God could never be predictably understood, by the spiritually infantile knowledge of His self-aware creations. Blind faith seems the only means for petitioning a personal God.

Further, if a personal God knows all, including what is best for His children, what happens when the answers to requested prayers, are unsuited for the individual's spiritual well-being? Will these spiritually sincere petitioners continue to pray to their personal God, disregarding His seeming indifference?

Assuming the prayers of individual, to their personal God, continue to go unanswered, is their spiritual understanding or faith weak? How does a personal God respond to a sincere follower, whose faith is spiritually weak? Is the strength of an individual's faith, in his personal God, more important than spiritual knowledge?

We, as individualized-Man, determine our deserved punishments and rewards. God remains forever indifferent to the consequences of our experiences of existence, not by His choice, but by His nature. God knows only Himself and His unfolding Beingness in the foreverness of His existence. We are the unknowingness of God; we are part of His Beingness that does not unfold.

All prayerful declarations of truth are answered, at the spiritual level of the divinely evolving petitioner. The appearances of truth realized always result from certitude of our correct divine understandings. Things spiritually received are divinely earned and deserved; anything else would be a mockery to the forever purpose of our infinite existence.

Praying to a personal God, from our human perspective is spiritually valueless. There has never been; there is not now, nor is there ever to be a God, who self-consciously loves us, either personal or non-personal. We must forever deal with that realization. Each one of us, alone and individually, is responsible for our infinite existence. There is comfort in realizing that we are all part of God's family, but each one of us is forever alone in the realizing of our divine destiny. We can choose to love God, but God does not Self-consciously love us now or ever.

Thus, repeating through the tears of forever sublime solitude, each of us, alone and individually is eternally and infinitely responsible for our spiritual destiny. As individualized-Man, we are divinely designed to receive God's forever love, but always by the way of our self-choosing, and it is always from our individualized divine spiritual perspectives. God's forever love is known only by each one of us individually.

Incidentally, there is one prayer a personal God will never answer, regardless of the depth of anyone's spirituality, or love of God. This unanswered prayer is the last prayer a person utters to be delivered, from an illness or circumstance, resulting in the final cause of their human physical death. As sincere as any prayer has ever been offered up to a personal God, that prayer remains forever unanswered.

Is a personal God a fair God?

Assuming a personal God created the individualized man, of this world, with a free will and individually created man utilizes his free will to disobey and reject his Creator and his Creator's Divine Plan. Then, he dies spiritually unredeemed. Now, the created man of this world is forever separated from his Maker, and that forever separation becomes his everlasting punishment?

However, how could individualizations of created man who become infinitely separated from their personal God-Creator possibly be considered divinely fair? No one ever asked to be created, and no one ever requested to be a part of any divine plan. If a personal God created the man of this world, He is responsible for the man of this world's infinite wellbeing, and He must do whatever it takes, to ensure the spiritual worthiness of His forever worldly man creations.

Therefore, the imposing of self-aware human existence by a personal God results in the self-awareness of living lives, where those self-aware lives, had no say whatsoever in their existence. It seems as though a personal God is saying: "I created you, and although you did not ask to be created, I endowed you a free will, now do as I say, or else!"

To my understanding, a personal God, who would punish anyone everlastingly for actions taken in an existence never self-consciously sought, is capricious, unfair, and unloving? All individuals should be held responsible for their actions committed in their self-conscious lives, but they should not be infinitely liable, for a self-aware existence never self-desired, self-sought, or self-chosen. Again, is it fair for a personal God to give created man self-aware life and then make him infinitely responsible for that never-asked-for life?

The living of life for many individuals is, in and of itself, a most unbearable punishment. If any individualized created man knew he was going to be punished everlastingly, for actions taken as a result of his free will choices, would he have rather chosen non-existence, if given that opportunity by a personal God?

Consider the unfairness of all those who are infinitely isolated from their Creator as a result of a self-aware life never self-consciously sought, never self-consciously chosen, or never self-consciously desired. All non-believers, in a personal God, should ask Him this question, when the opportunity arises: "Why did you create me to be punished infinitely for a self-aware existence, I would not be able to comprehend fully? I would rather not have existed at all."

Based on this realization alone, imposed everlasting punishment from a personal Creator-God demonstrates willful and unjustifiable unfairness. The only thing that could be considered remotely fair would be for a personal God to return all the spiritually unredeemed non-believers, to their pre-existent state of non-self-aware oblivion.

Further, if a personal God has infinitely existed and He is by definition all-good, all-powerful, all-knowing, and all-present; He has no choice regarding His forever existence. Then He creates individualizations of man with the purpose that His self-aware creations of man, choose to be faithful, obedient, and subservient to Him.

However, let it be abundantly clear that a personal God had no responsibility for His infinite existence, yet He expects and demands that His created individualizations of man be accountable, to their God-given reality. Where's the fairness and justice in the realization that God is not responsible for His Infinite Beingness, but He makes His created man responsible for his forever beingness?

As individualized-Man, we were never designed by God. One meaningful difference between us as God's expression and God's Self-knowingness of Himself is that we have a free will to make choices, in the experiencing of our existence. God makes no free will choices in the Self-knowingness of His existence. Thus, because we have a free will, we are forever responsible for our lives, and the fulfilling of our destinies. God has no free will, and He is not responsible for His forever existence.

Thus, due to our infinitely innate free will; we are the forever saviors and the forever punishers of ourselves. Our existence is an existence of infinite suffering, infinite joy, infinite punishment, and endless self-realized unconditional love. God never Self-consciously directly affects our unlimited and individualized free will.

We never had, nor do we have now, nor will we ever have a free will capability of forever divorcing ourselves from our infinite self-conscious existence. The only free will choice of consequence that each of us forever wields is the choosing of how we experience our infinite existence.

Our infinite objective existence evolves from our infinite existence in core reality, where we infinitely and intermittently come to know the monotony of harmonious blissfulness. Our self-conscious reality must eventually include challenges, or our infinite existence becomes a self-realizing state of forever boredom.

Assume, for example, every day of our infinite self-awareness consisted of indescribable harmony, joy, and perfection. Then, suppose one day, for some unknown reason it rained, coolness nipped the air, and the sun was occluded. Would there be any pleasure to be realized on such a day?

Our self-conscious awareness of our forever self-existence, continuing with the above hypothetical situation would, I believe, welcome such an unpredictable and unusual day. Thus, illustrating the realization that non-blissfully based interruptions, to our infinite ongoing blissful existence, may be welcomed respites to assuage the monotony of forever self-realizing of perpetual bliss.

Thus, as individualized-Man, we are perpetually impelled to answer this question: Is our infinite existence, an existence we never self-chose, an ongoing blessing of blissful self-realization? When our infinite existence turns to blissful boredom, are we required to exist self-consciously in objective reality, where untold blissfulness abounds, for each of us to experience? I say we are, and we have no choice in the matter. However, I resent being infinitely programmed, even if it is for my infinite welfare. That is why we have a forever free will; we can rebel against infinity's dictates.

Why would a personal God permit all the horrors of evil to exist?

Everyone has heard it said a personal God created man with a free will because He did not want to be worshiped by non-self-governing automatons. Therefore, the free will capability of created man gives him the ability to reject his Creator, and dismiss his purpose for being constructed into self-aware existence.

If a personal God created man with a free will, He gave him control over an infinite destiny, he never self-consciously sought or desired. Thus, a personal God gave his created individualizations of man unsolicited mortal lives and made them responsible for those lives. Thus, an all-knowing personal God created man whom He pre-knew would do evil.

From the perspective of a personal God, man has the free will choice to reject his Creator is the basis for all worldly manifestations of evil and sin. I agree that the self-conscious rejection of God is the source for all appearances of evil and sin. However, I deny a personal God created individual man and empowered him with the free will ability to reject His Creator.

For a personal God to do such a thing would be an exercise of divine injustice. Putting aside the significance of sin and evil, why should anyone infinitely be punished for using their personal God-given free will to reject their Creator? What sense does it make to give someone the gift of a free will, mandate how that free will gift is used, and then forever punish individuals for their sinful-evil use of their free will?

Should the gift a free will to created man have infinite accountability divinely attached to it? What seems fair to me is that each one of us is infinitely accountable to understand ourselves, interpret ourselves, punish ourselves, reward ourselves, and save ourselves. There is no God that can Self-consciously do that for us.

Why could not a personal God in His infinite all-knowingness, create only those individuals whom He pre-knew would use their free will gift to love, follow, and obey Him? Under that scenario, the gift of existence would truly be a marvelous wonderment and a miracle. Sin might still be a free will option, but the horrors of evil would forever remain unknown, for it is not a free will possibility to love God and do evil.

What is Heaven like to a personal-God?

Obviously, the created man of this present physical world has no knowledge or understanding of Heaven. However, that does not mean created man cannot speculate or ask himself heavenly questions. For example, are clothes and shoes worn in the heavenly environs? If so, how or where did they originate? If clothing and shoes exist there, who or what are the makers or providers?

The providing of heavenly clothes and shoes infers there must be some form of work-type activities there. Thus, if shoes and clothes exist in Heaven that assumes that there must be some types of machines there? If so, how did they originate, who designed them, who makes them, and who operates them?

Also, where did all the required heavenly material come from to make the holy machines, or to make anything for that matter? Also, are there heavenly supervisors, mechanical engineers, or hopefully industrial engineers, my profession? If holy work is necessary or required, are there rewards for completing work successfully? In fact, what would happen to divine workers who perform poor quality work?

I cannot believe that just because individuals make it to Heaven, which means they will automatically become efficient workers. What about heavenly rest breaks? What about heavenly coffee breaks? What about divine workers who are unable to get to work on time? What about compensation for divine workers? Is compensation based on skill? These are heavenly questions needing answers.

On the other hand, suppose a personal God supplies and manifests the clothes and shoes for everyone. In His infinite all-knowingness, He would know the various types of apparel each heavenly inhabitant would enjoy wearing. I assume that this provided clothing would never need cleaning; however, would that divinely provided clothing ever change or would everyone wear the same thing infinitely?

Even considering the seeming silliness of the above, it emphasizes the quandaries involved in speculating about the Heaven of a personal God's providing. After all, the spiritual deserving heavenly inhabitants, of a personal God's creating, who had successfully lived their God-based earthly lives, are going to spend their infinite existence in Heaven. There have to be activities to fill the time of infinity.

It seems logical for self-realized happiness to exist in a bliss-filled Heaven, there must be an infinite assortment and an infinite continuum of individual and collective challenges, activities, uniquely designed personal pursuits. Thus, Heaven, of anyone's understanding, must be a place full of infinite and divinely stimulating activities or self-aware existence would indeed become tortuous boredom.

Still, there are other heavenly problems. For example, would the overcoming celestial challenges always be successful? In not, would there be, such a thing as divine frustration? On the other hand, if the outcome of all contests were divinely successful, they would not be challenges. Thus, once again, does an infinite self-aware heavenly existence become tedious?

In a personal God's Heaven, would there be things to learn? If so, would everyone learn the same thing, or would there be choices in learning? Would there be heavenly schools? Would there be instructors? Who would train the trainers? If there is the acquiring of divine knowledge, does everyone desire to learn, does everyone learn at the same pace, what do individuals do with his or her learned skills? How would all of this impact an individual's personal proclivities and interests?

In Heaven, will individuals, who were known on earth, still be identifiable? Suppose someone disliked an earthly individual, will he or she still not like that same person in Heaven? Is everyone heavenly liked and loved equally? Do the annoying habits and ways individuals exhibit on earth, evaporate into heavenly ethers of blissfulness?

Also, assuming that a personal God has forgiven all His heavenly inhabitants, of their past sins and evils; would it also be required that all heavenly inhabitants forgive, in the same manner as their personal God forgives those who had caused great suffering and pain, to members of their human family?

Thus, could heavenly beings whose physical world children were abused and killed, by now present angelic co-heavenly residents, have God-embraced relationships with them, now that those physical realm degenerates, had been entirely God-forgiven? If that is possible, then the spiritual understanding of created man must come under some powerful form of spiritual regeneration, when he arrives in his personal God's heavenly realm. Imagine, happily going heavenly fishing with someone who had killed your innocent children, before they were able to find God?

However, forgiving is one thing, forgetting is another. Not all spiritually evolved individuals on the earthly plane are likable. Does their human unlikeableness stay with them, when they enter Heaven? There is no question that some people on earth can be spiritually minded, but not necessarily divinely likable.

So, in the heavenly environment, would it be okay to dislike another divine being that happens to have annoying habits? Perhaps they talk too much. Perhaps they are lazy, assuming it is possible to be lazy in Heaven. Perhaps they just do not like people, divine or non-divine? Maybe they always have to be right? Maybe they are sore losers when they bet on a heavenly football game, and lose?

Maybe they are the type of individual who is always complaining. On earth, although they were spiritually minded, they would often harp and carp on all varieties of things. Would that aspect of their personality continue with them, or change when they entered the heavenly realm? Can you imagine an individual saying: "All this constant bright light is becoming annoying" "The continuous music from everywhere is driving me bananas." "If I have to eat another heavenly peach pie, I will scream!" It seems likely to me that a personal God's heavenly abode will house many annoying angelic beings.

Do all heavenly inhabitants retain their self-ability to exercise a free will? If so, would it still possible for individuals, while existing in Heaven, to reject their personal God? Would a personal God allow someone to come into His Heaven that He pre-knew would eventually repudiate Him? If someone renounced God, while in the heavenly realm, where would that individual go?

If heavenly divine inhabitants no longer have a free will, how would that realization affect his or her infinite ongoing self-aware existence or how would they experience their divine individuality? Is it possible to have a divine free will and not experience some form of disappointment, especially in Heaven? Can there even be such a thing as heavenly disappointments?

In heaven, does everyone have the same potentialities, possibilities, and opportunities for experiencing their heavenly existence? In other words, does an individual who lived a horrid earthly life, yet still managed to receive His personal God's forgiveness and thereby be entitled to go to Heaven, experience Heaven in the same manner as someone who lived a love-filled, God-centered earthly life?

There must be varying heavenly rewards or the spiritual efforts exerted on the mortal plane would have little meaning regarding earned spiritual rewards. If there are varying heavenly rewards, would that result in some form of spiritual envy? If there are varying entitled heavenly rewards, would the inability of some celestial beings to experience the same spiritual rewards as others, be a form of divine heavenly punishment?

Even in heaven, due to the presence of infinite individualities, the ability to express love must vary from individual to individual. Also, the capacity to act spiritually must vary from individual to individual. We are what we are when our spirituality is self-known or self-unknown. It seems, even in Heaven spiritual understanding is not equal. How could it be? Some earthly degenerates make to Heaven through God's forgiveness while other God-based individuals prepare their whole physical lives to go to Heaven.

Questions and circumstances concerning the existence of a personal God's and His Heaven are virtually endless. However, even in a personal God's Heaven; there must be some heavenly method, preventing divine existence for created man, from becoming monotonous? For individualized self-conscious reality to be meaningful, it cannot become forever tedious.

What might a personal God say to two sinners on Judgment Day?

Individual A

God is speaking: "I have observed your life with sadness and heartache. You never valued the gift of life I gave you. You disrespected Me by your continuous desire, for depravity and evil sinfulness. You cared nothing for others and thought only of yourself. You have consistently scorned Me and turned your back to Me in your thoughts, and in your actions."

God continues: "Numerous times, I sent My messengers to you for you to see the wrongfulness of your wicked ways, for you to find, accept, follow, obey, and believe in Me. Can you imagine how frustrating it is for Me to love you unconditionally while knowing at the same time, you will never love Me?

Now, I will reveal to you how you consistently chose to reject My messengers and live your life in total self-conscious separation from Me. The sinful evilness of your actions I have tearfully witnessed. Now, I will now show you the life you chose to live, the life I lovingly gifted to you to enjoy."

After individual A sees his self-chosen life in review, God once again speaks to him: "Do you have anything to say for yourself before I banish you from Me always?" Individual A: "I am sorry, I was stupid, I did not understand, please forgive me!" God answers back: "Too late; I now banish you from My presence for the end of timeless time. You are unworthy to enter my Kingdom, and henceforth, I know you not.

Individual B

God is speaking: "I have observed My gift of life to you with particular interest. You valued the life I gave you. You attempted to live your life in a kind, thoughtful, and considerate manner. You even encouraged others to seek and find Me. You have many faults, but I have let others into My Kingdom, with flaws much greater than yours."

God continues: "However, this is what dismays Me. I sent you many of My emissaries to you that you may find and accept the true Me, but you rebuffed and rebuked each and every one, as I knew you would. Still, I sent them so when this time came; you would know I am a loving God, a caring God, a compassionate God, and a fair and just God."

God continues: "I must tell you how saddened and heartbroken I am because you never knew Me. I stretched my arms out to you, for you to accept My loving presence. I was always with you, and I was always calling to you. However, as My tears flowed, you rejected Me. Before I send you from Me into the foreverness of timeless obscurity; do you have any final words?"

Individual B replies: "Yes Lord, You know my heart, yet You send me away. Did I not always desire to seek spiritual truth and understanding? Was I not always determined to live my life, by the holy light revealed to me? Did I not always seek You? Surely You know I endeavored spiritually to do the very best I was capable of being? Am I not the free will outcome, You entitled me to be?

Individual B continues: "Father God, I forgive You for Your Self-absorbed intolerance of indifference. I forgive You for creating me, giving me a free will, and then sending me forever to be separated from You because I did not follow Your Divine Self-imposed Plan as You meant it to be followed and obeyed.

I forgive You for giving me an existence I never asked for, never yearned for, never desired, never chose, or never wanted. If You were a truly just God, You would know my faults and judge me on the sincerity of my dedication, to be faithful to the person, You created and endowed and empowered, with a self-governing free will.

In conclusion, as we turn away from the concept of a personal God, we begin to understand ourselves as the individualized and indestructible wholeness of God in forever expression. If God did not exist, each of us as individualized-Man would not exist. Our individualized existence and God's infinite wholeness of Beingness are interdependent and provide the meaning for our individual and united infinite beingness.

Because God exists, each one of us individually is infinitely blessed with a self-actuating self-consciousness giving each of us, as individualized-Man, the ability to understand, interpret, and experience all the glories, wonders, and infinite unknowns of our never-ending existence.

In the objective realm, the gift of self-consciously understanding and experiencing our reality is our forever gift. God is personal to each one of us because the infinite-Us is composed of God's infinite essence. We are the truth of God infinitely knowing and infinitely understanding the reality of God.

Thus, we infinitely exist to understand our divine selves and thereby we infinitely exist to realize God. However, we can do neither without the existence of all aspects of ultimate reality. The blessing and the curse of our infinite existence are that we shall never totally understand God, ourselves, or ultimate reality. We exist on an endless trail of understanding that never vanishes into the horizon.

CHAPTER II

Man, God's Unknown Self-Beingness

We are not human beings having a spiritual experience. We are
spiritual beings having a human experience.

Pierre Teilhard de Chardin

What does it mean to say that the mortal man of this world exists?
Rene Descartes famously proclaimed: "I think, therefore I am." That
statement is truth encapsulated into the minimum amount of words.
Self-conscious thought implies the self-consciousness of self-awareness.
Self-conscious awareness suggests self-conscious existence.

If we self-consciously exist, our existence must be infinite, otherwise
how, where, or why did our self-consciousness originate? It seems self-
evident that our self-awareness could not evolve from non-self-aware
existence. Even if we evolved or we were created into existence, we
would have no self-awareness of our non-existence. This book describes
the infinite process of endless self-aware existence as existence, and as
existence as the living of life.

We forever self-consciously inhabit two infinity's aspects alternately.
First, we abide in core reality, as individualized core-Man, self-knowing
our unending self-identity within God. Second, we exist in objective
reality, as individualized objective-Man. We enter the objective realm
without knowing our identity, purpose, or destiny. It is the objective

realm where we infinitely rediscover ourselves, our future, and our basis for self-aware existence.

Thus, it is our twofold infinite divine nature that provides the purpose for our self-conscious existence. The purpose for our infinite objective existence is to experience, understand, and interpret our divine nature. If we could never experience a self-living reality, our self-aware non-experienced forever self-aware union with God would become the spiritual staleness of permanent blissfulness.

In core reality, our unlimited existence is our pure divinity self-knowing itself. In core reality, we forever self-consciously know our infinite immersion, in our God-bound blissfulness. In core reality, we cannot be anything other than the knowingness of God, in the foreverness of our self-conscious awareness.

In core reality, God's unfolding nature is distinctive to only God. The unfolding nature of God, forever within Himself, is the spiritual process that makes God, God. In core reality, we do not and cannot understand or interpret our self-conscious identification with the unfolding allness of God's nature.

As individualized core-Man, we self-consciously know the unfolding reality of God's Beingness, but God's unfolding nature is not unfolding within the collective core-Us. Thus, God's existence of forever Self-knowing Beingness is the reality of complete wholiness and wholeness. Our existence, as individualized core-Man, is the forever incomplete self-knowingness of God's wholeness of wholiness.

In core reality, each of us is infinitely self-aware of our existence, as that part of God unknown to Himself. In core reality, we do not interpret our core selves. Here, the purpose for our existence is self-consciously infused with the Self-beingness of God. Here, we are infinitely self-aware of our divinity, as part of God.

In core reality, there are no challenges to our spiritual self-awareness; there is only our self-knowingness of God's reality, our self-knowingness of harmony, and our self-knowingness of the wholiness of perfection. Our infinite self-knowing core-existence requires no spiritual expenditures of effort.

Core reality provides us with the effortless knowingness of our perpetual unification with God. However, there is a question to be answered: Is our infinite individualized core-realm existence requiring no spiritual effort on our part, a forever blessing or a forever curse? Therefore, is an easy, unchallenged, infinite self-consciousness existence something to be infinitely desired?

I believe that our individualized presence in core reality is assuredly desirable and assuredly a blessing, but it cannot be the only knowingness of ultimate reality because there's nothing in core reality to do, except to be blissfully happy. In a spiritual sense, core reality is an imposed divinely divine blissful self-aware existence, from our living of life in objective reality, where we forever evolve in our understandings, of ourselves and God.

If core reality were the only component of ultimate reality, our individualized beingness would be our self-aware existence, without any meaningful purpose, other than the knowingness of God-ordained blissfulness. Our blissfulness, in core reality, must be earned through the objective experiencing of our lives. Thus, our earned core-realm blissfulness is always finite-infinite.

An effortless infinity of self-knowing blissfulness, although divinely stimulating, would be an infinite existence which was never self-earned or self-chosen. For our individual self-existence to realize a meaningful purpose, each of us must self-control the direction of our forever objective destiny.

Our ultimate existence demands fulfilling joy, not unsatisfying blissful boredom. Thus, when our self-known blissfulness becomes divinely unbearable, we are impelled and compelled into the objective realm of ultimate reality. This divine process is automatic and requires no self-effort or self-choice, on our part.

In core reality, we only know bliss-filled harmony. In the objective realm, we are now constrained by a reality filled with ongoing obstacles, barriers, and difficulties that must be overcome. The design of objective reality requires no one is to be infinitely bored. If boredom were a constant component of any portion of ultimate reality, our infinite self-aware existence would be that of unbearable torturous tedium.

When blissful boringness impels us out of core reality, our inviolate self-conscious union with God is suspended, and we embark upon our individual finite-infinite adventures, in the discovering and the rediscovering, of our existence, as indestructible divine beings. Our forever destiny now becomes that of experiencing our forever lives, through eternities ongoing.

In objective reality, we are still core-Man individualized, but now that we are in the objective realm, our core identity has been occluded from our now self-conscious awareness. In core reality, we forever increase in our absorption of divine beingness; however, in our existence in the objective realm, we increase in the absorbing of our understandings of life as existence.

Each of us is a forever intermittent but forever real component of objective reality, and core reality. However, the experiences we self-consciously actualize into existence, in objective reality, are not real. In core reality, we do not and cannot create experiences. Thus, our immortal-Man existence is realized both as a non-creator in core reality, and creator, in objective reality.

In core reality, we have no divine to realize or attain. In the objective realm, our continuing self-conscious re-reunion with God is our destiny. In the objective realm of reality, we seek to re-acquire the self-aware existence we had previously known in core reality. However, it is only through our self-willed efforts, in the objective realm, that we can understand the meaning and purpose of our infinite self-aware existence.

In the objective realm, when we realize the fulfilling of our divine destiny, through the all-powerfulness of our understanding, we eventually self-consciously return to core reality. Thus, the cycle of infinite existence is fulfilled, waiting to be revealed once again, in the everlastingness of infinity.

Only in objective reality, can we create experiences giving each of us the capability for the understanding of our existence and all reality, which includes God. We do not and cannot create anything into infinite real objective reality. We do not and cannot create life. We cannot create a purpose for our infinite existence; we can only interpret purpose into our infinite existence.

We are the only aspects of ultimate reality capable of creating unreality as experiences. Therefore, our self-conscious awareness is capable of understanding, and interpreting non-real reality. In the experiencing of our forever existence, we continuously understand reality; but, also we simultaneously comprehend and non-comprehend infinite unreality.

Our infinite spiritual history consists of our past infinite divine traveling-treks through objective reality. Thus, we have spent eternity's endless understanding the foreverness of our infinitely incorruptible existence, with each eternity seeming like the foreverness of infinity. Thus, in the objective realm, we experience infinities eternities.

Our present-evolving spiritual history consists of the experiencing ongoing objective eternities. Our future spiritual destiny consists of continuing sojourns into objective reality, to forever discover and rediscover, to interpret and reinterpret, to experience and re-experience, to overcome and re-overcome, and then to enjoy and re-enjoy the infinite rewards our spiritual existence, infinitely gifted for each one of us, to realize and experience.

As we correctly understand and interpret God; we understand and explain ourselves to ourselves. The most important truth to self-consciously know and self-consciously embrace is that we forever exist inside of God's Beingness, as the individual expression of God, and we forever exist outside of God's Beingness, as individualized immortal-Man.

As we truly and divinely self-consciously desire to understand and interpret the experiencing of our forever real objective selves; we are self-prizing and self-praising the allness of God. Our self-aware existence, as objective-Man, brings all-powerfulness to the nature of God, through each of us, through our forever increasing understanding of foreverness of reality.

Our nature and God's nature are unchanging, infinite, divine, and indestructible. However, each of us, as God's unknown expression of Himself, possesses the ability to discover, and to understand our infinite capability of self-expression, as God's representative to all things real.

Thus, our individual and shared divine identities are the fulfilling of that part of God that is only understood by each of us individually.

We are the infinity of God's divinity experiencing the wonderment of self-expression. Our forever developing understanding of spiritual truth is the sole deliverer from the fogginess resulting from the continuous inbred trumpeting of godless unreality, demanding our knee-bending recognition, acceptance, and obedience.

Our innate gifted ability to self-think has no infinite goodness or non-goodness attached to it. We experience the creations of our thought-desires. All created experiences are unreal, but they are inter-connected with the forever endowment, of our self-conscious self-actualizing capacity to think independently, of the functions and functioning of objective reality.

Each of us is a forever unique expression of our real and forever existence. Each of is destined to understand and interpret ourselves as the Godness of our self-everlasting divinity. The uniqueness of our present self-conscious experiencing of life results from our interpretations of the eternity, we are now occupying, which is part of the infinite progression of eternities.

Thus, infinity consists, in part, of infinite, eternal expressions of uniqueness. Thus, each one of us defines infinity by our endless interpretations of eternities. Therefore, a major portion of infinity is composed of perpetually created eternities, which can only be self-consciously understood, interpreted, and experienced, by each one of us.

In a sense, through our interrelationship with physical eternities, we forever understand ourselves into objective existence. Unfortunately, the physical realm includes a divine destiny which involves the constant overcoming of godless unreality, stabbing incessantly at our spiritually evolving self-awareness.

Our true and never changing fate is understand ourselves self-consciously, as the self-consciousness of God, discovering, exploring, interpreting, and traversing eternities endless. Through each one of us, as self-recognizing expressions of God, the God of ultimate reality is experiencing the infinity of existence, through us.

However, as long as we continue to follow the lured and naked-clad sirens of godless unreality, we remain in a mind-numbing depraved state of objective self-conscious awareness. We become self-consciously numb to all things real as we self-willing inject unreality into the purity of our endless self-recognized divinity.

As individualized Man, we possess the capability of misunderstanding the nature of God, and thus misunderstanding our nature, as God's nature self-consciously individualized. In our self-experiencing of existence, there are always conflicts and contradictions between what we understand as truth, what we interpret as reality, what we accept as truth, and all things we never know at all.

Still, now and forever, in the objective realm, we are always expressing the understanding of self-awareness. Only through our forever unchallenged power of amassed knowledge, can we infinitely demonstrate the trueness of our forever eternal and infinite divine self-identity. Our self-infinite divinity was never a created existence, it forever was existence, it forever is existence, and exists forever to be existence.

Forever illuminated within each of us, is the pathway for understanding our divine selves. As divine beings, our spiritual progress is the forever exponent of our divine unfoldment. The infinite celestial murmuring within the realm of our individualized self-conscious awareness forever seeks its re-reunion with God.

Our individualized self-conscious awareness gives objective reality meaning. Our ultimate existence is a mysterious marvel, a marvel never to be sated or divinely apprehended. Our infinite divine lineage is our never-ending divinity in forever beingness. However, our individual and commonly united divine destinies are always and forever to discover and rediscover the divinity of our consecrated self-identities.

The spiritual imperative of our forever existence is to understand ourselves from the ever changing perspective of experiences. The purpose of self-consciously experiencing life is to reveal our spiritual identities to ourselves. If we never self-consciously experience the understandings of our existence, we could never progress spiritually.

In the objective realm, we seek an understanding of all that we are and of all that we are to become, through the progressing and sometimes regressing understandings of ourselves. Our self-understanding is the power of the foreverness of our divine self-effort to understand our forever selves in relationship to our infinite never-asked-for existence.

Embedded within our objective reality is the inherent need to self-understand ourselves, and to self-understand the reason for our existence. The importance of this realization is the recognition that each of us becomes self-consciously responsible for the evolving and unfolding, of our short-term and long-term spiritual destinies.

In this discovering effort of understanding, each of us is a forever creator of experience. We create the experiences in our self-evolving understanding of existence. In a sense, we are the creators of ourselves, even though we have always existed. The force we exhort to create objective unreality is the same effort that returns us to the reality of our core existence.

When we inhabit objective reality, we become the creations of the understanding of ourselves. Thus, we create the experiencing of ourselves, in the image of our ever evolving self-understandings of ourselves. The difference between our real selves and our non-real created selves is our spiritual commitment to the realizing of our divine destiny.

We create experiences by our self-actuating self-consciousness importation of all the components of objective reality, into our progressing self-understanding, through the unreality of our self-created experiences. Our creations manifest as unreal-real expressions, in the realm of experience. Unreality exists as the creating function of our objective self-consciousness.

Therefore, our self-conscious ability to create experiences is an independent purpose of ultimate reality, because each of us is an independent functioning component of ultimate reality. All ultimate reality is dependent upon our infinite self-conscious functioning. In other words, it is our forever nature that provides divinity, to all of the infinity of ultimate reality.

However, the created experiences of our self-conscious self-actualizing thoughts are not an independent function of ultimate reality, because all self-consciously designed experiences have no absolute attachments to their appearing-world identities. All things made manifest as creations are unreal, in relationship to the independence of ultimate reality.

The truth of objective reality is only capable of being interpreted; it is never capable of being altered, impacted, or changed by our self-consciously creative thinking-thoughts. Created experiences are only our shadowy sandy-skeletal interpretations of objective reality, from our individualized perspectives. We are the forever interpreters of the infinite gradations of reality; we perceive in all things.

To each one of us, self-created experiences are as real as the realness of reality itself. But to objective reality, all of our self-consciously created experiences are non-real and non-existent, because they are not part of the infinite real processes of forever actual ongoing creations, devoid of beginnings and endings. From the perspective of objective reality, there is no such thing as creative creations; there is only one creation in infinite expression, and that is the entirety of objective reality.

Simply put, in objective reality, we choose to experience the outputs of our self-conscious thoughts, but the thoughts that we outwardly manifest have no real independently-based appearances. Real experiences result from objective reality's automatic and forever functionings.

These functioning operations occur without any self-coordinating effort, direction, choice, control, or volition, by any independent non-self-conscious power, or independent self-conscious power. The functions, within the reality of objective reality, operate on an infinite continuum of beginnings and endings.

These individual uses have no objectifiable realm identities. We, alone and individually, give the beginning-ending meanings to the functioning operations in objective reality, meanings which only have significance, from our self-conscious perspectives. Objective reality exists for our infinite interpretations, to understand our infinite selves.

As we forever exist in core reality, we know existence as total infinite bliss and harmony. However, as we objectively experience life, we infinitely experience heartache, pain, and all manners of suffering.

Self-aware ongoing pain is the forever price we pay for experiencing existence. We experience non-truth to exercise the power of real truth understood.

Is the price we pay, in the bottomless buckets of sorrow for our self-undergoing of infinite objective existence, worth experiencing the foreverness of our infinite existence? Thus, I ask once again: Is the experiencing of our self-conscious life a blessing or a curse? Is an infinite existence, so often containing various degrees of sorrow, a desirable forever life? Only increasing spiritual understanding can uplift our infinite existence to make it infinitely desirable.

However, whether or not our self-aware objective existence is a blessing or a curse, we have no choice as to whether or not we experience our forever reality. In the final reasoning for our self-conscious existence, each one of us is a self-identified soul in ultimate reality. In a sense, each one of us is the forever product of ultimate reality's forever existence.

The spiritual present of our destiny is to experience the eternity we are now occupying, through the singular eyes, of our ongoing divinity. In our current objective self-bruising journey through the entirety of eternity, it is never possible for any of us to transcend beyond our self-evolving spiritual understanding of God.

However, we are forever expressing an existence requiring self-effort; a self-effort filled life that God is incapable of expressing. In other words, we use our self-actuating self-consciousness to understand ourselves, through the experiencing of our self-understood selves. God is not capable of Self-consciously understanding Himself or us.

Our short-term destinies are always alterable by the self-conscious directing of our thoughts. However, our long-term fate is never alterable, never in doubt, and is forever being fulfilled, in our finite-infinite wandering throughout the eternities of objective reality. Thus, each of us is a forever nomad searching for the elixir of understanding, known only in the objectively real oases of our transbeingness, to comfort our infinitely troubled travels of experiencing existence.

Our objective purpose for existence is to joyfully and self-consciously experience the expression of life through our ever increasing understanding, interpretation, and acceptance, of our true divine nature, as the individuality of God in our self-chosen active expressions. To see Godliness in all things is our finite fate surrounding our infinite destiny.

However, throughout all the realms of our spiritual discoveries, we forever retain the capability of self-consciously rejecting our divinity. Still, each of us is forever preordained to discover, interpret, understand, experience, and self-know the infinity of our divinity, or the spiritual deity of our infinity.

As we experience existence, each of us has the option to be the expression of morality or to be the appearance of non-morality, to be just or unjust, to be sinner or saint. However, from the vantage point of objective reality, each one of us remains perpetually pure, forever incorruptible, forever indestructible, and forever changeless.

So it is with the real reality of God, forever pure, forever incorruptible, forever indestructible, and forever changeless. Actual reality, separate from God, consists of the timelessness of change, with unreality comprised of time-filled and change-filled arcs of experiences proclaiming their self-beginnings and their self-endings.

In our self-aware existence, we possess self-conscious desire-power, self-conscious choice-power, and self-conscious understanding-power. Thus, each of us has the power capability of self-consciously deciding to accept or reject godless unreality. If we choose to take godlessness, we become godlessness in outward appearances.

However, in divine truth, we never become godlessness because the untrue has no real existence, at any time, at any place, or in any reality. Still, our self-aware acceptance of the godlessness of unreality becomes an actual reality to us, as individualized-Man. Thus, the understanding of our infinite objective selves is an enigma. Unreality is real when its unreality becomes real to us.

Each one of us is the wholiness of God's forever Beingness in expression. The continuous arching rainbow of our divinity forever brightens our soul and persists throughout the sacred process of our infinitely divine objective forever revealment. It is to each one of us alone, the sacred responsibility of unveiling our infinite divinity to ourselves.

The totality of this realization must forever remain down deep, within our uncertain-certain self-consciousness identity continuingly pushing us along journeys endless, throughout the forever-lengthening finite-infinite understandings, of our physical selves in the perpetually manifesting stages of unreality.

If we choose to reject our true identity, we consign ourselves to experience the wrongfully untrue. Even so, we are self-consciously experiencing an existence which is real and unreal, but forever meaningful to our endless divine self-evolving. It remains forever true that our individualized self-existence provides meaning and purpose, not only for ourselves but, also, for all of the absoluteness of reality.

Even when our self-consciousness is shrouded in a canopy of darkness, the deific spark, within us, continually seeks our divinely wakeful acknowledgment, connectivity, and receptivity to our inwardly realized divinity. Our destiny to understand ourselves remains forever the experiencing of our objective existence, in ever increasing harmony and joy, while at the same time knowing the non-reality of experience.

Whatever we choose to experience in the living of life is our individual interpretations of changeless objective reality. Experiences of happiness without an awareness of the ever-presence of God, limit our self-consciousness, to the binding-burdens of godless illusions. Because the forever reality of divine joy is part of God's infinite essence, we can understand and experience the reality of God. If divine joy were not in God's Beingness, the self-realizing of divine joy would forever be unknown.

Only experiences of happiness, based on the understanding of our real identities, provide us with authentic experiences of joyfulness, in expression. False happiness is the fulfilling of unfulfillment in our assertions of self-beingness. True divine happiness results from our understanding the God-joyful connection of our forever oneness with God, with the divinity of our self-identity.

The sacred pathway of our eternal, infinite, and forever spiritually emerging journeys, through objective reality, cannot be forever altered. Each one of us makes the choices determining the degree of unreal bumpiness caused to our forever spiritual awakenings, by our self-acceptance of the non-real imperfections encased in our self-knowingness, as we progress ceaselessly onward.

Our spiritual progression demands our self-conscious dedication and rededication, to obey the wholiness of goodness that forever enshrouds us. Within each of us, the pure presence of God washes away the godlessly grown roots of unreality forever claiming, climbing, and clinging, to our self-awareness, watered by the ever flowing cascade of our tears, as we experience life as existence.

Our spirituality, self-consciously understood, makes level the rockiness of our divine travels, as we steadily progress along the holy highways, byways, and pathways, in the continuing discovery and exploration of our infinite existence. The understanding of our self-existence provides the power to our God-soul.

Struggles are the forever byproducts of our self-conscious experiencing of existence through our attempts to understand, interpret, and obey the directions we individually and collectively take, in the discovering and rediscovering of our objective destinies. We are forever destined to experience our existence: there is no escape from this purpose for our forever beingness! If we were ever completely understood all aspects of our forever beingness, we would have the power to end our self-conscious awareness, in ultimate reality. Who among us would choose that option?

Still, all struggles are blessings realized and unrealized, as they impel us onward and upward, into new realms of divinity, in our forever waking wakefulness. If there were no life-struggling lessons, in the experiencing of our existence, we would be incapable of interpreting the forever ongoingness of our divine destiny, in the revealing of our forever divinity, to our forever self-awakening selves.

In the realizing of our objective reality, we are constantly pummeled by the stinging hailstones of unreality. As we experience life, struggles result from our misinterpretations of objective reality. All efforts in fighting the non-realities of existence represent forever spiritual benchmarks achieved, in the continuous streaming of our divine self-consciousness.

In the forever streaming of our spiritual self-awareness, the Divine River, which forever floats our souls, is the same in all of its infinite moving currents. To the infinity of our individual self-aware existences, there is no difference between any of us. We are divinely divine, God is the source of our forever divinity, and we are infinitely indestructible.

All struggles provide us with a new spiritual impetus to understand and demonstrate the real reality of our divine destiny. Without our experiencing of struggles, we could never realize the understanding of ourselves as infinite divine beings. Thus, we infinitely struggle to understand endlessly that which we forever are throughout all infinity.

To objective reality, our struggles are non-existent. To the spiritually minded among us, struggles are interpreted as our self-consciousness of divinity, in the action of divine understanding. In our evolving spiritual understanding, would we appreciate and value our objective existence, if no spiritually mental effort was required, to overcome struggles?

All struggles are byproducts of our self-divinity not understood. Without struggles, there would be no self-evolving of our spirituality because there would be no method for us to evolve spiritually. That is why in core reality, the knowingness of ourselves is without struggles because, in core reality, our self-realized existence does not advance through any divine form of overcoming the struggles of objective beingness.

Without struggles, our angelic wings for our spiritual ascension remain powerless, to lift us ever upward, onward, and forward towards our finite-infinite spirituality self-acknowledged, interpreted, understood, and demonstrated. The overcoming of struggles by way of our divine identifications to the divinely real brings each of us the blessings of truth confirmed, understood, accepted, and obeyed.

Spiritual rewards are bestowed only upon the spiritually deserving and divinely worthy. Spiritually emerging individuals, who self-consciously and divinely choose to overcome the struggle-tangling claims of non-reality, earn their spiritual rewards, with their self-conscious desire to see the power of truth understood and accepted, manifest in the realms of appearance.

All our spiritual culminations, as we trek through objective reality, are infinitely finite. The spiritual evolving process of self-consciously experiencing our existence consists of forever divine portions of goodness and non-goodness, intermixed, accepted, or rejected. Our objective realm destiny is to experience goodness only, without any self-awareness of non-goodness.

When our self-conscious awareness agrees with our inner divine nature; the essence of God permeates our self-understanding. Our self-conscious spiritual unity with God rightly directed, keeps us on the spiritual path, understanding illumines our steps, and wisdom sanctions the steadfastness of our spiritual journeys. Our self-aware objective existence consists of ongoing and infinite eternal victories.

Thus, when struggles in the physical realm, are no longer seen as life-fighting efforts, to be spiritually fought and overcome, we become divinely victorious, in our present sojourning into and through objective reality. In other words, when the appearance of struggles is no longer challenging to the material evolving of our spiritual understanding, we return self-knowingly and self-unequivocally to God.

Our trek through the habitats of ever evolving eternities is our self-consciousness forever experiencing the gift of our objective existence. Our continuous self-evolving existence is our individual self-awareness of life acknowledging itself through the non-real realm of experience. Each one of us is a representative of the self-conscious advancement or non-advancement, by all members of God's perfect divine family.

Our individual divinely correct interpretations of our physical experiences bless the entirety of God's family members. The reality of truth understood by all divine family members is truth made increasingly available for all of us to experience. Each of us is the individualized mind and the individualized expression of God.

Our forever ability to experience life is a blessing to our evolving self-conscious awareness, even though it does not always seem a blessing. It is each one of us, alone and individually, who is solely capable of making the experiencing of existence, a self-realized blessing, or a self-realized non-blessing. The blessings we incur, in the living of our lives, are the forever ever-present gifts given to us, for divinely honoring our self-aware existence, by cherishing divine understanding.

If there were no real blessings to be received, in the process of living our self-active existence, there would be no experiences of real joy. If there were no such a thing as the experiencing of real joy, our self-realized lives would be bereft of the quality of divine happiness self-realized. If that was true, who would desire such a self-conscious existence, devoid of the experiencing of happy-joy? However, in the actual living of our lives, joy is a real reality for each of us to experience.

Thus, during our divine and infinite procession through objective reality, there are ongoing spiritual Heavens of joy-filled rewards, waiting for our self-conscious habitation. However, we must spiritually earn entry into these Holy Heavens, through our divine victories, resulting from our forever battles, endlessly fought, endlessly lost, and endlessly won.

We earn the self-conscious experiencing of divine joy, by our successful winning struggles, to understand the foreverness of our infinitely innate divine beingness. Thus, the forever understanding, of our infinitely subjective divine reality, results from our struggles overcoming the non-understandings of our divinity. As we save ourselves, through real spiritual knowledge, we earn our receptivity to things joy-filled.

The mentally unworthy, unprepared, and ungodly can never experience the joyfulness embedded in the forever divine essence of God. Unless God is sincerely sought, loved, obeyed, and cherished, in our self-awareness, undeserved spiritual blessings, are never bestowed to the unworthy. For anyone to desire undeserved divine joy-filled blessings, demonstrates a form of infinite blasphemy which dampens the purpose, for the experiencing forever self-aware existence.

All of our actions in objective reality are the cumulative result of our evolving, objective realm understandings. Our experiences in the non-reality of objectivity, become our self-acceptance of thoughts made visible, in the realm of appearances. Our ability to experience non-reality is the spiritual growth gift, bestowed upon us, for our continuous and infinite self-aware experiences of existence.

To objective reality, there are no judgments placed upon our self-actions as experiences self-accepted and self-realized. In other words, to the objective realm, there are no sinners, saints, or doers of evil things. From the objective viewpoint, we only exist to experience non-reality, in the forever real surroundings, of the objective realm.

Thus, to objective reality, there is no accountability required for our unreal-real actions eternally accruing, in the experiencing of our existence. However, the infinite actions occurring in non-reality, resulting from our countless expressions of our self-aware lives do not go unnoticed, and can never be removed for self-aware identities, except by each of us alone and individually, in the sanctum of our self-conscious knowingness.

We, alone, notice and determine the accountability of our self-enclosed, self-focused, self-derived, and self-determined actions, in the infinite interpretations, of our infinite objective existences. Again, this represents the fairness in our experiencing of reality, inculcated into our forever expressions of life.

Is it not infinitely fair that we alone and individually, must be accountable for our actions, punished for our wrongful actions, and rewarded for our divinely accurate derived sense of divinity? When it comes to evaluating our forever lives, in our experiencing of existence, no God is necessary, to evaluate our infinite lives. We sit in judgment of ourselves, and we judge ourselves more harshly than any God would ever judge us.

We, alone, can only understand and interpret the wrongness and rightness of our actions; we alone realize and suffer the consequences, of those actions, in our non-compromising sense of self-awareness. Through the experiencing of our self-chosen living of our lives, we alone in the infiniteness of all existence, are capable of understanding the complexities of our forever lives, which makes each of us infinitely unique, in our inescapably honest unflinching evaluations of ourselves.

It should be noted; infinity gives us non-judgmental non-designed rewards, for our mere self-conscious experiencing of existence, unrelated to spiritual concerns. For example, the non-spiritual reward of good health is granted to individuals who each healthy foods, exercise, and do not abuse their bodies with drugs, alcohol, et cetera. However, infinity's designed spiritual rewards are earned through the self-directed understanding of our forever divinity, or our forever destiny has no meaning to our forever beingness.

Still, regardless of our individual spiritual evolvement or lack thereof, life withholds nothing divine from us. However, we are only self-consciously prepared to accept life's sacred offerings, as we are spiritually entitled. Even so, sometimes spiritual rewards are shown though not to be experienced because we are not divinely prepared to receive them. The revealing of future spiritual rewards to the spiritually unworthy is one of the gifts of infinity to God's family, to encourage our self-discovery of our self-divinity.

These gifts are revealed to us to make us aware of the spiritual blessings of forever self-awareness, which are forever waiting for our spiritual receptivity, when we choose to seek, understand, and accept our forever self-divinity, instead of choosing to wallow self-consciously, in the grimy, dusty, withering shadows of unreality.

Our forever power-filled understanding of existence controls or enslaves our divine destiny. Either way, we power and empower the realization of our forever divinity. However, regardless of the exercising of our infinitely realizing power of understanding, we forever remain unchanged. The more we rise in spiritual knowledge, the more we embrace our self-divinity. The more we understand our self-divinity, the more divinely humble we become in the realizing that our existence, in the consciousness of God, is forever unfathomable.

Each one of us has an ongoing divine and a non-divine destiny to fulfill. Our continuous waking prayer should always be to attain the self-understanding realizing, of our divine destiny. The only real purpose for our existence is to realize that our destiny is the forever discovering of our self-divinity. Imagine what the experiencing of reality would be like if everyone understood, realized, and accept our real and forever divine destiny? Our self-aware existence in Heaven would be ever present, ever presently.

We exist to experience our forever existence, but why? From our individualized perspective, why is each one of us infinity's chosen one, so to speak? To infinity is our real infinite existence any different, or of any greater value, than the forever life immensity of a rock or the idea of a rock? To infinity, do any of us possess any specialness? I think not! We put the specialty of our self-aware existence into the interpretation of our self-aware living of life and reality.

In all eternities, our self-conscious experiencing of existence demands all ungodliness be replaced, by the self-accepting our awareness of our divinity, through our finite-infinitely divine self-awakenings. Our infinite self-existence is a maze-filled dream from which we can only divinely hope to awaken self-consciously finite-infinitely when we self-consciously embrace our forever divinity.

Experiencing existence as the living of life is the self-conscious purpose for our infinite existence, but it is our receptivity to things divinely sought that produces our receptiveness to the blessings bestowed upon our forever self-awareness. If we experience spiritual relapses of understanding, where the blessings of life seem withheld, it only means that we have not consciously uncovered a steadfast understanding of our true divinity.

The spiritually correct understanding of our self-conscious experiencing of existence is forever enabling the expression of God through us. There are no spiritual relapses in our self-sturdy divine self-awakening process of our spiritual unfoldment. All things properly understood unite for the success of the sacredness of our God-derived destiny.

Spiritual understanding is always knocking at the door of our self-awareness, but often we choose to ignore its knock. It is not possible to separate ourselves from God, strive as we infinitely may. God forever realizes Himself as infinite. We acknowledge ourselves as infinitely finite-infinite. Our spiritual successes are permanently seeded, in our endless unfolding pathways of our divinity self-realized.

Our forever capacity, to understand or misunderstand truth, is based on our free will, an aspect to our beingness that nothing else in ultimate reality possesses. When it comes to our understanding and acceptance of truth, there is no such thing as old truth or new truth.

There is only truth understood, at the level of our individual spiritual perception, unfoldment, and receptivity.

Each one of us has the power to reject our divinity, our destiny, and thus the purpose for our forever existence. However, we have infinity to discover forever and re-discover who we are, what we are, and why we exist through the infinite non-real appearing vibrations of the things we infinitely are not. It is the power of our understanding that gives authorization, for the claims of the endless unreal, to announce their birth into objective reality.

The marvel of it all is that in the actual understanding-knowingness of ourselves, we are forever, untouched, inviolate, and indestructible; regardless of the things we do and do not understand as reality. Each one of us chooses the forever expressions of our forever existence. Each one of us is the all-powerful god of ourselves; thus, each one of us has total non-influenced control over the infinity that is within the forever evolving of our self-beingness.

The experiencing of existence challenges our understandings of our forever selves. Our free will choices become entirely subjugated, by our steadfast resolve to adhere to the path of divine transcendence. The sumptuous temptations of existence lose their 'come hither' power, to infect our self-conscious receptivity, with the exotic aromatic candles of unreality, which permeate the spiritually stifling bondages of illusions.

Each one of us is an infinite composer providing the music for our individualized self-styled dances, through the experiencing of existence. The foreverness of infinity's ever present music vibrates the infinite harmony of beingness throughout the chambers of our self-knowingness. The vibrating notes of disharmony are the expressions of godless unreality attempting to create music of its own. In response, we use our forever free will to cleave the ungodliness of unreality from our self-awareness, and we use our same forever free will to cleave the goodliness of Godliness to our self-awareness.

Without the power of our individualized self-conscious free will, we would be incapable of discovering or understanding ourselves, including our innately designed destiny. Thus, our forever unfolding future of intended purpose, inherently branded into our individualized objective beingness, requires our individualized free will to overcome all perceived limitations, as we forever uncover, discover, rediscover, and experience our self-revealing existence.

In the experiencing of existence, our collective subconscious includes a vast array of our individualized understandings of idea realm ideas, spanning the interpretations and conceptualizations of perfection and non-perfection. It is only our self-powered firm determination, to the ever acquiring of spiritual knowledge, which prevents the commonality of erroneous suppositions from gaining a foothold, in our self-conscious awareness.

Let each one of us be the self-controlled God-authorizer of our expressing divinity. Our individual existence as a divine family member involves both non-spiritual weakness and spiritual strength. However, more often than not, we allow our group-common subconscious urgings and promptings to dominate our free will choices, and then regale ourselves in the creating appearances of ungodly apparitions. We understand our spiritual progressions as we understand that the commonality of our existing self-aware thinking is falsely based.

Our spiritual destiny is solely and self-consciously designed, for each of us to determine our thoughts holding a power sway over our free will choices. In contrast, there is nothing in infinite existence that has the capability of any sway-influence on God, who is devoid of a free will. Therefore, God is non-dominated and non-burdened, by anything expressing reality or unreality, thus illustrating another difference between our individualized realization of existence and God's total realizing of His for existence.

We are forever revealing our true or non-true destiny as we exercise the power of our free will choices. We are destined to experience our divinity throughout the ongoing creations of eternities, but we are not designed nor intended, to be consistently and infinitely spiritually minded. In the truth of understanding, from our individualized perspective, the realizing of our non-true destiny is the temporarily realizing of our true destiny.

It is the foreverness of our individualized free will prohibiting our successful ongoing submissions to the continuous callings of our inner divinity. Thus, our infinite existence demands that each of us is free-willingly destined to understand our forever spirituality through the non-understanding of our forever spirituality.

Our free will choices forever determine our receptivity to things divine. The practice of thinking and expressing kindness begets its spiritual rewards; there is no other way. Any free will attempt to possess a sense of unearned spirituality does not result in the attaining or acquiring of self-evolving spirituality.

Sometimes a sense of spirituality is simply realized, but the simple realization of spirituality must be self-validated, in the realm of experience. Spirituality cannot be a self-confirmed achievement by way of mere desire, lacking any spiritual effort. To appreciate the beauty of a painted picture is one thing, but to paint the beauty into the picture is another.

Thus, we are only able to share in the spirituality we all self-consciously desire to cherish, as we are self-realizing our individual spiritual identities. Even as become captured and lost in the throes of ungodliness, it is always Godliness we seek, because we are forever divine beings, forever in search of the real understanding of our divine selves.

Our free will enables us to rebel against our nature, and against the nature of ultimate reality itself. As we self-consciously and directly control our free will, we are revealing and fulfilling the purpose of our infinite destiny to our infinite selves. Still, it is the realizing that our infinite existence is infinitely spiritual that provides comforting gratefulness for our infinite existence.

Thankfully, as we freely and self-consciously embrace the ungodliness of things unreal, we are still fulfilling our divine destiny because we are still self-consciously experiencing our forever self-aware existence. The reality of governing our infinite existence does not determine the manner we experience our infinite existence. Naturally, if the realizing of our forever existence were predetermined, we would not possess a free will.

Our infinite free will determines how we choose to experience our self-awareness of our infinite existence; but, still, there is a forever divine design, within each of us, impelling us to seek, find, obey, and follow the God of our individual understanding. However no matter how deeply embedded is the divine design is, within us, if can be forever overruled by our free will choices. If that is not true, the realizing of our divine destiny would be effortlessly unwarranted spirituality.

Infinity has no sympathy concerning our infinite existence. To infinity, our infinite divinity remains in forever chilled abeyance because our destiny is forever being realized, by way of our free will choices. To infinity, our self-conscious existence is what we free willingly choose to make it. Our self-conscious reality only has a correctly interpreted meaning, if we self-consciously value and desire the understanding of God.

We, alone and individually, make our infinite existence meaningful and worth self-consciously experiencing. However, from our individual and infinite perspective, we are forever burdened by the uncertainties forever involved in the living of our lives. We are immortal, indestructible beings. It is only our stumbling spiritual weakness that can make that certainty, uncertain.

Our free will choices determine the manner of how each of us individually understands, interprets, and experiences our destiny. Thus, it is only our self-conscious spiritual evolving that can protect us from the unpredictable influences of chance, opportunity, randomness, and general unpredictability.

We each have an eternal and infinite divine quest to be forever realized. That spiritual quest is to divine comprehension of the meaning of our infinite indestructible existence. This forever journey requires a free will. Without a free will, we would have self-awareness of our forever divinity, but the forever evolving experiencing of our divinity would not be possible.

If we were unable to experience our infinite self-aware divinity, our infinite self-deity could not be understood; therefore, the question of God's forever existence becomes moot. The successful spiritual realizing of our forever reality requires our self-conscious understanding of God. It is our understanding of God's nature that provides the power for our infinite ability to understand.

Non-divine attachments to the self-consciousness of our divinity last as long as our self-accepted separation from God continues. We cannot elect to become divine; we are divine. Even if we choose to reject the foreverness of our self-conscious divinity, we remain infinitely divine beings.

Our free will choices never affect the existence of our forever-given divinity. All things that are forever divinely permanent belong to each of us. All things that are forever non-divinely permanent also belong to each of us. In our infinite foreverness, we always have been, we always are now, and we shall always forever be, the outcomings of our self-conscious thoughts, permanent or non-permanent.

Within each of us, our individualized self-awareness harbors the truth of our divine heritage. As members of God's family, the commonality of our sacred heritage is the forever binding unity of our forever togetherness, in our individually infinite but commonly shared unchanging existence.

In the final summation of our infinite divine existence, each of us exists as forever part of God. As we forever understand our infinite existence, God forever recognizes His infinite existence through each one of us. We are God's unknown expression of His all-Beingness.

Through the self-conscious understandings of our divine heritage, we are continuously discovering, rediscovering, and rejoicing, in the foreverness of our existence. If we self-choose to reject our holy heritage, we still can rejoice in our experiencing of life, but without the self-aware presence of God. However, real joy can only be experienced through the understanding that our infinite self-driven life is our endless God-driven life.

Our sacred imperative is to mold our divinely inspired desires, to obey the nature of God, at the level of our ever increasing spiritual receptivity. When we self-consciously choose not to see our true divine nature, we allow ourselves to become mired in the turmoils of unpredictability, and we become eternally and spiritually lost.

As we spiritually allow God, to be revealed to our self-conscious awareness, we adore, we praise, and we give thanks for the God-essence of our forever beingness. Our finite-infinite spiritual journeys are continuously self-determined by our motivations, whether self-consciously God-driven or non-self-consciously God-driven. We exist to praise God in the expressions of our understandings of His forever Beingness.

The inviolate and forever purpose of our lives is to understand God's true nature, for each of us to experience the divinity of infinity. Each one of us is the foreverness of God infinitely unwinding in the divinity of our forever self-evolving understanding of ourselves.

The ever-present potential of the untrue jousting for appearance and acceptance by us drives us to the seeking of things divine. All the challenges to our self-aware existence are forever understood and continuingly overcome within the eternities of our continuous self-realizing spiritual evolving.

All spiritual successes ever achieved in our forever evolving long-term divine destiny are the spiritual byproducts of challenges overcome, through the realizing of the divinity of truth, in our self-determined actions. Divine truth understood always has been, is now, and forever remains our constant savior from the stealth-like thrusts of unreality.

Our ultimate existence and the foreverness of ultimate reality guarantee our continuing spiritual success. Still without an active self-conscious awareness of God, the experiencing of life remains misunderstood. Our self-capability to understand the foreverness of ideas powers into the light of wholiness, encircling, in and out, of our self-conscious awareness.

Our continuing self-aware diminishment of God results in needless repetitions of afflictions, turmoils, and raucous expressions of disharmony. Without God, our existence flows in withering states of cascading sorrows, heartaches, miseries, and desolation. Without a self-consciousness of God, we remain lost in the realms of illusion. Only the understanding of our divinity provides the divine validation to our self-conscious existence.

We have eternities endless to discover and re-discover our true self-conscious identity. Also, we have eternities endless to deny and reject our true identity. Often, how we choose to experience existence makes our self-conscious evolving expressing of beingness, a blessing or a curse.

Self-conscious existence without the acceptance of God always leads to an ever devolving downward spiral of unsought spirituality.

The mere fact that we infinite exist mandates that we experience existence, both divinely and non-divinely. The golden truth permeating our individual divine selves is to understand our unasked-for infinite beingness, from the viewpoint of being ongoing and perpetual wrongdoers, sinners, and evil makers.

We are self-consciously capable of freeing ourselves from all things, especially from our sinful-evil bondage to all things unreal, claiming existence in our forever emerging self-awareness, but there is never an infinite finality, from the incursions of godless unreality because our interpretations of non-reality are forever and infinite.

We are only free as we understand and accept our forever self-divinity, but the understanding of our forever self-divinity is the forever processing of our infinite existence. Thus, our infinite understanding always involves our incessant graspings of things we do not understand. In short, non-reality must be infinitely known and ongoingly overcome.

Thus, we require the ongoing spiritual purification of our thoughts and deeds. Our self-purification results from our self-driven desire to turn from the rivers and streams of the ungodly, and self-consciously embrace the wholiness of God. When we finally evolve to the place where we no longer require the realizing of our divine self-salvation, we have become the spiritual conquerors of this present sojourn through the objective realm. Thus, our eternal destiny in objective reality has been fulfilled.

We should never have confidence in a God whom we believe is willfully influenced, by our myopic, selfish, foolish wants, and desires. Rather, we should trust in a God based on our understanding and acceptance of His infinite, unchanging divine nature. The one God of forever real existence makes no Self-choice to love us. This true God is forever expressing through us, as divine love in perpetual action.

While each of us possesses the capability to interpret and experience our divinity; God does not and cannot Self-willingly experience His divinity. God's Infinite Beingness never changes and cannot be influenced, by any aspect of ultimate reality. All that God truly is resides within each of us as the total forever reality of divinity. Thus, we are the infinite expressions of God, forever and infinitely Self-knowing Himself through us.

Our successful spiritual evolvement rests on an ever increasing understanding of God's forever divine nature. Without our confidence in God's unchanging beingness, we have no assured divinity to discover, fulfill or experience. Real spiritual success is not possible in our experiencing of existence if we misinterpret or reject the forever indwelling of God's purity of divinity.

Our evolving destiny is only meaningful to our existence as it leads us to an acceptance of God's nature, forever enshrined within each of us, as our forever soul. Thus, as we experience existence, we evolve to the realization that our self-consciousness is the Self-consciousness of God, in forever-active realization.

We are never able to understand our self-divinity until we discover and identify ourselves with God. If God did not exist, we would be the self-proclaimed gods of infinity, lost in our self-conscious existence, having no basis, purpose, or ability to apprehend our infinite beingness. We would be infinite gods ruling over realms of utter unpredictability, without a coherent destiny to achieve.

Without God, our existence would be the torture of experiencing infinite never-ceasing misery. Thus, our present self-existence infers that there must be an infinite God because, without the existence of God-divinity, our self-existence would be infinitely undesirable and there would be no divine basis for infinite goodness.

Even with our self-conscious accepting of God, much of the expressions of our lives remain sorrow laden, but still our lives are not consistently sorrowful. It is the strength of our connection to God that is the sole determiner for the happiness, experienced in our lives. We are all spiritually myopically weak in our reliance upon God; thus, bouts of misery are going to be continually included, in the experiencing of our existence.

Thus, without an ever increasing self-conscious connection with God, the forever enticing callings of godless unreality will continually drag us, into the throes of unhappiness. Therefore, without a self-accepting awareness of God, we are doomed to experience sorrow ceaselessly.

With our myopic self-acceptances of God, we are still condemned to experience constant misery unhappiness, based upon our waxing and waning strengthening reliances upon God. Our forever infinite existence is a nightmare of unhappiness until we dedicate ourselves to consistently and unswervingly, seek forever increasing understandings of God.

The forever destiny of God's family is realized both individually and collectively. Every member of God's family must love one another, or our progressing spirituality lingers uncontrollably, in our together bankrupt and stalled spirituality. As we look outward into the Godless world, the muddiness of ever engulfing depravity is triumphantly splashing for our spiritual acceptance, into our self-awareness.

Still, our infinite existence guarantees that no one is ever left to drift endlessly and aimlessly in the perilous seas of rejected spirituality. Regardless of what seemingly occurs in the objective dream-filled experiences of our existence, no members of God's family ever lose their inherited divine identities. In the infinity of experiencing our divinity, we sporadically self-choose to abandon God; God never Self-chooses to abandon us.

Even though God is the Father of our infinite existence; we are not His children. He never depends on us; however, we forever depend on Him. Properly understood, we are forever dependent upon our understandings of our divine selves, which are in truth, our understanding of our interdependency upon God.

Still, it must clearly be understood; our individual self-consciousness is infinitely distinct, separate, and independent from God's Self-conscious knowingness. We are capable of understanding God, by understanding His infinite divine nature. God is not capable of understanding His nature or our nature, which is His nature.

We share God's nature but with a separate impulse for understanding, which powers our self-awareness, in the forever understanding of our existence. God and each one of us, relates separately to the reality of our beingness. God infinitely Self-knows His Infinite Beingness. We are forever and continually self-understanding our existence.

Our soul remains forever changeless, but our individual bodies housing and encasing our God-soul varies, from one physical worldly experience of life to the next. The only thing of eternal, supreme, and infinite spiritual value is our individual self-conscious connection with the divine purity of our soul, which is the undiluted presence of God.

We experience truth in varying forms of its presentations. All the spiritual truth forever needed, by the individualized-Man of God, is forever presenting itself to each one of us, at our self-conscious level of divine receptivity. Thus, as we prepare ourselves to accept the God of our understanding, the God of our understanding appears to us, as the Savior to our self-knowingness.

Truth often seems to appear differently, but there is forever and always only one infinite ascending divine truth. Any presentation of the reality of truth leading to our understanding and awareness of the presence of God is the divine revealing of a perfect divine representative of the one true and forever unfolding divinity of truth.

We are realizing our divine destiny, as we self-consciously command the authority of our self-conscious awareness to understand, to interpret, to experience, and to share in the everlasting pure goodness of God, which comprises the infinite us. As we share in the understanding of whom and what we infinitely are, the entirety of God's family is blessed.

Interestingly, in the objective physical realm of progressively experiencing our spirituality, our evolving spiritual understanding of spirituality is mandated to be shared with all members of God's family, to assure the continuous spiritual growth of the collective-Us. However, when we come into the spiritual realm, we have the eternal option to experience our evolved spirituality with others, or completely alone.

Often our evolving spirituality attempts to experience life in the darkness of error, and with the godlessness cherished in our thoughts. Without our self-conscious willingness to seek, understand, and obey the inner light of our forever divinity, we often welcome the darkening of error as glittering speckles of truth, and therefore our self-conscious spiritual experiencing of existence as life becomes delayed, depraved, and enslaved into the corners of non-reality.

Each one of us understands and experiences God individually. Our correct interpretation of God leads us to real understandings of ourselves. To self-acknowledge our unity with God brings the realizing of our salvation into the theoretical realm of experience. Thus, the only true spiritual allegiance there forever is, is for each of us to self-consciously assert that God is the divine authority governing the experiencing of our existence.

Our self-consciousness powered by our free will is the soul and the breath of our divinity. God, in the foreverness of His Divine Self-knowingness, never reaches down to us; however, we are forever reaching upward to Him, forever abiding in our self-rising soul. Thus, we are forever reaching inward for understanding the reality of our reality.

Each one of us determines the direction of our inner and outer journeys forever divinely homeward. We alone and individually understand, accept, and obey the foreverness of God's presence. Our ability to understand God determines our success in the spiritual realizing of our existence.

Our forever spiritual awakening is driven by God's infinite nature, not by His Infinite Self-awareness. The ever-presence of God is the unending pathway to our spiritual understanding, spiritual demonstration and the ever fulfilling of our divine unfolding journeys, into the discovering of our forever real self-beingness. In the objective realm, we are forever outwardly seeking our inward existence.

Within the nature of God resides the infinite presence of divine love. Wherever the loving-kindness of God, is self-consciously expressed through us, His existence is revealed to us. Our united and shared spiritual destiny is to understand God's love as the substance, soul, and heart of our foreverness.

Because each of us is individually progressing spiritually, God's love is expressed throughout all eternities, in the varying and endless depths of our ever evolving spiritual discernments. Through our individualized existences, we bring God's touch of love to all of life.

The infinite love forever emanating within the nature of God is without focus. Our responsibility is to focus, individualize, interpret, and integrate God's forever outpourings of love, as we dynamically experience ourselves, in the expressions of our infinite divinity, in the objective realm.

Anything that experiences existence is capable of receiving God's love. Thus, it becomes our destiny to share God's outpouring love to all of life. Therefore, all of physical life, experiencing existence, has the potential of being distinctly loved by God, through our infinite interpretations of God. Thus, all varieties of animals, insects, and vegetation experience God's love, through our expressions of God's forever love as kindness to everything living and experiencing existence.

Our expressions of kindness to all life, increasingly makes God forever real to us, as individualized-Man. It is each one of us that makes God's love a continuing blessing in our lives. In a sense, all of life exists to be loved by God's touch through each of us. We, as individualized-Man, are the only component of ultimate reality capable of expressing God's love and our love, which is God's love. God does not ever manifest love; God is love.

We are divine, and the self-realization of our divinity must be forever self-consciously treasured in the thinking of our thoughts. It is our unenlightened spiritual desires that always illicit our false interpretations of happiness. Without a self-aware acceptance of the presences of God, true happiness is eternally disguised and masked in rag-torn garments of godless unreality.

Without self-conscious anchoring to our identity in God, we will stray aimlessly and remain self-lost in the windowless cells of non-reality. Then, we allow the material spiritually-void manifestations of this world, to shout and chant, for our attention and adherence, to be interpreted as the providers of so-called desired worldly happiness.

Without our acceptance of God, our material-filled physical existence is limited, by our spiritually haphazard responses to chance, opportunity, randomness, and general unpredictability. When our self-discovered spirituality becomes the divine master over the torrents of unpredictability, we then realize the understanding power of our true divinity.

As we become obsessed with things material, our self-awareness struggles against the divinely real is much like a clenched fist unable to grasp the desired object. Therefore, the spiritual treasures of God remain non-valued, un-awakened, and non-accepted. Thus, our innate divinity continues to be forever challenged by the non-real experiences of our objective existence.

We are the interpreters of all ideas presented to our self-consciousness. Our sought-for interpretations of ideas have a direct correspondence to the strength of the desires we harbor and nourish, through our ever functioning free-will choices. Through our interpretations of ideas, we choose the understanding-powerfulness of our thoughts. In the realm of creative thought, we are forever gods over the reality of our self-aware existence.

Think of the enormous power embedded in the ability to interpret ideas. If we consistently understood ideas in consonance with their real purpose, function, and usefulness; infinite harmony would be self-consciously consistent, and ever-presently rooted, in the experiences of our lives lived.

As we spiritually progress, the power of our understanding forever increases. Ultimate reality exists for our individual and unique interpretation, and for no other reasons. The greatest power our self-aware intelligence possesses is that of understanding the pure reality of all of the aspects of ultimate reality. Each of us gives our individual and unique interpretation of our infinity of foreverness. Thus, as we comprehend all the components of ultimate reality, we transform it into an intimate self-realized reality of our forever self-making.

Our ability to interpret ideas is an infinite process. Thus, our ability to infinitely translate ideas into experiences means that we in a self-aware process of endless understanding. For the truth of our beingness to forever manifest, our ability to understand and interpret reality combines with our self-aware desire to possess the divinely correct understanding of our true spirituality. Thus, to forever evolve spiritually, in the physical realm, means that we must permanently overcome our misinterpretations and misunderstanding of realities falsely assumed to exist.

Our designed objective fate is to realize the outcome of our self-conscious desires, to experience only divine harmony, love, and joy. Our eternal destiny requires our obedience to the dictates of our divine nature, to experience only real harmonious visitations, of idea realm ideas.

Our objective existence continues until our self-conscious experiencing of objective reality lacks the challenges of spiritual strength exerted. Without the godless challenges of our inner reality continuously confronting us, as we experience our lives, no spiritual success is deserved, earned, experienced, or warranted. Our spiritual destiny is only realized, by self-consciously silencing the falsely interpreted sirens of godless unreality, which haunt and torment our forever self-conscious understanding of the deity encompassing our forever selves.

Eventually, perfect harmony is achieved in our experiencing of the spiritual realm. In the spiritual realm, all vestiges of disharmony vanish, leaving only the reign of peaceful harmony, in complete its incorruptibility. In this present eternity, as in all eternities, the spiritual realm is the heavenly outcome of our divine understanding. In the spiritual realm, we experience our divinity, in the self-realization of God.

Our self-acceptance of God always liberates us from the binding shadowy clutches, of all the false assertions of godless unreality. When we foolishly choose to bar God from our self-awareness, ideas descend from their holy place of harmony, and become engulfed in the tangled, mangled, and strangled garments of sin, evil, and nothingness.

Thus, sometimes ideas are misinterpreted to appear in their most awful insidious, hideous, filthiest and vaporous manifestations. However, these unholy vestiges of godless falseness quickly vanish as we fill our self-consciousness, with the active and persistent awareness of the presence of God. Wherever and whenever we embrace our self-Godliness, ungodliness will wane into its supposed existence, separate from our self-knowingness.

Rejecting our divinity permits the godlessness in our self-consciousness, to wander divinely untethered in the realm of experience.

This aimless expression of our meandering destiny does not necessarily require us to suffer the pangs of sinful evilness, although its poisonous presence slithers around and about us.

Thus, our designed and divine fate does not compel us to interpret, understand, and accept our forever divinity. If we self-consciously choose to deny our forever heritage, the experiencing of sin and evil takes the place of our divine destiny. More accurately, our divine destiny is now understood as the suffering expressions of sin and evil.

Thus, as we become lost in the hypnotic illusions of sins and evil's alluring enticements, we inflate and conflate ourselves to be as little smug-laden deities who are now non-spiritually experiencing their existence. Again, whatever we self-consciously accept, we self-consciously become in objective reality's arenas of experience, self-consciously interpreted by each of us.

Even if we chose to experience our existence in the ethers of sin and evil, the only intermediary needed between God and ourselves, is our spiritual awareness revolving, evolving, and dissolving into the self-conscious understanding and acceptance, of our eternal, infinite, and forever allegiance to God. In other words, forever divine truth is the only divine intermediary ever required between God and the self-corrupted us.

Thus, all of our divine salvation comes from God through our self-acknowledgment, understanding, and acceptance of His forever Beingness. Our self-accepting knowledge of divine truth is our forever Savior. Therefore, there is no God whom Self-consciously delivers us from the un-realness of experiencing our existence. Our forever ability to save ourselves is our forever comforter.

As we praise God, we exalt our self-understood divinity to accept the gift of existence. We are forever praising God, through our continuing spiritual victories, as we infinitely experience the eternities of objective reality. Our self-conscious awareness of God's divine presence brightens our footsteps, fills our flower laden sacred paths with petal-pearls of divinity, and harmonizes the realizing of our infinitely divine-based self-identities.

Our praising of God is our self-active divinity understanding, rejoicing, and experiencing our forever true identity. Thus, through the light of our spiritual understanding, we joyfully praise God. We praise Him as we continuingly and self-consciously desire to identify ourselves with His forever Divine Beingness. Then, all things unlike the spiritually burning essence of God evaporate into the evil hot steaming throes of godless unreality.

Because God is unaware of our self-acknowledging praise of Him, He cannot be pleased by our exaltations of spiritual understandings. Regardless of our elevated spiritual thoughts, it is not possible for God to know our praise-driven divine rhapsodies. God is eternally and infinitely secure in His divine knowingness, and requires no pleasing-praise from any of us, who forever remain the unknown self-expressions of Himself.

We praise God by successfully living a spiritually-based life. In the praising of God, we are the only participants self-consciously aware of that expression of divine appreciation. In our forever praising of God, we are self-acknowledging His infinite existence, as the infinite substance of our forever beingness. Without the existence of God, there would be nothing, in all aspects of the foreverness of infinity, worthy of our divine acknowledging praise.

Thus, without the forever Self-existence of God, we would have no divinity to seek, no divinity to find, no divinity to acknowledge, no divinity to understand, no divinity to accept, no divinity to obey, and no Deity to praise. Without the existence of the one forever God, our power of understanding would be impotent against fire-forging claims of unreality. Without the existence of the infinite God of forever Goodness, our self-knowingness of infinite self-aware existence would be determined by the windy whims of desires, without the blessings of divinity to confront and triumph over the horrors of a rudderless non-divine existence.

Thus, our forever self-existence would be infinitely and godlessly based in unworthiness. Our infinite existence demands the existence of the one infinite God. Without the existence of the one infinite God of Divine Goodness, the godliness of depravity, and the godliness of goodness would be the contending all-consuming gods of absolute reality, with the god of depravity ensconced comfortably on the meaningless throne of reality.

We are part of God, but we are not God. In our travels through objective reality, we can never fully see, never fully understand, or fully apprehend the allness of God. Thus, we are forever divinely limited in our understanding of God, which includes the understanding of our self-divinity. Our forever spiritual sense of limitation accounts for our acceptance of the presence of ungodliness, through misinterpretations of idea realm ideas.

The infinite freedom comprising our beingness is our forever capacity to make self-conscious choices. Our limited-unlimited self-awareness is the holding pen, for all of our self-revealing thoughts. We alone create and fashion the experiences required, for the realization of our ever unfolding spiritual finite-infinite destiny. We forever create the pathways to the realizing of our forever salvation.

God is forever absorbing His infinite divinity; we are forever expressing our infinite divinity. God forever and only realizes His infinite Self-Divinity. However, we are forever divine and non-divine, in our experiencing of existence. Thus, we are forever self-aware of our divinity, and forever non-self-aware of our divinity. God only knows the experiencing of infinite existence through each one of us, as His forever expression.

Our forever self-awareness is God forever Self-acknowledging Himself to Himself, through our individual and unique individualized God-identities. As we understand and interpret God, all aspects of objective reality become awakened to our self-driven desire to apprehend the divinity of our infinite existence. We are the self-conscious individualizations of God forever limited by the process of self-understanding. God, apart from each one of us, in the totality of His Beingness Self-realized, is never the expression of Himself, and He can never be Self-individualized.

The purpose of our forever reality is to self-consciously inhabit our forever divine beingness, as individualized core-Man, and to self-consciously understand our forever divine beingness, as individualized objective-Man. Thus, the purpose for our infinite existence is to know and understand the totality, of our infinite existence.

Thus, we can understand the purpose for our infinite self-aware reality, but we will never understand the 'why' of our infinite self-aware beingness. From the viewpoint of the foreverness of ultimate reality itself: Does our forever self-conscious existence have any more authority to exist infinitely than the physically expressed idea of a tree, forever manifesting and re-manifesting throughout objective reality's ongoing eternities?

Let me illustrate. Suppose there was an infinite, ultimate reality bag filled with never-ending ideas, forever having the potentiality to manifest in objective reality. Thus, this bag would hold all the ideas for dogs, cats, trees, flowers, insects, ideas of individualized-Man, so forth and so on – an infinite bag filled with endless ideas for the infinite existence of infinite physical realities.

Now, the selection begins to determine who or what is to experience infinite existence in ultimate reality. A gigantic hand, of no one's understanding, reaches into the bag and pulls out the idea of a dog, next it pulls out the idea of a tree, next it pulls out the idea of rocks, and finally the hand pulls out the idea of individualized-Man. Note: all the ideas selected for actual existence had the same opportunity and potentiality of being randomly selected by chance.

Again I ask, from the viewpoint of ultimate reality: Disregarding the nature or substance of anything experiencing absolute real existence, does anything have a superior claim to infinite existence, over anything else claiming infinite existence? Thus, do we, as self-conscious individualized-Man have a greater claim to chance-existence than that of a gnat? In this illustration, everything has the same potential for actual existence. Thus, in the understanding of everything that forever exists, there should be no hierarchy of infinite existence, except for individual-Man who can lay claim to being the self-appointed protector of all things infinite.

So, it could be argued that self-making a claim to a superior existence, superior to all other infinite realities, should be based upon the potential self-willful ability to impact all aspects of ultimate reality.

We, as individualized-Man have the potential capability of doing and accomplishing anything in the realms of ultimate reality; therefore, we must be the most superior infinite existence. Thus, we are the chosen-unchosen gods of the universe. Thus, we define what infinite existence is, and we alone determine how it is to be understood and experienced.

Therefore, each of us is realizing our divinity as we understand and interpret our divinity. As we acknowledge and accept our true identity in God, we recognize the purpose for our existence. We exist to learn and experience our forever God-identity. In this manner, all of forever reality is subservient to our understandings of our self-God identities.

Our self-accepted destiny is to experience all eternities as the eyes of God, beholding the wonderments of created and non-created experiences. If we are non-spiritual in our thoughts, we are non-spiritual in our actions. In our desire to experience our infinite selves, we are consigned to experience our infinite non-selves.

To be infinitely non-spiritual potentially possible and our present self-aware existence seems to indicate that potentiality to be a distinct possibility. However, in the infinite truth of understanding, we can only be non-spiritual for one eternity at a time. We can continue to be non-spiritual in ongoing and consecutive eternities, but due to the fundamental design grafted into our infinite nature, each will eventually triumph spiritually.

As we experience our thoughts, God forever sees only the unfolding of harmony and perfection through our eyes. If we allow truth and illusion to comingle within the margins of our self-understanding, even when truth is in the ascendency, the crippling and binding strengths of myths always attempts to drag us down, into accepting the non-spiritual unreal realm of godlessness, as our forever eternal home.

Thus, the unrealities we accept into our self-consciousness claim their self-power to mold and shape our thoughts and desires. Unreality has no self-governing power except the power we cede to it through our non-acceptance of things spiritual. We are not in control of our destiny when non-spirituality becomes a welcomed guest in our self-awareness.

We are God's infinite warriors. Our battles are spiritual and involve the trouncing of all things godlessly unreal, back into the netherworld of their forever nothingness. Thus, it is in our forever physical realm battles, that we defeat our false acceptances of unreality. As infinite warriors, we are battling ourselves to self-realize our forever divine selves in God. We forever win and lose the battles of self-realized infinite existence, but we forever lose the war in the total understanding of our infinite self-beingness. Thus is our divine destiny.

We experience life as a holy war zone where all battles are won or lost, within the perimeters of our individual and forever self-evolving self-consciousness. Our victories are assured as we accept God and banish all things ungodly, for our self-awareness. Thus our objective experiencing of existence is twofold: to forever be spiritually victorious and to forever be divinely battle-scared.

As members of God's family we must seek, find, and accept our spiritual identity and fearlessly choose to do Godly right, and reject godlessness of unreality. If we never understood the rightness and wrongness of our actions, we would remain spiritually lost, in deserts of lifelessness self-consciously experienced. Still, we have eternities endless to gild our spiritual redemption with divine truth self-accepted.

Our destiny in the realm of experience is forever determined, by our free will choices. If we are foolishly acting wrongly, we must replace our wrongdoings with our spiritually-chosen right doings. Self-consciously taking correct spiritual actions secures the spiritually evolving portion of our progressing spiritual awareness. The self-willed doing of divinely propelled efforts is the challenging part of infinite spiritual evolving understanding self-consciously accepted.

If we cannot demonstrate the understanding of our spirituality, in the realm of experience, we see only the rewards of our self-acceptance worldliness. We do not understand that worldly rewards represent our self-allegiance to the callings of non-spirituality. As we choose to understand and accept the God the within us, our choices become spiritual; our salvation assured, and we spiritually taste the glories of goodness self-realized, in our expressions of divinely received rewards.

Still, we should always be thankful for seeing and recognizing our wrongdoings of our actions as wrongdoings. If our wrongdoings were continually unrecognized, they would remain in the realm of our self-conscious false understandings of ideas, chiseling niches into our self-awareness. To understand our real selves, we must understand the non-reality of our self-falsely accepted ideas of ourselves.

If we were never objectively to understand our false appearing selves as unreal, we would experience a world of constant turmoil, which we seemingly do so often. However, the seeing of our wrongdoings is not the same as the understanding of our wrongdoings. To see wrongdoing without the power of divine self-awareness is to give our wrongdoings a claim of self-existence they never had.

To be the self-acknowledged rightfully entitled heirs of God, we must understand the harmony behind all the wrongdoings of our actions. Wherever and whenever the balance of peaceful harmony is apprehended and accepted, wrongfulness evaporates into the vapors of designated nothingness.

The spiritual self-regeneration for our wrongdoings not only requires our self-recognition but is also requires our self-remorse. Without self-remorse, there is no self-forgiveness. Self-forgiveness embodies our spiritual advancement. Our spiritual progression is infinite; therefore our spiritual need for forgiveness is infinitely endless.

There is no forever salvation to be received from any God. It is our divine destiny to finitely and infinitely save ourselves. Still, God forever remains the non-Self-conscious source of our infinite salvation. God's mind individualized understands Himself, through each one of us, and that is the forever source of our infinitely required salvation, for experiencing an earned self-conscious spiritual existence.

All things, seemingly devoid of harmony, which appear to us, in the physical realm of our objective existence, are teaching lessons. Thus, all things physically experienced and spiritually understood are infinitely designed, for each of us to strengthen the divine understanding of our infinite beingness.

Before salvation, our spiritual evolvement requires spiritual guidance. Teachers coming to us in various forms provide us with the needed opportunities for spiritual guidance. Spiritual teachers may present themselves as individuals, circumstances, or the randomness on unpredictability. Learning opportunities, through the teachers of divine reality, gives us the opportunities to discover, rediscover, and uncover our divinity to ourselves, through practicing the lessons of kindness and goodness in self-expression.

Difficult as it may seem, in and through the realizing of our self-divinity, we must remain teachable to the thoughtless actions of others who continually and mentally tempt us, to swallow the barb-baited claims of godless unreality. Thus, as divine family members experiencing our lives, we become teachers to one another, on all occasions, all circumstances, and all experiences. If we self-consciously chose to be eternal students, our salvations decrease in our self-pain realized.

Without the accompaniment of the practice of kindness, life's lessons are hard fought; yet, the battles are never lost; and victories only delayed. So it is that our individual spiritual journeys must always include the seeing of truth, even when the shroud of unkindness veils before us as a false teacher, clouding our realizations of truth, with enticements of the ungodly unknown.

All spiritual victories are finite-infinite. When we see truth in all things, our spiritual battles are being won. However, for each one of us, infinity is a progression of spiritual battles infinitely won and lost. Final spiritual victory is a forever impossibility because we all experience existence endlessly, in the foreverness of timeless time.

Thus, in the successful spiritual experience of existence, everyone becomes a teacher and a student. Also, everyone becomes a student of things unpredictable. As mentors and students, we continuously function in a continuous and reciprocal manner for everyone to self-consciously continue to advance in spiritual progression.

This ongoing interdependent process continues to be our source for the divine reinforcement of the forever understanding that there is only one perfect, holy family, and God exists eternally, infinitely and ever-presently indwelling each one of us, as our ever-present Divine Teaching Soul.

All life's lessons are eternally motivated, and they become blessings to us when we understand them spiritually. It is the divine understanding of our thought-perceptions that make us the forever students of our evolving self-divinity. Thus, our eternal destiny is to choose to express the reality of our forever divinity. When we only self-consciously express our divinity, we truly become the self-knowing offspring of God.

When the lessons of life combine with our self-conscious expressions of kindness, truth is blossoming forth, in multi-harmonious sunlit rainbows of goodness. These multi-colored arcs of Godness light the pathways to the holy fulfilling of our self-derived destiny, in the eternal evolving of our realizations of truth. Thus, these life-lessons of experiences guide each of us to the ever increasing collective understanding of our forever unfolding divinity in self-realized expression.

Our responses to the wrongdoings of others should be in the same manner, as our responses to the interdictions of chance, opportunity, randomness, and general unpredictability. We should view all things, in our experiencing of life, as spiritual opportunities, to apprehend, demonstrate, and explain to the realization of our divine self-beingness. Thus, as we interpret the understanding of our divinity into the expression of our divinity, we have chosen to know God.

All wrongdoings result from the self-accepted denial of the presence of God. We must self-determine ourselves not to continue in our wrongdoings, lest we once again lose the self-awareness of our divinity. Thus, our determination becomes the momentum for the reawakening of our never-ending desire, to experience existence, as life spirituality enthroned in our self-awareness.

All the things we experience, divinely understood, point us to a self-conscious awareness of the presence of God. Our continuing spiritual understanding increases our capability, for refusing to accept the non-divine. Spiritual teachers do not come to us by chance. Rather, they come to us as a response to our self-conscious desires, whether spiritual or non-spiritual.

No divine family member, who understands his or her relationship to God's spiritual family, would self-willfully harm another holy member. The godless teachers, who praise only non-reality, come to us in disguise. These pagan teachers do not bring with them the light of goodness; rather they bring the false light of unreality's darkness. Teaching circumstances are different. They come to us as the rawness of existence challenging our self-evolving spirituality, to express the true and real understanding of ourselves. When we can interpret the Godness of reality into the godliness of unreality, we become the master-knower of our divinity.

Thus, when it comes to the persons bringing us spiritual teaching lessons, they have no realization that they are providing us with spiritual learning opportunities. When we see all individuals as coequal members of God's family, spiritually yearning for the knowingness of God, we become self-consciously divine students transmuting the tumbleweeds of bumpy unreality, into expressions of divinity self-realized.

As we evolve to the understanding that everyone and everything is a teacher, our forgiveness of others becomes unnecessary, because we can separate the wrongdoings from the wrongdoers. However, in the place of forgiving others, we can choose to recognize and accept them as divine family members, expressing their realization of spirituality at the shadowy level of their self-identity while spiritually urging them to become receptive to divine truth.

Therefore, all the circumstances we experience in life, especially those caused by others are spiritual lessons, prompting our self-evolving divinity, to understand, recognize, and interpret itself as evolving holiness in self-aware expression. However, from our individualized perspectives, the hurtful-harmful acts we do to others are always wrong, even as they serve as teaching lessons, to the spiritual wakeful.

I repeat, if everyone is a teacher to each of us, and we recognize his or her actions serve to promote spiritual awakenings and re-awakenings, to become divinely receptive to things spiritual; what is there in others to forgive? In the understanding of true divinity, there is nothing that any divine family member does to another that requires any self-conscious effort of forgiveness. In the foreverness of our divinity, all things impacting our self-awareness of existence are sacred blessings, if the self-knowingness of our divinity is what we value above all things.

In the forgiving of ourselves, we are self-consciously acknowledging our ever evolving spiritual understandings. Even as we interpret the wrongdoings of others as spiritual lessons, we are always in need of self-forgiveness. Our self-willful wrongdoings conclusively demonstrate our attraction to non-spiritual beliefs. Thus, we forgive ourselves for not self-consciously remaining loyal to our divine destiny, which is to obey and follow the goodness in our soul.

Objective reality never varies in the infinite totality of its forever existence, because objective reality is infinite, and our understanding of objective reality is infinite. Thus, in the foreverness of timeless-time, all the meaningful change that ever occurs is in the understanding of ourselves, in relationship to our forever and endless objective progressions, through eternities endless.

Alone and forever, each of us varies in our understanding and interpretation of the forever finite-infinite. We are infinity's designers never lacking for the self-designing of our created experiences. The things we design become the things we experience. Thus, we create expressions of harmony or non-harmony. The spiritual depths of our eternal designing inclinations determine the spiritual depths of our ever evolving spiritual understanding.

We mold and remold the direction our destiny takes us as we experience each eternity. However, the infinitely designed forever progression of objective reality is separate from our forever planned progress and is never molded, remolded, changed, altered, or influenced in any manner whatsoever, by us, God, or any other expressions of ultimate reality.

As individualization of Man, it is our destiny to paint beautiful pictures, write beautiful poems, play beautiful music, and dance to the rhythm of the stars. No one is ever deprived of any ability or talent, to express and experience the things that are truly self-consciously desired.

The difficulties, in experiencing the spectrums of our desires are based on the ever evolving understanding of our spirituality, in the revealing of our commonly-shared equality. Thus, even though our commonly shared existence in God is equally distributed among us, our individual understandings of our forever equality are not equal.

In truth, there is no talent or ability that any God family member possesses, that any other divine family member cannot have or replicate because the same ideas are available to all members of God's family without any bias towards anyone. The only thing preventing any member of God's family, making the same accomplish as another, is the depth of anyone's spiritual understanding.

All talents received, in the objective realm, are based on our ingrained receptivity, to the ideas that would actualize our desires into experienced existence. Our desires, combined with the depth of our developed spirituality, determine the realization of our desires. Thus, some of us may realize desires that others of us may never realize. We are all different in the depths of our forever evolving spirituality.

In the physical realm, each of us varies in talent, intelligence, physique, personality, et cetera, but our varying abilities, to express ourselves, are based on the constricting, and limiting factors of chance, opportunity, randomness, and general unpredictability. Still, in displaying the real qualities of genuine reality, we remain equally non-equal in our divine receptivity, to the forever expanding of spirituality understood.

Thus, there are degrees of spiritual equality in our now present understanding of our infinite divinity. There is inequality in the progressive unfolding of our immense individualized minds, due to the varying degrees of our free will desires. Also, each one of us possesses the forever infinite power of understanding, but that power of understanding is infinitely limited, by the spiritual depth, certainty, and direction of our individual divinely evolving thoughts.

Since the knowledge of things spiritual, is continuously realized individually, our personal spiritual existence does not seem fair. How each of us acts and reacts to the outside-of-us circumstances reflects our self-determined strength of spirituality. Our actions and reaction are not equal because our self-conscious awareness of our self-spirituality is not often on similar levels of spiritual knowledge.

There is no commonality of experiences caused by ever impacting conditions affecting our lives. Thus, seeming unfairness, in our self-exercising of existence, is directly proportional to our self-acquired depths of spirituality. The depths of our ever acquiring spiritual knowledge, determines our ability to make manifest the higher and higher realities of ideas.

The experiencing of our infinite existence is often unfair because each of us is individually uniquely and independently self-realizing the awe-filling dynamics, of our infinitely progressing soul-journeying through eternities. Thus, the challenges of life for some may be successfully met, while others languish in the unforgiven heartaches of self-realized existence.

However, within each one of us, there is equal potentiality to express the wonderments of existence, through idea realm ideas. Still, we are limited in our capacity to understand and interpret life. Thus, we each differ in our objective responses to the sin-dripped evil-plated fire tongs of godless unreality squeezing out of our self-awareness, the droplets of our forever divinity.

Thus, it is our responses to ingrained godless unreality that is the measure of our forward marching spirituality. Therefore, it forever remains for our advancing divine understanding to nullify the increasing randomness of uncertainty and unpredictability. Each of us is the self-consciousness of truth pushing aside the infinitely unreal curtains of false existence.

Because we are all spiritually equal, we share the same mind, the same inner God-presence, equal access to the idea realm, and each of us is eternal, infinite, and indestructible. We are each experiencing existence at the level of our spiritual or non-spiritual understanding.

As we each advance spiritually, we become increasingly self-aware that our forever existence is inseparable from God. As unequal as this world seems to be, the self-conscious acquisition of spiritual wisdom is our ever-present cherished desire to understand, interpret, accept, and demonstrate.

In the understanding or misunderstanding of our thoughts, we are the output of our self-thinking thoughts. In the foreverness of truth acknowledged, we are the infinity of divinity recognizing, understanding, interpreting, and experiencing our infinite self-existence. We, alone, create the realizations of goodness, for the strengthening of our spiritual enhancement.

We have the unlimited capability of understanding ourselves as divine, and then self-consciously rejecting that understanding. Thus, we are infinitely able to choose to express an existence, of non-accepted self-divinity. If ultimate reality could shed a tear, it would shed a tear for this self-realizing capability, of ours, to reject our divinity.

With our self-acceptance of God, our infinite existence is forever blessed by the certainty of goodness. Without our self-acceptance of God, our infinite existence is punctured by the incessant uncertainties of chance, opportunity, randomness, and general unpredictability. Still, these punctures of unpredictability represent spiritual learning lessons.

Our spiritual efforts determine the realizing of our spiritually victorious destiny. Our spiritual efforts rest on our choices, and our choices rest on our desires. God, on the other hand, exerts no effort, makes no decisions, and has no Self-conscious desires. God Self-consciously exists at the forever ends of total harmony Self-realized.

Our objective destiny is always to experience our real identity of self-beingness. The self-consciousness of God's Beingness is what the seekers of divine truth forever strive to obtain in the objective realm. That is the spiritual self-awareness we possess in our finite-infinite stays in core reality. Thus, the spiritual self-awareness we undeservedly possess in core reality is now the spiritual reality we seek, in our experiencing of existence.

Courage and steadfast resolve are essential ingredients for the realization of truth, as we tread pathways holy. Continuing spiritual success demands steadfast adherence to our true self-divinity when confronted with the forever falseness of the untrue. We need the courage to resist the godless temptations that continually assault our spiritual weak spots. To stand bravely when one's spiritual awareness is weak, in resolve, is divine courage. Affirm always: "I am the strength-power of my divinity understood, there is no other power."

Infinite temptation, unknown to God, is the price we each must pay, for the gift of experiencing existence. The entirety of God is infused within us to be forever revealed and made manifest. God never Self-consciously desires an inner-active communion with us. Whereas we individually and collectively, accept, obey, and demonstrate our willingness to commune with Him, through our self-acknowledging of His divinity the substance of our soul.

As I have often said, through each one of us, God is interacting with Himself, with only each one of us as the self-active and self-conscious participant. God is forever self-understood by each of us individually. Therefore, no one unique understanding, interpretation, and acceptance of God is the same as another's. In a sense, our infinite individual existence with God is the only interrelationship to God that exists, in all ultimate reality.

Our existence mandates God's existence. As individualizations of Man, we are now forever and always unknown to God. Each of us is the self-conscious realization of God, in divine and infinite individualized self-expression. Without the existence of God, we would be ultimate reality's chained slaves to an endless self-aware life. Our immense self-aware presence, without the existence of God, would be constant self-torture. The Goodness, existent in God, gives all reality its purpose and soul for its infinite expression.

However, in truth, each one of us is the pure divinity of God in the infinite self-conscious unfoldment of divine expression. We are God's presentation of Himself to all reality. Simply, all expressions of infinite beingness need the existence of God to provide the purpose for infinite reality to follow its inherent infinite design. It is a divine paradox: God forever exists with no Self-awareness of ultimate reality, and ultimate reality is oblivious to God's existence. However, without either one, infinite life and infinite non-life of any kind is meaningless.

The infinity of God's perfection is ever-present, and our forever destiny is self-consciously fulfilled, in the realization of God's infinite purposeful presence, within us. Our nature is God's nature. God is powerless; each one of us is potentially all-powerful. Still, each one of us is God individualized, and without our understanding of God, we would not be all-powerful. So, in that sense, God is omnipotent.

We are innately flawless. No infinite blemish ever scars our forever beingness. All imperfections which appear to us, in our self-conscious experiencing of living life, result from our misunderstandings of our divinity. We never misunderstand ourselves, if we understand ourselves in God, with God, and expressing as God individualized. Our self-realized existence is the presence of God Self-realized.

All reality within the nature of God exists within our individualized essence. For example, beauty is not something to be discovered outside of ourselves. Beauty resides forever in a niche of our soul, surrounded by infinite harmony, the essence of God. Our forever understanding of our divine selves enables us to bring the qualities of God, into contact with our experiences of existence.

All the beauty of God exists within our individualized self-awareness unperceived by shadows of fading density, yet forever waiting for our spiritual apprehension. In the physical realm, we only see the silhouettes of real beauty, as we chisel away unformed matter to reveal infinite individualized beauty, residing in the forever far-reaches of our commonly shared mind of God, and experienced in the commonality of our objective existence.

Thus, the Self-essence of God, within us, is forever seen as we express and experience life through the ever expanding understanding of our self-divinity. Therefore, all things in objective existence have the potentiality of revealing God's essence to us, as us, and through us. We are God's divine emissaries, to objective reality, to bring the spirit of God into and out of the realms of experience. Each of us is the individualized mind of God, seeing the essence of God, in the realm of Godless reality.

Although our nature and God's nature are intertwined, both realities function separately and independently. If we ever actually understood the totality of God beingness, we would be God instead of just part of God, but to totally and complete understand God is forever divinely unattainable.

Our ability to understand is an infinite process. If we understood the allness of God, there would be no forever challenges in our experiencing of existence. Without challenges, our infinite existence becomes meaningless. Interestingly, if we ever achieved the power of understanding over all things, in other words, we were to become God in Toto, our self-conscious existence would have no purpose for beingness.

As each of us forever discovers the understanding of our divine existence; God forever divinely knows and forever is His divine reality in expression. In short, we objectively exist to understand the forever ongoing infinitude of God. However, the depth of our spiritual God-understanding never increases, because God's knowingness of Himself never decreases, only increases.

I repeat once more what I realize is a painful acknowledgment. Although we are forever part of God and thus ceaselessly divine, we are never Self-consciously loved by God, never Self-consciously protected by God, and never Self-consciously blessed by God. God is Self-consciously aware of Himself and His forever divinely unfolding existence, and nothing more. The meaning of God's existence to each one of us is only meaningful and understood by each one of us.

Each one of us is an independent component of God inside, and outside of God's divine and infinite Beingness. We exist to understand God; God does not exist to comprehend us. God is the total and complete substance of all that we are. However, we are not the full and complete self-conscious content, of all that is God, and we never will be.

However, the wholiness of God is enveloping love, and it is up to us individually to seek His love, accept His love, be comforted by His love, obey His love, follow His love, and share His love with all things experiencing life. Our self-conscious understanding of God's nature is the forever source of God's forever-loving presence, in our experiencing of our forever existence.

Our experience of objective reality is forever tempered, by our understanding of our God-driven selves. The more we understand ourselves as individualized divinity, the closer we are to interpreting harmony as harmony, goodness as goodness, and truth as truth. The nature of God gives us the capability to experience real and everlasting joy, love, and happiness without having to be cognizant of their seeming opposites.

For each one of us to understand and experience what is true, we must be capable of apprehending and experiencing the non-true. Uncovering the forever untrue to reveal the everlasting real; is the self-consciousness of our divinity, in actual self-realization. Without the ability to experience our ever evolving understandings, we would be incapable of advancing spiritually, as the finite-infinite individualized transbeingness of Man.

Often, we interpret the indestructibility of our existence as freedom to acknowledge, and accept the godlessness of our false understandings which continually deluge our spiritually evolving self-conscious awareness, with the depravities of unreal, tangled, and debouched claims for existence.

These falsely accepted perceptions ignore our true destiny as a fate of continuous spiritual discovery, and thus we dethrone God of Goodness from within our self-aware throne of divinity. Then, the dethroning of God of Goodness diminishes our self-conscious purpose for the experiencing of life. Whatever we allow to separate our self-awareness from the presence of the one true God, we render false power, and we become slaves to the army of unreality.

Thus, regardless of the depth of our spiritual evolving, goodness and godlessness sit comfortably together in the sanctity of our self-awareness until godlessness is washed away clean and vanishes into the nothingness of existence, as we satiate our self-awareness with the ever-presence of God. To value the Goodness of God above all things is to live divine.

Forever experiencing life is our infinite self-evolvement expressing through us. Only to our forever selves is the experiencing existence meaningful; purposeful Self-Beingness is non-meaningful to God, except through each of us. As we are infinite and indestructible, our experiencing of self-beingness is infinite, indestructible, unchangeable, and immortal.

We determine the distribution of blessings in the realizing of our destiny as we tramp, stumble, bounce, and dance our way through the highways, byways, sideways, and pathways of objective reality. Blessings are given to us freely, but only as a result of our spiritually evolving self-awareness. We exist to amplify the meaning of infinity through our ever-evolving self-awareness of spiritual understandings. Nothing else in the infinity of reality is capable of doing that.

Our gift for the self-experiencing objective existence is to experience the grandeurs of life for our infinite pleasure and enjoyment. We have eternities endless to understand our physical beingness. Thus, each of us is an ever-ripening spiritual fruit, in the ever blossoming tree of objective reality. We forever exist to blossom forth our divinity.

In the following discussion, I highlight the primary differences between God and us. Throughout the entirety of this work, these differences are emphasized. Each one of us is the untouched and untarnished self-portrait of God divinely experiencing objective reality, and divinely knowing core reality.

God's Self-conscious identity does not include any process of understanding. God's Self-awareness is limited to the infinite knowingness, of Himself. In contrast, all aspects of ultimate reality, including God, are self-consciously understood, interpreted, and experienced, by each one of us individually.

God's Self-knowingness never expands beyond Himself. He is only infinitely Self-aware of His forever divine unfoldment. In other words, God's Self-awareness infinitely increases as a result of His forever, unfolding divine nature, within the reality of His own infinite Self-knowingness.

The mind of God contains no knowledge or self-active thought. In His self-awareness, there is only divine unfoldment, the reality of *now*, and Isness. God's Self-conscious Beingness is His Self-awareness. God does not need any aspect, outside of Himself, to validate, sustain, interpret, or interact with, to give meaning to the foreverness of His divinity, except for us as individualized-Man.

As individualizations of Man, we infinitely evolve in the spiritual understanding of ourselves. However, the things we understand spiritually never progress beyond a speck of divine knowledge, as we continue to be the only interpreters of objective reality. As we advance in our self-conscious spiritual understandings, our self-awareness of unknown forever realities also increase.

Objective reality consists in part of pure, undefiled, ever-to-be experienced eternities of existence forever changing in their non-self-conscious creative processes of expression. Our ability to self-consciously create existence is entirely unknown to objective or ultimate reality.

Ultimate reality was never created, and is never a creator, except through the expressions of each of us.

God's divine attributes comprising His divine nature provide Him with a never-ending knowingness of blossoming blissfulness, within Himself. The infinite attributes of God, consist in part of love, harmony, joy, serenity, peacefulness, and an all-embracing realization of non-opposed Goodness. All of God's infinite nature, including each of us, exists as the wholeness of harmony.

God's nature, attributes, and essence infinitely dwell patiently within us, awaiting our self-acknowledgement. God never utilizes His attributes, either specifically or non-specifically, to display His Infinite Self-Goodness. For each of us, God's natural divine attributes are to be discovered, revealed, accepted, and experienced. As individualized-Man, we exist to know and to experience the forever reality of God.

In the physical realm, there is a collective subconscious form of knowledge influence that combines truth and untruth and impacts each of us individually. However, this concept is not applicable, nor does it have any relationship to God. Our self-conscious or subconscious influences cannot impact or affect God in any way. Thus, we only interpret God; we never change Him.

Individually, we have the same mind as God; however, our individualized mind and God's mind have separate innate identity and purpose, with each having its distinct self-awareness. The infinite mind of God is without any need, other than the perpetual need to reveal Himself, to Himself.

Although our mind is God's mind individualized, our individualized-mind-need requires the understanding of our infinite selves, infinite God, and the infinity of ultimate reality. Our mind-need requires endless ideas to be forever understood and experienced. Our individualized mind of God exists to understand, God's mind exists to Be.

Our individualized mind, separate from God, has the capability of self-thought, and self-actualizing thought to create experiences through our self-knowingness, self-understanding, self-interpretation, and forever self-increasing self-awareness. It is our individualized, independent, unique capacity to self-think that gives meaning and purpose, to our self-realized forever existence.

To understand our self-conscious lives, we must possess the means, for the expressing of our existence. The ways of apprehending our forever self-aware lives are though our self-actuating self-consciousness bringing into the realm of appearance, the seeming reality of created experiences, by way of our desires and self-conscious choices.

Each of us chooses the manner in which we express and determine our divine destiny. Our self-conscious awareness is never to evolve to a total and complete awareness of infinite wholeness. Our forever self-awareness is in a forever process of divine wholeness in realization. Still, our self-conscious awareness of divine wholeness expands the divinity of wholeness, within our self-knowingness, for each of us to experience.

God's entire Self-knowingness lacks the capability of Self-actuating Self-conscious expression because His Self-awareness is infinitely whole, Self-known, and divinely unbroken. There is a sense, in which God experiences His existence: however, His sense of experiencing reality is without any self-creating ability to create experiences.

God is in a Self-conscious state of infinite receptivity regarding His divinely infinite unfolding inner divine nature. Thus, God's knowingness of Himself is Self-consciously receptive to the blossoming forth of His inner divine nature. God exists to be the source for all of our creations of expressed divinity, into the experiencing of our lives. Thus, God is the source of our expressions of the Goodness of Harmony and the Purity of Wholeness.

In opposition to God, we are in an active self-conscious state of infinitely understanding and interpreting our divine nature as revealed, to our ever evolving self-awareness. Therefore, the self-realizing of our existence is to be forever understood, endlessly explained, and forever receptive to God's indwelling essence, which envelopes and permeates the foreverness of our self-existence.

Our purpose for existence is always to seek, find, follow, understand, interpret, accept, and obey the experiencing of our divinity. The foreverness of our self-conscious expression is our self-divinity in search of our infinite self-identity. God's existence is the reality of forever effortless Ease of Beingness.

Our experiencing of reality, as the beingness of life, demands our efforts. Thus, each one of us, in the objective realm, puts forever effort into viewing ultimate reality from the center-point of infinity. In core reality, each one of us is effortlessly observing reality from the center-point of God. The center points of God's existence represent the individual starting points of each of God's family members.

Objectively, forever and always, our self-existence is the individualized self-consciousness of our divinity, in progressive realization. We are forever always in the process of consummating our finite-infinite spiritual existence and destiny. We infinitely exist to define and refine the understanding of our eternally divine selves.

We are forever evolving in the understanding of our spirituality. Thus, our destiny is always the present progression of our spirituality self-consciously accepted, understood, interpreted, and demonstrated, in the realms of our experiences. We are eternally and infinitely the spiritual outcome of our desired thought-choices.

In the foreverness of our beingness, WE ARE God, BUT WE ARE NOT GOD! As God is divinely and infinitely whole in His Self-knowingness, we are divinely and infinitely non-whole in our self-understanding. We can never be God because we can never be the self-understanding divine fulfillment of our forever existence.

Thus, as the individualized-Man of God, we are no more God than the sunlight is the sun, a drop of ocean water is the sea, or a child is a parent. Still, God's infinite existing substance and our always current substance are forever divinely intertwined. In the divinity of God's divine essence, we are infinite. However, in our understanding and expression of God's divine nature, we are forever finite-infinite.

Each of us is the realization of God, as God's Self-conscious process of infinite communion, within Himself. We represent the portion of God that understands Himself, infinitely and individually. As God's individual and unknown expression of Himself, each of us gives existence and purpose to God's forever Beingness.

CHAPTER III

TransBeingness of Man

There are three classes of people: Those
who see, those who see when they are
shown, those who do not see.

Leonardo da Vinci

In the objective realm, each one of us is given the capacity of self-conscious understanding and the capability of following our destiny of infinite discovery and understanding, through the four stages of our objective realm transbeingness as individualized eternal-Man. The four cyclical stages of our transbeingness, as eternal immortal-Man, consist of the following: formless-Man, physical-Man, purgatorial-Man, and spiritual-Man. Each one of these four stages of our individualized objective-Man's transbeingness represents an infinite function of our identity as self-conscious immortal-Man.

Leonardo da Vinci in his depiction of Vitruvian man provided a brilliant and helpful pictorial image for understanding the four stages of Man's objective realm transbeingness. In da Vinci's image of Vitruvian man, he depicts individual-Man with arms and legs outstretched and enclosed in a rectangular square. The rectangular square, enclosing man, then overlaps a circle, representing God. Also, the rectangular square is both within and outside of the circle, representing God. Thus, his pictorial image shows eternal objective-Man's transbeingness, in relationship to individual-Man's forever and eternal divine nature, which includes individualized-Man's relationship to the forever nature of God.

Thus, the rectangular square depicts individualized eternal-Man and symbolically represents the objective transbeingness of Man, expressing as the four stages of our infinite progression, through objective reality's evolving eternities. Each side of individualized-Man's rectangular square has a perceived beginning and a perceived ending. Objective individualized-Man's ability to perceive beginnings and endings is an innate quality giving individualized-Man the ability to interpret objective reality.

Thus, individual eternal-Man's capacity of viewing ultimate reality as inherently containing segments of real existence, possessing seeming beginnings and endings, gives individualized eternal-Man the ability to understand, interpret, and experience ultimate reality, in self-perceiving the segments of ultimate reality's wholeness.

The wholeness of ultimate reality is infinitely beyond any concept of present understanding. However, the infinite and forever enclosed arcs comprising the wholeness of ultimate reality are infinitely capable of being understood and interpreted by each of us, as individualized-Man. From the perspective of individualized-Man, ultimate reality can only be understood through interpreting the infinite arcs of infinity's wholeness appearing to us as experiences.

Thus, there are no beginnings and endings within the realness of infinity itself. Beginnings and endings consist of our interpretations of infinite arc segments, of objective reality's wholeness, self-consciously understood to give substance and meaning to all real and perpetual existence. Our individualized eternal-Man ability to understand, perceive, and experience ultimate reality is the sole purpose for our individual and infinite self-aware reality.

One of the basic premises of this book is that each one of us has infinitely and self-consciously existed. We are immortal beings expressing our infinite indestructibility. The purpose for our individual existence is to experience reality. Moreover, it is our forever free will choice as to the manner in which each one of us chooses to experience life.

The purpose for our existence is to experience a reality that is understandable to us. However, the question that has no reasonable answer is: Why do any of us have or deserve an infinite self-aware existence for any purpose whatsoever? Alternatively, an even a more fundamental enigma is: Why does anything that experiences life deserve the gift of existence? Our infinitely ongoing never created self-existence must remain a forever mystery. If we understood why we have infinite non-created self-aware life, we would truly be God. However, if that were the case, there would be infinite gods.

In da Vinci's pictorial, God is visibly depicted by a circle, without beginning or ending. The God circle composed of infinite arcs encapsulates the idea of God's infinite harmony and perfection. Also, the God circle denotes the unbroken Self-awareness of His infinite divine nature, forever revealing Himself to Himself. The allness of God is infinitely bubbling up within His Self-beingness. Thus, God forever knows the fullness of Himself, in forever unfoldment.

Da Vinci's pictorial depicts eternal-Man's limbs stretching out and touching both the square of his infinity, and the circle of God's infinity. Thus, as individualized eternal-Man, we are self-aware of our infinite connection to God, both inside and outside of His infinite presence.

The top side of the square represents our individualized eternal-Man objective existence as formless-Man. The left side of the square represents our individualized eternal-Man objective reality as physical-Man. The bottom side of the square represents our individualized eternal-Man objective reality as purgatorial-Man. The right side of the square represents our individualized eternal-Man objective reality as spiritual-Man.

Thus is the infinite and eternal order of our individualized eternal-Man transbeingness throughout the foreverness of the eternities, forever being objectively created and de-created. Each one of us, as individualized eternal-Man, is the totality of our transbeingness.

Profoundly important is the realization that the four phases of our individual eternal-Man transbeingness denote that our self-awareness extends beyond the circle that represents the totality of God. Especially notice the bottom purgatorial side of our transbeingness is entirely outside the Self-knowingness of God.

From the above, I conclude that our individual and collective destiny is to self-understand and interpret ourselves in relationship to the infinite reality, forever dwelling inside of God and to our relationship to the infinite reality, forever dwelling outside of God.

If we misunderstand and misinterpret our relationship to God, we relegate ourselves to wrongfully experiencing our infinite objective lives. To successfully experience our infinite, eternal existence as harmony objectified, we must be in a constant self-conscious communion with our forever relationship to God.

Each side of eternal-Man's square seems to have a starting and ending positions. Thus, our individualized eternal-Man nature appears to be innately and infinitely limited and constricted, in the understanding of our forever outer objective beingness. In other words, our individualized eternal-Man existence understands and interprets objective reality, in finitely-infinite chunks and pieces, in all that which is infinitely real.

This objective sense of limitation necessitates the inclusion of a free will, into our infinitely individualized eternal-Man divine nature. Thus, we use our free will to overcome the inherently designed limitation, objectively embedded within each of us, in our forever objective existence.

Thus, our individualized free will is a component of our infinite objective existence, but it is not an active part of our infinite core reality self-aware reality. Our objectively embedded free will gives the power to our material understanding. In our core reality existence, we have no free will, we have no power, and we have no directed purpose for experiencing the complete perfection of God-reality. Our self-beingness in core reality is never completely realized, in objective reality, until the last objective Heaven is attained and realized.

Individualized eternal-Man's square extends beyond the all-inclusiveness of God, demonstrating our capacity to experience objective existence, outside and separate from God's Self-knowing existence. Thus is a seeming contradiction in our perpetual existence: we are forever simultaneously within and without God.

Thus, our objective existence, as individualized eternal-Man, includes a portion of God's Infinite Self-beingness, combined with a portion of ultimate reality objectively existing outside of God's Self-awareness, and thus unknown to Him. In a sense, we forever know God, and we forever do not know God.

Our infinite objective reality as eternal-Man encompasses the wholiness of God, combined with a separate and unique identity, forever outside the wholiness of God. In the objective realm, we possess the portion of God's nature enabling us to understand, determine, and realize our forever objective destiny, through the experiencing of our objective existence.

Following are the sacred truths of our transbeingness as individualized-Man experiencing existence.

- There is only one God. However, that one God is understood infinitely, individually, and uniquely, by each member of God's family. From God's perspective, He exists solely to increase in the Self-knowingness of His infinite divinity. Our objective existence is to increasingly self-understand the inner-allness and outer-allness as part of God and separate from God.

- Each one of us has the real ability to increasing understand God, understand ourselves, and understand all of forever reality. Each one of us is a portion of God unknown to God Himself. Through our divinely accurate self-understanding of existence itself, we are all individually and uniquely the vibration of God.

- The realm of ideas provides the capability for each of us to self-consciously think. Our self-conscious thought-thinking process gives us the ability to understand and translate all the things of existence into spiritual meaningfulness. Inherent in our ability to understand and to interpret real reality and non-real reality is our free will. Thus, it is our free ability to apprehend and interpret all things real or imaginary that make each one of us a creator. However, the only things we create are non-real illusions imitating our self-understandings of reality.

- Ultimate reality is forever real to its infinite existence. In our transbeingness as individualized objective-Man, we understand infinite reality, infinite beingness, infinite progression, infinite glory, endless happiness, and infinite sorrow. Also, we are the objective outcome of the understandings of ourselves. Thus, our infinite divine existence is often expressed non-divinely.

- To each one of us, the appearing existence of sin and evil are based on that which we assume to be true because each one of us can interpret reality. The non-reality of sin and evil is a forever to-be-realized component, of our objective self-awareness.

- The creative processes for the emerging of physical worlds are functions of objective reality and only exist for us to understand, interpret, experience, and enjoy. When each physical world emerges into objective appearance, the purgatorial and spiritual worlds also come into objective existence giving each one of us the opportunity to understand ourselves as the forever individualized transbeingness of Man.

- Our individualized infinite beingness, demands to be experienced. Our lives represent the experiencing of existence. It is the physical realm of objective reality where we create experiences, with or without, a self-awareness of God. In the physical realm, each one of us is all-powerful in our creations of non-real experiences.

- The power of our ever-evolving understanding gives us the power to create. In the physical realm, we create the manifestations of experiences. We create self-consciously designed experiences for understanding reality and non-reality.

- God never punishes anyone. We punish ourselves for self-consciously deviating from our divine destiny. It is only our forever self-punishment that enables us to return to the realizing of our self-conscious divinity in expression.

- Our power of understanding gives each of us the ability to experience infinite happiness, through self-consciously desiring to experience our God-derived nature. Unfortunately, our ability to interpret and misinterpret reality also gives us the power to reject our forever God-derived divine identity.

- In the self-aware experiencing of existence, each one of us is superior to God because each one of us possesses the infinite power of understanding. God infinitely exists, but His existence does not include the power to Self-consciously understand, except through the individualized-Us, of which He has no infinite Self-awareness. Thus, God's Self-knowingness is forever Self-consciously receptive to the unfolding of the infinity within Him.

- In the experiencing of our lives, we should strive always to be kind in our thoughts and our actions. We should revere and respect all expressions of life. Moreover, we should seek earnestly to find and accept the God of our understanding.

Formless-Man

Our original entry into the formless realm from core reality is impelled, compelled, and propelled. We have no choice as to whether we enter or do not enter, into objective formless reality. When we are first born into the formless realm of objective reality, we begin a new journey into the objective realm of experience, a journey comprising limited and unlimited expressions of self-aware existence.

Our formless realm existence is somewhat similar to our formless existence in core reality. However, in core reality, we have no self-awareness, self-association, or self-relationship to the idea realm. Therefore, in core reality, we are not capable of self-conscious, independent thought, we are only self-consciously aware of infinite bliss.

In both core reality and the formless realm, we have no sexual identification. When we enter the formless realm, we are divinely coequal with each other in all respects. As we enter the formless realm, we become awakened to a new self-identifying realization of ourselves. Fortunately, divine family members, who are further along the path of experiencing their existence, introduce us to the workings of the idea realm.

In core reality, we had no infinite self-conscious destiny to realize or fulfill. When we enter the objective formless realm, we self-consciously embark upon our finite-infinite voyage into our self-realizing, self-understanding, self-interpreting, self-experiencing, and self-earning the blessings given to the spiritually self-deserving, of infinite self-aware existence.

Imagine what it must be like for us to go from a non-earned spiritual self-aware environment of blissful self-beingness to the objective realm, where we become self-aware of our infinite existence, and where the blessings of self-evolving spirituality, are earned through the experiencing of life. Thus, our objective finite-infinite destiny becomes the overcoming of omnipresent godless challenges, through the experiencing of living reality.

Our formless realm existence is mentally objective. We are incapable of externalizing our individual self-thinking process, through our self-actuating self-conscious interaction with idea realm ideas. However, our self-conscious realization of ideas instills within us a sense of yearning, to experience the ideas we perceive. Thus, we experience ideas rather than merely being subjectively perceived.

In the formless realm, we become students of self-aware existence as the living of life. Now, our self-awareness becomes wedded with the idea realm, giving us the ability to think thoughts self-consciously. In core reality, we exist without thinking thoughts about our existence, and our self-conscious aware has no power to wield. However, in the objective realm, we are given the potential of the infinite power immersed in the thinking of thoughts, the understanding of thoughts, the interpretation of thoughts, and the authority to make free will choices.

Thus, in the objective realm, we become awakened to our infinite and forever old-new existence. In the formless realm, we are shown how to self-incorporate the idea realm into our self-awareness, to create a pathway for our innate forever existence-given capability of self-aware thinking. It is the learning of languages that gives us the ability to express, understand, and interpret our thoughts, spiritual and non-spiritual.

Thus, languages are required for each of us to self-understand our infinite existence, God's existence, and the existence of all things. We need the capability to understand all aspects of ultimate reality to be able to create experiences. We need to create experiences to discover, rediscover, and infinitely fulfill our objective divine destiny, to self-recognize ourselves as the individualizations of God.

In the formless realm, we begin to understand reality and non-reality. Eventually, we make the choice to enter into the physical realm, which then becomes our physical inhabiting of eternity. At that time, we begin our progression through the remaining three stages of our immortal-Man transbeingness as physical, purgatorial, and spiritual-Man. When the eternity we are occupying ends, no matter where we may be in our transbeingness, we return to the formless realm.

As we reenter the formless realm, from the other objective realms, we retain no memories of our objective excursions through the physical, purgatorial, and spiritual realms. However, since we have already existed in the formless realm, we quickly readjust to our renewed formless existence.

In the formless realm, the purpose for our existence is re-revealed to our infinite selves through our interaction with ideas. In the foreverness of our circular reality, we have no choice other than to accept the experiencing of physical lives. Theoretically, we could remain infinitely in the formless realm, but our formless existence would become a reality existence of unfulfilled yearnings to express existence as life.

The ongoing bliss, we know in core reality, is not known in the formless realm. Also, we are never automatically forced out of the formless realm due to the realization of boredom. However, our formless realm existence eventually evolves into overwhelming yearnings, to experience existence as physical life.

When we first enter into the formless realm, we do not understand the meaning of experience. Once we comprehend its meaning, we are reborn into a new realization of our infinite reality. Thus, our immediate desired destination is the objective physical realm, for the purpose of experiencing physical reality. If never given the opportunity to experience physical existence, we would remain forever spectators self-consciously viewing objective reality, through a kaleidoscope of ideas, forever lacking the capability of being experienced.

Thus, our formless reality becomes a self-cravingness to experience life because only in the formless realm do we acquire the capability of self-conscious understanding. By obtaining self-conscious understanding, we could never continually self-consciously exist, in an environment where reality was only understood, not experienced.

When we self-consciously exist in the formless and spiritual realms, we are in the only two tributaries of our recycling transbeingness, whereby we unmistakably understand our infinite individualized divine nature. Thus, in these two realms of self-realized reality, we understand the purpose for our infinite existence.

As individual formless and spiritual-Man, we are self-cognizant of unreality's professed claims for existence. However, our clear realization of actual reality, in the formless realm and our real understanding and acceptance of God, in the spiritual realm makes us self-consciously impervious to the empowering of thought-substance, to the godlessness based illusions of unreality.

Thus, as individualized formless and spiritual-Man, our understanding of the real is so clear and self-evident that our free will capacity, to accept the unreal as real, remains untested. Still, as individualized formless-Man, we possess the self-conscious free will ability to reject God, but the rejection of God, in the formless realm, has no means of being experienced. When we become individualized spiritual-Man, our divine self-understanding has reached a sacred place of spiritual evolvement, where the rejection of God is no longer a free will possibility.

As individual formless-Man, we have the ability to recognize ideas. However, in our formless objective existence, we are not capable of experiencing the ideas we self-consciously acknowledge and accept; thus, we are limited to only self-awareness of idea-thoughts. Only in the objective realm of experience do ideas fulfill their purpose for existence.

Thus, in the formless realm, ideas are only perceived; they cannot be self-actualized into physical existence. If our self-awareness only consisted of the self-conscious awareness of ideas, without the capability of being objectified into experiences that would mean a portion of ultimate reality would remain forever dormant in purpose and realization, thereby making the existence of idea realm ideas meaningless.

Thus, if we were never able to experience our understandings of ideas, our self-aware existence would only consist of infinite unfulfilled yearnings. We would never be able to test the perceptions of ourselves because there would be no obstacles to overcome, and no challenges face. We would understand the purpose for our infinite existence, but we could not experience the meaning of that understanding.

Suppose in the formless realm, we become aware of an idea-thought, of some far off paradise, existing in the physical realm. This idea-thought is a serene sun-bathed paradise which pleases and entices our desire to experience its reality. However, if all we could do were to self-consciously envision that nirvana; that pleasant self-impelled inspiration would quickly fade, and lose its enchantment.

Thus, without the capability to experience objective existence, our self-conscious awareness of idea realm ideas, would quickly become tiresome and dull, meaningless and boring. Imagine self-aware existence, as physical life, in an environment of endless mental temptations in a realm of reality beyond that which is self-consciously known.

As individualized formless-Man, we understand that as long as we remain in the formless realm, we will never experience the understandings of our infinite existence, in the objective physical realm of our beingness. When the opportunities become available, we use our knowledge, of the idea realm ideas, for exiting the formless realm and entering the physical realm.

It is our transbeingness through the physical, purgatorial, and especially the spiritual realm, that enables us to experience our self-aware existence, in consonance with ideas. The unreal realm of experiencing reality gives each of us the ability to experience the infinite range of our interpretations of ideas.

There is a great dilemma concerning formless-Man, I have yet to understand. It seems even in the formless realm; there are members of God's family who self-consciously and self-willfully choose to reject God, and thus deny their divine heritage. Strange as it seems, the choice to experience existence does not necessarily coincide with a self-willingness to seek, understand and accept God.

These self-aware individualizations formless-Man understand their relationship to God, but still they reject Him. They reject God, even as they realize the perfection is pervading throughout all of the infiniteness of reality. Thus, a large segment of God's family consistently chooses to reject God, incomprehensible as that seems.

Until these divine rebels come to a self-realizing acceptance of God, their physical experiences of existence are forever driven, by the wanton gods of chance, opportunity, randomness, and general unpredictability. Thus, their infinite spiritual wings eternally remain untested, impotent, and non-desired.

Every evil act ever committed results from a self-conscious choice, to be separated from God. Thus, these errant divine family members are responsible for all appearances of evil. When we divinely understand, accept and choose a self-realized God existence, evil ceases its claims to be part of reality. When we decide to deny our self-God existence, evil smugly puffs about the runway of our evolving destiny, bathed in the ever darkening light of godlessness.

When these spiritual rebels become individualized physical-Man, they continue in their rejection of God. Thus, in the objective realm, they persist in their self-chosen evilness. Therefore, it is their continuing self-conscious desire to reject God that enables evil, to eternally proclaim its pretended existence.

If evil appears now in our present experience of reality; its supposed existence, has thus far been established and persistent, throughout all God's family member treks, into and out of, objective reality's eternities endless. Therefore, evil continues to maintain a seeming identity of its own, as long as God continues to be self-consciously rejected, by any members of God's family.

However, our inner divinity never abandons us. Thus, we are forever spiritual beings, whether or not our divinity is self-consciously acknowledged or rejected. The evilest sinner ever to exist has the identical divine nature, as the saintliest saint ever to have lived. Thus, if expressions of evil persist in perpetuity, evil's seeming existence is based on individualized-Man's self-denial and self-rejection, of his forever divinity.

When an eternity ends, no matter where we may be in our physical transbeingness, we return to our formless and mental self-conscious state, of spiritual self-awareness. Once returned to the formless realm, we remember nothing of our transbeingness in the physical, purgatorial, and spiritual realms of objective reality.

The formless realm is our forever non-evolving spiritual home, throughout the eternities of objective reality. When we return to the formless realm, we clearly understand and realize that nothing in objective reality has changed, or has been affected in any way, by our self-conscious sojourn into the physical, purgatorial, and spiritual realms.

When we return to the formless realm, we revert to the self-realization of our divinity. Still, the God rejecters remain members of God's family, who continue in their self-conscious repudiation of their divinity, and thus stay recalcitrant in their self-denial of God. Even so, the corporeal reality remains untouched by their individualized self-conscious self-actuating, encountering of existence.

When a new physical world is born into physical existence and ready for our self-conscious habitation, we once become capable of leaving the formless realm to enter into the physical realm. While in the formless realm, we self-consciously accept the idea giving us the understanding to go from the formless into the physical realm.

Thus, we are eternally and persisting fulfilling our infinite objective urges, to experience our existence self-consciously. Our experiencing of physical life is not something we have the capability of refusing. Our understanding of our infinite existence mandates our living of life, in the physical realm.

In the formless realm, no one denies the existence of God. However, in the formless realm, God is first as being infinitely impotent. In this understanding, some members of God's family choose to reject Him, due to His infinite divine impotence. Thus, they reject a powerless God and embrace the understanding of their all-powerfulness, and claim the reality of God, without the earned spiritual ability to understand their divinity in God. Thus, they choose to experience their self-existence without accepting the God of forever divine purity.

No one ever permanently retains the choice to remain in the formless realm, because staying in the formless would be a self-conscious repudiation of immortal-Man's forever designed destiny, to infinitely express the all-powerfulness of his infinite self-conscious understanding. No one in the formless realm is denied the potentiality of the all-powerfulness of understanding, as they progress through their realizations of objective reality.

Since everyone in the physical realm is experiencing existence, everyone has the endless possibility of finding and accepting the God of his or her understanding. However, our finite-infinite individual self-existence includes the forever option to be with without God. In the formless realm, there are no consequences for the mere self-conscious rejection of God. Consequences for our actions only result when our self-willed actions become branded into the experiencing of existence.

Still, it remains an uneasy realization that so many individualized members of God's family care little for how their experiencing of existence, is experienced. It seems they only desire to experience life on their non-spiritual terms. They continue to reject their self-identity which is their self-divinity in God.

Physical-Man

The objective physical reality is the independent, intact, and undefiled portion of ultimate reality. The objective physical reality is realized by each one of us, as a functioning continuum of ongoing eternities. It is here that each of us spiritually evolves to become the understanding of our spiritual incorruptibility, as we self-consciously prevent the phantasma of godlessness, to gain a foothold in our self-awareness.

The same door used to block the entrance of thing claiming reality is the same door opening into the *eternality* of our objective existence, enabling each of us to find and re-find the ever-presence of our divinity.

In the physical realm, all appearances of godless unreality represent an assumed reality which is continuingly tempting us, to deny our true divine selves.

As individualized physical-Man, our ability to think freely creates both our bondage and our salvation. Unreality remains forever real to our spiritually deficient self-actuating consciousness. The only divinely real way to know, understand, and experience true reality is to overcome the false presentations continually assaulting our self-realizations existence. Our deliverance from the unreal is achieved through our self-acquisition of spiritual truth understood, accepted, and obeyed.

All the challenges of life we forever face are infinity's gifts to our forever existence. Without challenges to be overcome, we would never experience our true divine selves; we would never experience our true divine potential, and never experience bona fide ultimate reality itself. Also, we would never experience our understanding of God, the sum, and substance of our forever and infinite beingness.

The realm of appearance eternally resides in the constructs of our self-awareness. As individualized physical-Man, the meaning of real existence is dependent upon the realizations of experiencing non-real reality. We spiritually evolve by understanding, reacting, and interpreting the physical realm of experience. It is our destiny to explain, into appearing existence, the self-consciously created molds of our understandings.

The concept of self-willful evolving only has real meaning in relationship to our evolving as individualized physical-Man, in the unreal and real realms of objective reality. Objective reality evolves by obeying the self-enclosed infinitely unfolding laws of physical realm beingness. We also are destined to obey those physical laws. It is spiritually possible, in the potentiality of our all-powerfulness to transcend those physical laws. Since we start a new spiritually evolving existence, in each new sojourn into objective reality from core reality, who knows what we may have spiritually accomplished in previous sojourns.

The self-realizing of our divine destiny is finite-infinitely endless. Thus, our existence is non-stoppable, incorruptible, and divinity infinite.

We are finitely forever experiencing the understanding of ourselves. Thus, our infinite objective reality is a forever challenge to reveal our immense spirituality to ourselves.

In our present physical life, we are preparing ourselves, through experiencing the non-real realm of projected reality, to eventually find our eternal abode in the spiritual realm. In other words, we understand our real divine selves, in the way we interpret ourselves in our relationship to non-reality. We realize the successful evolving of spirituality when we no longer harbor any fears, from the claiming appearances of godless unreality.

To this end, there are no short cuts; we must earn our divine admittance, into the spiritual realm, by way of our firm commitment to realize, accept, and self-consciously obey the nature of our inner divinity. Our earned existence, into the spiritual realm of heavenly wonders, is only achieved in one eternity, at a time.

As physical-Man, our objective destiny is to awaken self-consciously to the understanding that the presence of God, within each one of us is our forever soul, as members of God's family, driving each of us to the realizing of our non-alterable destiny. We realize our evolving future as we understand, interpret, and experience our existence through infinite ongoing objective eternities.

Our spiritual evolvement infinitely increases and decreases in the divine sputterings of our divinity being self-understood. Thus, the understandings of our objective physical existences are forever spiritual fluid and forever spiritually static. Our physical self-existence is a continually molded enigma forever requiring our divine interpretations.

In the objective realm, there is an ongoing linkage of cycles of existence before spiritual victory is assured. In the measure of earth-time, one cycle of actual objective existence may consist of tens thousands of years, of spiritual self-evolving, spiritual self-understanding, and self-interpretations of our forever identity in our forever divinity, before our objective realm spiritual victory is won.

Objective physical reality makes no judgments upon our free will choices. As we continue in the self-conscious seeking process of spiritual enlightenment, we understand that objective physical reality is continuingly encouraging each of us to experience new challenges, new opportunities, and new joys through the progression of eternities endless.

Our infinite self-aware existence is meaningless if it cannot be self-understood. The spiritual things we seek to accept self-consciously are the realizations of our divinity, at the level of our divine unfoldment. There is never any outside authority that judges the choices we make, in our infinite self-aware existence. We alone are the justices of the choices we make.

However, as we realize our divine destiny, in concert with the God of our understanding, we provide the actual meaningfulness to our infinite existence. The blessings given us, for the exercising of our infinite self-conscious awareness, are the result of our accepted divinely real self-understandings of reality.

There is no infinite relief from the self-conscious prison we make out of our sinful and evil actions. Without the power engrafted into our self-consciousness self-realization of God, and our self-acceptance of God the dissolving pf our self-imposed limitations, into their non-real realm of divine nothingness is not possible.

As I have said previously, we are capable of denying our infinite existence, but we are not capable of dislodging our infinite existence, out of the ever presence of ultimate reality. Our forever non-chosen destiny is to understand ourselves as infinite beings. Thus, in the objective realm, we experience the understanding of our infinite existence. We exist forever to live forever.

This understanding of ourselves remains forever, a blessing or a curse. For reasons unknown, we are infinite spiritual enigmas in a self-aware existence we never chose. If we exist, in self-aware reality we never self-consciously chose, why and how did we become the selected ones of infinity? The unknowable reason is that each one of us has infinitely existed, within infinite God, within infinite reality, infinitely.

As we spiritually understand the meaning and purpose of our forever physical lives, we are automatically gifted with the blessings our spiritual understandings have prepared us to receive. Our divine destiny, without the God of our understanding, becomes our divine destiny, providing us with deserved penalties of pain, sorrow, and heartache.

We are forever choosing our thoughts and experiencing the material soul of our understandings. Without a sincere desire to find and accept the God of our self-realization, the things we envision become manifest as our self-accepted material world soul, as pictured forth into the realm of experience, and we become the gods many, of created experience.

As divine beings, we are compelled to tread and experience the forever pathways of existence. The divine compass which is our self-realized beingness forever remains the power of truth acknowledged and understood that determines our successful demonstrations of our divinity in action, in the continually revealing destiny.

At times, the burdening pressures of experiencing life seem overwhelming. To prevent the devouring of our spiritual unfolding iniquity of evilness, we must hold tight to the unbreakable divine truth that we are now and always the individual, incorruptible, and indestructible expression of God. We are the infinity of divinity in self-realization.

As each of us physically progresses in the understanding of things divine, we retain our ongoing developed sense of spirituality. This accruing of inner-influx of spirituality is necessary for the successful self-conscious continuous rediscovering of our forever divine destiny. We discover our destiny, as we self-acknowledge our destiny, to the goodness of our beingness.

This developing sense of spirituality is our self-conscious receptivity to things divine. Since we are infinite spiritual beings, our receptivity to spiritual understanding is infinite. Thus, we exist in an infinite circle of forever completeness. Our spiritual evolvement begins anew with each new objective reality we enter to experience.

Thus, we exist to attempt forever an understanding of our existence that is never to be comprehended, in its finality. We are forever divine prisoners of infinity, continually breaking the illusionary crippling chains of ungodliness, to understand ourselves as divine conquerors. Through the power of our increasing spiritual understanding, we create the image of ourselves, whether it is God-like or non-God-like.

These ongoing infusions of developed spirituality enable each of us to find, acknowledge, and accept the God of our understanding compatible with our ever increasing immense sense of spirituality. Without a self-acceptance of God, the purpose for our self-conscious existence remains unrecognized, and we become lost in our power of understanding choosing to seed itself in the wrongful unknown.

The infinitely real qualities of God are only experienced, through our self-consciousness acceptance of God, combined with the understanding that divine truth is always consistent, unwavering, and unchallenged, by anything claiming the opposite. This realization occurs as a result of our faithfulness to our continuing self-conscious understanding that we forever exist in the ever-presence aura-wrapped goodness of God.

As we enter into a new objective physical eternity, we become subject to belief patterns implanted, into our universal subconscious collective mind, through the continually evolving and experiencing life, as God's forever and perfect family.

These belief patterns impress upon us, both spiritual and non-spiritual proclivities, which shape our evolving or non-evolving individual and group understandings of life as experienced existence. These subconscious nomads of mental influence continually seek acceptance, in the individualized-minds of physical-Man.

Thus, we are significantly influenced by the consensus of accepted agreed upon collective beliefs. This consensus of beliefs acts as a mesmerizing force to attract interpretations of idea realm ideas. Then, in the experiencing of our objective existence, we become continually besieged by the real and false collective consensus beliefs of the entirety of God's family.

These mass-collected interpretations of existence float through the collective and individual subconscious and conscious mind of physical-Man. To the spiritually ill-prepared mind, these interpretations of beliefs find lodgment, adhered to in varying strengths. Once accepted, these rumbling and rambling ideas often become self-contorted, and their actual meanings become lost, in the uncontrollable variances in undergoing the perils of life as self-aware existence.

Experiencing life successfully always remains challenging because it requires total allegiance and reliability upon accurate understandings of God when the distortions of this world continuously seek our bowing allegiance. Doing the right thing is often easier than understanding what the right thing to do is. Again, in our spiritual understandings, weak or strong as they may be; we always have the power of choice. We can choose to act in a spiritual manner before we understand the spirituality of our choice making.

Through the correct realizations of our divinity, we discern things divinely. Through the incorrect understandings of our divinity, we perceive things non-divinely. Thus, the forever challenge, in our experiencing of existence is to develop a sense of spiritual discernment, which continually reveals divine truth to our receptive self-conscious minds.

Our correct sacred perceptions become our spiritual understandings in appearance. Thus, our developing ability to discern divine truth saves us from all things godless. How do we know if we are living up to our spiritual potential? We are always living up to our developed spirituality, but we are more often than not, we are living up to the awareness, of our non-developed self-awareness of spirituality.

These impinging collective subconscious influences combine with chance, opportunity, randomness, and general unpredictability. The collective self-conscious provides much impetus for the numerous and continuous challenges each of us must encounter, experience, and overcome, as we advance and adapt, to the objective physical realm.

For our actual and real existence, to be revealed to our self-awareness, we must withstand the onslaught of godless thought-barbs bubbling-up from unreality. For each one of us to advance spiritually, we must be self-consciously equipped to separate the trueness of ideas from the falseness of ideas. Our capability to understand, if self-consciously motivated to seek things divine, gives us the self-conscious separating ability of spiritual discernment.

We are not destined to be imprisoned, in the shadowy bonding constraints of non-reality. Rather, our divine destiny is to experience our existence centered in the self-awareness of our God self-beingness, and in our God self-assertions. The greater our identification with God, the greater becomes the realizing of our divine destiny.

We are infinitely impelled and compelled to realize our forever divine existence. However, each one of us has the free will to deny that inner-divine impetus, which pushes each of us ever onward, in the self-realizing of our forever divinity. Thus, the fundamental edict for our infinite existence is that we experience our infinite existence. How we experience our infinite existence is the forever choice, we each judge.

Our sinful failures eventually become subdued by the divine winds of truth, surging us ceaselessly onward into the successful experiencing of existence. Our ever evolving spiritual self-awareness unshackles the tightening of unreal reality, and our finite-infinite victories forever become consecrated in our self-knowingness.

In our present foray into objective reality from core reality, we will experience eternities endless. Eventually, through our irrevocable and unchallenged understanding of our oneness with God, we will achieve redemption, only our infinite existence enables us to accomplish. As God is forever, we are forever, and our redemptions are forever. Imagine we infinitely receive redemption, for infinitely experiencing the purpose of our existence, an infinite self-aware reality we never chose.

When that occurs, we have experienced but one single heartbeat, in the infinity of heartbeats. Imagine in the timelessness of time, each unique world we inhabit seems like infinity. All the individual worlds we experience, in our spiritual overcoming of this objective reality, appear to us as an infinite infinity. We live a tortured forever existence, with timelessness as our only forever Savior.

Each time we understand, interpret, and experience a new physical world, we realize the purpose of our infinite self-conscious objective existence. As we self-acknowledge ourselves as divine beings, we empower the understanding of our divinity to self-recognize a new understanding of itself.

Each one of us is a portion of God that is all-powerful based on our capability of understanding. Presently, all of us are unworthy of the infinite power we potentially possess. Our developing spirituality keeps us from abusing the power that only spiritual understanding issues to us. Conversely, our undeveloped spirituality, represented by our unharnessed free will, allows us to abuse our existence. When our spiritual self-awareness is spiritually encased, in the presence of God, it is not possible to self-willingly abuse any expressions of life. All of us are in the shadows of that spiritual understanding.

Still, by accepting the recognition that God is the substance of our forever beingness, each one of us is entitled to be spiritually sovereign over our present realm of experience. The destiny for each one of us is to command all the aspects of ultimate reality, to seek an infinite future to be forever realized but never attained.

As we take our first breath in the physical realm, we become individualized physical-Man. As innocent newborns, we are presenting our divine credentials to objective reality. We enter the physical realm to experience once again a physical existence we have self-consciously experienced infinitely.

Each entry into the physical realm is a new adventure in the discovering of our self-divinity or rejection of our self-divinity. In the physical realm, we eternally attempt to understand who and what we are, and continue to construct the self-understanding of ourselves. Thus, in the physical realm, we continually determine the expressions of the interpretations of ourselves.

At the time of our entrance into the physical realm, we are spiritually unblemished. We possess no self-developed receptivity to evil or sin's pretended ability to engulf our self-awareness with the falsity of godless unreality. However, now we are subject to the wielding life-changing and unpredictable powers of chance, opportunity, randomness, and general unpredictability.

It should be kept in mind, that when we self-consciously enter the physical realm, we bring with us the depth strength, and spiritual evolving, of previously amassed spiritually grasped understandings. It is this attained spiritual depth of conviction that determines the resisting strength of our responses, to the callings of the godless unreal.

As we evolve to use our free will to temporarily self-consciously separate ourselves, from the presence of God, evil and sin state their claims, for our self-recognition and acceptance. Because each one of us possesses the free will ability of understanding, our choice-making power enables us, to forever overcome those infinite claims of sin and evil.

The great blessing of physical existence is that our spiritually evolving self-conscious interactions with reality strengthen our understandings of ourselves and our lives. In the physical realm, our divinely mandated beingness spans the spectrum, in our forever discovering of our self-divinity, through understanding, rather than knowingness.

When it comes to our individual spiritual evolvement, there is no right or wrong way to seek, find, and follow God. Each of us realizes our unique destiny, in the spiritually flowered sanctuary of our individualized self-awareness. Forever and always our relationship with God is understood individually and uniquely.

In our relationship with God, our physical world journeys are forever individual, yet never departing from the collective journey of God's perfect family. All false understandings of God eventually lead sincere God-seekers to the correct the individual and non-influenced understandings of God.

As physical-Man, it matters not how God is understood, as long as we self-consciously desire a relationship with Him, by learning to experience an ever widening understanding of His divine nature. To the spiritually mindful and sincere, the God of their understanding is revealed in the light of spiritually comforting truth and thus the God of Goodness is only revealed, to the proven spiritually worthy.

This enlightening recognition of God uplifts us spiritually and prompts us to see the Goodness of God in all things. To bring our knowingness of God, into our interpretation of all things, empowers our divine self-awakening, to accept, follow, and obey the God of our understanding. If we follow the God of our perception with kindness, our infinite self-aware existence becomes a blessing, albeit it is temporary.

Thus, the infinity of our divinity is before us to eternally discover, rediscover, and understand our foreverness in God. There is only one way to the Deliverer God of our understanding. That one way is to seek kindly-good, interpret kindly-good, do kindly-good, and be kindly-good in all experiences we create. It is our self-willed desire and ability to infuse kindness into our self-consciousness, which justifies our infinite existence.

Expressing kindly-good is the loving understanding of God made visible. Thus, the expression of gentle kindly-good is to reveal ourselves in a manner causing no harm to ourselves, to others, or to anything experiencing existence. Thus, we demonstrate the status of our evolving spirituality by our depth and strength of our ability to impress kindly-good into the experiencing of life.

God is not in some far off distant place; rather, God and the goodness of God are forever within each of us. Through our desire and commitment to seek good, to be good, and to act divinely, we are self-consciously harmonizing ourselves, with the presence of God within us. Thus, our continuation in the doings of good things is the ever evolving self-discovery of our forever divinity.

Only by holding firm to the realization of our divine beingness and always striving to be kind, tolerant, just, and Godly prevents the godlessness of chance, opportunity, randomness, and general unpredictability from determining the expressions of our self-realized divinity. As we control the pincers of unpredictability, we come to realize our divine destiny as the self-accepting realization of the God of our individual understanding.

It is possible to be consistently kindly and good, without the self-acceptance of God, but for such individuals, there are no eternal spiritual rewards. Self-conscious existence without God is not a desirable self-aware existence because life without the knowingness of God self-realized is the living of life without divine salvation and heavenly rewards.

Our determined desire to do good be good and experience the Goodness of God delivers us from phantom claims, of evil and sin, whether or not God exists. Whatever enhances our experiencing of life is good; whatever diminishes the experiencing of life is the self-realizing of a tainted understanding of self-existence. Thus, what we choose to experience is our destiny realized, in the light of goodness, or our future realized in the slumbering of darkness, forever surrounded by the light of God-knowingness.

Goodness desired, cherished, and expressed is our gateway to the spiritual understanding of life, as divine existence. All things understood spiritually begin with the enlightened of divine desire. Thus, we cannot show goodness without the desire to manifest goodness. Even if God is self-consciously absent from our thoughts, the desire to reveal goodness in place of God points to a recognizing acceptance of God.

To possess unswerving trust in God is to bring the power of God to our self-conscious understanding of our divinity, as we reveal our divinity to ourselves. Our faith in God is our continuing self-acknowledgement of God's presence, purifying the realm of experience, with His undiluted wholiness. Faith is our steadfast reliability upon truth when untruth, expressing as reflected light, glistens its pretended alluringness.

Each one of us is the existence of God understanding God's existence. Our realization of spiritual truth is a ceaselessly expanding power, both individually and collectively. As we spiritually evolve, we choose to dwell in the company of the holy God-minded. Not holy God-minded in the sense of sharing the same spiritual understandings of truth, but holy God-minded in the sense of sharing the common spiritual desire to find, love, and obey the wholiness of God.

Although we may choose, to self-consciously hide in the shadows of the godless unreal, the divine spark driving our forever instilled existence never abandons us. Thus, at various times in our experiencing of life, similar situations often present themselves, for our spiritual re-evaluation. Even though these learning situations are seemingly worldly random, we alone interpret the similarities of their circumstances.

Our understandings result from our experiences. Our experiences result from our choices. Our choices emerge from our desires. Our desires produce our realizations or non-realizations of our God-identity. Therefore, with or without God, we forever determine the realizing of our destiny. However, the recurrences of similar learning situations are required for our spiritual edification.

This process of objective existence occurs to our self-conscious awareness because, in previous circumstances, we made inappropriate and spiritually uneducated choices. Thus, we are now provided with new opportunities to make divinely correct decision. This desire to divinely improve our spiritual understandings is a gift grounded in the structure of our infinite existence, to guide us in the realizing of our divine destiny.

Thus, physical existence continually provides us with ongoing opportunities to make morally correct and spiritually appropriate decisions. How we respond to these opportunities determines the pace of our heavenly spiritual ascension, *goodward*, and Godward. This infinite corrective self-process for spiritual understanding eventually enables each of us to realize and inhabit the infinite, eternal Heavens throughout the foreverness of eternities.

Each divine Heaven experienced is a temporary spiritual haven, in our continuing spiritual realization of our experiencing of existence. Therefore, our infinite existence consists of self-consciously imbibing in ongoing heavenly havens, and infinitely self-realizing the corrupted *havenly* hells, also forever manifesting in the objective realm.

Our continuing desires for wrongful doingness overrides any of our desires to find God. If we continue to make spiritually void choices, our spiritual progress becomes self-trapped in the false appearances of self-accepted illusions, and we continue to suffer the consequences of our self-active godlessness.

Thus, our impulse efforts to find God remains unfulfilled to our circularly entrenched self-evolvement and thereby unheeded. However, even in this non-divine stagnation, of our non-evolving spirituality, we remain forever divinely pure, yet lacking the spiritual understandings to guide our heavenly steppings, towards the self-realizing of the goodness of our beingness.

Feelings of remorse serve to awaken our desire for things spiritual. Our wrong choices activate an inner self-conscious stirring of spirituality. These feelings of remorse promote a form of spiritual prompting guiding us to an inherent need to seek good, find good, and accept good so that we may experience the goodness of our divine nature.

Feelings of remorse accompany our desire to take correct spiritual actions and never again allow spiritual opportunities to go unnoticed, unheeded, or unappreciated. To recognize these spiritual opportunities, in the living of life, and then to take the appropriate spiritually enlightened actions, denotes our evolving recognition of our evolving understanding of spirituality in the realm of physical appearance.

Our self-existence, without an awareness of things divine, results in continuous godless interpretations, of our individual self-consciousness of existence. Without God-awareness anchoring our ever evolving self-understandings of existence, we remain rudderless vessels of self-awareness, in the often turbulent waves, of objective existence.

Through divine understanding, we are forever saved from our falsely self-accepted selves. These undisciplined waves of non-spirituality invariably break in upon the self-realizing of our divine selves. Thus, our objective existence is encrusted in constant turmoil, and this eternal turbulence forever requires the welcome quelling of our self-acknowledging and self-accepting of our God-identity.

We may deny the existence of our spirituality, but we cannot deny our spirituality out of existence. God is our soul. Nothing ever enters into or is ever removed, from the temple of our divinely derived and commonly shared soul. Thus, our infinite soul-nature is forever emblazoned with the essence, power, and goodness of God.

Thus, in the forever purity of our individualized-soul, nothing ever changes, modifies, alters, or denies that understanding, not even the false interpretations of ourselves. We are infinite and indestructible, but unless we truly self-accept that understanding, that realization remains forever challenged by the gods of whim and unpredictability.

Divine spiritual knowledge always guides us to a self-acceptance of God's forever non-focused will, through our ever-evolving spiritual self-awareness. We are the understanding of God, seeking the knowledge of God, as the understanding of God. Thus, our forever objective destiny is to be the self-realization of God, in self-active expression.

The unreal often appears to us as a beggar, at the door of our self-awareness, forever in humble begging for our acceptance. The great spiritual gift to ourselves is to acquire the self-conscious ability to deny the unreal, entrance into the enclosure of our self-divinity, through the effortless knowingness of divine truth.

When falsity in its myriad of enchantments parades before our evolving self-consciousness; it is the out-picturing of the theoretical deeply embedded within our accepted self-identity, trying vigorously to replace ever-present divinity, with godless unreality pleading and clamoring mightily for recognition and acceptance.

Until the time comes when our total self-conscious self-will is directed to experience only the real, is the unreal denied its self-expression, in the non-real realm of experience. Unfortunately, none of us ever progresses to that holy place of divine fulfillment, until we have objectively and self-consciously demonstrated our spiritual mastery over this present venture of experiencing existence.

Our housing of God is our understanding of God. Our destiny is to be the self-realization of God embracing all things real and making invisible all things unreal. Our past, present, and future remain inseparable from the presence of God, accepted or not accepted. Our forever present and ever always abode of beingness is the creating of the house of our self-everlasting divinity. This abode of self-divinity is a house we self-consciously construct and reconstruct, within our self-knowingness of changelessness.

We each have the infinite capability of increasing or decreasing, in the self-realizing, of our divine identity. We must evolve spiritually to a place where our interpretations of existence, validates our uniquely expressing divinity. The sole purpose for our existence is to understand our real divine selves and then experience the joys resulting from that infinitely divine understanding.

When our interpretations of truth, lack desire for spiritual understanding we become lost, in a labyrinth of non-directed self-conscious thought influences, tearing down the walls of our self-evolving divinity. Thus, we self-destruct ourselves, into the realms of unreality, where we continue to experience existence, without desiring a self-conscious relationship to God.

Although spiritual truth itself is absolute, our individual interpretation of reality makes the divinity of truth about our understandings. Themes of truth, devoid of any sense of divine morality, breed the unruly clouds of false perceptions, which appear ever alluringly above us and below us.

Our destiny is to strive forever to understand the absoluteness of truth wrapped in divinity. In our ongoing understanding of divine truth, each one of us is a dedicated cornerstone supporting the forever substance of infinity, with our self-realizing of infinite existence.

Regardless of how we interpret our destiny, there is one primary spiritual absolute, applicable to all members of God's perfect family. This spiritual absolute is unequivocal and mandatory for our successful experiencing of existence. We must always choose to follow the highest divine worthiness of our evolving spiritual understanding. If we fail in that endeavor, we corrupt our evolving spirituality and become the corrupted and immoral pawns of this world.

As divinely growing members of the forever emerging family of God, we self-consciously demonstrate the truths we understand. However, assimilating the understandings of truth and expressing those perceptions are not necessarily the same divine substance composing our self-evolving beingness. For example, understanding the wrongfulness of our selfish acts and still choose to act selfishly is our understanding of spirituality circling itself in a corrupted contradiction.

We must always choose and make the self-conscious effort, to demonstrate the highest spiritual awareness of our understanding. It requires our unwavering holy divine effort to express ourselves at the level of our spiritual evolving. Thus, the challenge of our objective existence is always to externalize the highest understandings of our self-divinity in expression.

Absolute truth is never to be fully understood by any of us. Absolute truth is only recognized, in segmented golden rainbows of our divinity, in expression. Each rainbow arc only represents a tiny, infinitesimal grasp of reality. Thus, our demonstration of the highest spiritual good varies from individual to individual, because we are at irregular progressions, in the spiritual understanding of ourselves, as we climb the ladder of experiencing our forever unfolding self-realized existence.

Our highest spiritual welfare self-acquired expresses through the strength of our pure and holy convictions. Above all things, the demonstrations of our spiritual understandings represent the self-consciousness of our divinity, in our material stream of expressions.

When we self-understandingly and self-willingly express our developed spirituality, as treasured divine nuggets of spiritual purity, we become in self-conscious expression that which we are in self-conscious divine truth.

All spiritual demonstrations equal the degree of our spiritual receptivity to the divinity of truth. By obeying our highest understanding of self-accept, we self-consciously accept the God of infinite and utter kindliness, in our thoughts and actions. Thus, we glorify the presence of God which is the pure substance of our forever beingness in divinity.

It is often possible for us to become lost in vain spiritual foolishness, but our true spiritual destiny remains forever intact. Unfortunately, there are many so-called followers of God devoid of the recognition of kindness, understanding, compassion, and tolerance. They trumpet their interpretations of spirituality, through an array of self-announcing flat notes of depravity.

The foolish creators of the non-genuine quickly reveal their false perceptions of things divine. Still, if we to allow it to be meaningful to ourselves, these false chest-thumping teachers and preachers may serve as a spiritual impetus as we follow our self-understood spiritual paths. With our eyes spiritually focused, we can choose to see through the fogginess of falsely presented spirituality; rather, we can decide to see only the God of divinity "in smiling repose" as Ralph Waldo Emerson so aptly described Him.

Thus, it is our forever choice; we can opt to be spiritual victims, or we can choose to exercise the power of our divinely evolving understanding, and drive all false claims of spirituality attacking the sanctity of our ever developing spiritual understandings of ourselves, to the far rims of oblivion.

Wherever disharmony is perceived, the authentic God of our individual and independent revelation is not being self-consciously acknowledged. It is not possible to understand the whole and real God of our divine yearning while dishonoring the God of our understanding and acceptance.

In the spiritual evolving of God's family, the spiritually homeward bound always realize the God of their divine awakening. Thus, the one true God has is realized in infinite and progressing mystical and non-mystical realizations. The God of our understanding which promotes the wholiness of harmony in all things in existence is our forever faithful, everlasting, and ever obedient God.

Each of us is punished for our actions if our actions are shown to be thoughtless, selfish, harmful, and self-serving. We cannot fool ourselves by pretending to act in a spiritual manner, while those actions do not represent our highest self-realization of good. To surely understand God is to do the highest good of our self-knowingness notwithstanding the consequences. To self-knowingly do the highest good is the action of a spiritual warrior, unafraid, undaunted, incorruptible, and serene.

There comes a time when our courage to accept only God-based truths delivers us into a spiritually humble acceptance of God's Beingness. At this moment, God becomes our Servant because He provides to our self-knowingness, all our spiritual needs. This spiritual understanding scuttles the tentacles of bondage, resulting from our self-imposed limitations having burdened the understanding progression of our spirituality.

Thus, our increasing understanding of God's nature brings our increasing deliverance from the false bonds of godlessness which continuously seek to badger our self-awareness for acceptance. Each one of us is representative of God's continuing existence, in the objective realm of experience. God suffers His Self-existence through each one of us. Thus, we are the forever part of God's nature bearing the suffering of infinite existence.

We manifest God's presence in the realm, of our self-actuating experiences. By doing good, we impress the presence of God onto things we objectively experience, as we are self-willingly experiencing existence as life divine. Divine goodness self-accepted in our self-consciousness of God actively expressing through us.

Through the goodness of our spiritual self-evolving, the power of God banishes all godlessness of unreality, from the vacillating of our defining un-evolved spirituality. Thus, our continual doings of things good leads us to our eternal and infinite salvation, forever and only temporarily understood and realized. Everything entailing the realizing of our perpetual experiencing of existence requires endless salvation.

Spiritual transformation and salvation result from our eternal and infinite self-consciousness of truth, experiencing unchanging reality. Our spiritual transformation results from our spiritually developed un-encumbered divine self-awareness. It is our unencumbered acceptance of divine truth forever liberating us from the cobwebby anti-gods, thrashing about, in the bottomlessness of infinite existence.

Spiritual transformation and salvation, which comprise many levels of spiritual awakening, seldom occur quickly. Our self-developing sense of spirituality comes through our self-conscious cultivation of our forever divine self-awareness which is encouraging us forever onward.

No one can save any of us, but ourselves. We alone determine our divine right to self-exist harmoniously. Our infinite and individual lives require understanding the needs for the infinite saving of ourselves. In the ever increasing of our awareness and divine self-receptivity to the wholiness of God, which is infinitely reverberating through us, our forever need of salvation is fulfilled.

Our progressive salvation requires humility and receptivity to things divine. Salvation occurs as our self-conscious sense of godlessness is unveiled to reveal our ever-present unfolding divinity, as the inheritors of self-consciously experiencing life. Thus, each one of us is an observer and an actor throughout objective reality's endless eternities, at the increasing level of our continuing spiritual reawakening.

Each one of us is on a camel ride throughout the infinity of our beingness, roaming from one heavenly oasis to the next. The self-acknowledging of our divinity, along with our overriding desire to understand the infinite progression of our soul is our forever spiritual journey of self-discovery, self-realization, and self-unfoldment. There is no escape from our destiny to know ourselves infinitely.

To understand that each one of us is the expression of God's goodness is to understand that our infinite existence is an unearned blessing, which each of us must spiritually evolve to understand, accept, and to realize. However, each one of us alone and individually determines which parts of our infinite existence, we will experience as blessings.

Thus, each one of us gives meaning and power to the infinite expression of our infinite existence. Absolute reality cares not a whit about the free will choices which cause our sufferings. Our sufferings are unknown to infinity because infinity does not interpret itself. Suffering is unknown to God because He is not capable of understanding Himself. We alone, in all of existing reality, understand the meaning of suffering.

Only one of our choices entails lasting meaning. We can choose to be forever finite-infinitely Godlike, or we can continually decide to be finite-infinitely non-God-like. Our infinitely innate ability to make free will choices gives us the capability for attempting to understand the why and the wherefore, of our forever self-conscious existence.

All the spiritual transformation we ever experience is incremental, as we evolve in and through the understanding of our divine existence. Our spiritual transformation and salvation is the forever outcome of our infinite attaining, claiming, and maintaining of the never culminating realization of the fullness of our divinity.

Our unique individuality in God determines the path of our spiritual awakening and reawakening. To self-consciously experience the divine fulfilling of our individualized physical destiny is to demonstrate the presence of God's love, in our self-active choices. We are self-embracing our divinity, as we choose to express the divinity within us.

In the physical realm, our spiritual understandings evolve infinitely; the refining experiencing of our spirituality is infinite. Suffering the consequences for lack of our divinely based perceptions is infinite, and the rewards for our genuinely accepted spiritual beliefs are also infinitely endless.

The above conclusions are valid because we infinitely experience objective physical realities, in our forever excursions through objective reality and objective realities. It is interesting to note that we have the potentiality of experiencing, in the physical realm, all that we can experience in the spiritual realm. However, given the understanding that we have existed infinitely, how spiritually pathetic we are, in the acknowledgment of our infinite existence as pathetic spiritual creatures?

All the things we forever experience are the things we experience because we are forever spiritual beings, in the process of endlessly presenting our divine credentials, to the physical realm. The authenticity for our right to proffer our holy credentials is the presence of God, forever indwelling our forever self-beingness.

In the physical realm, our self-immersed self-centered selfishness attempts to obtain things non-deserved. Our foolish myopic forms of non-divine understandings delude and denude our spiritual undertakings. Selfishness is the ignorance of divinity because it brandishes the non-realization that we are infinite spiritual beings, possessing the infinite ability to amass knowledge, which is the forever fulfiller of our forever desires.

In our firm understandings of God, all things divine, are freely given to the God through our ever-evolving perceptions of reality. We receive spiritually only the things we divinely acknowledge and embrace, by the strength of our conviction to self-assuredly absorb ourselves, in the presence of God. Would there be any fairness, to anyone's infinite self-awareness, if the religiously non-deserving received blessings not spiritually entitled to receive?

There is no saving divine spiritual power attached to anything in the physical realm, and there are no shortcuts to our spiritual salvation. This present physical world is sadly awash with religious gimmicks serving only to delay the realization of our true spirituality.

Spiritual gimmicks are easy to identify. Anything or anyone that promises spiritual rewards requiring no divine effort, other than a nodding acceptance of an eager desire for spiritual rewards, denotes a gimmicky religious practice. We must see in our actions, the depth, quality, and character of our evolving spirituality or we become seekers of unmerited spiritual blessings.

In the objective realm, if spiritual understanding required no effort, the experiencing of existence would be unnecessary. We experience existing reality to validate our evolving perceptions of things divine. In our physical-Man existence, we continuously demonstrate the power of evolving understanding. Our self-existence requires our self-understanding, and that requires effort. We are unable to know our infinitely self-consciously divine selves if we are not able to understand our infinitely self-consciously divine selves.

There is nothing in all existence that possesses a sacred key, which enables us to secure our divine destiny, unencumbered by the illusions of unreality. Our divine fate is only realized in surges of spirituality, overcoming the trials and tribulations of experiencing our lives, as self-aware existence in expression. A great mistake we all make, in the living of life, is to cede to others the power for determining the spiritual direction of our unfolding divinity in expression.

We exist to understand and demonstrate our infinite existence with God. We should listen kindly and attentively to all those who speak truth with kindness, but we are only obliged to obey the divine foreverness resting securely within our soul. God never abandons us; thus, divine truth and salvation are forever present and forever ours. Each one of us has an individual relationship with God, separate and unique from the Godly relationships of all others.

With our God-lit self-consciousness, we reject the false appearances of ungodly-inharmony and transform those false appearances into harmony realized. The strength of our self-aware understanding of things divine determines our spiritual success in the divine experiencing of our forever existence.

In the correct understanding of reality, all things having real permanence manifest their self-aware or non-self-aware existence.

In the realm of experience, harmony is the distillation of Godliness through our eyes, observing our obedience to the self-conscious cultivation of divine certainties. Only in our spiritually evolving understanding of divine truth can we see wholeness, balance, and harmony in all things expressing existence, as reality in infinite flux.

Our spiritual potentialities are infinite, but will remain forever undiscovered if there is no impetus for their self-conscious discovering, accepting, and demonstration. We coexist with God in the foreverness of His innate divine nature. If there were nothing left of our divinity, to understand, our existence would lose the transforming power to overcome the endless throbbing challenges of godless unreality.

Thus, God and our individualized self-beingness are eternally and infinitely sacredly combined, yet sacredly separate. Still, our desire to understand God forever guides us through the experiencing of our infinite existence. In our understanding of God, we alone and individually, choose to make Him our Forever Guide.

We are the self-accepted perceptions of all things we experience. The realm of our spiritually evolving experience mirrors our conscious and self-conscious thoughts, based on the strengths and convictions of our mind-bred conceptions of reality. The choices we make revealing experiences of harmony reveal the self-evolving of our spirituality.

The experiencing of our destiny continues, to be fulfilled and unfulfilled, throughout the vastness of eternities experienced. As individualized members of God's family, each of us is infinitely linked with one another. Although our divine destiny, forever understood by each of us individually, is infinitely bound together to the entirety of God's family. Through each one of us, God has known, is knowing, and forever knows Himself, in the timelessness of infinity.

We all share the same divine soul, the same divine mind, and the same divine purpose. The present realizing, of our destiny, is always to be spiritually fulfilled in the eternity we are occupying. However, our spiritual victories failures are infinite, and our understanding of all reality is infinite because we are infinite. The infinity of our existence as reality is forever God-based.

Why does each one of us possess infinite self-awareness? There is no answer to that question. There is a purpose to our existence, but that does not explain the reality of our forever self-awareness. True, each one of us is the expression of God, and God knows Himself through each of us. Still, that does not explain why we have individual and forever self-conscious awareness.

One of our present eternal physical realm needs is to eliminate all tinges of sorrow, heartache, trouble and unhappiness, by self-consciously identifying with our divine nature, and with the wholeness of ideas. Our infinitely holy instinct is to exalt experiences of joy, through our self-evolving understanding of harmony, as the substance constituting the reality of ideas, accepted, realized, and utilized.

Again, it is our ability to understand all the intricacies of the actuality of existence that powers the fulfilling of all of our expressions, in the hypothetical realm of experience. Thus, this understanding ability gives us supreme authority over all things real. If we cannot understand our infinite existence, we cannot determine the spiritual path to the fulfilling of our divine destiny. There is no escape, we infinitely exist, to infinitely understand, an infinite existence, we will never infinitely understand.

Truth externalized always corresponds to the depth of our spiritual understanding. Our forever self-recognized existence is spiritually realized, through the certainty of our spiritual thoughts. It seems paradoxical that while our infinite self-existence is real; our infinite understanding of our forever continuing self-existence is self-consciously understood and interpreted, in the infinitely non-real realm of experience.

The perfect divinely designed structure embedded into the reality of our infinite existence enables each one of us to self-identify as a sinner, evildoer, or saint. As sinners and evildoers, we are always challenged to define reality falsely. We design the sins we allow expression through us, as we continually progress in our whimpering experiencing existence.

What are sinners and evildoers? Sinners and evildoers are saints self-expressing as sinners and evildoers. Thus, sinners and evildoers are the infinite non-real shadows of divinity. Looking at the totality of our infinite self-aware existence, in the objective realm, the primary difference between sinners, doers of things evil, and saints is the spiritual rewards given only to the saintly and the meaninglessness of life revealed to the sinners and evildoers.

Our immediate compensated destiny for each one of us is forever realized, in our ever-evolving thoughts, whether morally good, sinful, or evil. Can there be any greater self-realization than to acknowledge and understand that each one of us is in control our forever destiny and how our forever destiny is to be self-realized? Our choice to be a sinner, an evildoer, or a saint is infinite and infinitely realized.

There is never a spiritual finality to our infinite self-aware existence. Our infinite self-aware beingness is finality in and of itself. Thus, each one of us is infinitely self-aware of our real and unreal divinity. Still, in our self-choosing acceptance of non-divinity, we remain infinite divine beings, although not acknowledging, not wanting, not desiring, and not cherishing the foreverness, of our divine reality.

Our free will choices forever determine our finite-infinite destiny. Thus, our infinitely revolving spiritual fate is to be experienced as the reality Godly understood, or godless unreality self-accepted and assumed. It is always our understandings and acceptance of God that provides the spiritual quality in the self-beingness of our self-existence.

Thus, we are the determiners of our forever unfoldment, in the non-real real realm of experiencing life. In the fullness of actual objective life, we are forever sinless and evil is fangless. In the fullness of false objective reality, we are forever sinners and evildoers, with the fangs of evil continually piercing our deific desired thoughts, as we flounder in the throes of attempting to understand the experiencing of existence.

Only through the non-real realm of created experience does godless unreality assert its unreal existence. Still, it is the non-real realm of experience that enables us to understand and demonstrate our forever evolving spirituality. The purpose for our infinite existence is only recognized and validated in the unreal realm of experience. We exist to experience our real divinity, but the experiencing of our real divinity is not real.

We cannot deny our divine nature and reap the spiritual joy-filled benefits ensuing from our self-identification with our inner divinity. Thus, we cannot go directly from the physical realm into the spiritual realm. After our journey into the physical realm is complete, we enter into the purgatorial realm. Here our eternal destiny is purged, evaluated, determined, and judged by each one of us individually.

When the eternity we are self-consciously occupying ends, everyone returns to his or her individual formless state of transbeingness. In the formless realm, the once physical realm saints, sinners, and doers of things evil continue to coexist equally, in a self-consciously aware forever harmonious mental environment, where experiencing self-aware existence is not possible.

Understood or not understood, each of us is God's love in active self-expression. Our collective destiny is a golden bond forever blending all of our individual and unique interpretations of God. We exist as distinctly unique and divinely gift-endowed members of God's family who is forever expressing endlessly, individually, and uniquely.

Our collective spiritual destiny is to reveal the love of God forever. For all the spiritually like-minded, the self-aware acceptance of God is a universal blessing to be universally shared. Except for our existence, in core reality, there never comes a time when all members of God's family possess a self-aware purity of divinity, in the forever self-thinking of existence.

Experiencing physical reality is our divine destiny. We are fulfilling our purpose for our existence, as we experience the reality of life. The endless self-actuating self-conscious expression of our self-awareness is in the forever process of interpreting and understanding ourselves, through our creations of experiences. Thus, each one of us is the endlessly creative in our understanding of our preordained destiny.

Our experiencing of the physical realm requires the continuing evolving of our developing and redeveloping of our self-understandings of ourselves. One of the most important of these understandings is the recognition that we attract to ourselves the cherished properties of our thoughts.

If we cherish a desire to welcome the callings of godless unreality, the finger-curling sirens of sensuality entice us to turn from our innate divinity, and accept the goddesses of unreality, swaddled in emanations of dancing shadows. Unreal reality forever appeals to the vice-ridden senses of our crawling self-awareness, rather than to divine understandings of our spiritually strengthening self-awareness.

However, if we cherish the desire to seek always and only the divinity of supreme truth, we attract avenues of spiritual guidance, which serve to awaken and reawaken our spiritual yearnings, to be faithful to the discovering of our forever divinity. The infinite existence of non-reality is continuously seeking to drive us into a closed-eyed godless slumber, a slumber we can only be awakened, by self-consciously identifying ourselves with the divine light *flamelessly* illuminating our soul with the presence of God.

Our forever divine existence, in objective reality, is the presence of God in expression. As we evolve in our spiritual undertakings, we learn to protect ourselves from the bewitching enticements of the godlessness of unrealities, by cherishing the understanding that our forever divine destiny is to experience the foreverness of our divinity.

We always remain infinitely holy even as we turn our backs to the truth of our divine beingness. True happiness realized is never based on false physical quicksand realm god-denied understandings. In the experiencing of existence, we realize true happiness, by unconditionally understanding and accepting the divinity that is forever enveloping us, as the very essence of God.

Thus, true happiness results for the self-acceptance of our real divine selves. The only thing of lasting consequence is to know that wherever we may self-consciously be, in body, mind, or soul, we are in the presence of God. The painful realization that we all must overcome is that when we experience life, as our non-real selves, we believe that we are experiencing life as our real and true divine selves. Only through pure spiritual understanding can we identify as the authentic expressions of God.

True happiness is only fulfilled through the purity of God understood. Our forever choice, in the experiencing of life, is to experience life with or without God. In the physical realm, we realize God through the limitations of growing understandings. Thus, our understandings of God are sloshed with hypnotic and beguiling sprinklings of unreality, continually assuring us that we have found that for which we forever seek. Only when we strive to identify with God, at all times, have we found the self-consciousness we divinely desire.

Each of us is in an alternative state of spiritual evolvement, development, and progression. We always view objective reality from an individual perspective. Just as beauty is in the eye of the beholder, truth is in the eye of the beholder. The marvel of our existence is that all the goodness and beauty of truth forever resides within each one of us. It is the harmony of goodness forever within us that we seek to understand, experience, and be known to us as the presences of God.

As individualized physical-Man, we can see and appreciate beauty, but the beauty we see, in the physical realm, is a mere shadow of the things divinely beautiful, we are destined to experience in the spiritual realm. The depth of our capacity to see and enjoy beauty is forever linked to our ever-evolving ability to self-consciously, and unquestionably adhere to the indwelling presence of infinite goodness. We forever are the spirituality we yearn to be.

Thus, the beauty we see about us is incomparable to the forever beauty residing within us. As the sculptor shapes and cuts his chosen stone, beauty is unveiled. This vision of grandeur had remained dormant in the lifeless stone. When we self-consciously identify ourselves with the presence of God, the beauty we see emerging from the eternal stone is the outer revealing of God's inner nature, and thus we realize God at the level of our understanding. We see beauty in an object as the reflection of our divinity. We feel the beauty in an object as the introspection of our God-derived divinity.

Experiencing existence is the fulfilling of our destiny as we self-understand it individually. When our self-created experiences are continually devoid of the understanding of our forever divinity, they become enveloping anacondas of evilness, strangling and squeezing our self-conscious separation, from an ever active awareness of the presence of God. Evil's audacity to be accepted is its claim that it can squeeze God out of existence.

Forever evilness results from our infinite free will capability to self-consciously separate ourselves from God. The things we allow to separate our self-awareness, from the presence of God become the triumphs of evil, dancing and clapping gleefully, by our self-acceptance of its mesmerizing presence. Thus, evil exists as a forever free will choice but has no real existence separate from self-knowingness. We are the evilness we create into the godless unreality of experience.

False beliefs continually challenge the steadfastness of our understanding of God. The assertions of godless unreality bombard us because our desire to discover spiritual truth necessitates spanning the spectrum, of our limited evolving perceptions of truth, or sense of doubt. However, unwavering faith in God renders false perceptions of truth impotent.

We forever experience doubt because we are in the forever divine process of understanding ourselves. If we ever actually experienced the fullness of our divinity, self-doubt would never be an accepted into our thoughts. Our self-conscious existence would become void of challenge and purpose. It that was ever to happen, we would no longer seek any understanding of ourselves, and our lives in the objective realm would no longer have any infinite meaning. We would then be the self-infinite knowingness of pure divinity, with nothing to motivate us.

Incredible as it may be, for all of our stumbling faults, poor choices, and spiritual myopia; we forever remain eternal, infinite, and indestructible. However, we will forever stay in a self-conscious denial of our true selves until we reawaken to the realization that we are God's divine messengers, always and forever presenting our spiritually empowered credentials to all aspects of objective reality.

Without the God-presence within each one of us, the entirety of ultimate reality could never be interpreted through the realization of God's nature. We are individually and collectively the self-aware soul of God's presence. It is our forever understanding of the depth-beingness of God which enables us to interpret goodness, beauty, harmony, perfection, and joy into all of objective reality's real expressions.

How we think and how we act may seem different, but they are identical twins in relationship to our evolving spiritual sense of beingness. The realm of physical experience is the forever proving grounds for the reflecting back to us, the depth of our spiritual advancement, enhancement, and enchantment for things divine.

We are forever self-consciously expressing our objective understandings or misunderstandings of ourselves and our existence. Each one of us exists to understand our existence, and then to self-consciously, experience our existence. The realization that there is no explanation for our infinite self-aware beingness strongly indicates that we infinitely exist.

If there were an explanation for our infinite existence, that would presuppose the existence of some form of intelligence, outside of ourselves. If there were an infinite intelligence, besides us, we could never be in absolute control, in the evolving understanding of our infinite beingness. For our infinite existence to have a meaning, we together and individually must give it the infinite worthiness of meaning.

If we justify our wrongful, hurtful, evil and sinful acts, we devalue our existence. Thereby, we devalue the experiencing of life. Even though the experiencing of reality is an unsought gift, we must create the understanding of our infinite existence. Thus, each one of us must forever determine, for ourselves, what our forever beingness means.

Our correct or incorrect interpretations of our infinite existence have absolutely no impact upon the infinite-Us. We forever self-consciously choose to be that which we forever self-consciously desire to be. Obviously, that is both a gift and a curse. Imagine each of us has an infinite self-conscious untouchable existence that we can choose to experience in any manner whatsoever. If we were determined to consistently experience, godless unreality, would our forever self-conscious suffering of life, still be considered a gift?

All sin and evil is the chomping and gnawing of ignorance vying for our self-conscious attention and acceptance. In the physical realm, our understanding is infinite; therefore, our ignorance is infinite. Thus, sin and evil are infinite in their ever presence to grab at reality. The forever problem each one of is required to negotiate endlessly is that our forever understanding of actual reality requires our forever understanding of non-actual reality. In this process of perpetually acquired understanding, we give self-power to each, until we enthrone God into our self-awareness.

As we remain, sinners and evildoers, we remain spiritually unworthy to appreciate the gift of our forever existence, because we are continually misinterpreting things divine. Although God's nature is to seek forever unification with each of us, we are the only ones capable of interpreting and understanding that forever spiritual unity.

We need God; God does not need us. Without each of us, God remains non-understood, and His existence is devoid of any purposeful realization, other than to Himself. Without God's existence, we would have no sacred identity to realize, embrace, fulfill, and empower. Thus, our infinite existence and God's infinite existence are infinitely intertwined, but only from our individualized perspective.

Our understanding of the nature of God allows for the interpretations of ultimate reality. Our developing spirituality is our receptivity to things divine. God's nature is forever calling us; however, we must actively seek His call before we can respond to His call. Thus, our successful experiencing of existence requires the seeking of God and receptivity to the nature of God's calling. Our divine receptivity to God's nature is how we save ourselves. Paradoxically, we are forever infinitely saving our lost selves, who are never infinitely lost.

Our forever salvation is the realizing and the accepting of our oneness with God. Our self-accepted identity in God is the power of divine truth saving us from the engulfing swamping torment of self-accepted falseness. Thus, in the objective realm, we are continually being immersed by the sucking-sands godless unreality.

We harmonize our evolving understanding as we increase our awareness of God. As our free will choices return to us, as our self-aware understandings and acceptance of God, our destiny is self-realized, in the realm of experience. If we have no desire to use our free will to seek God, God does not exist, God's nature does not exist, and God's comforting presence does not exist to us.

However, it is our divine destiny to use our free will to become spiritually receptive to the greatness, the goodness, and the Godness of the divine truth forever revealing itself into our self-awareness. Moreover, fortunately, spiritual opportunities are ever-present, but still, it is the lack of our free will spiritual receptivity which often allows those golden spiritual opportunities, to go unnoticed.

Without a persistent desire to understand God, we use our will to imprison ourselves, in a self-conscious labyrinth of godless unreality. As we choose to accept God, our free will choices become blessings, as the self-known source of our divinity. To make a conscious decision not to experience the goodness of God is to choose to experience the godlessness and lifelessness of non-divinity.

When our self-consciousness becomes imbued with an active awareness of the presence of God, we are spiritually rebirthed into a new understanding, of our objective reality. Our self-conscious love of God eventually elevates our free will to the place where choosing to experience any desired existence contrary to the nature of God is an impossibility.

We spiritually protect ourselves by strengthening our understanding of our forever divinity. Bad things happen to good people because they have not protected themselves from accepting misinterpretations of the forever roaming ideas. The idea realm ideas move, in and around our collective self-consciousness, both in their purity and in the covered vestments of our false perceptions.

All infinite idea realm ideas are innately harmonious. However, it is forever possible, for our ever evolving self-conscious awareness, to inharmoniously interpret, shape, and mold ideas, into the non-real realm of experience. Now, unreality becomes a component of the non-real realm of experiencing existence, and thus we experience unreality as reality.

Thus, ideas appear to our self-realizing awareness as something other than their real nature. Still, no ideas are ever harmful when we spiritually progress to the place, where we self-consciously refuse to accept any false representations or interpretations of ideas. In our evolving spiritual understanding, we experience our understanding of ideas to understand God, ultimate reality, and our infinite divine selves.

To protect ourselves, we must understand our pure divinity to interpret ideas in their true spiritual and harmonious natures. All appearances of disharmony result from our spiritually fragmented self-awareness mixing the forever real, with the forever unreal. Thus, bad things happen to good people because they have not been diligent in uprooting their falsely interpreted assumptions about seeming reality they are experiencing.

With God as our infinite self-realized companion, we are forever participants in the wondrous treasures involved in the experiencing of existence. We are the self-conscious portion of God's divinity, in forever divinely unfolding expression, whether we understand or not understand our forever divine existence. We can never escape from the progressing of our divinity. However, we are always capable of not choosing to accept the goodness of God's Godness. The godless members of the divine family interpret their infinite ability to choose, as making their infinite existence superior to God's infinite existence.

Real spiritual progress results from the purification of our thought processes, as we dismiss the false assertions of godless unreality sending them back to their non-reality of nothingness. As our spiritual choices self-consciously mingle with our non-spiritual decisions, our spiritual progress inches along, at varying degrees of non-spiritual darkness interspersed with alternating arrays of spiritual light.

The unreality of nothingness is the depthless abode for all the false assertions of somethingness. As we understand the nothingness of unreality, we understand the somethingness of reality. Again, our free will ability to comprehend our forever existence enables us to interpret unreality, into the realm of experience.

The continuing infusions, into our self-consciousness, of divine graspings of truth serve as a never-ending process for our ongoing spiritual reawakening. We are forever spiritually objectively driven to rediscover the divinity within ourselves, forever derived from God. When we interpret objective reality, in concert with our forever God-identity, we put deity into our physical reality.

Each of us is unique in our choice of mystical paths. We embark upon our individual journeys as we self-consciously increase in our understanding of God. Within each of us is a spiritual compass forever pointing to the understanding of our infinite divinity, forever to be self-consciously activated, as we continue to fulfill our destiny, in the physical realm of existence.

Our divine destiny is to be the Self-conscious expression of God understanding His forever Self-divinity. If there were no such thing as self-conscious physical experience, we could never understand or interpret our divinely mandated destiny, forever implanted into each of us, as presently understood as our forever spiritual destiny.

In the experiencing of physical existence, each of us is self-fulfilling of God's Self-conscious knowingness of Himself. Our existence requires the fulfilling of our destiny. The successful fulfilling of our divine destiny requires the exultation of God, in our self-awareness.

Individuals who allow their free will to be influenced by others relinquish control of their free will existence. Without a self-controllable free will, we are not able to find the God of our understanding. Without embracing the God of our understanding, our free will actions are destined to cause harm to others. There can be goodness express without Godness, but that is a rarity, in the experiencing of existence, and represents spirituality in stagnation.

To cause real spiritual harm is to encourage others to do harm and to turn away from God. Still, the doers of things harmful, and the receivers of harmful things are both spiritually blind. To attempt to harm others spiritually shows the seeking of divine truth is not a personal priority. For those who allow themselves to be recipients of harmful things also indicates that their seeking of divine truth has not been an essential personal priority.

Even when evil and sinful acts serve as teaching lessons, we cannot raise higher, in our spiritual awareness, from the purposeful expressions of evil and immoral deeds. Even though we may allow others to influence our actions, we are always responsible for our thoughts.

If we do not seek the truth behind our sinful and evil wrongdoings, nothing has been spiritually learned, and our spiritual progress remains in the cesspool, of humanity's non-spiritual mental landfill of depravity. As we accept the claims of unreality, our awareness of spiritual knowledge is retrograding, but still progressing as the experiencing of existence. If there ever is an appearance of spiritual relapse, it is due to the lack of mental firmness, in the realizing of divine truth.

To intentionally try to spiritual harm another is a total disrespect of God and disrespect for the gift of life. Any attempt to spiritually harm another is non-spiritual darkness thickening around another's free will. All non-spiritual darkness endeavors to cover the personness of our divinity, striving to make itself understood.

All the godless unreality we ever encounter, in the realm physical, results from misinterpreting ideas. The persistence of these misinterpretations constructs, within our self-awareness, a sense of godlessness continually powered by our uninvolved spiritual perceptions. If we do not see our forever beingness as a blessing; God's existence is incapable of providing us with the self-acknowledgement that we are divine.

As sinners we often become so crunched and contorted by grief, we drench ourselves in numbing pain and lose sight of our divine heritage. Still, we must persevere in the light of inner divinity. Still, we must never lose sight of our God-identity. Still, we must enrich our self-awareness to the realization that we are the individualizations of God in active harmonious expressions.

Our God-driven selves know nothing of pain, heartache, and sorrow. We are forever the indestructible self-knowingness of God. We exist to exalt our divinity infinitely. We are our God-divinity pounding godless unreality into non-recognizable non-existence. We are the forever shouting thunderings of God subduing and subjugating anything, unlike our divine selves.

As long as our perceptions of godless unreality persist, we only partially acknowledge God. However, as we open the door of our self-conscious self-awareness and see only the God of infinite perfection, we deliver ourselves into the divine light of truth realized. Thus, we are in forever control in the realizing of the direction our destiny, and thus, we remain the forever source of our infinitely needed salvation.

Our ability to continually understand our lives as a divine gift forever unfolding, forever unique and forever self-actualized. In the experiencing of existence, we never able change what we truly are; we only modify the understanding of our true selves to ourselves. We modify ourselves to understand our forever existence with God, or we modify ourselves to understanding our forever existence without God.

Although our forever destiny is secure and intact, the pathways to the realizing of our destiny are forever fragmented, by the limitations of our evolving understandings and by the constrictions of our non-disciplined misunderstandings. Our infinite ongoing sojourns from core reality into objective reality denote the infinity of our existence being finitely and infinitely experienced.

Our forever existence is always tripping over and through the realms of the unreal. In our physical experience, the divine light of our inner divinity shines brightly, when the understanding of spirituality eternally remains self-sought. However, when our self-sought spirituality combines with our self-sought non-spirituality, it remains a cold, lifeless speck of divinity.

In our physical existence, if we choose to identify with our divinity, we self-consciously become the wholiness of God experiencing the wholiness of existence. As we express as the individualizations of the Man of God, we are individualizing God Himself. Forever and always, each one of us is knowing, unknowing, and re-knowing the allness of God.

It is not possible to rid ourselves of our true spiritual identity; however, we can become lost in our godless understandings, for the eternity we are self-consciously occupying. After being expatriated from core reality, if any member of God's family were to become eternally lost permanently, that would mean that a member of God's family, was removed from core reality, to experience an objective existence, not capable of being spiritually interpreted successfully.

Still, there is some sense of truth to that realization because as we look outward from within ourselves, we see the claws of depravity ripping and tearing ceaselessly, at our self-aware existence. Thus, if possible to appear spiritually lost, if anyone is incapable of rising above unreality's relentless attacks, upon the divinity of his or her beingness.

However, such spiritual abomination cannot be part of ultimate reality because we are infinitely designed to know God, understand God and self-consciously experience the reality of our spiritually. Each one of us possesses the infinite capability of ruling over our unique and personal inner infinity, but only as spiritually evolved beings.

Think of what it would mean, to our self-conscious presence in infinity, to choose infinite separation from God? We would exist infinitely without self-identifying with our true divine nature. Who would possibly desire such an existence? Unfortunately, many are those, of God's divine and perfect family, who self-consciously choose to make that the realization of their self-desired destiny.

Our forever objective purpose for our self-conscious physical existence is to return to a self-awareness of God, through divinely directed understandings as we traverse through eternities endless.

Experiencing reality without a self-awareness of God results in a non-disciplined form of so-called happiness, clinging to a false divinity of its making.

This form of self-accepted false divinity is always a distortion of our forever divine nature. Without a divine self-acceptance of God, we remain in a self-aware mental state of corruptible indestructibly. Even though the experiencing of existence is not real, the fundamental innate process, residing in each one of us, for our experiencing of life, is infinitely real.

To uncover, uproot, and dismiss things false, requires the acquiring of a disciplined spirituality based on a continuing desire to accept only God, as the divinely controlling source of our forever beingness. Wherever God is divinely self-accepted by us, godless unreality loses its inflated power, for announcing a life of its own.

To the spiritually minded, there is no such a thing as failure. However, failure remains a steady component of the ever evolving experiencing of our existence. In the truth of our existence in infinite objective reality, the experiencing of failure is required so we each eventually acquire the understanding of our forever spiritual self-evolving.

When the time comes that we no longer see failure in the circumstances we experience, our self-conscious awareness has been cleansed of all accepted appearances of unreality. Our present trek through objective reality no longer leaves footprints, in the sands of timelessness. When that occurs, we stay in the spiritual realm, until once again we self-choose to impel ourselves back into core reality.

Failures are blessings for the understanding of our spiritually. We divinely win our eternal destiny through the progressively spiritual outcomes of our failures. No failure is a failure when spiritual knowledge transforms that failure, into a self-conscious connection with the presence of God.

Each one of us objectively exists throughout the infiniteness of reality. Our forever existence is infinitely realized in our understanding, experiencing, unfolding, and self-determining of our divine destiny. If our self-existence wallows into a permanent cascade of sorrows, heartaches, and pains, then our forever self-aware existence becomes a curse, to our self-identities. It must be firmly understood; we forever exist to know reality and to understand unreality, to be able to identify ourselves as part of God.

Our divine spiritual progressions, as members of God's forever perfect family, remains infinitely individual, in the self-understanding of ourselves. As we look outward from within the Soul of God, the manner we choose to experience existence determines the level of happiness and joy, we discover, uncover, and recover within ourselves. All self-realized happiness, separate from God, renders our infinite self-aware survival in the realm of experience eternally tortuous.

Each eternity we spiritually experience expands the infiniteness of the self-discovering of ourselves. We forever exist to understand ourselves forever. In our self-understanding, each one of us is the all-powerful god of our infinite existence. However, our unlimited potential for all-powerfulness degrades into spiritual impotence, if our self-initiating power harms anyone or anything. Also, without our self-acceptance of God, our spiritual power, the only power that can be self-directed, has no divine authority to be made manifest. The strength of our trust in God is the strength of our power in God.

In our experiencing of eternities, spiritually advanced and progressed divine family members encourage wayward members of God's family, to recognize and undertake their spiritually evolving destiny. The common thread of our God family spirituality infuses each of us, with the same divinely intertwined soul. Either we become spiritually one in our self-known divinity, or our individual paths to true spirituality found long, arduous, and exceedingly painful until we attain total self-reliance on our understanding of God.

Thus, this joint sacred bond of our shared spirituality requires each one of us, as evolving divine beings, to spiritually encourage one another, at whatever level we are self-consciously experiencing our spirituality, to ensure that no one continues in his or her spiritual loneliness, blindness, and self-defeat.

We are forever divinely linked; there is no escape from that realization. We are forever united in the experiencing of existence. Thus, it is imperative that each of us manifest the kindness of spirituality to one another. As long as any member of God's family remains divinely lost, all members of God's family stay self-consciously incomplete, in their objective physical-realm self-aware existence.

Thus, our individual ongoing spiritual progression, through the objective realities we forever experience, is not possible without spiritually assisting the struggling members of God's perfect family. Thus, it is ceaselessly mandated, in the realizing of our divine destiny, that we divinely comfort and support the faltering of God's lost, struggling to understand the evolving of their spiritually.

Spiritual illumination dwarfs intellectual, spiritual understanding when it involves our spiritual progress. Our spiritual development is the combination of our self-conscious choices, combined with an active realization of the presence of God. Without a spiritually humble acceptance of God, the purpose of experiencing existence remains undefined, unfulfilled, and defiant.

Unless we remain forever humble in the understandings of our evolving spirituality, we will never realize the spiritual potentials, engraved into our individually and infinitely realized existence. For the spiritually reckless, the endowments of infinity are automatically withheld. Our evolving spirituality should always be cherished, never assumed.

Our never-ending attainable and non-attainable spiritual destinies are to experience all aspects of ultimate reality. However, our infinite capacity to understand all things real forever restricts our infinite existence because there is always something new to learn and experience. Thus, our understanding infinite reality is the forever condensation of infinity's forever nature, being self-realized by each of us.

Purgatorial-Man

In the non-physical purgatorial realm, we review our lives lived, and our lives potentially lived. Here, we suffer all deserved punishment for all of our harm doing to ourselves and others. This self-punishment is absolute, mandatory, and inescapable. Punishment serves as the source of our salvation; it guides to the understanding of the purpose for our infinite objective existence.

Punishment is the divine process resulting from our acceptance of limitation, constriction, and restriction which had seemingly bound our self-identity to the illusions of godless unreality. Our punishment is mandated because we have clothed our self-awareness in the glittering vestments of unreality. We covered over the purity of our divinity with the impurity of godlessness self-accepted.

The concept of punishment is unknown to all portions of ultimate reality devoid of self-awareness. Punishment only results from abusing the infinite structure of our infinite reality rooted deep into our infinite beingness. When we abuse the divine truth concerning our infinite selves, we are divinely punished to understand and accept the reality of our infinite divinity.

Our self-actuating self-consciously created experiences resulting in a continuing self-conscious denial of our divine perfection creates the development of a godless self-aware consciousness. Punishment received in purgatory is the result of our spiritual disobeying of our self-conscious purpose for experiencing life. To experience existence as a blessing, we must understand ourselves as spiritual beings, and obey our true divine nature.

There is no escape from the slightest degree of deserved punishment. All punishment is the result of our ungodly self-conscious abuse of life, in the experiencing of our forever existence. All of our self-conscious, self-actualizing false choices follow from our non-God-based decisions finding a means of expression. There is no escape from the slightest degree of deserved punishment. All punishment is the result of our ungodly self-conscious abuse of life, in the experiencing of our forever existence.

All evil and sinful wrongdoings deserve punishment, but we as individualized-Man, are the only components of ultimate reality possessing the self-awareness that requires punishment to validate, affirm, guide, and protect our self-consciously evolving existence, from being lost in the oblivion of aimless and groundless self-self-conscious choice making.

Therefore, our self-punishment enables us to understand and interpret our life to proclaim our undeniable reality to ourselves. If there was no such thing as self-punishment, there could be no such thing as spiritual learning. We achieve divine education, as we self-consciously empower our understanding, to manifest the qualities of God, into objective reality, to bring harmony into the realm of appearance.

In core reality, our self-awareness has no free will capability of understanding. In objective reality, our innate self-awareness is gifted with a free will. Without punishment, we could never channel our free will choices to guide and lead us, to the breathless vistas, summits, and pinnacles of our spiritual destiny.

Our cycles of existence have beginnings and endings, but still, they are forever without beginning or ending. All purgatorial punishment serves as a fire-burning catalyst to purge our self-conscious awareness, of all the ungodly penetrations of unreality. When our evolving understanding no longer requires eternal purgatorial punishment, the purgatorial realm becomes the repository for the non-compromising resisters rejecters of God.

In the understanding of our free will ability to make choices, there is good news and bad news. The good news is that even though we possess the infinite capacity of exercising a free will; our free will choices never put a scratch, dent, or stain in the foreverness of eternal, objective, or ultimate reality.

The bad news is that our repentant and unrepentant commissions of our free will sinful and evil acts of wrongdoing are thoroughly self-punished, without exception, whether or not those wrongful acts were intentional or non-intentional. We experience self-punishment to understand and interpret the wrongfulness of our ungodliness in expression.

When we first leave the physical realm and move into the mental only physical realm of purgatory, we still retain a sense of our physical world bodies. The first thing which occurs in this mental realm of purgatorial limbo is the reliving and reviewing of our just ended objective physical existence.

During our first life review, we self-consciously experience all the suffering for all the wrongdoings, evils, and sins we committed to ourselves and others. This self-punishing also includes wrongdoing to animals. Only through the self-conscious experiencing of pain are we able to self-acknowledge our wrongful actions.

Our evolving spirituality demands our respect for all life. Everything that lives is a blessing to our existence, for each of us to discover. Anything experiencing life as existence is capable of being harmed. Thus, we even feel the pain, of our evolved or non-evolved spiritual ignorance, due to our intentional or non-intentional abuse of the living environment. We are the guardians and protectors of all life because nothing else in all of ultimate reality is capable of that divine charge or authority.

If we never received punishment for our sinful and evil wrongdoings, there would have no spiritual obstacles to overcome because there would be no incentive to overcome them. Thus, our self-aware experiencing of existence would be void of the urge to acquire spiritual truth, understanding, and evolvement.

It is only through suffering the wrongfulness of our sinful and evil filled actions that paves the way for the understanding of our wrongdoings. Thus, we cannot begin our endless journey toward God, until we suffer and atone for all of our non-Godly behaviors. The atonement for our wrongdoings becomes our self-forgiveness. To understand our need for self-forgiveness enables us to understand ourselves spiritually.

We are punished for all of our wrongdoings, whether or not we perceived those wrongdoings as right doings. So many of the wrongful things we do in the physical realm, we attempt to self-justify to ourselves. Therefore, while we are experiencing the physical realm, we are often incapable of correctly self-identifying our sinful actions: hence, our need to self-evaluate our experiences in the physical realm, in our experiencing of the purgatorial realm.

When we move into the purgatorial realm, we experience all the physical realm pain caused by us, whether or not we self-consciously realized, and understood the harmfulness of our hurt-filled actions.

Thus, in the purgatorial realm, we self-realize how we knowingly and unknowingly caused hurt and pain to ourselves and others.

In the purgatorial realm, our self-punishment decreases and ceases, as we evolve to the realization of the wrongfulness, of all our actions. Here, we dedicate and re-dedicate ourselves to the renewal of our desire, to self-knowing be the spiritual inheritors, of our infinite existence. In other words, here we realize that we self-consciously exist to know, understand, and be the knowingness of our divinity in self-active expression.

The spiritual understanding of our destiny mandates that we will only finite-infinitely overcome our forever self-acceptance of godless unreality. Our self-active self-aware existence is in a forever war of opinion, understanding, knowledge, and interpretation eternally contesting the real, with the non-real real.

Before continuing, I wish to discuss an interesting and important concept. In the objective realm, due to the ever-present unpredictability of chance, opportunity, randomness, and general unpredictability, I present this theory that we all experience numerous potential lives. If that is not a correct understanding of our experiencing of reality, there is fairness to our self-conscious experiencing of life.

In the physical realm, we simultaneously self-consciously live multiple upon multiple potential lives. We are self-aware of each possible life as we realize it, with each life seeming as though it is our only life. Thus, in the living of actual or potential lives, we are continuingly encountering what I refer to as life-forks of unpredictability. When life-forks occur, possible "what if" lives become alternative lives self-realized. Thus, in the purgatorial realm, we understand the meaning and purpose of "what if" lives.

In the purgatorial realm, all actual and "what if" lives lived are equally reviewed and punished. Therefore, all "what if" lives self-consciously lived are accountable for all life choices made, whether they are good or non-good. Throughout all lives lived or potentially lived, the seeking, finding, and accepting the God of our understanding is our greatest life-meaningful accomplishment. Without accepting and obeying the God of our understanding, our infinite existence pales to insignificance.

All self-conscious existence must be evaluated and accounted for, to enable our immortal-Man selves to realize our forever spirituality. Thus, our "what if" lives coexist with our actual lives lived. In all lives, real or potential we have increased opportunities to seek, find, and follow the God of our understanding.

There is no spiritual difference between a real life lived, and a possible "what it" life lived. In reality, strange as it seems, even though we believe that we only live one life, we live hundreds or more lives, as a result of our ongoing life-altering encounters with the unpredictabilities of chance, opportunity, randomness, and general unpredictability. Each "what if" life is a life we could have lived, if not for the life-impacting forces of the unforeseeable.

Here is an example of a "what-if" life-fork. Suppose a young man around thirty years of age is happily driving along a beautiful scenic coast highway. Unpredictably, the hillside collapses and his crushes into shambles of scraps. If the young man dies or lives, what are the consequences? Either way, his self-conscious awareness is exposed to alternate directions of the living of his life, either he continues to live his life unharmed, he continues to live life in a life-altering injured manner, or he dies.

The above example illustrates how all the living of all lives, includes the living of potentially lived lives. The consequences of this understanding are monumental, both spiritually and non-spiritually. The experiencing of potential lives means that we self-consciously experience the living of life in so many ways, heretofore unknown.

I theorize that all real and potentially possible "what-if lives" are recorded, in some unknown manner and some unknown realm of ultimate reality. This recording of actual or potential lives only applies to life self-aware of itself. This forever information is an adjunct, to all immortal-Man's infinite existence to assist him in his forever understanding, of the reason for his infinite beingness. The above material seems to be a variation of the so-called Akashic Records.

However, if an all-knowing God exists, an all-knowing God would also know how all of the "what-if" lives lived.

No one is ever deprived of self-consciously experiencing the divine self-discovering of his or her forever existence. Babies, who die in the physical realm and then enter into the purgatorial realm, continue to relive their potential lives, in the same manner as anyone who self-consciously lives and experiences the physical realm.

Think of the interesting possibilities of the above theory. Suppose a baby dies, and then lives a "what-if" life, if the baby had not died. Now, in this "what-if" life, the individual discovers a cure for cancer. Thus, everyone having cancer, in this individual's "what-if" life, is cured. The infinite possibilities for the experiencing of everyone's "what-if" lives are unimaginable. Each "what-if" or "life-fork" life becomes a reality of its own.

As we review potential lives lived, these lives are also subject to the constant influence of chance, opportunity, randomness, and general unpredictability. Therefore, our mental reliving of possibility lives represents opportunities endless, to experience self-conscious existence. How interesting it is to realize that the ongoing experiencing of potential lives lived is how we finite-infinitely understand the nature of ourselves, in just one eternity inhabited?

It is unknown how many potential lives each of us may experience, but the potentiality of lives lived seems exhaustive. The continuing influences of chance, opportunity, randomness, and general unpredictability continuously provide the endless means for the possibility of self-aware alternative lives.

For example, due to unpredictability we do or do not accidentally meet someone. We win, or we do not win the lottery. We are injured, or we are not injured. We are talented, or we are not talented. We are athletic, or we are not athletic. We are charming, or we are not charming. Thus is the appearing of ongoing possibilities and seemingly endless opportunities, for the living of life, from a continuing variety of perspectives. Each unpredictable happening represents a "what-if" possible life, to be lived.

We review each of our possibly lived lives until we truly determine the desired understanding, of our eternal single-life, which includes countless "what-if" lives. However, it is the aggregate spiritual evolvement of our potential lives lived, which determines our eternal destiny. In other words, we do not experience countless spiritual destinies. For each eternity, we only experience one destiny, after our self-aware existence in the physical and purgatorial realms, based on the accumulated spirituality, or lack thereof, of our "what-if" lives.

Embedded within each of us is the unflinching design of our forever existence. All of our infinite objective existence is designed for each one of us to find God, and thus find our forever destiny in our forever divinity. All potentially lived lives blend to develop the depth of spiritual understanding, and receptivity to things divine. Thus, all possibly lived lives contribute to the evolving of our spirituality.

All possibly lived lives are reviewed, punished, and rewarded spiritually or non-spiritually. In all potential lives lived, it is still each one of us making all of our free will decisions. Experiencing possible lives gives each of us the possibility to understand our existence ever anew, from varied perspectives of experiencing life. Thus, one of our great gifts to our forever existence is this tremendous gift of unlimited opportunities.

There is a seeming built-in unfairness in our experiencing existence resulting from the continuing functioning of chance, opportunity, randomness, and general unpredictability. In other words, any one life lived may appear fairer or more unfair than another. Thus, due to the above factors of unpredictability, the opportunities for living lives levels out the unfairness of any individual life self-consciously lived.

All purgatorial lives mentally relived, reviewed, and suffered the consequences of wrongdoings committed, were continuously influenced by the factors of unpredictability. Thus, it is our spiritual overcoming and re-overcoming of our sinful and evil acts, committed in the physical realm, which is the source for all of our purgatorial spiritual progression.

It is a sobering realization that so many of the not predictive factors, in our physical lives are based on the seemingly uncontrollable influences of unpredictability. However, as we spiritually evolve, we become the spiritual masters over the sudden, unpredictable whims of chance.

Our potential for realizing and living our self-divinity is forever presented, to each one us. When we confirm, to ourselves, our unflinching divine loyalty to spiritual truth, the throes of unpredictability become powerless to affect the eternally resolute spiritual knowingness of ourselves, as divinely indestructible. Thus, our infinite salvation is assured, infinitely.

Our living of potential lives is a counterbalance to the unpredictability of experiencing existence. No single life which includes the forces of unpredictability determines anyone's eternal spiritual worthiness. Thus, fairness and unfairness are eternally made level in the living of our lives, actual or potential.

If lone unpredictable events, in the living of our lives, decided our finite-infinite spiritual understanding, progression, and unfoldment, our free will capacity to guide us divinely, would be severely encumbered. The experiencing of existence must be fair, or existence itself is incomprehensibly unfair.

Our self-conscious living of potential lives is a significant part of our objective realm destiny, by providing us with the gift of increasing opportunities to husband ourselves spiritually, to realize our inherent destiny, and thereby to become forever grateful for the gift of our infinite existence.

Living potential self-conscious lives demonstrates our innate spiritual feebleness because we require countless opportunities for overcoming the endless claims non-reality thrusts upon us, through predictable and non-predictable events. For our infinite existence to be spiritually determined, we must forever dethrone, within our self-awareness, the non-real claims of godlessness, to spiritual enthrone the divinity of God into our self-awareness. The living of potential lives provides such continuing opportunities.

As sinners and evildoers, we gratefully acknowledge the numerous opportunities, provided us to correct our wrongful choices. Thus, whether we are sinners, evildoers, or a combination of both, living potential lives continually provides opportunities to welcome sustained spiritual understanding, into our self-accepting self-awareness.

Thus, as sinners and evildoers, we are continually given opportunities to seek, find, and accept redemptive salvation, through developing a God-centered self-awareness. However, the spiritually wayward who regularly express themselves as doers of things evil, are eternally lost in their ungodly chosen destiny. In most of their potentially lived lives, they steadfastly chose to reject God. Sometimes the function of chance offers them the opportunity to choose to live a life of goodness: however, most of they opt to deny God, regardless of the influences of unpredictability.

Thus, evildoers consistently reject God, reject life, and reject life's gifts. However, before they become eternally lost, in their mostly consistent rejections of God, their individualized self-conscious awareness is always free to move through the gripping drizzle, frazzle, and dazzle of godless unreality, into the light of God-awareness self-accepted and realized.

However, even as evildoers continue to fulfill their non-divinely embraced destiny, they still recognize the hereditary design of their infinite existence. They are not Godly stupid; they are stupidly not Godly. They choose to attempt to experience their unlimited potential power without God.

Evildoers possess infinite existence but choose to remain unworthy of their forever divinity. For them to self-consciously accept divine salvation, they must self-consciously reunite with their inner self-divinity: this they refuse to do. Evil doers would rather deny their divinity than allow any spiritual control over their free will. Thus, their punishment for the godless living of their living of their lives lasts until either; they choose divine self-redemption or their callousness towards God remains reaffirmed.

All purgatorial punishment is for causing harmful wrongdoing only. There is no punishment for wrongful but non-harmful free will choices. For example, there is no purgatorial punishment for self-accepting the calculation of 2 plus 2 equaling 5. In the same manner, there is no purgatorial punishment for self-consciously merely choosing to reject

God. If no harm to done, in the living of any life, there is no punishing penalty.

Thus, for the poor choice of self-recognizing infinite life without God, there is no punishment. Infinite reality does not demand a self-aware acceptance of God. However, the self-conscious non-acceptance of God prevents evildoers from using the nature of God, to alleviate the constraining effects of godless unreality.

Non-God choice makers drift into godless realms of unmanageable unreality, most often resulting in the doing of evil deeds, for which all punishment ensues. However, these evil doers understand that their purgatorial punishment will eventually end, and so they continue in their self-conscious rejections of God.

Fortunately, most of us are eternal sinners, not consistent or persistent doers of things evil. After the number of our required life reviews are completed and we repent for our sinful wrongful wrongdoings; we accept all required punishment; we forgive ourselves and choose to unify ourselves with the presence of God. We have now prepared ourselves to receive the spiritual gifts, for recognizing and realizing, of our enlightened and holy self-existence in and with God.

As individualized purgatorial-Man, we self-evaluate ourselves for the eternity we are experiencing. Alone, each one of us is the only judge of our eternal destiny. The administering of purgatorial punishment is fair. There is no difference in the suffering penalties for all possibly lives lived and reviewed.

We only perform the life review process upon ourselves, to wash away all the sinfulness and evilness self-acquired, by our self-conscious awareness, in the living of our actual and potential lives. Most of us learn from the purgatorial realm, to make our self-conscious experiencing of existence harmonious beneficial, which then validates our infinite survival as an infinite being.

Our self-conscious life becomes spiritually meaningful to ourselves when we self-consciously re-unify ourselves with God. The self-acceptance of God is not a requirement of our infinite existence; even though each of us is forever in God, and God is our forever reality.

Thus, when we deny God, we deny the reality of our forever presence, in infinity.

Our self-consciousness is the controlling substance of ultimate reality. Our self-punishment guides us to the realizing and the fulfilling of our divine destiny. Without punishment, our existence could never be interpreted spiritually or accurately. Each one of us houses the only individual self-conscious power to interpret, understand, and make relevant all choices made, in the experiencing of our lives.

In our forever romp through the realizing of our self-existence, our self-realizing understanding is wandering unruly, without our desire for the divinity of convictions. Still, with or without God, our infinite capacity to understand and interpret existence shapes the reality of our experiences.

Thus, as we replace our acceptance of godless unreality with a genuine understanding of infinite reality, our divinity becomes self-consciously enshrined into the gifting of our forever existence. If we refuse to understand our existence, as a divine gift, we become heirs to seeming endless eternities of torment, heartache, and pain. For evildoers, this may be acceptable, for us sinners it is not.

One of the primary purposes, in the realizing, of our infinite existence, is to interpret objective reality. In our purgatorial experiencing of our potential lives lived, we objectify those lives, into our self-aware self-consciousness, making the experiencing of those lives seem like real lives happening in real reality. However, it does not matter if the reliving of our lives is actual or potential because everything we ever experience occurs within the forever interiors, of our individualized self-awareness.

Through each potential life relived and reviewed, we self-consciously experience our responses to new circumstances, situations, and confrontations. In possible lives lived, we self-consciously and continuously interact with others, and we are still subject to the myriad influences of unpredictability, and including forces of physical-Man's collective subconscious.

As in all things relating to our objective existence, the only thing of real spiritual significance is our eternal progression, self-realized. Thus, in the foreverness of our spiritual evolvement, there are no actual divine differences in living real objective lives, or potential lives. In the self-aware living of all lives, the whims of the non-predictable remain mandatory to our experiencing of our existence.

Not only does purgatorial punishment upright us in our forever spiritual journeys, but our spiritual worthiness is also eternally determined. If the spiritual worthiness, of our purgatorial selves, is successfully achieved, we are sent to the spiritual realm, of our transbeingness. If we are deemed divinely unfit, for the spiritual realm, we are consigned to remain in mental purgatory, or sent to purgatorial hell, for the remainder of this eternity.

If we are spiritually determined unworthy, for the eternity occupied, our spiritual unworthiness will most likely continue to be spiritually unworthy through future eternities. Still, eternal spiritual worthiness only evolves through the understanding of our divine destiny, in one eternity at a time.

The manner in which we interpret our punishment determines our destiny. However, it should be reaffirmed that after all purgatorial punishment has occurred; no further punishment is given to us in the eternity occupied. Purgatory exists not only for the administering of self-punishment, but it also the bridge to the spiritual realm, and also the eternal home for all who reject God, and their divinity in God.

Experiencing the joys of spirituality understood, accepted, and cherished is eternally and forever temporal. After we mentally experience all self-deserved punishment, forgive ourselves, and accept God, we experience our spiritual non-punishable existence, in the spiritual realm, as our reward for realizing and affirming our self-conscious unity with God.

The purgatorial realm drives our self-conscious spiritual learning by self-experiencing of heartache, pain, suffering, and happiness we have caused. However, we also spiritually learn from the things we cherish in our self-knowingness: understanding, acceptance, and experiencing things divine. To love our forever divinity is to love God, and God's nature.

Thus, for our spiritual understanding to continually evolve, the reliving of happy-filled experiences is as important as the reliving of non-happy experiences. Thus, we not only feel the pain, heartache, and unhappiness we have brought to ourselves and others; we also feel the joy and happiness we have given to ourselves and others. The self-experiencing of life is fair.

The realm of experience is not real; therefore, we do not punish ourselves for thoughts and actions having any real existence. It is only our self-thoughts and actions occurring in the non-real realm of experience, which receives punishment. The self-punishment we individually endure in the purgatorial realm is solely for our spiritual benefit.

Thus, we punish ourselves for allowing sin and evil to influence our self-conscious choices, by self-accepting non-spiritual understandings, through our non-spiritual options. When we choose that to happen, sinful-evil becomes our self-expressions and our purgatorial self-punishment is divinely ordained.

All sin and evil result from our desire to prefer to experience our non-divine self-identity instead of our divine identity. No deserved punishment for any wrongdoing ever committed is pardoned. Our forever destiny is to understand all things divinely. Our forever future is subservient to our free will. Therefore, we are capable of choosing to express, the forever non-reality of ourselves.

Even though we are, in objective reality, that which we think ourselves to be, we are forever and infinitely divine. The only reality of significance to each one of us is the reality of our self-understanding, self-awareness, or self-identity. The wrongful deeds we commit are the externalizations of our thoughts. It is always and only the sins and evils instilled in our thoughts and actions that are the source for all of our self-imposed punishments.

Our present commonly shared evolving spirituality is minuscule because so many of the divine family are choosing to reject God; thus, not all self-punishment leads to spiritual understanding. Some members of God's family accept punishment as validating their self-chosen existence without God.

Punishment may last for eternity, but that is unlikely because our self-consciousness would have to remain in an eternal state of spiritual non-decision. In each eternity, we must eventually choose to accept God, be ambivalent to the existence of God, or forthrightly reject God. Thus, our eternal destiny of punishment is decided by our self-conscious relationship to the existence of God.

From the perspective of infinity, the rate of progression of our advancing spirituality is meaningless. Thus, to infinity, the worst evildoer, and the most advanced saint are infinity's equals. To infinity, there is no such thing as the self-conscious advancing of spirituality understood. In our self-consciousness of infinity, we are not punished for mere recognitions of non-spiritual thoughts. However, merely noticing godless unreality, without giving it any power, denotes our spirituality which is only inching forward from our perspective, but standing still from infinity's perspective.

Our self-punishment forever guides us towards our spiritual evolvement. However, whether we learn or do not learn from our wrongdoings, all of our physical realm wrongdoings are punished in the purgatorial realm. Punishment leading us to the acknowledging of our divinity is a blessing. Punishment resulting in a physical purgatorial existence without God is the self-deserved experiencing of total godlessness.

Through our self-punishment, we understand the wrongfulness of our thoughts and actions. When this understanding combines with a desire to find and accept God, salvation is nigh. Eternal salvation results from our increased spiritual understanding which enables us to go from the mental realm of purgatory into the objective spiritual realm.

Some members of God's family, although they see the wrongfulness of their actions, still desire no relationship with God. For them, there is no eternal salvation to be realized in the spiritual realm. They do not interpret self-aware existence, as a spiritual gift to be desired, treasured, and experienced joyfully.

Punishment reinforcing a self-conscious sense of godlessness is retribution for self-consciously denying the gift of divine self-aware existence. Divine self-aware existence may be denied and rejected, but never divinely rewarded. The only reward, if one chooses to use that term, for the rejection of one's self-divinity and thus God, is total and complete experiencing of their eternal rejection of their self-divinity.

The question of spiritual importance for all lives lived is this: In each real or potential life lived and reviewed, do we seek spiritual understanding, guidance, or support? How each of us experiences our eternal destiny depends on upon whether our free will decisions, in our potentially lived lives, bring us to a realization and acceptance, that we are divine derivatives of God wholiness and the offspring of forever goodness.

This realization and acceptance must be accompanied, with self-forgiveness combined with a self-awareness of the presence of God. Until this divine pattern is consistently validated or not validated to the judgment of our self-awareness, we will remain in the mental self-active punishment realm of purgatory. We continually review our potential lives lived, until we self-consciously accept, reject, or remain neutral in our eternal relationship with God.

When we are self-consciously experiencing our existence, in the objective physical realm, the spiritual understanding of ourselves, is based upon a combination of reality and non-reality. Therefore, we often spiritually fool ourselves. However, in the purgatorial realm, it is divinely impossible to fool our infinite self-awareness.

If it were mentally possible to deceive our purgatorial selves, our infinite self-aware existence would have no soul. We would merely remain self-aware of our existence, unable to understand who, what, and why we exist. It is inside purgatory that we discover and accept our infinite identity.

Thus, because we are reviewing countless lives lived, there must evolve a self-realizing spiritual or non-spiritual consensus of divine direction. Thus, in countless possible lives lived, we spiritually favored in some, and in some, we are spiritually disfavored, due to the caprices of non-controllable unpredictability.

It is the overwhelming majority of the mental reviews of our potentially lived lives that determine the actual evolving of our eternal spirituality. To judge anyone's eternal destiny based upon one life lived would be infinitely and inherently unfair. Thus, the consensus of our free will decision making in many multiple lives lived is the only spiritually reliable method for determining anyone's spiritual or non-spiritual eternal direction or outcome.

This purgatorial process of life reviews continues until the certainty of our eternal destiny is firmly determined. As we self-empower our free will to accept and obey only God, spiritual victory is won in the eternity we are occupying. Also, if we self-empower our free will to reject God, our godless victory is won in the eternity we are occupying.

Also, through potential lives lived, the free will choices of others continually bring us new opportunities to understand ourselves and our existence spiritually. Thus, it is recognized that even in living potential lives, we are always interacting with members of God's family. In our living of possible lives, others are also living their possible lives.

Purgatorial reviewed lives which seemingly occurred, in the objective realm, are not representative of the presently accepted understanding of reincarnation. Reincarnation is usually understood, as someone who had previously lived, perhaps many lives, and was reborn into a new body, and into a new environment. Individuals who have said they experienced this type of reincarnation talk of remembering their previous lives.

My theory, of living continuous "what if" lives, is not a form of reincarnation. Even though we may mentally experience numerous potential lives lived it is always the same self-consciousness of self-awareness living those lives. The realizing of our potential lives lived becomes virtually inexhaustible, due to the unpredictability of life-forking, in our multitude of physical lives, lived.

Each of us chooses the pathway for the realizing of our destiny. In all potentially lived lives, we make the choices. Eventually, these life reviews establish a pattern of our evolving or non-evolving sense of spirituality, which is for or against the essence of God. Thus, each of us is given countless opportunities to acknowledge, find, accept, and obey the God of our understanding.

In the living of purgatorial potential lives, each one of us continuingly experiences the seeming evilness indelibly wedged into objective non-reality. However, to objective reality there is no good or evil, there is only the permanent and persistent displays of harmony and perfection. Outside of our individualized self-awareness, no form, substance, or authority for disharmony exists.

When we awake to the divine understanding of ourselves, as the self-consciousness of divinity in expression, we realize that our self-conscious Godly understanding of objective reality becomes ultimate reality's interpretation of itself, through our individualized mind-seeing. Each of us forever beholds ultimate truth from our inner beingness seeing outwardly, through experiencing inwardly.

In the mental realm of purgatory, we are punished for our physical lives lived, and our potential physical lives lived. Is it fair to be punished for potential lives we never actually lived? Assuredly, however, fairness is irrelevant because we possess an infinite indestructible existence requiring the necessity of being self-consciously experienced, and spiritually evaluated.

Our individualized minds interpret all experiences. Thus, the meaning of reality becomes our understanding of reality. It seems self-evident that the more opportunities we have to experience reality as unreality provide us with more opportunities to discover and understand our real selves.

We are simultaneously the captives of our existence and the captains of our existence. Each one of us realizes reality at the center of self-awareness of reality. Therefore, the understanding of reality is infinitely comprehended individually because each self-conscious center of reality is perceived, from a unique perspective, only applicable to itself.

If we embrace our God-identity, our interpretation of reality is uniquely individual and harmonious. If we reject our God-identity, our understanding of reality is individually and uniquely inharmonious. Whatever the possibilities of existence entail, we have no choice, but to obey the divine mandate of our infinite self-aware beingness.

In this understanding, the question may once again be asked: Is our infinite self-conscious existence a gift of ultimate reality? If our existence is a gift, it Isa gift we could never have self-consciously desired, sought, or embraced, because it is illogical to believe we could choose to exist.

Thus, we infinitely exist, and we endlessly endure. Nothing or on one created us, but why do we unbelievably possess an infinite self-awareness. For me, our forever existence is a puzzle, with no possible understandable solution. If we understood why we exist, we would understand the absolute allness of ultimate reality. That is not possible because that would then make our existence meaningless. Then, again the question: How can there be such a thing as meaningless reality?

If experiencing pure divine happiness is our absolute objective, we have no choice but to seek, find, and obey our divine destiny. In a sense, our destiny is a forever free will and a non-free will outcome, for each one of us to experience; hence, our struggles, sorrows, and punishments. Also, our redemptions are infinite. Carved into our forever beingness is our permanent destiny to experience sorrowfulness and joyfulness, in the realizing of our forever indestructibility.

The design of our individual and collective beingness is so that there is never a time that we are to experience objective existence, in unbroken divine harmonious perpetuity, without the accompaniment of punishment, except when we become entirely and self-consciously God-based, God-driven, and God-certain victors, in our objective experiencing of reality.

Our destiny is to realize that the gift of our existence as a gift to be infinitely self-valued. Thus, even though none of us were ever given the choice to exist infinitely, we are infinitely infinite. In core reality, our self-conscious existence comprises our certitude of ultimate reality knowing itself and pronouncing itself "Perfect, harmonious, and whole."

The uncertainties of objective existence provide endless possibilities for potentially lived lives. The overall consensus of our self-conscious experiencing of life determines who and what we understand ourselves to be. Our understanding of ourselves involves the understanding of how we will act, react, and adjust to the ever-present impingements of unpredictability.

We realize our true destiny, as we understand ourselves to be divine beings forever enveloped in the wholiness of God. We forever objectively strive to become self-consciously that which we already are, in ultimate existence. In the forefront of our self-consciousness, we must always understand and realize that we are infinite indestructible divine beings.

Our infinitely active self-aware presence in ultimate reality is God ordained, through the understanding His divine nature. We exist because God exists. In the truth of our foreverness, we are holy, incorruptible, and perfect, just as God is. We exist to understand God and describe God's purpose for infinite existence. To know what God is must include understanding what God is not; hence, our divine destiny revealed.

We are infinite. Our understandings are infinite, and our knowingness is infinite. Our ultimate existence requires constant effort. Thus, it is our expenditure of persistent effort that makes our continuing existence infinitely uniquely understood. How we choose to utilize our individual effort determines the worthiness of our self-conscious divine reality. Our efforts of expression power the self-realizing of our soul.

Our self-conscious thought-choices determine the realizing of our infinite destiny. Thus, for all lives lived, actual or potential; our human future is to strive self-consciously, to experience our infinite beingness, which forever abides, in the foreverness of God. We exist to experience, to understand, and to seek the knowing of the infinite unknowable.

Each potentially lived life review is independent of ones previous. In the purgatorial realm, we only retain a self-conscious awareness of the immediate past life mentally reviewed, experienced and punished, whether actual or potential. Our infinite self-awareness provides for the accepting valid totality of our choices. Is there anything more infinitely fair?

However, whenever we garner life lived self-conscious spiritual understanding, we carry over this accrued sense of spiritual development, in the form of spiritual receptivity, to all things divinely genuine. Due to the unforeseen factors of objective existence, this form of developing spiritual sense manifests differently and separately, for each of us, but it is still the culminating accruing of our progressive spiritual evolvement and awakening.

This carryover of a developing sense of spiritual receptivity promotes within us, a sense of continuing spiritual growth and progression. If we did not retain this sense of spiritual progress, we would forever remain objectively lost, in a land of uncertainties, unable to control the directions of our self-divinity realized.

Our self-conscious existence, without a developing sense of receptivity to things spiritual, would be the ongoing self-consciousness of godlessness. If we did not develop a spiritual-based sensitivity to the vagaries of objective existence, we would be incapable of maintaining and sustaining a consistent sense of any physical realm morality. Without a developing sense of morality, our expressions of spirituality in the object world are spiritually rootless perceptions.

The infinite certitudes governing our self-conscious existence are all things forever divinely real, indwelling the infinite presence of God, and thus indwelling each of us. Without our innate impulse to drive our way through uncertainties of life, we would lack the effort to understand our self-conscious relationship to the expression of life. Unless the certitudes of life replace the perplexities of life, there is no finite-infinite salvation, for us individually or collectively. Our forever salvation rests on our self-knowingness and our effort to understand our self-knowingness.

The experiencing of possibly lived lives is real to each of us but is not real to objective reality. Each purgatorial potential life we self-consciously review is a new life presented to our self-awareness, born from the uncontrollable influences of unpredictability. Each potential life self-consciously reviewed is indistinguishable from any actual physical existence.

Thus, in our self-conscious purgatorial self-reviewing process, we never know if we are living a real life or a possibly lived life; but, that does not matter in the slightest. Our forever destiny is to understand ourselves in the timelessness of forever. The processes involved in the understanding of ourselves are always subservient to our spiritual awakening and reawakening. Nothing is more important to us than our evolving spiritual self-awareness as we exist in forever reality.

There are times we will experience punishment even if we had not caused physical harm to ourselves or others. The penalties for non-harmful physical acts are welcomed punishment because in that punishment we readily recognize the wrongfulness of our actions. The punishment we endure for our painless indiscretions is the sense of guilt we feel, in disappointing ourselves and others.

We cannot disappoint ourselves unless we recognize the wrongness of our actions. For those of us who are self-consciously aware of the needfulness of our spiritual evolving, this guilt-ridden punishment manifests as a self-aware stepping-stone, to increased spiritual understanding and receptivity, to things divine. Thus, not only do we punish ourselves by feeling the harm and pain we have caused to ourselves and others, but we also feel the uncomfortable nagging pangs in disappointing of ourselves and others.

Here is an example of non-physically painful punishment. Suppose someone inadvertently walked out of a store with a small unpaid item. Instead of bringing the item back and paying for it, the individual just left. Later, when that person self-consciously reviewed their indiscretion, he or she readily regrets the temporary lack of honesty and is panged by remorse.

Even though we are forever divine, we have the infinite choice of accepting or rejecting our divinity. Objective reality is entirely indifferent to our interpretations. The reviewing of potentially lived lives does not necessarily include all possible lives lived. Each of us individually determines the number of possibly lived lives we will review, by the speediness of our self-aware acceptance of our God-identity.

We eventually acknowledge and accept that which we have self-interpreted ourselves to be. In other words, there comes a point in the purgatorial reviewing and punishing process where we self-realize and understand the progression or the non-progression of our spirituality. In short, we purgatorially understand and accept our eternal destiny.

If it were possible to fool ourselves, in the judging of ourselves, we would be eternally and hopelessly lost, in the bottomless pit of objective, eternal existence. There would be nothing to impel our self-realizing spirituality onward. If we become spiritually lost in any eternity, we will eternally self-dwell in the presence of godlessness.

However, eventually, our infinite existence guarantees that we will fulfill our eternal and infinite divine destiny, by self-consciously accepting our divinity in God, and thus choosing to recognize our self-conscious existence, as our emersion in the presences of God. Still, in the objective realm, we eternally struggle to discover and understand the divinity forever arching our beingness.

Make no mistake about it; it takes spiritual effort to understand, accept, and dwell in the presence of God. Our understandings of God are forever finite-infinite. The experiences in our interpretations of God are forever finite-infinite. Our beginning-ending experiences in objective reality are forever finite-infinite. Understanding our forever existence is finite-infinite. Because we finite-infinitely self-realize our infinite existence, we will never fully comprehend the allness of our reality.

The realizing of our forever enhancing self-reality, dwelling in the presence of God, is to be self-understood, by each of us infinitely. There are ongoing finite-finalities to our objective existence, but there is no finality to our forever self-existence. Finality, in the experiencing of our infinite objective existence, occurs as we return to the foreverness of core reality. In core reality, we exist as one final realization of our oneness with God, among infinite final realizations of our oneness with God.

In all potential lives lived and reviewed, we continue to make free will choices. We continue to attract learning experiences, and we remain subject to the spiritual outcome of our struggles resulting from the relentless besieging of chance, opportunity, randomness, and general unpredictability. Until the realness of truth is objectively solidified, in our self-conscious awareness, our self-experienced objective destiny vacillates from eternity to eternity, yet always moving towards our divine destiny.

We individually and unitedly are the self-conscious wholiness of God, combined into the wholeness of individualized-Man, experiencing the fullness self-aware existence. The actions of the individuals we encounter in the reliving, of our potential lives, are the actions of other fellow members of God's family, who are also reliving their potential lives. Thus, how magnificently intertwined, we are with one another.

Thus, all of our objective progressions of spirituality ceaselessly intertwine. It is interesting to note that each one of us is experiencing existence individually and collectively. Thus, our individual and collective lives are eternally and infinitely intermixed. Our personal thoughts affect our collective thoughts, and our collective thoughts influence our singular thoughts.

The understanding and expression of our spirituality mandate that our individual spiritual expressions include our collective divine demonstrations. We may choose to self-exist as an island of spirituality. However, islands by their very nature are isolated and surrounded, by unknown waters. Self-spiritual isolation limits our understanding of our infinite divinity. In truth, we are forever isolated in God, but our isolation is in our commonality with God.

Regardless of what we experience in our potential lives lived, the purpose of mentally experiencing those lives is to increase, in the spiritual understanding of our forever destiny and confirm to ourselves whether or not, our eternal sense of self-spirituality is progressing. Regardless of our choices in life making, it is purgatorially not possible to misjudge our spirituality.

Our continuing spiritual self-evolvement is the sole purpose for our objective existence, as realized and understood by the experiencing of life. Thus, our life existence is forever spiritual. Godlessness self-embraced is the rejection of the recognition that we experience objective reality to understand ourselves as the God of our beingness in Self-expression.

It is through punishment that we come to the self-realization of our forever divinity. Thus, all self-imposed punishment is the active source of our spiritual salvation, if we self-choose it to be so. If a self-relationship with God is not a desirable spiritual end, punishment does not lead to salvation; it only validates godless self-existence.

Our interpretation of ourselves is our understanding of ourselves. We must understand ourselves as divine beings, or our existence has no redemptive value. We are divinity in infinite expression, whether or not it is self-acknowledged. Imagine some of us infinitely exist without a desire to experience our self-divinity?

Some of us look at the mirror of our mind and believe what we see. We become mesmerized with our self-creations of imperfection. We see in our mind-mirror the creation of our thoughts. Why would not we accept these visions of ourselves, if we created them? Only our desire to understand our forever divinity breaks the self-mesmerism of our false self-accepted definitions of ourselves as life self-realized.

Through punishment, we come to understand our constant need to find and accept God so that we may eradicate the stingy-stringy onslaughts of godless unreality. We punish ourselves to guide ourselves to the necessary spiritual understanding, for successfully experiencing existence, as divine representatives of God.

However, we are never able to escape the realization that we are eternally and infinitely punished, for our self-aware expressions existence in a self-aware reality none of us ever willfully sought. If God could think as we think, He would say to Himself: Why do I have a forever ultimate existence? Each of us and God exists forever, but the answer to that question remains forever unanswerable.

We often lose faith and trust in our forever God-identity. Many times we choose to do wrong, even though we understand the correct choice, to be made. Too often we give into to the temptations to reject the things we spiritual know but refuse to acknowledge. Thus, the knowingness of things spiritual is one thing; the doing things spiritual is another. When we are aware of the correct action to take but do wrong, we are witnessing the primitive evolving of our spirituality.

Thus, one of the banes of physical existence is to know the goodness of goodness and then act in the badness of badness. Thus, understanding the right thing to do is not particularly spiritual, although it is most often easier than doing what is right. The right thing to do, in all situations, is willfully express the highest realization of our divinity. For the ungodly, the right thing to do is a self-understood good, which has no foundation in self-evolving spirituality.

However, as we self-consciously choose to make spiritually correct choices, our objective divine destiny successfully unfolds before us. Understanding our destiny as spiritual is the spiritualizing of our thoughts. When we realize our destiny as spiritual, we compel ourselves to make spiritually perfect choices.

Also, as we understand the need for punishment, we understand the need for forgiveness. Thus, our spiritual thoughts do not always equate to our divinely desired actions. Forgiveness is an integral process for the understanding of things spiritual. We forgive ourselves for our spiritually flameless self-willingness to misinterpret reality.

Thus, our self-forgiveness moves us from spiritual darkness into spiritual light. We must earn our spiritual understandings, and we do that through forgiveness. Without self-forgiveness, our evolving spirituality cannot be earned because our self-recognition of our wrongdoing has not been self-accepted. If we do not accept the understanding of our wrongdoings, how can we evaluate our spiritual destiny?

In the objective realm, we have the capability of self-conscious thought. With self-conscious thought comes understanding. With self-conscious understanding comes interpretation. With self-conscious interpretation comes misinterpretation. With self-conscious misinterpretation comes the need for salvation through self-conscious forgiveness.

Salvation through forgiveness is eternally required because we are endlessly self-accepting the interpretations of the non-real impediments to our individualized spiritual understanding. For the understanding of ourselves, salvation forgiveness is eternally needed. If there were no such thing as salvation and forgiveness, we would infinitely and unceasingly experience the pings, pangs, and pains of ultimate existence, without the coexisting realizing of painless and harmonious life.

In our physical lives, our salvation is forever finite and infinite. All salvation results from wrong thinking. Salvation dissolves the misinterpreted stickiness of wrong thinking from attaching itself to our self-awareness. We save ourselves through our allegiance to and acceptance of divine truth, along with the forgiveness of ourselves for accepting and acting upon things untrue.

Salvation results from the correct spiritual understanding of our existence. The real understanding of our existence requires the understanding of our God-identity. Entrenched in our ongoing understandings of God, lies our forever salvation, in our forgiveness of our spiritual ignorance.

We are the infinite Saviors of ourselves because we infinitely misinterpret the experiencing of our existence, and each of us is forever responsible for the realizing of our divine destiny. Our objective salvation is always our self-willingness to return to our self-awareness and an acceptance of the presence of God. Therefore, each one of us in the sanctuary of our self-conscious divine self-dignity determines our eternal and infinite salvation, in the self-forgiving of our ungodly actions.

Thus, our self-forgiveness for all wrongdoings we have caused to ourselves and others, combined with our self-acceptance of the presence of God is the only source of our salvation. In the realizing of salvation, we are affirming that our infinite existence is a gift, albeit an unsought.

I repeat something I discussed earlier, but this time from the point of view, of our infinite transbeingness. Suppose an infinite, all-powerful God created each one of us. Then He showed us the consequences of our infinite created existence would entail. Then, He showed us that we would forever experience immense sufferings along with endless joys.

Then He asked each of us: Is this existence one you would like to experience forever, if not I will return you to non-self-aware nothingness? How many of us would choose that forever self-aware reality of infinite pain and joy? I would not. To me, the pains, sorrows, and heartaches of the infinite experiencing of existence outweigh the joys and happiness.

Through self-suffering for our wrongdoings, we realize that we are evolving spiritual beings; we accept our self-forgiveness. Thus, this healing of our self-awareness becomes the beacon to our divinity apprehended, but still our self-forgiveness must be accompanied by a self-acceptance of God, as the source of our forever divineness.

Self-consciously experiencing existence without God is possible, but experiencing the gifts of infinity without the self-acceptance of God is not possible. We exist to understand and experience the joyfulness infused into all reality. Unfortunately, reality's joyfulness is meaningless if it is not spiritually observed and deserved. We are the only components of reality capable of interpreting the joyfulness implanted deeply into all shades of reality.

For the sacred understandings of ourselves, ample opportunities are provided to abet our spiritual development, which is our relationship to God, through potential lives, lived. Our aggregate purgatorial lives lived and reviewed establish our free will propensity to seek things spiritual, accept things spiritual, and demonstrate and share things spiritual.

If that were not so, the heavenly spiritual realm would become a corrupted repository, for perpetual sinful evildoers who had self-consciously buried themselves, in disastrous repetitions of their non-spiritually evolved lives, actual or potential. Infinite existence without God would be a sinfully evil reality claiming a divinity of its own.

Thus, one potentially good life lived, cannot be substituted for numerous potential evilly lived lives. We must affirm to ourselves, that our evolving spirituality must be self-consciously in unison, with the God of our understanding, or our experiencing of existence is divinely fraudulent.

In some of our potential lives lived, we may have been evildoers due to chance, opportunity, randomness, and general unpredictability, but we have countless opportunities to live possible lives enabling us to find the divinity that is forever connecting our infinite beingness. Therefore, we should never judge the spirituality of anyone. Someone appearing as an evil doer may be an overall saint and a spiritual blessing to God's perfect family.

However, if our overall potentially lived lives were spiritually evolving, no singular evil lived life would deter our eternal self-aware understanding of our spiritual progression. Thus, contradictions to our demonstrations of kindness and goodness, by acting evilly in one life lived, are mitigated by the living of numerous potential lives where we were kindly in expression.

Thus, no single chance at life is ultimately meaningful, in establishing anyone's spiritual worthiness. The continuing uncertainties of unpredictability provide the means for some members of God's family to consistently choose to remain in an evil sin-filled drenched self-awareness.

Infinite unpredictability is infinitely unpredictable. Thus, our evolving spiritual understanding must transcend the forever waging campaigns of unpredictability or our experiencing of existence, is not objectively fulfilled. When the steel-like clutches of unpredictability, no longer influence our free will choices, unshakeable spirituality is divinely elevated in our self-conscious awareness.

Our objective reality is continually and eternally unfair until our self-understanding becomes spiritually realized, divinely embraced, and divinely demonstrated. The overcoming of unpredictability requires a divinely focused free will, understanding God's nature, and the desire to be Godlike in self-expression. It is through suffering the pains of our sins and evils that our self-directed free will seeks spiritual comprehension, through our desire to be self-consciously wedded to God.

Contrary to the expressers of godliness, for the vast majority of us, it is easy to review potential lives lived, experience the pain caused to ourselves and others and sense guilt, even extreme guilt. However, our feelings of remorseful guilt, for the pain we have caused in potential lives lived, is not necessarily indicative of our spiritual regeneration, or spiritual progress.

Thus, many of us feel remorse for our wrongdoings, but have we understood and accepted the wrongfulness of our actions? If we desire God-based understanding and act wrongly, we are unfaithful to our evolving understanding of spirituality. Unfaithfulness in spirituality is doing the wrong thing while at the same time understanding the correct spiritual thing to do.

Unfaithfulness for the Godly minded is a non-total trust in God. We are all weak and non-deserving of our ultimate existence. We are wretched in our unfaithfulness. We are impotent in our love of God. We are weak in the desire to know God. We are merely scratching at the door of the divinity; we cannot open it. The main difference between the godless evildoers and sinners is that in the dregs of sinners divine self-conscious beingness; they do not desire to be godless.

Each one of us, as sinners, represents a primitive spirituality, sinking in a cesspool of godlessness. We await our eventual eternal and infinite salvation while we continue to pay the price for all abuses which occurred in our self-conscious existences as lives lived or possibly lives.

Have we learned and understood that all divine success, in the reliving of all of our lives must include a self-desired renewal of the holy understanding that our self-aware existence requires that all of our actions be grounded in kindness, forgiveness, tolerance, and respect for all things living? To honestly understand God is to see love permeate all of our self-created actions. All harm-filled experiences, in the reviewing of our lived lives, must be transformed into harmony through our seeing through the eyes of God. We are regenerated as we see the eternal harmony in all ungodly things, especially in our lives.

Do we divinely understand that in the living of life, no harm must be caused to anyone, including ourselves, or to any living thing? A simple objectively lived existence, centered in the self-awareness and self-acceptance of God, is a life of goodness, self-realized. A life lived that intentionally causes no harm is a spiritually fruitful self-actuating life, which is embracing a destiny of spirituality found.

Forever woven into God's all-encompassing divine family is our self-aware, independent beingness. We are forever blessed and forever limited as individual members of God's family. Thus, our objective existence often requires the wholiest of God's family to befriend us, encourage us, and love us unconditionally.

Whenever potentially lived lives occur, inconsistencies in the living of life are forever present. Life is unfair. However, due to our existence, as self-conscious members of God's infinite family, all inconsistencies eventually even out. The experiencing of life is fair if viewed from the viewpoint, that the greatest obstacle in the living of life to overcome becomes our greatest spiritual lesson, for the understanding of our infinite divinity. What price would we pay for our divine disobedience if that rebellion of spirit led to the self-conscious exercising of the power of divine understanding?

The consistent realizing of spiritual knowledge, spiritual progress, and divine faithfulness encourages us to move spiritually onward. The reliving of potential lives removes the problem of age-shortened lives lived compared to age-lengthened lives lived because, in age-shortened life spans, there is less opportunity for individual spiritual evolvement.

It would be spiritually unjust for anyone to enter the spiritual realm, based on the good intentions and good actions, of a single age-shortened life, or even a single age lengthened life. Thus, the reality of potential lives lived is virtually endless for any one individual. Think of all of the countless possibly lived lives?

Each potential life lived has life-forks of life opportunities to be randomly determined. These randomly determined life-forks continue from potential life potential life. Each eternal life lived has infinite possibilities, to be lived in an endless possible combination of existences. Forked lives are often lived simultaneously. What is interesting is that when an individual is self-consciously living a forked-life, he or she has no reason not to believe that the life they are living is not reality based.

In actually lived lives or in potentially lived lives, some members of God's family may or may not have lived moral, ethical, or spiritual lives, and died at an early age. In these age-shortened lives, spiritual lessons are barely noticeable. Except for their early death, who knows what spiritual lessons may have or may not have learned had their lives been lengthened by time?

This concept applies to all life experiencing existence. Suppose a redwood tree, in its birthing stages of growth, is killed by a thunderous storm. The redwood tree's potential for experiencing its life gone. Had that baby redwood been allowed to grow to its designed destiny, it would have become a tower of beauty, majestically praising existence itself. Thus, all of life has the same potential to fulfill its purpose for existence.

In the design of life, there is no difference between actuality and possibility. Why should there be a difference in the realizing of life? The same factors applying to actually lived lives, apply to possibly lived lives. What is of supreme importance is the glorification of life, through the respect of spiritual acknowledgment. In the realizing of all life, the things that promote harmony, joy, and beauty are infinity's treasures.

Many individuals, who had been living spiritually ethical and moral lives and died early, had they continued to live, may have ended up living non-spiritual horrid lives. Conversely, many individuals who had been living non-ethical and non-moral lives and also died young had they continued to live may have become spiritual benefactors, to God's family.

Thus, it is not possible that any one life briefly lived can reveal anyone's degree of spiritual self-worthiness? I define spiritual worthiness as a continuous and sincere development of spiritual understanding, based on demonstrations of kindness, understanding, tolerance, and respect for all things living, combined with love and acceptance of God.

Thus, the determining of spiritual self-worthiness is achieved in the reliving and reviewing of countless potential lives lived. In each eternity we traverse, our spiritual unfoldment, combined with our self-conscious desires, must be firmly self-established, to experience the spiritual rewards that the spiritual understanding and acceptance of our forever divinity provide.

Each potential life lived and reviewed is separate and unique from any previous life review. Fortunately, spiritually advanced members of God's family may provide guidance and encouragement, in actual or potentially lived lives. These divine family members sacrificed experiencing the gifts of existence, to spiritual minister to spiritually wayward members of God's forever family.

These spiritually advanced members, of God's family, are evolved spiritually ascended angels who bring spiritual comfort and encouragement to urge us, one and all, to seek the understanding of our true selves which returns us to the realization of our infinite self-identity in God.

Even for the spiritually advanced members of God's family, they experience sadness, in their self-awareness. They understand the truth of reality but still they tear. They understand that all experienced suffering, real or non-real, is suffering nonetheless. The cause of all suffering is spiritual ignorance self-consciously accepted. Thus, they choose to encourage others to discover the truth of their divinity.

It is still divinely valid, regardless of the spiritual encouragement we receive, as members of God's perfect family; the gift of objective existence would not be a gift if we did not possess a free will. Thus, any and all spiritual encouragement received remains eternally subject to our free will choices.

Understanding the infinite supremacy, for the forever ability to make free will choices, brings to light a disturbing realization. Spiritually advanced members of God's family have the capacity to know future free will choices individualizations of physical-Man will make. Their spiritual progress has enabled them to accept self-consciously idea realm ideas giving them the ability to know future free will choices of those who are experiencing the physical realm.

Thus, these divine helpmates know who will benefit from their spiritual comforting, and who will not. Still, these helpmates comfort the stubborn unchanging, spiritually lost members of God's perfect family, much like spiritual compassion given to a godless dying man. They minister to the unreality of suffering, disregarding the realization that suffering is an infinite illusion.

Although no one is ever permanently lost, some of us may use our free will to become hopelessly and spiritually mired, in the ongoing timelessness of time, for eternities ceaseless. To be consistently eternally lost in the experiencing of existence turns the gift of life into a curse of continuing sorrow.

Still, due to our innate free will, our incontrovertible destiny forever guarantees the progressing availability of our spiritually evolving life. Thus, through our continuous sojourns through objective reality, we always retain the self-conscious capability to de-realize all so-called errors, in our experiencing of life.

All the delays in the realizing our divine destiny result from misunderstandings and misinterpretations of our forever divinity. Thus, we are forever interpreting ourselves in objective existence. Of course, only as we correctly define ourselves as self-divinity in expression do we spiritually justify our existence.

Our evolving spiritual understanding is an ever-present and infinite process. If that is not true, our objective existence will continue to be eternally lost, as thus it seems for many. Many of God's family feel infinitely lost. However, their salvation is the recognition that their existence is infinite, and they have infinity to become spiritually unlost.

We can never become permanently spiritually lost because, whether we realize it or not, we are forever fulfilling the divine mandate forever sustaining our existence, by continuously understanding ourselves through the process of experiencing life. All experiencing of life must eventually lead to God-awareness as we prepare ourselves to be receptive to all things divine.

In the purgatorial realm, our self-conscious experience of pain is real, even though pain itself is unreal. Physical world experiences seem as real to us, as if godless unreality was a real component, of our physical world lives. Thus, I maintain, sustain, and proclaim that our self-conscious self-actuating experiences have no real reality attached to them.

Each one of us determines the number of potential lives to be self-consciously reviewed and punished. We cannot fool ourselves. We fulfill our eternal destiny by experiencing what we have consciously and steadfastly adhered to our self-identity. We evaluate possible lives lived until we consistently accept or reject our forever self-divinity in God.

All things involving the experiencing of existence must be seen spiritually, for us to understand and fulfill our divine heritage. Spiritually understood, all the challenges of our physical existence combine to encourage us to realize, follow and obey our internal design propelling us onward, into the forever reaches of discovering our self-divinity.

To become self-consciously spiritually worthy is the fulfilling of our divine destiny, and results in the gift of experiencing the spiritual realm. Thus, our potential possibly lived lives bring us new understandings, new opportunities, and new challenges. Therefore, the numerous opportunities for experiencing possible lives lived; determines our spiritual worthiness.

I re-emphasize, our entry into the spiritual realm must be spiritually deserved and earned. Good actions, good deeds, good ethics, and good morality are not enough. To divinely realize the spiritual realm, the infinite goodness of God must be self-consciously sought, found, obeyed, and enthroned, within our individualized self-awareness. Thus, there are no other means for attaining and realizing the heavenly wonders of experiencing our successful evolved spirituality.

Therefore, as individualized purgatorial-Man, we cannot progress to individualized spiritual-Man until we have self-consciously repented for all of our wrongdoings, and earnestly seek to dwell self-consciously in the presence of God. The spiritual realm is reserved, for the God-minded, who are no longer capable of using their free will to do anything but to obey the workings of their self-divinity.

To make ourselves spiritually and self-consciously worthy is to understand ourselves as divine. Regardless of what forms of godless unreality we have accepted in the reviewing of possible lives lived, our essential divine and unchanging nature remain forever unblemished.

God has no role in our spiritual self-evaluation. In some reviewed lives we develop a sense of spirituality, in some we do not. For all of our infinite existence, each one of us forever chooses the manner of our relationship to God. God makes no judgments on anyone, at no time, at no place, and for no reason.

Our successful spiritual progress self-understood means the pain, heartache and unhappiness we have created require not only our sincere repentance, but it also requires our dedication and re-dedication to acknowledge and accept only the presence of God as the reality of our self-awareness.

There are some kind-hearted individuals who, in the reviewing of potential lives lived, continue in their refusal to acknowledge and accept God. Their eternal life reviews are not continually unpleasant even though they self-willfully choose their self-conscious existence without God. Thus, they demonstrate that the experiencing of life may be somewhat pleasant, by accepting ideas of goodness, while simultaneously self-rejecting God.

As these kind-hearted individuals continue in their desire not to seek a self-accepting understanding of God, they interpret the goodness of existence, without the Godness of existence. They prefer a self-determined life without a desire to have any relationship to or with God. That is their infinite free will choice. However, imagine being part of God and choosing to have no self-aware relationship with Him?

Thus, these kind-hearted individuals continually elect to experience their lives without any desire for acquiring self-conscious God-awareness, but still they have not hardened their thoughts towards God, and they have not self-consciously rejected Him. They have decided God is unnecessary for the experiencing of existence.

They continue with their possible lives lived reviews until they have suffered and repented for all their sins and it becomes firmly established that they are not going to seek a relationship with God, in the present eternity occupied. At that time, they will continue to remain in the non-physical purgatorial realm, but they will suffer no more eternal punishment.

Thus, when the steadfastness of their non-willfulness, to seek God, is confirmed by their consistent self-conscious free will choices, their eternal purgatorial punishment ends. At that time, they enter into an eternal slumber lasting until the end of the eternity they are occupying.

When the eternity they are residing in ends, these sleepers in eternity revert to the formless realm. In the formless realm, they continue their self-aware existence without self-God identification. In the formless realm, they continue to reject a desired knowingness of God. Still, they are not practitioners of things evil.

The other group of individualized purgatorial-Man is those who self-consciously and continuously choose to reject God. After completing their life reviews and receiving all their deserved punishment, and even though they remain self-consciously hardened towards God, their self-punishment ends. Thus, even for the vilest of self-aware creatures, eventually, eternal punishment ends.

At that time, they automatically enter the physical realm of purgatory to experience their existence objectively without God. Now their experiencing of reality becomes the lifeless experiencing of life. Now, they have nothing to look forward to except ungodly existence self-realized.

These individuals understand God exists; still, they self-consciously and willfully choose to reject Him. For them, the pain and suffering they caused and the pain and suffering they received define their self-accepting existence. They replaced any desire to understand God with the spiritually unrestrained exaltation of their free will. They exist to be the gods of their pitifully self-accepted non-spiritualized self-accepted identities.

They regaled themselves in a puffed-up defiance of their misdirected self-divinity and continued in their jubilant rejection of God. They desired no God, sought no God, accepted no God, and obeyed no God. They demanded control of their self-aware existence with total disregard for the consequences of their self-aware actions.

For them, God has nothing to offer. They become evil, deranged gods of their making. Even though they will eventually return to the formless realm, they choose only to identify their self-existence in the physical and purgatorial realms. For them, the acceptance of God is a threat to their self-acknowledged beingness.

Those who reject God self-glorify themselves in their godless experiencing of existence. Those who reject God give no value to the meaning of life. Those who reject God are the self-consciousness of their divinity in divine rebellion, a rebellion lasting for endless eternities. The innate spirituality, in those who reject God, eventually wins out, but their spiritual battles are long-fought and fiercely defiant.

For those of us who remain faithful to God, we recognize ourselves as the self-conscious heirs to all things divine. Thus, for the considerable majority of God's family, in the purgatorial realm, the heavenly awakening within our self-consciousness occurs, as we continue to realize and accept ourselves as the wholiness of God. In purgatory, our self-conscious desire is to return to the experiencing of our self-awareness, in divine unity with God.

In conclusion, the purgatorial realm is where we experience the joys and the pains of objective existence, through our actual and potential life reviews. Here, we spiritual meet all of the divine requirements for entrance into the spiritual realm.

It is our purpose in the purgatorial realm to uproot, repent, and reject all of our deliberately self-accepted deceptions, to eternally reveal a consistent and sincere understanding and unity with God. Without our purgatorial method of life reviews, to determine how we handle the predictable and unpredictable challenges of life, we could never understand and fulfill the needful requirements of our forever evolving sense of spirituality.

As we self-consciously identify and embrace our oneness with God, we move on into the spiritual realm. Thus completes the divine purpose for experiencing our purgatorial existence. We judged ourselves and deemed ourselves to be in paradise with God. We have now earned our temporary finite-infinite stay in the deserved Heaven of our divinity self-known and understood.

However, each eternity is only one eternity of the endless eternities we will traverse. Many of God's family will fail spiritually and not make it beyond the purgatorial realm. Eventually in the experiencing of eternities endless, these non-deserving spiritual foot-draggers will become victors, in the discovering of their divinity in God. They will join God perfect family in the voicing of rejoicing.

The only failure there in the infinite experiencing of ultimate existence, is the inability to understand and accept ourselves, as infinitely divinely whole spiritual beings. Thus, the divine understanding of our existence makes the experiencing of our self-aware lives a forever blessing. Without our self-accepted recognized beingness in God, our infinite existence continues to be a self-conscious curse.

Only as we win the spiritual battles that mold and shape the understanding of our self-conscious identity, will we eventually understand ourselves to be reality's holy conquerors. However, from the viewpoint of infinity, we have never won, lost, or tied a battle. To infinite existence, we have no battle scars. All of our spiritual battles occur within the confines of our self-conscious awareness. Infinity is oblivious to our self-awareness of ourselves.

From our individual perspectives, spiritual conquering always involves the overcoming our self-sense of embodied existence in the objective realm of uncertainties, unpredictabilities, and the challenging of challenges. We exist to know, understand, and challenge our infinite existence, to prove our spiritual worthiness to ourselves. Infinity exists to be its existence, unencumbered by any sense of self-awareness.

Thus, from our individual vantage speck-point of infinity, we are constantly winning and losing battles. However, our ability for the successful foreverness of spiritual victories is infinity's gift to us, because we are the self-consciousness of existence, infinitely self-consciously understanding, experiencing, and interpreting itself.

As spiritually prosperous purgatorial inhabitants, we accept and identify ourselves in the presence of God, and all self-conscious stings of our ungodly, sinful, evil acts vanish from our self-awareness. Now the understanding of our divine existence replaces the harmful unreal in our self-awareness. Our self-existence is now a divine blessing to be experienced.

Thus, the most important aspect of the purgatorial realm is the realization that the spiritual realm is unattainable until God is consciously acknowledged, accepted, and enthroned in our self-consciousness, as the substance of our true identity. If we consciously choose to deny that we are part of God, our experience of existence remains self-consciously chained in the realm of unreal and depthless godlessness.

Spiritual-Man

Divine understanding is the only power behind our infinite experiencing of existence. When our spiritual knowledge is self-consciously and consistently divinely motivated, we pass through the physical and purgatorial realms, into the spiritual realm. In the spiritual realm, our spiritual understanding of existence and our experiencing of reality are realized, without any spiritually limiting influences of a faithless doubt.

As individualized spiritual-Man, we continue in the never-ending process of self-consciously demonstrating our forever divinity. Now, we completely understand, without the limiting restraints of uncertainties that our object existence is for the purpose of experiencing our divine nature, which is the presence of God.

When we enter the spiritual realm, we have achieved our purpose for existence. We now exist to experience unfettered joy, without the self-acceptance of non-reality. The divine gifts for self-consciously choosing to accept our spiritual selves become available for each one of us to experience, in the finite-infinite heavenly playground, we understand as the spiritual realm.

We reach the spiritual realm based solely on our free will choices; to understand, accept, and obey our forever divinity divinely entrenched in our self-beingness. Without making spiritually correct decisions, the bluster-filled shouting's of godless unreality would continually shape and contort our divine understanding of ourselves, into grotesque images of our divinity lost.

We remain forever sacred, whether or not we understand it, accept it, embrace it, or experience it. In the spiritual realm, we are fulfilling our spiritual destiny, through our self-conscious realization of the wholiness of God, as the purity of divine happiness and joy. Here, the false lurings of the physical realm are replaced with our desire to experience existence, in the light of our forever God-individualized wholeness.

Spiritual-Man is the objective realization of each of us as immortal-Man experiencing existence. As we successfully pass through the purgatory's portal and move on into the spiritual realm, we reawaken to the realization that we are all individual members of God's family, who are eternally and infinitely bound together as one divine unity, through the collective sharing of our spiritual identities.

In the spiritual, we are spiritual victors. Alone and commonly we have trumpeted spirituality and followed the rising crescendos of our forever divine self-awakening. We have individually defeated the enemies of our divinity, those forever enemies of godlessness. Now we can enjoy the spiritual wonderments of our divinely recognized existence, without the cumbrances of challenges.

However, here is a heart-gnawing question: How could anyone depart the physical and purgatorial realms, and be content in the spiritual realm realizing that his or her loved ones continue to suffer greatly, from the vise-gripping clutches of grief, heartache, sorrow, and unhappiness? How can any of us, as individualized spiritual-Man, be content when so much unhappiness retains a remembrance in our thoughts?

The answer to the above must be understood spiritually. When we enter into the spiritual realm, we are reborn into the realization that all experiences, in the physical realm, have no infinite realities attached to them. Now, we totally and comprehensively understand that all suffering is unreal.

Now each of us understands that our loved ones are infinite God-beings without beginnings or endings. The immortality of our cherished loved ones is never touched, impacted, or tarnished, in any way, by the so-called miseries of godless unreality that forever attack self-conscious thought. Each one of us, alone and individually, must find our heavenly way; we cannot do it for others, not ever our for earth-realm cherished loved ones. Infinity is the home where all of us, alone and individually, must make our beds.

As individualized spiritual-Man, we have familial ties binding us to each another. From our new divine perspective, we understand that in the truth of our self-beingness, there are no fathers, no mothers, no children or no relatives of any kind. Our relationship to God is the only forever lasting familial relationship each one of us will ever possess.

Thus, we are all coequal members of the one divine familial expression of God. However, throughout the infinite traversing and experiencing objective reality, we each become forever fathers, forever mothers, forever children, and forever divinely related to each other, in our infinite experiencing of existence.

We understand that the divinely significant progression for all self-aware life is the progression of our self-aware spiritual understanding. Now, we self-confidently realize that all who self-consciously experience the living of our reality are divinely indestructible.

In the spiritual realm, we appreciate, understand, and accept the infinitely spiritual divinity of all self-awareness existence. We fully understand that our loved ones are experiencing existence to realize the purpose for their forever indestructible divine beingness. If we ever really knew why we infinitely exist, we would cease to be infinite self-aware beings, because the purpose for our infinite existence would no longer be something to seek in ultimate reality.

Our common destiny, although being experienced separately and individually, is divinely intertwined with one another. Throughout the infinity of our forever self-aware existence, that interweaving interdependence of experiencing reality can never be abridged. Thus, all divine family members are recognized, accepted, and understood as co-beings, spiritually indestructible and infinitely connected to God.

The purpose of our self-conscious understanding of our divine beingness is to express our divine nature objectively. As individualized spiritual-Man, we have arrived at the Heaven of our spiritual self-knowingness. Now, our self-conscious experiencing of existence cannot be corrupted by misinterpretations of idea realm ideas.

Thus, as individualized spiritual-Man, we only experience the resounding joys of our spiritual knowingness, without the disruptive piercings of godlessness vying for our attention. Now we are truly and purely able to realize the essence of God, in the objective spiritual realm of experiencing existence.

We now experience divine reality with the fullness of God. Ungodly things no longer respond to the mental desire-power for expression. In the spiritual realm, we are no longer tested or challenged, by the spring-back coils of non-reality. Now, the only challenge we have is self-determining what heavenly treasures we are capable of experiencing.

As individualized spiritual-Man, God's real qualities are combined and experienced with the awareness that divine truth is always consistent, always unwavering, and always unchallenged. As individualized spiritual-Man, we are the self-consciousness of our divinity without the flaws of a spiritually unbalanced self-aware existence.

This realization occurs as a result of our proven spiritual steadfastness to our acceptance of the ever-presence of God. In this heavenly spiritual realm, our understanding and our spiritually divine interpretation of objective reality are combined to experience our eternal existence, at our level of self-consciously evolved spirituality.

As individualized spiritual-Man, we are equally unequal. That means that even though each of us has fulfilled our spiritual destiny, by finding, acknowledging, and accepting God, the depths of spiritual understandings vary. In other words, we not all equal in the absorption of divine knowingness. Thus, in the spiritual realm, some of us are in heavenly kindergarten, and some of us are advanced students.

Our place in the spiritual realm is proof once again that we are infinitely unique, and thus, each of us has our individual and distinctive understandings of God. Even though we all have the same infinite spiritual abilities, none of us we ever self-consciously experience our divinity in forever degrees of equality. Still, we are all equal in our capability of receiving things infinitely divine.

However, we remain infinitely unequal, in our receptivity to the receiving of things divine, because infinite spiritual rewards must be infinitely deserved and earned, through our individual and infinite progressions through eternity. Thus, each one of us is forever evolving in the length and depth of our spiritual understandings.

As individualized spiritual-Man, we are no longer self-consciously capable of causing harm to anyone or anything. We only realize, understand, and accept the divinity of truth, and nothing, unlike divine truth, has any power to entice our self-conscious awareness, away from the forever pure, the perpetually real, and the forever everlasting. Now, our free will choices are based solely upon our accepted-knowingness of God.

As individualized spiritual-Man, we only embrace the divine truth behind our thoughts. Our self-consciousness is self-knowingly powered, by our self-acceptance of God. Thus, our knowingness of God is without any opposition, from the objective world of phantoms, who ceaselessly herald their pretended existence.

In the spiritual realm, unhappiness is non-existent. Here we are filled with self-conscious harmony, and we totally self-acknowledge and self-accept God's will for each one of us, as we understand and accept our divine beingness in Him. God's will as correctly and divinely interpreted, from our perspective only, is our self-conscious experiencing of His divine nature. Without our self-aware existence, there would be no such thing as understanding the will of God.

As each of us expresses our infiniteness, our individual identities are being revealed to us infinitely. Our objectively obtained spiritual bodies are the spiritual realization of our physical bodies. Our spiritual bodies are perfect and flawless. In the spiritual realm, our outward physical appearance manifests and remains in appearance, at the approximate physical age of twenty-five.

As individualized spiritual-Man, we are in an eternally perfect environment of beauty, harmony, peacefulness, joy, et cetera. Our divine nature is continually being impressed to experience the forever cascading yielding of celestial wonderments. There is never any separation from the ever-presence of divine bliss, self-consciously understood, realized, and accepted.

Each of us harmoniously experiences the eternity we are occupying, in our personal, unique, and individual manner. Infinity exists for us to experience individually, and if so desired commonly. The realizing of our spiritual destiny and the non-spiritual destiny in our knowingness of infinity is inseparable.

In the spiritual realm, we are eternally and self-consciously wrapped in the exuberance of our divine existence. The vibrations of pure divinity harmoniously and joyously bound and rebound within the self-knowingness of ourselves. In the spiritual realm, we each experience harmony in varying degrees of expansion, but it is still the same God being self-realized by us as harmony.

In the spiritual realm, our objective divine existence is self-consciously realized. In the spiritual realm, taunting flickering shadows of light are no longer perceived, known, or experienced. There is only the harmonious intensity of divine brightness forever beckoning us, forever bathing us, and forever soothing our sense of divinity. Now we self-knowingly bask in our divinity self-revealed as we experience our divineness.

As individualized spiritual-Man, there are no obstacles or challenges to overcome. Now, our acquired depth of spiritual progress provides the basis, for our self-consciously deserved spiritual rewards. Regardless of the depths of our individual self-acquired spirituality, each of us has the remainder of eternity, to experience the range of our spiritual desires.

Spiritual understanding and progress is a never-ceasing process. We interpret, and experience the spiritual realm from our individual divinely evolved perspectives, combined with our self-conscious identification with God. In the spiritual realm, as individualized spiritual-Man, we are fulfilling our divine destiny to be self-knowingly spiritual.

Our spiritual understandings and the spiritual experiencing of our pure knowingness are infinitely individual and forever ongoing. Each one of us in the aloneness of our self-realization accepts and interprets God, based on the intensity of our desire to know God. Thus, we forever self-consciously realize ourselves to be, that which we forever self-consciously desire to be. In the spiritual realm, we desire to be explorers in the spiritual realm of infinity's perfection.

This spiritual realm we come to inhabit self-consciously is eternally and forever temporary. It may seem like a final spiritual destination, but it is just one perfect spiritual oasis, in ever ongoing divine resting places for those who are spiritually successful, in the realizing of their divine destiny. The length of existence for the eternity we are occupying determines the spiritually earned time we abide in the heavenly wonderland.

Interestingly, just because we are spiritually entitled to experience our self-earned spiritual rewards, in this Heaven, does not necessarily mean we will choose to do so. Our infinitely divine uniqueness provides all possibilities for the interpreting of our heavenly residence. Some divine inhabitants prefer to be eternally alone in the self-knowingness of their spirituality.

Thus, for some, even in the spiritual realm, the gifts of infinity remain unaccepted, at the doorstep of their self-awareness. Thus, even in the realm of things spiritual, our spiritual individuality spans the spectrum of our divinity self-understood and self-accepted. Just because someone values the understanding and self-acceptance of spirituality, does not require that individual to be sociable.

All members of God's family traversing the spiritual realm self-consciously love and accept God. Thus, our spiritual objective for experiencing existence is fulfilled. Even so, the depth and intensity of our personal love for God varies; therefore, no two individuals have the same identical love of God. Thus, in the spiritual realm, our particular and unique love of God mirrors the self-knowingness of our evolving divinity.

Therefore, the self-conscious experiencing of our spiritual rewards varies individually, uniquely, and eternally. Every spiritual wonder, experienced by each one of us equals the depths of our spiritual evolvement. In this manner, we reaffirm to our evolving spiritual understanding, that in the experiencing of things divine, all thing must be spiritually deserved.

Thus, our individual experience of earned spiritual rewards is always fulfilled, to the maximum of our self-realized spirituality. Not one of us ever totally and comprehensively self-realizes the love of God, except in core reality. However, in core reality, our spiritual self-awareness is not earned; it is forever a divinely-blessed underserved gift realized as our infinite self-consciously blissfully aware existence.

As spiritual-Man, we never fail in achieving anything we desire. Of course, our spiritual desires are determined by our spiritual evolvement. It is not possible for any of us to desire anything beyond our self-amassed spiritual depth. Thus, here we realize the harmonious culmination of our evolved spirituality, in the controlled demonstrating of our divine essence.

In this spiritual reality of our divine beingness, we never know a sense of loss or incompleteness. Spiritual-Man exists in a free will state of divinity where there is never any self-awareness, self-acceptance, or self-understanding of failure, lack, uncertainty, limitation, or insecurity? Here, our free will is harnessed to our infallible and divinely evolving spiritual understanding of ourselves and God.

As spiritual-Man, unbridled joy is our ever-present reward for correctly understanding and accepting our unity with God. The possibilities of joy-filled experiences for each of us are individually and universally endless. Each of us understands the fulfilling of our spiritual desires as a divine gift to be experienced.

There are some similarities between our transbeingness as individualize physical-Man and our transbeingness as spiritual-Man. For example, in the spiritual realm, our bodies retain their same physical world identities. Thus, male and female forms are still identifiable in the spiritual realm, but gender identification has no other significance. The spiritual realm continuum of our gender is for continuity only, for the experiencing of our eternal reality existence.

As individualized spiritual-Man, we still partake in some physical world enjoyments. For example, in the spiritual realm, we are still able to enjoy the taste of a succulent apple. However, now our sense of apple tasting becomes our self-conscious experiencing of the idea, of the taste of a delicious apple. Tasting a spiritual realm apple is far more pleasurable than tasting a physical realm apple.

As individualized spiritual-Man, our once physical world bodily functions are unnecessary. For example, in the spiritual realm, the experience of eating requires no need of digestion. Spiritual-Man is never hungry, never tires, and never needs exercise or sleep. In the spiritual realm, rest is our ever-present self-realization of perfect harmony. Spiritual-Man is in an environment where only the reality of perfection is self-realized.

Again, I re-emphasize that in the spiritual realm, we only desire to experience the things we are divinely entitled to experience. Still, it is not possible to desire anything beyond our self-developed self-attained spirituality. Thus, our desire for spiritual experiences varies, due to the uniqueness of our physical realm evolved spirituality.

However, the overall joy, harmony, and spiritual excitements of experiencing the spiritual realm are common all; even though experienced they are experienced at varying depths of divine self-awareness. In the spiritual realm, as in all objective regions, everything that we experience is realized in our individualized self-conscious awareness. Thus, infinity is always experienced individually and uniquely, within the confines of our self-knowingness.

Spiritual-man is a self-expressing note in the divine and infinite symphony of God's rhythmical expressions. Thus, as independent divine beings, we are knowingly contributing to the perpetual harmony which forever manifests. In the spiritual realm, we individually, consciously, and collectively pulsate to the forever rhythm of God blessing our self-awareness, with sprinkles of harmonious perfection.

Thus, we vibrate in complete unity with the harmonies of God, which are echoing throughout the forever expansiveness of God's family. In our individual self-awareness, we are God-individualized, viewing and experiencing a portion, of ultimate reality's divine infinitude of unimaginable symmetry. Now, we are self-knowingly experiencing objective reality with God. Thus, God is forever Self-glorified though each one of us.

The continuingly fulfilling realization of our divine destiny forever occurs in our spiritual forays, into our ever increasing divine knowingness, of the objective spiritual realm. Our individual spiritual destiny is without limit, and our spiritual gifts are countless, within the range of our developed God-awareness.

Symbolically, let the infinite range of our developed spirituality be contained in the infinite range number one. Likewise, if the number two includes the infinite range of our developed spirituality, its unlimited range is twice the infinite range of number one. So it is understood; we are infinite spiritual beings, infinitely experiencing and expanding our self-developing spirituality. Thus, some of us are at number one in our spiritual development, some of us at number two, and some of us are destined to be number 100, and so on. Thus is our forever spirituality increasing, in our individual understandings and expressions of the infinity of our divinity.

As individualized spiritual-Man, anything we are capable of imagining, we are capable of experiencing. Suppose, for example; we desired to view the universe from the perspective of an atom or an electron? There's a spiritual idea or a series of ideas enabling the fulfilling of that desire.

Wherever we are experiencing our transbeing existence, we are always destined to express love. Thus, suppose we had a cherished animal companion in the physical world, and we desired to be united with it once again. There is an idea or series of ideas that would allow us to demonstrate that spiritual desire. Imagine the joy of once again sharing life and love with our beloved pets? Animal pets are infinity's gift us to encourage the self-awakening of our spirituality through the expression of love.

Another example, suppose someone has a desire to play a musical instrument. That yearning desire, combined with idea realm ideas, makes the playing of a musical instrument an effortless joy. The taking of lessons is not necessary because, in the spiritual realm, there are no failures in the accomplishing anything divinely desired. In the spiritual realm, learning is the experiencing of our spiritual desires.

As individualized spiritual-Man, the experiencing of time is meaningless and is subservient to our wishes. Thus, we are now capable of observing the ongoing evolving of our physical world. Therefore, we can witness all manners of this world's created manifestations, from dinosaurs to our physical evolution as primitive animal man.

In the spiritual realm, many of the mysteries of our present existence can now be readily apprehended. Imagine sitting on a verdant knoll observing a herd of dinosaurs graze, or seeing how primitive animal man adapted to his environment? Here, we are even capable of witnessing the moment when the evolving of animal man became self-conscious physical-Man.

As individualized spiritual-Man, we harmoniously experience the infinite real foreverness of objective spiritual reality. Everything which appears as creation exists for our joy, pleasure, understanding, and experience. Thus, all evolving seemingly creative forms of experience have an inherently designed purpose, and that purpose is for our self-conscious realization and enjoyment.

How we, as individualized-Man, choose to experience any aspect of our spiritual existence remains our individual and personal self-choice. We always retain our different, unique, and individual divine proclivities. Thus, spiritual understanding does not necessarily equate with a sense of spiritual adventure. Some of God's family members are content to wait out eternity surrounded by the ease of harmony, beauty, and the ever-presence of divine music.

In all circumstances, our expressions of spirituality are self-desired, self-wanted, and self-determined. What would our individual self-existence mean, if we all chose to experience the expressions of reality, in the same manner? Thus, some divine family members are content in the self-realizing of relatively limited spiritual desires, while others of God's family stretch their spiritual desires, to the borderlands of the infinity of eternity.

As individualized spiritual-Man, we are still capable of recognizing sin and error, but in the spiritual realm, sin and error have no sustaining power or ability, to enrich their self-chimed existence. As spiritual-Man, our firmly rooted spiritual knowingness prohibits us from using our free will to do anything but to obey the innate dictates, of our divinity, forever encircling and permeating our soul.

We are all members of God's family; we are all infinitely interconnected. In the transbeingness of our forever objective existence, infinite soul mates do not exist? My definition of a soulmate is an individual who is in total harmony, in all aspects of the living of life with another, including, disposition, point of view and sensitivity. Due to our nature, as individual divine family members, it might seem as though we all meet that soulmate criterion.

A good example for the understanding of physical realm so-called soulmates is what occurs in marriage. It is interesting that often individuals marry someone who is at their same place of spiritual evolvement or non-spiritual evolvement. However, that does not necessarily mean they share the same spiritual or non-spiritual understandings.

Rather, it refers to a basic level of spiritual receptivity or non-spiritual receptivity to things divine, or non-divine. In this way, we validate, to ourselves, the understanding of ourselves, by the individuals that we attract into the environs of our experiencing of life, as existence.

If we observe the spiritual perspective of our marriage partner; that perspective usually shows the level of our spiritual progression or lack thereof. We naturally gravitate to individuals who share our outlooks on the living and expressing of life. There are exceptions; this is just a general observation.

Thus, due to the commonality of experiencing existence, some divine family members temporary become eternal soulmates and may even share some eternities together. However, since everyone's infinite spiritual evolving is unique, there is no such thing as a forever soulmate. Thus, no two divine family members could ever consistently and endlessly unfold at the same rate of spiritual progress, and understanding; ergo, there are no infinite soulmates.

However, we are always sharing temporarily existence with other divine family members even as our infinite existence remains self-solitary. To each one of us individually, we are the only self-conscious reality there is, in all the infinity. In this understanding, ultimate reality is forever individual and uniquely understood and experienced, there is no infinitely sharing of infinite existence.

Each one of us is the center-point of infinite existence, and the understanding of our existence only increases as our understanding of infinity increases. Thus, we are forever remaining uniquely stationary in our infinitely evolving beingness. Still, no unique motionless point of infinite reality is the same as another. Thus, infinite soulmate compatibility is not infinitely possible.

Regardless of our state of transbeingness, we have the forever choice of experiencing existence with or without others. There is no divine edict requiring that the spiritual experiencing of reality must include others. Still, imagine the unrealized happiness of experiencing spiritual reality as a sole individual? For some of us, that remains an option.

It is self-obvious, that experiences of joy, harmony, and beauty are greatly enhanced when shared, with other spiritually like-minded members of God's family. If our choice is to be alone while traversing and experiencing the objective spiritual realm, we deny ourselves the enriching of our knowingness, of our spiritual existence.

Still, strange as it seems, some forms of potential spiritual happiness may go unrealized infinitely. Thus, even in the known spiritual Heavens of divine perfection, there is no certainty for the experiencing of everyone's spiritual fulfillment. Thus, forever in our individual understandings of our desired expressions of our spiritually, there is fulfillment.

Consider the existence of God. God cannot choose to obey or deny His nature. He is alone in His wholiness, and nothing ever alters that Self-realization of Himself. Throughout all of forever reality, God is only aware of His Self-unfolding divinity. Thus, does He possess some sense of divine isolation or infinite loneliness?

Perhaps if God does possess some sense of divine isolation, it is assuaged, to some divine degree, by our individualized God-derived existence? The only supreme assurance of certainty there is, concerning the nature of God, is that He is infinitely Self-realizing the wholiness of Himself.

Thus, it could be assumed that God is infinitely secure within His forever existence. However, our individualized truth is that each one of us, as the self-aware beingness of God, is forever to be self-understood, self-known, self-interpreted, and self-experienced. God is forever divinely settled, into His infinite existence. We, as members of God's family, are forever finite-infinitely unsettled in our infinite existence. We are capable of knowing all things, but we are not capable of self-knowingly becoming that which we forever are in our infinite existence. That is the infinite reality of our infinite existence.

In our individualized spiritual-Man existence, we are forever at the end and the beginning of our spiritual progression, unfoldment, and realization. We are at the end because, in any eternity we spiritually and successfully occupied, we found, accepted, and obeyed God, as the substance, heart, and soul of our divine beingness.

Still, we are at the beginning of our spiritual-Man existence, because the spiritual evolving cycle of our objective existence never ceases. Thus, the realizing of our individualized destiny is a never-ending process of self-realization, self-experience, and self-knowingness. We exist to understand the beginning and endings of things, in an infinite universal reality, where there are no beginnings or endings to reality.

CHAPTER IV

Idea Realm

Ideas are the source of all things.

Plato

Plato first postulated the existence of the idea realm well over two thousand years ago. In the objective realm, ideas are ever-present and infinite, and they contain their own and individual inherent self-power, driving them to objectify their purpose for existence. Besides our relationship to ideas, they integrate themselves into the objective realm processes of reality, for the purpose of creating new physical worlds and universes.

As individualized immortal-Man, we are infinitely born into the objective realm, which includes the idea realm. Ideas come to us, either to our self-conscious or our subconscious, for acceptance, understanding, and interpretation. When God is self-consciously neglected, denied, or rejected, our free will combined with our self-conscious activating ability to interpret and misinterpret ideas becomes the genesis, for all the appearances of evil and sin.

In the objective realm, each one of us is capable of self-aware thought. As such, each one of us is the soul-awareness of ultimate reality. Our capability for self-aware thinking is the result of our infinite self-consciousness awareness interacting with the infinite objective existence of idea realm ideas. Without our ability for self-conscious thought, ultimate reality's existence would be infinite existence without relevance, meaning, or purpose.

In the formless realm, we first encounter the idea realm. In the formless realm, ideas give us our ability to think in a language. Our ability to language-think gives us our ability to understand, interpret, and adapt to objective reality. Also, our ability to comprehend the substance of the forever existence of all things gives each of us the potentiality for being all-powerful.

Thus, though the existence of ideas, we have the ability, availability and opportunity to understand all aspects of objective and ultimate reality. In a reciprocal manner, objective reality gives us the environment to experience the acceptance, interpretation, and understanding of ideas through our objective self-aware existence.

Ideas are ever-present throughout objective reality. Ideas solely exist to be made manifest and thus to be experienced. Ideas provide us with the capability of understanding God, but to God, ideas remain unknown. God is incapable of Self-conscious thought and incapable of experiencing existence. Therefore, idea realm ideas have no relevance in relationship to His Self-realizing of Himself.

Also, ideas provide us with the understanding core reality. Core reality and God occupy independent sections of ultimate reality and have no relationship or interaction with the objective realm. However, God has a Self-unknown relationship with objective reality through each one of us, as forever carriers of the presence of God.

Our capability of self-conscious thought and understanding provides the only real power to our self-conscious, self-aware individualized existence. The self-wielding of our self-powerfulness depends on the forever widening and broadening depth of our spiritual understanding. Thus, each one of us is all-powerful in our unique and individualized expression. Since idea realm ideas are infinite in reality, our ability to understand reality is infinite.

There is always constant newness and freshness to ideas ceaselessly seeking receptivity, in the objective realm. Infinite ideas have the infinite potentiality for expression. There is no limit to the number of times ideas may appear, cease to appear, or reappear, in their forever accepted functionings, utilizations, and manifestations.

We cannot control or determine which forever ideas will seek entrenchment in the sphere of our self-consciousness. At times, we allow random ideas into our self-consciousness, in the guise of false spirituality, and provide those ideas with a temporary mental abode. The acceptance and interpretation of random ideas occur because we have not stood diligently against the enticing misinterpreted aromas of unreality.

Our realization of truth is directly proportional to the strength of our desire to understand the divinity of our objective existence. As Physical-Man our free will is self-destructive when we choose to displace God from our self-awareness. For the harmonious expression of ideas, through our transbeingness, a true love of God must be self-consciously and self-continuously cultivated, accepted, and obeyed.

Our free will exercise of all real power must be the outcome of free will desire and decision to know God, and follow the reality of our divine beingness. When our free will power is used to express goodness and harmony, it forever increases giving us the ability to make increasingly accurate spiritually correct choices. This type of mental power seems magical because, with it, we are capable of overriding the physical laws of reality. Thus, all of ultimate reality is our obedient servant.

Through punishment and forgiveness sins are redeemed, but our redemption is not complete unless it includes our self-conscious acceptance of the presence of God. This entire process requires ideas for the understanding and implementation of our infinite redemption. Without ideas, all processes of existence would be unknown, and existent reality itself would be unknown and without any infinite knowable value.

There is only one mind possessing the capability of self-awareness. That one mind is God's mind, and it is the one consciousness we all share, and individualize together. We are one and all, self-aware of our divinity, just as God is Self-aware of His. The difference between our self-awareness of our divinity and God's Self-awareness of His is that our self-awareness evolves infinitely and individually through the understandings that the idea realm provides each of us.

Thus, we are endlessly emerging in the understanding of ourselves, through our relationship with the idea realm. God evolves, but His evolving does not include the understanding of ideas. The evolving of God is His infinite nature in forever Self-expression. Thus, God possesses Self-awareness without understanding.

Each of us possesses the capability of attracting only the trueness of ideas based on our individual spiritual proclivities and desires. Our interpretations of ideas always correspond to the degree of depth reached or the degree of non-depth reached, in our spiritual desires, understandings, and evolvement.

Without a self-conscious awareness and acceptance of the presence of God, we will self-consciously continue to experience unreal existence, as godless unreality echoing its pagan-reality proclamations. Our self-power of understanding, through the mental assimilation of ideas, gives each of us the capability for infinitely understanding the reality of truth and understanding the unreality of non-truth.

Our continuing evolving of spiritual understanding requires continuous interaction with idea realm ideas. Infinite knowledge is infinite in its limitation because our unlimited capacity to understand is in a forever process of understanding. Thus, we are forever limited by the things we do not know and forever constrained by the things we do know. Thus, this is one of the paradoxes of our infinite existence.

God does not have any idea understanding of Himself; God is Himself, and thus His nature is forever Isness. God cannot interpret His nature because He possesses no means for Self-interpretation. It would be infinitely limiting for God to have any Self-knowingness of ideas because that would presuppose an outside-of-Himself motivation, to contemplate reality.

The idea realm enables each of us to describe, interpret and experience God as love, beauty, perfection, joy, kindness, harmony, et cetera. We alone experience the qualities of God; God cannot experience His qualities. He is His qualities. The nature of God is infinite, and it is the idea realm that provides each of us, as objective-Man, with the opportunity and ability to infinitely understand God's nature.

In the objective realm, our experiences of the love, beauty, and harmony are ongoing and eternally increasing. Thus, due to the idea realm, we are infinitely encountering the foreverness of God's infinitely unfolding nature. Our infinite existence centers on our understanding of God. Without the idea realm, we would never know the God of our forever beingness.

To our self-consciousness, the understanding and interpreting of ideas in the real and unreal realms of reality determines what we understand ourselves to be. Our understanding of ourselves and our interpretations of ourselves become the rubbery contortions of our objective self-realized existence.

All appearances of evil are the externalization of perfect ideas wrongly interpreted and accepted by our self-consciousness when we allow ourselves to self-consciously accept misinterpretations of godlessness. The doers of things harmful self-consciously choose to reject their divinity and enter into a self-chained state, of self-conscious ignorance projecting appearances of evil, into the physical realm of our experiencing of existence.

Objective reality is real, but our self-conscious experiences of objective reality are unreal. It is our forever dependency and interdependency on the idea realm that enables us to experience and to understand our infinite existence. We recognize and interpret ideas to understand the foreverness of our physical lives.

Thus, we have objective reality interpreted and expressed by each of us individually interacting with objective reality constructed by idea realm ideas, resulting in our self-conscious awareness of objective reality, as understood by each of us, in the non-real realm of our self-conscious self-actuated created experiences.

We, as individualized objective-Man, do not and cannot create ideas, we only accept, understand, and interpret them. The idea realm forever gives our individualized soul infinite thought nourishment, for the revealing of our infinite objective destiny. Ideas are seeds for our experiencing of objective realm existence. Thus, the idea realm enables us to interact mentally with the formless, physical, purgatorial, and spiritual realms.

The evolving of ideas is only meaningful as interpreted by our individualized self-consciousness. Our self-conscious awareness of ever evolving ideas is simply new realizations of how ideas are understood and utilized. Individual ideas themselves never evolve.

The apparent evolving of anything in the objective realm is merely one idea replacing another in a series of individually unique ideas building upon other unique ideas. Thus, the concept of complexity is the understanding of the relationship of ideas to one another, in their continuing process of self-integration.

Therefore, from the perspective of objective reality, as expressed through the idea realm, nothing is easy or complex in design; there is only the infinite manifestation of wholeness. All infinite real existence is in truth, the highest idea-realization of harmony showing itself to itself, as understood and interpreted by each of us.

Alone or united, we possess the capability to increase or decrease the appearance of harmony, into the seemingly real realm of experiencing existence. Thus, as we experience harmony or disharmony, in our self-awareness, these harmonious or non-harmonious ideas are projected into the realm of experience. In this manner, each of us ongoingly experiences harmony and disharmony.

The experiencing of objective reality often seems mysterious. These seemingly magical or mysterious expressions are simply ideas whose purpose for existence has not been understood or only understood by a few. Therefore, in our excursions through eternities endless, we are as little children forever anticipating new and exciting magical adventures. When we perceive existence as enchanting, our self-awareness of ourselves is seen as a blessing.

For example, thousands of years ago the idea of a light bulb existed, but physical-Man had not evolved to the place, in objective existence, where he could recognize and incorporate the concept of a light bulb, into his experiencing of reality. However, if primitive physical-Man ever were to see a light bulb, he would certainly think it was magical. Ideas only retain their magical allurement, until they are understood.

Our infinite understanding of existence gives purpose to our experiencing of existence in ultimate reality. Thus, through each of us, ultimate reality is to be forever understood and to be forever experienced. The marvel of our forever individualized beingness is that we are endlessly learning, interpreting, and experiencing the ideas that define the who, what, and why of our infinite existence.

Thus, our understanding or non-understanding of ideas determines our finite-infinite spiritual destiny. Even though we have forever existed, we are presently and self-consciously bouncing about at a fledgling state of myopic spirituality in expression. We are now infinite spiritual beings, choosing to accept and interpret ideas which turn us into unspiritual shadow-dancers gyrating in non-reality.

Our ability to infinitely understand and interpret ideas highlights the realization that there are no final spiritual victories. Our forever existence is experienced finitely-infinite. In our forever experience of our beingness, how many times have we used and re-used the same ideas to understand our infinite selves? Our infinite existence consists primarily of our forever understandings of the ideas concerning our forever nature and the experiencing of our forever reality.

We self-consciously exist to interpret our existence. Through ideas, we can interpret our real existence and real non-real existences. Since we exist infinitely, we understand, interpret, and experience ourselves infinitely. However, no idea, can ever touch, affect, impact, or harm our individualized, indestructible, and infinite God-identity. It is through idea realm ideas that we can describe our existence to ourselves.

We understand our existence as we experience our interpretations of idea realm ideas. In our objective existence, we use ideas to create experiences. Thus, all knowledge results from our self-conscious interpretation of existence, through our self-conscious interaction with the idea realm. Idea realm ideas exist solely to augment our self-existence. Thus, the idea realm infinitely augments our forever existence as individualized-Man.

We exist objectively to understand and experience our forever divinity. For each of us, the experiencing existence goes through the endless range of our self-conscious thoughts. The idea realm provides us with the ability to self-think. We can only understand the ideas receptive to our self-evolving. Thus, our self-awareness of ideas is the reflection of our desires, which then provides the understanding of our desires that we seek and find.

Ideas are forever whole, whether or not objectively expressed. Ideas have no innate ethics, morality, or spirituality. Ideas are non-self-aware. They know nothing of how they are being understood, interpreted, or used. In the infinite spirituality of our existence, ideas are the expressions of perfection without the substance of spirituality.

There are no ideas for the existence of sin and evil. It is our individualized renderings of these non-reality based ideas that bring into the objective realm, all the appearing constructs of sin and evil. It is only ideas wrongly discerned that enable so-called sin and evil any authoritative claim for existence. Thus, the misinterpretation of ideas is the forever source of sin and evils seeming influence over us.

Some idea realm ideas exist to support ultimate reality's infinite structure. Some exist to abet in the creating of forever evolving of universes. Some exist to understand ourselves and God. Some exist to be used in the physical realm, to create experiences. Some exist to establish an understanding of the purgatorial realm. However, idea realm ideas have no objective function in the actual physical portion of the purgatorial realm.

Some idea realm ideas are specifically designated, for each of the seven Heavens, in the spiritual realm. Some idea realm ideas exist solely for the purpose of understanding ultimate reality. Thus, some idea realm ideas function independently of immortal-Man's self-consciousness, but most idea realm ideas have an inter-functional relationship with individualized immortal-Man's self-consciousness while traversing objective reality.

The self-actualizing powers of ideal realm ideas forever wait for objective existence. All things infinitely real consist of designed ideas manifesting as the fulfillment of their purpose for existence. Also, idea realm ideas are the catalytic source for all objective expressions of evolvement.

Thus, the wholeness of all real existence consists of infinite and unique self-enclosed ideas endlessly creating and shaping all the functionings of objective reality. These non-self-aware idea realm ideas are the source for all of the powers expressing in the infiniteness of ultimate reality.

Objective reality is the infinite evolvement of wholeness. All objective experiences appear as extrusions of reality which we interpret, with idea realm assistance, as having beginnings and endings. However, all things real, devoid of our self-conscious interpretations, are a continuum of the infinitely segmental and evolving components of objective reality.

Disharmony has no independent existence. Any acceptance of the appearance of disharmony is our spiritual evolvement self-acknowledging our self-limiting level of spiritual apprehension. All seeming appearances of disharmony are the presumed existence of a reality outside of our self-conscious self-evolving awareness.

Disharmony or seeming chaos results from our self-imposed illusions manifesting as our self-accepted free will understandings, as we navigate through the unreal realm of experiencing existence. Any form of disharmony is the misinterpretation of an idea our self-consciousness has accepted as reality.

The potentiality for the existence of all falsehoods concerning our infinite existence resides forever within each of us. It is our spiritual understanding that destroys the non-destroyable falsehoods of non-reality. There can be no destruction of non-reality because it has no real infinite ideas to give it existence reality. However, each of us spends infinity defending ourselves from the non-real realm of unreality.

As we express and experience ideas, in their true innate wholeness of purity, our divine destiny is realized. All appearances of disharmony result from our misinterpretations of our idea-thoughts. These distortions of reality continuously create false appearances, in the realm of non-real experiences.

Then, we interpret and accept this godless reality and encounter it as truth; whereas, reality self-consciously understood, by us, as truth must manifest as truth, in the realm of experiencing our existence.

Non-reality is not real, but it persists in its claim for existence due to our infinite capacity to misinterpret ideas.

We create and are responsible for all the struggles we encounter in our experiencing of life. Through our misunderstandings of God, disharmonies are created as experience. Our correct understanding of God is our salvation from all appearances of perceptions of disharmony.

Thus, we are forever saving ourselves by accepting, into our self-consciousness, the actual ideas of God's infinite nature. If we existed without God, our salvation would not be possible. The idea realm provides us with the understanding of God's nature. Thus, it is the combination of ideas correctly understood, and the nature of God that forever saves us from the misunderstanding of our existence.

The idea realm enables us to understand and interpret our eternal, infinite, and forever self-conscious existence, the existence of God, and the existence of ultimate reality. Ideas give us the ability to understand that experiencing life requires the ongoing overcoming, of our self-imposing of struggles.

If we were unable to discern the purpose of our infinite existence, we would be incapable of understanding the forever meaning that our struggling efforts fulfill. In the infinite idea-evolving of the forever ongoing understandings of our divine beingness, we are forever struggling to realize our divine destiny.

Thus, our objective destiny is to idea-understand our infinite divineness, but our immortal divineness can only be followed by infinitely increasing in the power of our forever evolving spiritual understandings. Thus, our divine destiny endlessly demands the subjugating of the infinite misinterpreted idea-strangling tentacles of unreality.

Unreality is forever accepted and infinite rejected by each one of us. Our free will takes us away from our divinity, and our free will returns us to it. To understand ourselves as infinitely divine beings would be never to self-consciously accept any false idea-interpretations of non-reality. The only time unreality is not idea-interpreted into existence is when we self-consciously exist in core reality.

Objective reality always correctly manifests idea realm ideas according to their purpose for existence. Ideas, in their association with objective reality, create only real experiences. Thus, within objective reality, there are infinite combinations of real experiences to be infinitely created, in the endless evolving of the objective realm. The experiences that we create, as physical-Man, are non-real because we self-consciously create them with prescribed beginnings and endings.

The idea realm provides the means for all non-self-aware real life forms to make their appearances. Ideas express themselves as real experiences in the forever real activities of plants and animals. These real objective experiences are independent of each of us, as individualized objective-Man. However, these real idea-manifestations require our understanding and interpretation, to give purpose and meaning to their existence.

Predetermined randomness is one of objective reality's aspects. Thus, in the non-self-conscious environments of objective existence, ideas manifest as real experiences, through chance, opportunity, randomness, and general unpredictability. However, it remains our physical destiny to interpret the objective expressions of ideas so as to understand the workings and complexities of real existence. We alone define and interpret the reality and unreality of ideas.

The objective manifestations of ideas are the expression of reality. Our interpretation of the worldly expressions of ideas creates the seeming appearance of non-reality. Our interpretations of ideas include true and untrue representation of their existence. Thus, appearances of unreality often combine with appearances of reality. If that was not so, our forever spirituality could never be self-understood.

All real existence is permanently implanted, in a reservoir of infinite unknown fields of planted joyfulness. Thus, everything occurring in objective reality is the fulfilling of the expressions of joy. Still, all the joy permeating all reality needs each of us, to be known through our created experiences.

Thus, our individualized self-awareness is the only aspect, of ultimate reality, capable of acknowledging, understanding, and experiencing the joyfulness of existence. The nature of ultimate reality needs each one of us as immortal-Man, to confirm the purpose of its infinite inherent nature, unknown to itself.

Therefore, our infinite objective existence enables the purpose for non-self-aware existence to be realized and understood. All the meaning there is to all of the reality of life resides in the infinity of ideas, waiting for their futile ground to be received and experienced.

The infinite substance of joy enwraps all idea-based existence. As we forever interpret ultimate reality, through our acquisition of ideas, we are forever understanding or misunderstanding the gift of self-knowing joy-mandated existence. Our capacity to know and experience joy exists at all of our self-evolving realizations of our forever divinity.

The gift of our forever existence is to understand ourselves infinitely and experience ourselves as immortal divine beings. If we appreciate living life as a gift of joy, life must forever be capable of being comprehended and explained. Thus, if we are infinitely understanding and experiencing our existence, our infinite existence must include non-stop new understandings, new interpretations, and new forms of self-awareness.

The idea realm is infinite and complements our infinite objective beingness. If our material existence was infinite, but the idea realm was not, we would eventually interpret and experience the existence of idea realm ideas. If that were possible, it would mean that our understanding and knowledge of infinite reality would be infinitely limited, and our infinite existence would lose its infinite quality of self-understanding.

However, idea realm ideas are infinite, our individualized existence is infinite, and the experiencing of our beingness is infinite. Our infinite objective self-conscious reality is many things, but consistently boring it is not, because we are forever confronted, with the grueling challenges of chance, opportunity, randomness, and general unpredictability and ever new vistas in infinity.

So, as long as we are making self-conscious objective choices, whatever those choices may be, we realize an objective destiny of non-boringness. Still, we forever retain a free will choice to seek boredom, experience boredom, and be boring, however contrary, to our forever existence that may be. However, whenever we choose boredom; we are self-denying the purpose for our existence. We exist to experience the joys of our spiritually-based self-conscious interpretations of reality.

Ideas, in relationship to each of us, forever await our developing receptivity. Imagine, presently we only comprehend a minuscule portion of ideas for the understanding of our ever evolving self-sense of divinity. Whatever ideas we self-consciously apprehend expands our knowledge and understanding of experiencing existence.

Each one of us is infinitely standing still, in our individual and forever-claimed center of ultimate reality. Each of us has infinity to progress spiritually. However, our spiritual growing progression is an illusion. There is no such thing as self-aware spiritual progress viewed from the perspective of infinity. We interpret spiritual progress into the understanding of spiritual development.

Our infinite self-awareness of our infinite existence evolves but never increases in self-awareness. Our destiny is to understand our infinite divine beingness, but our infinitely divine beingness is never capable of being wholly understood or explained. We embrace the gift of existence, by understanding that our infinite divinity is forever evolving. If that were not true, our ultimate reality of existence would have finality, in our forever self-comprehension, and then our self-aware existence would become purposeless.

The forever understanding of ourselves requires ideas. As we understand ourselves, we know God; however, God's Self-awareness is forever expanding beyond the reality of our perceptions and understandings. Our individualized self-consciousness forever existence persists in the process of understanding our infinite existence and in understanding our infinite nature as God's nature.

We will never completely comprehend the ideas of reality. The godless unreality of ideas relentlessly shouts for acceptance within our real and non-real identities. The presence of our self-consciousness must be forever understood, because the claims of godless unreality forever infect lives, to take ownership of our self-aware existence.

As individualized-Man, our objectively waged non-real battles are infinite. Our forever war, within our self-consciousness, pits absolute reality warring against our acceptance of the forever unreal real. Thus, our infinite existence is a perpetual spiritual battle. Our infinite beingness is not a clash between good and evil; it Isa forever war, within our self-consciousness, for the supremacy of spiritual understanding.

The perpetuity of unreality's false existence is the result of our misinterpretations of ideas. I ask again: How can we understand what we truly are, if we do not understand what we truly are not? Therefore, the understanding of our infinite selves requires the understanding of our immense capabilities for the doings of good and the doings of non-good.

Thus, the authentic understanding of the foreverness of our existence requires the misunderstanding of the foreverness of our non-authentic existence, strange as it seems. If that is not true, we would never really be capable of understanding our true self-identities. We would accept the definition of ourselves, by the things we experienced in the outer objective realm, interpreted by our individualized minds, in the inner realm.

The shadows of unreality are blurred and denied expression, as we fill our self-awareness with the light of the forever real and genuine. Thus, we vanquish the appearances of godless unreality by understanding the ideas of actual reality, not by continuing to misinterpret the ideas as unreality. The gift-bane of our forever existence is our ability to misinterpret ideas into non-real appearances and experiences.

Our objective self-awareness is to understand forever and accept the wholeness of ideas. How we perceive and experience existence is forever and entirely based on our free will choices. It is our free will that injects morality into ideas. Thus, how we choose to accept and interpret ideas determines the directions we take, in the fulfilling of our objective realm destiny.

Our experiencing of objective existence is the product of the evolving understanding of ourselves. Spiritual knowledge must be desired, sought, and learned. In our self-conscious spiritual experiences of our self-beingness, the ends never justify the means. In other words, we should not embrace false interpretations of ideas of truth, to attempt demonstrations of spirituality. Never seek undeserved spiritual rewards; we must spiritually work for them. We spiritually work to understand our real selves; we work to understand our non-real selves, and we work to know ourselves as divine.

To intentionally do wrong, in the name or nature of God, is spiritual blasphemy that leads to the paralyzing of spiritual advancement, for all of God's family, and drives individuals into the realms of spiritually depraved darkness. If we succumb to unholy dishonesty, we lose the power of understanding to rectify ourselves divinely.

At all levels of our self-awareness, the trueness of our spirituality must be practiced. Our spiritual goal is to be divinely consistent, or we realize our destiny in warped and confused self-accepted illusions. To self-fool ourselves in our relationship to God is to be eternally lost in the wilderness of non-spiritual uncertainties. To understand God with unshakeable certainty is to express all-powerfulness, in the realm of appearance.

To our evolving objective self-awareness, our existence always seems to exist in shadows of divinity mystically darkening and clearing in intensity. Until we are spiritually able, to understandingly remove the shadows glazing over the divine realizing of ourselves, we are destined to remain godlessly chained to ongoing progressions of eternities.

The present world we inhabit is often difficult to fathom. Sometimes it seems as though good and evil are walking hand in hand. Ideas accepted by a self-consciousness which is divinely receptive and teachable, to things forever pure are understood in their eternal divine wholeness. Being teachable requires the desire, willingness, and understanding to interpret ideas in the wholeness of their expressions rather than succumbing to their enticing echoes of truth.

There is no salvation from the forever temptation to misinterpret ideas into the seemingly godless reality of experiencing our self-existence. To be spiritually mindful is to begin each endless objective journey, cultivating a spiritual awareness of divine receptivity, in the form of divine teachability. Anyone who remains non-teachable, concerning things divine, is choosing to stay loyal to their godless non-spiritual undisciplined choices.

Idea realm ideas come to our self-awareness in three ways. First, they come through the agencies of chance, opportunity, randomness, and general unpredictability. In other words, ideas are forever wandering and forever seeking opportunities for receptivity, both in self-aware and non-self-aware environments.

Thus, our random thoughts are merely the self-conscious recognition of random ideas, temporarily finding attention in our self-awareness. Often ideas enter into our self-awareness, and we dismiss them quickly. For example, presently I am randomly self-consciously aware of the silly idea of a frog wearing a polka dot bow tie. I gave this self-conscious awareness no thought-glue, and it quickly departed from my self-awareness. In a similar manner, we choose our strength of receptivity or non-receptivity to all ideas.

Second, ideas come to us through so-called laws of attraction. The strengths of our accepted beliefs, within our individualized self-consciousness, attract some specific forever wandering ideas. Thus, we draw ideas to us, corresponding to the strength of our mentally directed thoughts.

Therefore, the increasing intensity of our thought-desires provides the greatest drawing force for bringing ideas to our self-awareness, for our self-acceptance. In this manner, the things we attract and accept, display our objective self-evolving understanding of ourselves.

We entice evils to ourselves when our self-consciously entrench ourselves in the auras of evil. We draw progressed goodness to ourselves, when our self-awareness is rooted, in the auras of goodness. In this manner, we are forever determining our divine destiny which is self-consciously and spiritually realized, with our ever-increasing self-awareness of goodness.

Third, we willfully attract ideas for specifically designated purposes. In other words, we self-consciously self-actuate the process for creating experiences. Thus, we are continuing to fulfill our destiny, by self-consciously directing the purpose of existence, through our self-willed desired incorporation of ideas, into the experiencing realm of physical reality.

The foreverness of objective reality provides the infinite potentiality for the realization of the wholeness of ideas. Thus, from the vantage point of real physical existence, there is no such thing as our self-interpretation of ideas. To the objective realm, all ideas are infinitely real and whole. It is only our self-awareness that distorts the wholeness of ideas, into the non-real realm of experiences appearing in the physical material realm.

All non-self-consciously driven real experiences are the genuine and infinite functionings of objective reality's nature. Infinite objective reality is the forever seemingly randomness of reality, in the wholeness of expression. If we did not self-consciously exist, the expression of ideas would always manifest in their infinite wholeness, without the capability of being misinterpreted.

However, without our self-conscious existence, the expressing wholeness of ideas would exist in a reality of meaninglessness. To objective reality, the idea realm's existence is whole and undivided, a continuum of forever harmony. When objective reality is viewed, by each one of us, it is perceived in broken segments of reality's wholeness. Our external divine destiny is to see and experience only the wholeness of reality in our interpretations of segmented objective reality.

Without a humble reverence for God-awareness and acceptance, it is not possible to consistently apprehend the true harmonious state and nature of ideas expressing in objective reality; therefore, it is not possible to correctly understand ourselves, in our true divine identity as individualizations of God who is experiencing existence.

In the physical realm, we are capable of creating godless unreality and surrendering to it. Always and always, our awareness of the goodness of God is required to separate true and divine interpretations of ideas, from unreal interpretations of ideas. We must understand and accept our innate goodness in God, to deny the whispering chants of non-reality trying mightily to enter our spiritually evolving self-conscious awareness.

Because the idea realm gives us the forever ability to understand God, we have the infinite capability of changing our false interpretations of reality into genuine understandings of reality. We desire to know and self-consciously evolve towards God, as long as we recognize the need to overcome our receptivity to things godless.

The progressions of our physical existences are spiritually complete when all of our self-desired thoughts embrace an imperishable awareness and acceptance of the presence of God in our thoughts. Total reliance on God occurs when we have spiritually evolved to the understanding that we longer have any choice-desire to follow any pied piper dragoon of godless unreality.

When we desire only God, we have self-consciously unified ourselves with God, in our objective and eternal existence. Still, it must remain clear, that we infinitely exist to experience and overcome the falsely driven claims of unreality. However, when we realize our spiritual success over the kings of forever falseness, we have only spiritually conquered one sojourn, out of countless sojourns, into objective reality.

Imagine our infinite actual existence as a divine prizefight, in an ongoing contest for spiritual understanding and supremacy? In some rounds we are victorious, and in some rounds, we lose. Thus, as we fight infinitely, we will experience infinite intervals of godless unreality as sorrow and pain, as well as endless interludes of spiritual triumph.

Regardless of the number of times, we are knocked down and out; we eventually return to resume the endless battle for the understanding of our infinite spiritual existence. Finally, after seemingly endless rounds, we render our opponent helpless. The purpose for our infinite existence is validated, and we no longer experience the suffering pains of a fight-driven existence.

Temporary-infinite punishment forever results from our fighting bouts with non-reality. There are no ultimately complete spiritual triumphs in absolute reality. Some of the endless rounds of pain are greater than others. Some endless rounds of spiritual victory promote greater divine understandings than others. Non-reality is infinite in its ability to be known by us, but each of us has the mental capability of experiencing non-reality out of our self-aware existence.

We succumbed to the powerless poundings of unreality, each time we are knocked down. Our pain-filled sufferings resulted from our inability to understand our opponent. The fight has no time limit. Therefore, we have infinity to realize our final objective spiritual victory. Bloodied and bruised, we finally vanquished unreality. Thus, our finite-infinite victory and salvation have been achieved, in our imposed existence in the objective realm.

In the above illustration, objective reality houses the fighting ring. Each one of us represents an infinitely unbeatable spiritual champion. Punches and counterpunches are ideas understood and misunderstood. Our opponent is unreality. The pounding gloves represent thrusts of godless unreality finding their receptive targets.

The ringing of the bell allows for the advancement of self-conscious spiritual progress. As we rest between bouts, we refocus upon our forever divinity. Throughout our objective fighting rounds, we bob and weave from the thundering shadow-punches of non-reality. All the punches we feel are the false claims of godless unreality that have pounded themselves into our self-accepting understanding.

In the trueness of ultimate reality, each one of us is a dedicated spiritually prized fighter armored and sustained by the forever presence of God. We infinitely fight to understand ourselves and the purpose of our forever existence. However, the primary difficult of being a forever spiritually prized fighter, infinitely fighting to win things spiritual, is that we are forever sentenced to infinitely of life without the infinite assent of our approval, desire, or will. We have absolutely no choice but to obey the dictates of our infinite existence and accept the consequences.

After the finality of our physical realm fight, for our spirituality to be triumphant, we return once again to core reality, to rest in total self-unity with God, until we once again we are assigned to become objective reality's fighting warriors, subduing the spiritually menacing phantoms of non-reality. Thus, our divine destiny cannot be denied, altered, or aborted, out of our infinite experiencing of our existence.

Our next fight becomes our next excursion into objective reality to self-consciously determine the spiritual outcome of our material realm existence; we have no choice but to fight. Ideas give us the capability to battle successfully, for the spiritual realization of our physical lives.

Thus, the idea realm makes the fighting experience of our self-conscious existence possible, in our mental understanding and interaction with the physical realm. Without ideas, no physical world or universe could evolve into organized, objective reality. Thus, the purgatorial and spiritual worlds would also be non-existent.

Again, each one of us fights to realize the purpose of our self-conscious existence; we must experience our existence in the formless, physical, purgatorial, and spiritual worlds, of objective reality. Again, our ability to understand and interpret ideas makes for the creation of the unreality of experiences, which enable us to understand correctly and explain our real existence.

Ideas accepted by a universe manifest through non-determinable occurrences of chance, opportunity, randomness, and general unpredictability. Thus, due to the randomness of evolving of universes, ideas are unique and unpredictable, except for the fact that they must obey the overall idea-plan, for all self-aware and all non-self-aware existences.

For individualized-Man's self-aware existence, the inherent infinite idea design for each evolving physical world automatically channels the forces of randomness to evolve the predestined evolution of physical man, to prepare for individualized physical-Man's appearance. Without ideas, nothing can be experienced in all of ultimate reality.

The idea realm is based on and consists of infinite harmony. In the realm of ideas, no judgments are ever made regarding our infinite self-aware existence. We exist to understand our existence. Idea-concepts enable us to understand our reality as self-aware existence. Ideas provide us with ever increasing understandings which give us the possibility of becoming all-powerful.

The idea realm is forever subservient to our infinite individual free will. Without idea-thoughts, our free will would be valueless in the understanding and interpretation of existence. If the idea realm did not exist, our ability to make free will choices would be rendered powerless and meaningless. For the ability of our free will to function, the understandings of ideas must be made manifest. Thus, the idea realm provides those understandings.

To possess infinite self-aware objective existence without the ability to determine the content of our self-aware reality, by way of idea realm ideas, would mean that we would have an infinite predetermined non-understandable destiny to follow. If that were to be our actual self-aware reality, our objective existence would be preordained and meaningless chaos.

We have a designed destiny to fulfill, but our divine destiny is forever being fulfilled, in the fulfilling of our divine destiny. Our divine destiny is to understand ourselves as part of God and not part of God. Without the idea realm, the non-part of our self-conscious awareness would be unable to experience existence.

Thus, ideas enable us to fulfill our divine destiny to experience life objectively. When we are spiritually successful in the idea-understanding and experiencing our divine destiny, we are divinely rewarded. When we fail to understand objectively and realize our divine destiny, there are no divine rewards.

We must be totally free in our self-aware choices, or our infinite existence could never have any spiritually earned value. In the understanding of ideas, we are infinitely able to accept or reject our God-nature. If we affirm God, the joys of infinite existence are spiritual gifts, to our forever experiencing life.

If there were never any spiritual rewards, in the experiencing of our existence, our existence would be an existence of infinite uncontrollable suffering, pain, heartache, and depravity. Who could envision an infinite self-awareness of life that did not include the enjoyment of earned spiritual rewards?

Therefore, even with the realization of an infinite God, there are godless ologies and godless isms that foster a sense of spirituality that enable sincere of godless individuals to achieve some inner sense of pagan peacefulness and atheistic fulfillment. Thus, the existence of God is not a necessary prerequisite, for experiencing a spiritual type of reward.

Thus, for all infinite self-conscious free will-driven existences to be grounded in an infinite sense of fairness there must be a sense of spiritual comfort or reward provided to all of self-aware existence, whether or not God is self-consciously desired. However, all spiritual rewards, God-based or not, must be spiritually earned.

The recipients of godless spiritual rewards must be sincere non-harm making godless members of the divine family. Thus, in the physical realm of our transbeingness, there are comforting isms, ologies, and systems of thought, not required to be based in the self-acceptance of God. Therefore, there are spiritual rewards for the sincerely good but godless members of the divine family, but these rewards are realized only in the physical realm.

Now I will give an example of a godless ology of which I have some familiarity, the atheistic ology of astrology. Many, even most individuals believe astrology to be silly, inane, nonsensical, and the epitome of foolishness. Quite often that seems valid. However, in fairness to astrology, something that has been around as long it has been around deserves thoughtful observation.

Some critics assert that astrology to be the embodiment of evil. That assumption is nonsense. If astrology appears evil, evil is interpreted into it. The study of astrology may be helpful to some individuals; I emphasize 'may be' for those who possess a searching sensitivity for things spiritual without belief in any God, yet sincerely desire to practice a form of non-divine spiritual helpfulness.

Thus, many individuals who believe in astrology do not believe in God. Of course, many individuals practice astrology and devoutly believe in the God of their understanding. Thus, the realm of astrology provides individuals having no belief in God and individuals having varying beliefs in God, to discover for themselves a meaningful expression, for their spiritually desired yearnings.

In my youth, I studied and practiced astrology and found it to be interesting and spiritually rewarding on helping others understand the impediments of life. However, I soon came to realize that its seemingly benevolent allure was an obstacle to my spiritual sense of purpose. I realized that studying and practicing of astrology was not for me.

Astrology is the idea realm's reflection of divine light without the understanding and sustaining source of a God-realized divinity. The practice of astrology echoes a form of false spirituality. It is false spirituality in the sense that it does not overtly encourage the seeking of God. Any seeming spiritual truth appearing in the practice of astrology results from the sincere and non-malevolent misunderstanding of the practice of Godless goodness.

I recognize that in our physical-Man existence, many individuals find a sense of spiritual fulfillment and purpose in astrology. The mechanical interpretation of celestial movements seems to provide them with searching answers for our human-based experiences. Astrology is individualized physical-Man's attempt to impose and interpret an infinite distinct celestial design into human existence, a design interpreted into its practice by its practitioners.

Our inner impulse-sense of seeking spirituality, with or without God, is a desire to understand the seeming unfathomable. Thus, astrology's attraction is that it offers understandings of comfort, for the seemingly incomprehensible questions concerning our physical realm existence. Simply, astrology is wrong because it assumes the existence of an independent knowledge and power separate from us, which determines our destiny and thus renders our free will impotent.

To accept a so-called spiritual belief system, such as astrology, devoid of a God-basis is a denial of our divine purpose for existence, but it is not evil, it a spiritual misuse of our non-divine free will. Most evils result from the intentional desire to reject God and encourage others to do the same. Thus, evil always results from actions associated with a self-conscious repudiation of God. Astrology is neutral on God's existence.

To believe in and accept any godless-based teaching is a free will option each one of us forever possesses. How we interpret our infinite existence is our forever choice. The biggest problem with astrology is that even individuals who believe in God and believe in astrology, place astrology ahead of God. It is astrology that they turn to for answers, not God.

Each one of us is infinitely empowered with a free will. There is no infinite mandate requiring that God must be sought, found, accepted and obeyed. However, without the self-acceptance of God, the real joys of existence cannot be attained. Astrology fools the spiritually minded into always making God secondary. Still, for non-God orientated individuals, the understanding and practice of astrology may provide some physical realm comfort.

Let me be unequivocally clear. I do not recommend that any God-seeking or non-God seeking person study astrology. Astrology is a trap that combines good-will authoritarian motivations, intellectualism, and ego, with a sense of divine certainty, but it lacks a recognized and comprehensible God-based foundation.

For those who seriously study astrology, their study of astrological data gives them their highest sense, for the interpreting of objective reality. In essence, they replace the need for the understanding of God, with calculations of the relationships of the celestial bodies to one another.

In my study of astrology, I encountered many spiritually minded individuals. Many were kind, loving, and non-judgmental. They sincerely cared about the well-being of their fellow man. If these persons were ambivalent to God's existence or they accepted God, their study of astrology was harmless. However, astrology is spiritually harmful to those individuals who sincerely desire to seek, find, and know God. For them, God-based spiritual evolvement is delayed, perhaps for eternity.

Still, for most people who practice a Godless form of astrology, they attain a sense of spirituality. For them, astrology replaces a seeking of God, with a form of comforting intellectualism. For them, the belief in any God is secondary to their knowledge, faith, and acceptance of astrology.

For the truly spiritually minded, to rely upon a mechanical and celestial understanding of existence, without God, is to dishonor the forever gift to our self-aware lives. Still, ultimate reality provides rewards for the Godless practitioners, who practice a sense of encouraging goodness. Ultimate reality rewards the practice of kindness, encouragement, and comfort, with or without a self-acceptance of God.

Astrology imitates truth. The interpretations of idea realm ideas give astrology its seeming credibility, in the describing of objective reality's influence upon human existence. Components of astrology are interpreted differently depending on the skill level of the astrological practitioner.

Individuals are comforted by astrology because astrology gives them a cause and effect understanding, for the non-understandable occurrences in their lives. The experiencing of life seems more bearable if experiences can be understood, through the influences of outside factors. Whether or not there is any spiritual validity to that type of comfort, the caring-for-others practice of astrology provides it.

However to study astrology is to replace the desire to understand God with the desire to know the workings of astrology. The study of astrology boosts and flaunts an individual's ego by their seeming ability to answer the unanswerable. Thus, it is harmful to anyone's spiritual progression because astrology bestows an aura of confidence which is hard for anyone to surrender.

Thus, adherents of astrology do not need God because astrology seemingly provides the answers to life's questions? In astrology, spiritual blessings are sought and accepted without the required divine preparations of earned spirituality. Astrology is representative of the ongoing spiritual problem which is the desire to experience spiritual blessings, this time in the form of spiritual understandings, without the divinely required effort to attain those understandings.

Hence, one of the attractions of astrology is for someone to garner unearned spiritual understanding, without divine effort. Interestingly, since we attract things to ourselves, at the spiritual level of our spiritual receptivity, some of the wrongful things we attract may provide with a sense of comfort. Again, our free will choices are not judged, by any component of ultimate reality, except ourselves.

To accept the workings of astrology is to admit spiritual limitation. As it is with all things, to endorse the beliefs of astrology is our objectively evolving understanding, reflecting back to our individualized selves, at the spiritual level of our spiritual self-evolving. Simply, astrology is an accepted form of benign intellectualism, rather than reliance upon the understanding of God.

The danger in studying astrology for the spiritually minded is in the sense of control that it gives to its practitioners. In other words, individuals seeking answers, under the influence of astrology, will cede their free will to others and allow others to determine their future choices.

Thus, practitioners of astrology and the ones being *practitionered* upon are on a downward spiritual spiral. Unfortunately, any comfort astrology seemingly provides, strengthens an individual's self-conscious separation from God, but still infinity provides support and encouragement for those who freely choose forms of desired harmless godlessness.

Now, I will turn from the subject of astrology. In the spiritual realm, we experience our divinity at the level of our divine self-understanding. Since we are infinite, our self-understandings are infinite and thus, our harmonious experiencing of ideas is infinite. This concept is similar to a string of random numbers expressing infinitely with never any finality, to their forever unfolding. So it is with each of us.

When we reach the spiritual realm, there are no misinterpretations of ideas. In these heavenly pastures of self-understood and self-accepted divinity, our collective and eternally evolving divine destiny is realized. In our experiences in the spiritual realm, ideas are accepted without any interpretations.

Thus, in the spiritual realm, when any divine realization is unquestionably acknowledged and welcomed, ideas are only known in the purity of their wholeness. At this time, the gift of existence is surely recognized, understood, accepted, and experienced. In the spiritual realm, we embrace ideas specifically allotted to our divine placement.

Turning to the physical realm, our incorporation of ideas provides the shape, meaning, direction, and function, for the peaceful developmental expression, for all physical phenomena required to create physical worlds and universes. Since all ideas, in the reality of ideas, are infinitely unique; all created physical worlds are infinitely unique, but they still must obey the overall infinite idea-plan, to provide homes for their self-conscious and non-self-conscious existence.

Physical worlds provide the needs and expressions of our individual spiritual progressions, in the realizing of our individual and collective divine destiny; therefore, each progressing physical world gives us opportunities to understand and experience our existence in perpetual newness and uniqueness.

The forms and directions for the making of physical worlds and universes manifest as a result of endless idea realm ideas forever emanating from the reality of ideas. These ever-present ideas continually seek a means for their physical or non-physical expression, depending upon their inherent designed purpose for existence.

All physical universes contain self-creating evolving worlds or eternities, existing solely for our individual and collective experience. The same pre-expression state of existence, for each new physical world, is based on the same changeless formless matter. The state of matter in formless flux is infinite, and its ability to forge and shape new physical worlds and universes is infinite.

All phenomena, appearing as objective creation result from the interaction of an evolving physical universe and physical worlds, with the reality realm of ideas. Thus, ideas represent the non-divine demiurge or afflatus for all visions of creations. God creates nothing, knows nothing of any creative process, and is not Self-functioning part of any creative-type reality.

Finally, each one of us has an idea in the idea realm that contains the knowledge of our infinite beingness in God. As an infinite idea, each one of us is infinitely whole, perfect, and indestructible. Also, each one of us is infinitely unique, No two ideas of the individualization of Man are the same. It is our forever destiny to use our self-conscious ability to understand and forever delve into the infinite reaches of our immortal identities. It is the idea realm that enables each of us to understand the reality of ourselves, as the forever expression of God.

CHAPTER V

The Physical, Purgatorial, and Spiritual Worlds

Physical World (part of our universe)

> Evolutionary cosmology formulates theories in which a universe is capable of giving rise to and generating future universes out of itself.
>
> Robert Nozick

The present universe burst into existence approximately 14 billion years ago without assistance from any God. The now prevailing cosmological hypothesis for the creation of the existing universe is the Big Bang Theory. Indeed, that is how our universe was born, and that is how all evolving cosmoi come into existence.

Each newly created cosmos is tangible and real and evolves into reality, through its self-sustaining energy, and is representative of the never-ending process of self-creating universes. Each universe is only one universe among a string of infinitely ongoing progressions of universes.

Each universe is an eternity obeying and fulfilling its purpose and mandate for existence. The creation of cosmoi is a designed function of objective reality. Each cosmos evolves without influence or direction from any self-consciously inspired God-type will. As cosmoi evolve, they evolve through a continuing symbiotic relationship with the idea realm.

Each new universe is an eternity and an eternity lasts as long as a universe lasts. Each new universe develops its individual uniqueness, identity, and destiny. The evolving nature of a universe results from its cooperative functions and interactions with idea realm idea-seeds, in their infinite harmonious development, unfoldment, and expression.

Within the created universe, our physical world is created, There is only one purpose for the existence of our physical world, within a universe, and that one purpose is for our self-conscious experiencing of existence, by us as immortal-Man transbeing as physical-Man, in the physical world. Thus, physical worlds allow for the capability of transbeing physical-Man to experience objective existence.

God's presence is Self-independently non-existent in any creating energy process of newly evolving universes. However, through our physical-Man's individualized self-conscious awareness, God's nature is objectively made manifest; but, the actual presence of God's nature is forever, foremost, and always understood by each of us individually, wherever we are self-consciously experiencing existence.

The infinite matter-substance required for each Big Bang expanding explosion is the non-changing formless physically infinite malleable substance-matter basis of objective reality. As a universe or eternity ends its expanding process of actual physical existence, it constricts in upon itself and devolves into its infinite native state of formlessness.

This constricting process provides the new creative self-activating generating power needed for creating the next Big Bang explosion, to burst forth and propel a new universe into objective existence. In this manner, the material realm process for creating universes is infinite.

Each new cosmos provides a means for ideas to project their identities, into the real tangible realm of objectivity. Without the existence of universes, ideas would lack the capability for manifesting their forever purpose, for their necessary contribution to the functioning of ultimate reality. Without universes, ideas could only provide our self-consciousness, with a sense of existence, never to be experienced.

The random migration and integration of ideas accepted and made manifest in each evolving universe formulate its individual identity. Each new universe evolves from its interaction with ideas. Still, each new cosmos evolves uniquely based on the unpredictability of ideas interacting with evolving physical universes, through the channels of chance, opportunity, randomness, and general unpredictability.

Each one of us, possessing self-conscious awareness has the divinely transbeing mandate to experience existence infinitely throughout the endless progressions of objective realm worlds existing in universes. Through the experiencing of life, the infinite overlays of our struggling divinity are revealed to us for our understanding.

The evolving structure of each physical world, created in the creating process of a universe is eternally unique unto itself, for the duration of its objective realm manifestation. Because each physical world is infinitely unique, our interrelations with each physical world are infinitely unique. Thus, our infinite experiencing of existence is forever unique.

Imagine each one of us has our forever unique understanding and interpretation of eternal worlds, universes, and realities? Thus, no two members, of God's family, experience or interpret objective reality in the same like manner. Thus, ultimate reality is infinitely and uniquely being understood individually.

When a Big Bang occurs and begins the process of forming a new universe, including our physical world, a new purgatorial and a new spiritual world also come into existence. The purgatorial and spiritual worlds are separate from each other, yet yoked by the seeming creative process in the bringing of a new physical world into existence.

Just as the physical worlds come into existence, for each of us to self-consciously inhabit and self-consciously experience, the purgatorial and spiritual worlds evolve into their objective place reality, for each of us to eventually occupy and self-consciously experience. Thus, objective reality's creations, of physical, purgatorial, spiritual worlds, enable each of us to fulfill the transbeing experiencing of our objective existence.

Also within objective reality is the existence of the formless realm. The formless realm is an infinite non-creative functional realm within objective reality. Its significance is that when physical, purgatorial, and spiritual worlds cease their identifiable objective existence, all divine family members, experiencing objective as the transbeingness of Man, return to the formless realm.

Of course, the formless realm is also the repository, for each one of us as immortal-Man, as we are impelled from core reality into objective reality, as our entry into the objective realm. Thus, the formless realm is our genesis link between core reality and entry into objective reality.

Without the existence of the formless realm, we would be unable to experience our phenomenal objective reality. Also, the formless realm is our self-conscious returning home location, when infinity completes is objective existence. When an eternity ends, and we, as the individualized transbeingness of Man, return to the formless realm, all memories of our past physical, purgatorial, and spiritual world excursions vanish.

Once our individual transbeing existence returns to the formless realm, each one of us as individualized formless-Man, awaits a new opportunity to experience a new self-aware beingness, through the creation and evolvement of the next physical world. When a new physical world is ready for our arrival, we choose the time to relocate ourselves.

In this manner, we experience worldly eternities ceaselessly, until we totally and uncompromisingly understand ourselves to be the spiritually uncompromising self-aware expressions of God. The number of times we relocate from the formless realm into the physical realm in one our sojourns, from core reality into objective reality, is unknown and varies from individual to individual.

Inherent in the design of all physical worlds is a provision providing for the creation and evolution of natural animal man. When this creative evolutionary process is complete, individualized formless-Man enters into evolved physical animal man, to bring self-awareness into physical-Man.

Thus re-begins the continuing eternally cycling of immortal-Man's physical transbeing existence. When evolving animal man is given self-consciousness, he spiritually awakens to his actual physical existence. Thus, as the human man physically evolves, he is not divine, but when he becomes infused with self-awareness of formless-Man, he becomes physical-Man and now he begins to understand himself as individualized infinite divinity, in self-expression. The man of this world is now divinely understood.

When individualized formless-Man's self-awareness enters into the human animal man, objective reality becomes awakened, to a new interpretation of itself. Thus, we as individualized physical-Man now become objectively capable of understanding our divinity and our destiny, through the self-conscious process of experiencing our existence.

Without the capability of evolving animal man to acquire a self-conscious identity, the evolutionary process of animal man would remain purposeless. Thus, the evolutionary material animal human creature would just be another evolving non-self-aware animal wandering randomly in the wilderness of objective reality.

In the awesomeness of physical material existence, there appear to be endless forms of evolving creations. However, anything seemingly objectively created is only an infinite segmented portion, of an infinite objective physical process, expressing in its infinitely-finite reality, of its infinite wholeness.

In objective reality, there are no beginnings and endings; there are only the infinite manifestations of finite-infinite existence. To each of us, the orderly functions within objective reality are interpreted as experiences and all experiences, from our individualized perspectives, are time-driven because all experiences have prescribed beginnings and endings, notably the experiences we self-consciously create.

From our infinite individual perspectives, the objective processes of creation seem to have beginnings and endings. However, the perpetual methods of reality appearing as creations are forever without beginnings and endings. It is only in the infinite processes of seeming creations that we identify and interpret the appearances of beginnings and endings.

Here is an example to understand the concepts of beginnings and endings. Within the circumference of a circle, there are infinite possibilities of potentially existing arcs having seeming beginnings and endings. These individualized arcs are interpreted into existence, by each of us, while at the same time; we recognize the unbroken wholeness of the circle's circumference. Each arc is attached to reality. Our interpretation of each arc is a non-real reality.

Thus, the interpreted potentialities for our understanding of the existence of arcs are time-driven and are understood, by us, as having beginnings or endings. However, the reality of objective reality is its wholeness which comprises infinite possibilities, from our perspectives, of endless arc-type beginnings and endings. To objective reality, our interpretations of time-based arcs are meaningless.

Thus, all seeming real manifestations of self-evolving creation occurring in each physically evolving universe demonstrate the inherent functionings of objective reality, evolving infinitely within itself. Basically, to ultimate physical reality, creation is a mechanical process of unfolding material existence which is forever part of the infinite Whole.

All seeming forms of creation are time-driven interpretations we each make as we observe and interpret the allness of reality. As individualized immortal-Man, we are not capable of completely understanding the wholeness of reality. We are only capable of discerning portions of the wholeness, in the forever evolving reality within itself, and provide interpretations which are only meaningful to ourselves.

Thus, all objective occurrences expressing as real experiences are infinitely encapsulated happenings, signifying finite-infinite streamlets of forever actual and real processes. Thus, all non-self-conscious material creations are the infinite functionings of objective reality, in forms of segmentally time-wrapped experiences of seeming randomness, which we infinitely interpret and provide meaning.

Therefore, all things objectively appearing as creations to us are segments, of the infinitely expanding encirclement of objective reality. Thus, infinity is forever increasing, but it only increases within itself. Infinity encompasses all of the ultimate reality of existence; therefore, there is nothing outside of infinity, including nothingness. If nothingness existed, nothingness would be somethingness.

Objective reality itself is incapable of any form of self-determined focused type creation. From objective reality's perspective, there is only the infinite churning energy of real creative-type manifestations. Each of us interprets the happenings within objective reality which appear to us as self-evolving creations. Thus, real experiences, expressing as creations in the wholeness of reality, seem to us as created portions within the wholeness of infinity.

The one and only purpose, for all real existence, is for each one of us to understand and interpret. In this manner, we describe our lives into our self-conscious understandings of ourselves. In short, we infinitely self-consciously exist to understand that we infinitely self-consciously exist, and we exist to understand ourselves in our individual relationship to our self-individualized interpretations of ultimate reality. All creations seemingly occurring in ultimate reality comprise the forever expressing wholeness of ultimate reality. In all ultimate reality, we as individualized immortal-Man are the only sources of creation.

In objective reality, we are never to understand fully or wholly our experience of existence, from the viewpoint of infinity's wholeness. As infinite divine beings, we are infinitely whole, and non-whole. We are forever whole because we are a part of ultimate reality, and ultimate reality is forever whole. We are infinitely non-whole because we are in the forever infinitely divine process of self-consciously understanding our existence, ultimate reality, and God.

Our persistent and ever-present destiny requires us to strive continuously for understanding, as we forever occupy the objective realm, in infinitely broken progressions of reality, towards the fullness of infinity. In the objective realm, we interpret our existence by way of ideas, interacting with chance, opportunity, randomness, and general unpredictability.

Our infinite self-aware reality demands that we forever seek the understanding of ourselves, but it does not require that we understand ourselves as spiritual. We are infinitely divine, but we can choose not to see or understand ourselves as divine. Look about; everywhere we see the choice to embrace and accept godless non-divinity as our reality. Hence, the great ruse of infinity; we are unshakable in the realization of our infinite divinity, but we are not unshakable in the acceptance of our divinity as we self-consciously experience our existence.

The general unpredictability of each evolving physical world provides new challenges for each of us to overcome. Thus, we persist in our struggles of self-consciously experiencing our true divinely unbending, eternal, infinite, and everlasting existence, as the self-consciousness of God interpreting Himself.

We experience life through ever new and continuing lifetimes, in the progressively evolving of physical worlds. Each new physical world gives each of us the opportunities to discover and rediscover the uniqueness of our self-actuating self-conscious awareness. Thus, each new physical world allows the infinite real to be experienced by the infinite real through creative experiences that are infinitely unreal and created by each of us.

Our experiences in an eternity only become meaningful through our understanding and interpretation of time. It is the concept of time that makes the understanding of our existence possible. Thus, in each physical world or eternity, the idea of time emerges as a necessary component for our understanding of our existence, and for the understanding existence itself.

Time becomes real to us as we progressively and self-consciously experience objective physical reality. However, time is meaningless to our overall infinite non-experienced existence. It is through our interpretations of time-driven experiences that give us the power underlying our ability to understand things real and non-real.

Thus, we interpret each newly evolving external world through our self-conscious constructs of time. Therefore, time, as it relates to our experiencing of existence, results from our understandings and interpretations of physical eternity's orderly progressions of infinite evolvement. Without our ability to construct time into the experiencing of existence, we would be unable to think self-consciously.

We are forever self-understanding our destiny, as we forever self-continuously fulfill our destiny. Our present collective and individual destiny consist of continuously struggling with struggles, losing to struggles, overcoming struggles, and then reaping the spiritual rewards, for our victories over struggles. Through the experiencing of struggles, we reveal our divinity to ourselves. Thus, struggles represent a divine catalyst for our spiritual evolving.

The realization that we are forever fulfilling the understanding of our divinity is one of infinity's sacred gifts to us, for divinely experiencing our existence. As I have said, our ultimate spiritual success is only achievable, in finite-infinite gradations through eternities endless, divinely sought, divinely found, divinely experienced, divinely fought, divinely understood, and divinely conquered. Each of us is on infinity's treadmill of beingness, and there is never to be any debarkation. Thus, we are the self-aware divine hamsters of infinity.

Our final spiritual success in any single struggling trek through objective reality is just one last spiritual success among ongoing spiritual finalities. Thus, our physical existence remains infinitely understood uniquely, interpreted uniquely, experienced uniquely, and spiritually conquered uniquely. Each one of us gives unique and individualized meaning to infinity.

Our ongoing eternal lives continue until the challenges delaying our self-conscious spiritual realizing of our destiny, cease their demanding influence over us. Then we leave objective reality and return once again to core reality, where we self-consciously reunify with God. In core reality, we unknowingly exist to God, as God's individualized self-aware family.

The self-conscious process of understanding our existence must include the non-understanding of all aspects of our beingness. In core reality, we know our divine reality without understanding our forever divinity. Thus, it forever remains for each of us to determine, for ourselves, the desirability of our infinite self-conscious existence. However, that is meaningless because we can do nothing about our infinite existence and the infinite processes we must follow to experience our infinite reality.

I quote from the immortal words of the Bard of Avon: "Nothing is good or bad, but thinking makes it so." Our ability to self-think gives us the power of understanding. Thus, our self-directing power of our self-conscious thoughts determines whether or not our infinite existence is a blessing or a curse.

Purgatorial World

The purgatorial world consists of two realms: non-physical purgatory and physical purgatory.

Non-physical Purgatory

The non-physical portion of the purgatorial realm is entirely mental. Our self-existence in the realm of experience demands punishment, or we would be unable to understand or tolerate ourselves, as evolving spiritual beings. It is here that all punishment for our evil and sinful wrongdoings occurs.

Purgatorial punishments for our non-spiritual wrongdoings guide us to our spiritual self-evolving, as we trudge ever onward through the myriad pathways, highways, and byways of eternities endless. I discussed purgatorial punishment in detail in the purgatorial-Man section, in the chapter on the Transbeingness of Man.

Physical Purgatory

The substantial portion of the purgatorial realm is for all individuals who self-consciously and continuously choose to reject God. Here, they spend the remainder of eternity self-consciously occupied with godlessness. They purposefully chose to experience a self-conscious existence combined with their self-conscious repudiation of God. Thus, their desired godless self-existence becomes their eternal purgatorial profane home.

In a sense, the physical purgatorial realm of reality is the opposite of core reality. In core reality, our awareness of God is self-known. In the physical reality of purgatory, God is self-rejected and unknown. In core reality, individualized-Man's existence is infinitely blissful. In the physical reality of godlessness, individualized-Man's non-experiencing of life is infinitely not blissful.

Anyone choosing self-aware existence without God is rejecting their self-divinity, identity, and divine destiny. For all those purgatorial decision makers who decided to remain eternally unrepentant in their self-conscious denial and rejection of God, they are automatically deposited into the physical realm of purgatory.

For them, physical realm purgatory is not a self-determined punishment because existence without God is their desired form of eternal reality. In purgatorial Hell, there is no self-desired salvation from self-garnered ungodliness. These Hell dwellers understand that there is no God to fear and that they are in forever control of their destiny, through limited severely by their lack of self-attained spirituality. For them, the gift of infinite existence is not a spiritual gift.

In fact, in this realm of purgatorial reality, salvation cannot be desired, cannot be sought, and cannot be received. However, these God rejecters will eventually receive their non-desired salvation. When that non-wanted salvation comes, it is automatic, unearned, and undesired. For all those who reject God, the unwanted, unearned, and undesired, salvation comes about when the eternity they are occupying ceases its existence, and they return unblemished, to the formless realm.

In the purgatorial physical realm, objective existence is entirely experienced without God, an awareness of God, or even a desire for God-realization. Here, they have already received punishment for their harm-causing godless actions. Now they are truly the self-governing gods over the wastelands of godlessness.

Living life without any desire to know God remains a forever free will option for everyone. Still, there is no designed punishment for their self-willing self-conscious rejection of God. Although each of us, as individualized-Man did not choose our infinite existence, we have the forever option of choosing how we realize our forever reality. Thus, there are some who of us who desire to realize their infinite self-existence as existence without God.

However, those who choose the realizing of existence without God are rejecting their divinity, their identity, and their destiny. Unmistakably, they are rebelling against the gift of a God-based existence. If they had the choice, they would choose to eliminate God from reality. Of course, if God did not exist, that would also mean they would have no self-aware existence in ultimate reality.

In a sense, the physical realm of purgatory is experiencing non-existence because the stimulating life-forces of their objective reality are no longer relevant, to their self-conscious experiencing of existence. If there was ever such a thing as infinite divine loneliness, it is now their self-cherished desired realization.

For these God rejecters, experiencing existence is an eternal and ongoing self-aware godless death. Without a purposeful grounding and understanding of their true divine nature, the waves of godlessness, intoned in their self-awareness, uncontrollably slosh about in the knowingness of themselves. Still, this is not punishment. Physical purgatory is the self-realized culmination of their godless desired destination.

Again, how or why should anyone be punished for self-consciously rejecting an unsought self-aware existence? In purgatorial Hell punishment, if one chooses to use that terminology, is experiencing the reality of non-creative life, non-experienced joy, or lack of desire to accomplish anything construed as edifying. In other words, here in the physical realm of purgatory, no one has any determinable control over his or her self-awareness. Here, the ungodly impotently rule over the godless realm they cherish.

Because the purgatorial Hell dwellers have allowed all manners of evil and sinful wrongdoings into their self-conscious acceptance, they accept their self-ordained godless existence as a natural reality. Their self-accepted rejection of God ceaselessly exhorted them to replace all self-awareness or self-reliance on God with their unchallenged desires.

Now, they shout into the purgatorial wilderness of their God-barren existence:" I am not divine, and I need no God!" Now they understand nothing; they control nothing, and they create nothing. They now experience a non-self-actuating existence. Here is eternal barrenness without God and life. Now, they bury themselves in their repudiation of reality itself. Now, they are self-consciously experiencing non-purposeful existence.

In physical purgatory, reality becomes self-awareness incapable of self-actualization, because there is only the ever-presence of godlessness and lifelessness. Here is the chosen abode for those embedded and entrenched in a self-godless desired reality. Who would possibly crave such an existence? Still, this godless locale is the desired eternal home, for the purposeful God rejecting members of the divine family.

In the non-physical section of purgatory, self-punishment for evil and sinful acts becomes the impetus for spiritual understanding for those who desire a willingness to seek, find, and surrender themselves to the understanding and acceptance of God. For them, punishment brings divine salvation, which brings them their reward-filled spiritual blessings.

However, in physical purgatory, there is no self-instilled repentance. They will not repent for their godless and evilly lived lives because that is their self-desired realization of their divine destiny. Therefore, in physical purgatory, there are no earned spiritual blessings to be realized. However, now the mental processes of understanding the wrongfulness of their evil and sin-filled actions are non-existent. Even that is not a blessing because they see nothing wrong with their godless desired existence.

In purgatory's physical realm, there is no earned eternal salvation from the commissions of wrongdoing. Here, eternal salvation is not required. Here, eternal self-aware godless existence is purgatorial-Man's godlessly desired form of salvation. In the purgatorial realm, godless salvation is purgatorial-Man's realization that he forever exists, but he is no longer punished, by the torments of his self-judgments, which are only momentary lapses into the sensitivities of self-aware existence.

Here, evil or sin does not exist; therefore, there is no need for understanding the goodness of divine truth's ability to triumph over evil and sin. Here, there is no goodness and no Godliness. Here, self-conscious existence is realized without desire for any God-awareness.

It is through our self-punishment that self-awareness of our divine nature emerges, for those who self-willingly choose to reunite themselves with their divinity. However, in the physical realm of purgatory, there is no divineness to accept, no deity to seek, no divinity to find, no spiritual understanding to experience, and no divineness with which to be reunited. Here, the infinite unbroken cords to their inner connections to their divinity are self-consciously encased in the chill of godlessness.

All evil and sinful actions deserving of punishment occurred in the non-physical realm of purgatory. All eternal self-conscious existence that chose to reject God and desired no relationship with Him lead to purgatorial-hell self-consciously absorbed into self-realized reality. For these purgatorial malcontents, Hell is godless contentment.

So it is that self-conscious existence in the physical purgatorial realm is not a Hell-filled realm of punishment, torture, evilness, and sin. If the physical purgatorial realm is interpreted as hellish suffering, it is hellish suffering resulting from self-consciously choosing eternal existence, devoid of the active awareness of the presence of God.

Physical purgatory is the eternal abode for all those who God, but the rejecting of God, itself, does not illicit suffering; rather, physical purgatory is a hellish self-aware eternal existence without the comfort of God's Beingness. Here, spiritual, comforting support is unknown. Imagine, individualization of divine beingness existing in an environment where they self-consciously repudiate their reality?

In the physical purgatorial realm, these godless inhabitants wander aimlessly, as trembling shadows realizing their lifeless dance of self-accepted existence. Here, these temporarily lost divine family insurgents are doomed to wander hopelessly and wretchedly, throughout the wastelands of their purgatorial God-barren preferred reality.

In this lifeless and godless environment, individual self-awareness is entirely engulfed in ubiquitous godlessness. Here, individualized purgatorial-Man is incapable of appreciating or experiencing existence, except as godless reality. These participants in Hell rule over their godless reality with a frozen sense of gleefulness.

All awareness of the physical senses associated with the experiencing the self-conscious self-activating realm of objective reality is gone. In the self-aware purgatorial realm of godlessness, there is nothing to create, smell, or enjoy. Godless self-awareness without the capability to create experiences is self-existence in a meaningless reality. If this were the only self-aware existence in ultimate reality, the existence of ultimate reality would be a mockery infinite undesirability by all.

For purgatorial-Man, self-aware existence is experienced as self-conscious death. Here, there are no flowers, no trees, no growth, and no living creatures of any kind. Here, except for the infinitude of immortal-Man, all life is designed to be voluntarily absent. The only sense of experience self-consciously realized, is the awareness of godless self-existence.

Thus, the godlessness of self-awareness is the only identity individualized purgatorial-Man recognizes and consciously experiences. Physical purgatorial-man eternally self-consciously experiences lifeless death. This form of self-conscious death is not punishment; it Isa self-chosen eternal destiny. In the commonality of our infinite existence, each one of us has most likely spent some eternities in this reality.

Since there is no self-actuating experiencing of existence, there is nothing to understand or interpret. Here, there is no self-conscious interaction with the idea realm. Individualized purgatorial-Man is only capable of retaining a self-aware acceptance of his godless self-identity.

Here, there is only self-conscious existence without design or basis for beingness, except for the endless choice, to be self-consciously void of God-awareness. Here, self-existence consists of the continuing self-conscious realization of isolation, emptiness, and spiritual privation.

Self-awareness in this dead habitat lacks any desire or purpose for expression because there is nothing self-enhancing to express. Hence, in this spiritually barren world, there is no motivation to experience the reality of living, because individualized-Man's self-actuating ability to create experiences no longer functions.

Only the deadness of rocks, dirt, deserts, glaciers, oceans, et cetera comprises the lifelessness of this godless environment. The only reoccurring transformations taking place are the continuous gurglings, rumblings, tumblings, and crumblings of lifeless corrosion and erosion.

In physical purgatory, the tranquility of life is unknown and not present. Here, the transforming operative functions of chance, opportunity, randomness, and general unpredictability are relegated to empty-negative non-meaningful mechanically-dead actions. Here, objective reality is realized without the capability of being spiritually interpreted.

In this eternally deathless world, the realization of tranquility is not capable of being self-desired. Only in the self-active living of life is the tranquility of thought realized. Here, in the godless physical realm, there is never any self-thought of tranquility because here, the unreal tranquility of godless existence is the only reality self-realized.

Here existence is without effort, and thus without purpose. Here, there is no effort because there's nothing to achieve, acquire, or attain. Here, there is no capability to exert any effort of any kind for anything, except for the self-realizing effort of realizing one's self-aware existence.

In this lifeless realm, the realization of God is not wanted, not desired, not experienced, not relevant, and non-existent. Physical purgatory is a God-dead reality waiting for the steadfast and godless-minded, to make their appearance. Many members of God's family spend eternities upon eternities, basking in the death-cold appearances of this God-barren existence.

The warmth of fire is unknown because there is nothing to burn, and the physical senses are dead to the allurements, and the utility of experiencing existence. Here, the processes for the experiencing the sufferings and joys of life are dead. Therefore, the self-aware experiencing of life is not possible.

Purgatorial-Man has a death-shrouded ability to see, but lifelessness is all he sees or knows. He can touch, but all that he touches is lifeless. He can hear, but all he hears is lifelessness of nothing. He retains the sense of taste and smell, but all his senses are now dead. Purgatorial-Man's physical realm senses have been replaced, by a desolate coldness of self-aware existence.

Life alone provides the means for experiencing sense-derived existence. Non-life expresses purposeless non-sense aware existence. Who would choose to exist eternally and self-consciously without the purpose of exploring the inner and outer realms of reality? Some divine family members continually desire to make that choice. They will eventually find God, and then their death-filled self-aware existence ceases to be a memory.

Rocks express their solidity; sand presents its granularity, the wind shows its force, water displays its fluidity, and so forth. Here, experiences are not interpreted. Existence is mechanical, random, and undeterminable. Purgatorial-Man's physical self-existence is without purpose except to remain in a non-evolving state of self-awareness eternally separated from God.

Here, self-conscious existence becomes lifelessness identifying itself. There is no hope to hope, no dreams to dream, no expectations to meet. There's only a godless destiny to be fulfilled continuously. There are no challenges to overcome, no victories to win, and no impetus or desire to realize the divine mandate that requires the self-evolving self-consciousness experiencing of existence.

Now, self-existence has no value, no choices, no power, and no aspirations to be met. There is only the desolation of self-conscious awareness without expectations, without joy, and without happiness. Thus, self-existence is self-realized meaningless. Here, the pleasures derived from self-conscious awareness, along with the experiencing life are not wanted, not valued, and not desired.

Sadly, now self-conscious reality is purgatorial-Man's eternal deprived and depraved destiny. Still, this self-desired destiny is not punishment; rather, here there is only self-conscious awareness without God. This self-acquired existence cannot punishment if it is the desired reality for the godless to experience.

Here, there is no desire to experience the wonders of reality. Now, the wonders of a God-derived life are rejected and replaced, by a streaming self-realization requiring no recognition of self-divinity or God's divinity. Here, the awareness of all understandings of divineness is repudiated, unsought and unwanted.

While residing in this purgatorial realm, the foreverness of purgatorial-Man's inner divinity remains unreachable. Memories of the past experiences of existence fade into the dead coldness of their godlessness, as purgatorial-Man accepts his present state of godless reality. Each individualized purgatorial-Man has chosen to make his home in this refuge of godlessness, for the remainder of eternity.

As individualized purgatorial-Man embraces his self-accepted godless destiny, he is incapable of desiring anything beyond his present existence. Even though the physical realm of purgatory is not any imposed punishment, it may be interpreted, as punishment, depending on how it is perceived and understood.

For divine family members who have chosen to identify themselves with God, this godless purgatorial realm would be punishment so unbearable that non-existence would be far preferable. However, for these physical inhabitants of purgatory, no punishing sentences are given because they have self-chosen to abide in this godless-driven reality.

For causative punishment to take place in this godless domain, the capability of experiencing existence would have to be present, be recognized, and be meaningful. However, it is here that the purposeful experiencing of life as existence goes unrecognized, unwanted, unrealized, and unexpressed.

Here, there is no self-conscious ability to create experiences. All punishment results from self-consciously abusing the experiencing life. Where there is no self-ability to experience the abusing of life, there are no self-conscious punishing penalties imposed. In the physical purgatorial realm, self-aware experiences are coldly mechanical. Here, there are no harmful or joyful reactions to the purgatorial realm's lifeless expressions.

In this purgatorial realm, purgatorial-Man's self-conscious access to the idea realm is unavailable for the duration of eternity. Thus, no new ideas can be perceived or received. The capability to find God no longer exists. Purgatorial-Man retains an awareness of his physical world existence, but his thoughts cannot be enhanced upon, improved upon, or self-experienced as any form of happiness. Here, thoughts are realized in the deadness of their coldness.

Here, any form of spiritual progression is not possible. The concept of causing harm to others has lost all relevance. Also lost is any desire to love others. In this godless environment, there is nothing requiring care of any kind. Here, purgatorial-Man's self-awareness of his existence is self-awareness of lifelessness.

Here, there are no choices to be made and the free will that once empowered his individual immortal-Man beingness no longer functions. Here, there are no free will choices to be made. Also, physical purgatorial-Man has self-separated himself from God's family, and thus self-separated himself from any spiritual assistance, comfort, and encouragement that God-loving divine family members could provide.

Physical purgatorial-Man realizes his self-conscious godlessness without challenge, guidance, or opportunity. For all who have chosen to scorn and self-willfully reject God, there is no spiritual assistance. While abiding in this physical purgatorial realm, the possibility of expressing love or receiving love is not in the godless realm of capability.

These temporary godless members of God's perfect family consist of self-aware soulless souls, who share the common desire of non-God self-awareness. For them, the concept of spirituality has no relevance and meaning. The eternal futility of their non-focused aimless wanderings drives purgatorial-Man's self-aware reality. Thus, they all share the non-relevance and worthlessness, of self-conscious existence.

Among themselves, there is little interaction; each purgatorial-Man exists in a self-imposed godless prison, where the experiencing of existence, is denied, unrealized, and unattainable. Although the presence of God remains their soul forever, purgatorial-Man's presence is eternally incapable of self-recognizing, self-accessing, or self-activating any relationship with God, even if desired.

There is no dancing, singing, banquets, or camaraderie. The joys of experiencing existence are no longer present or desired. The awesomeness of sunrises and sunsets remain dormant and forever cold and distant, to their self-awareness. They are no longer capable of appreciating beauty because they can no longer sense the infinite beauty that abides in their foreverness.

Thus, encrusted in their self-denial of God, is their once self-aware sense of inner beauty. Now, all conceptualizations of beauty are eternally gone from their self-awareness. Their desire for a godless existence is the only desire there is for them to fulfill. In the physical purgatorial realm, godlessness is their soul.

Here, no comfort is given, and none received. The healing balms that once blessed their self-conscious existence are no longer present, and no longer soothe. Here, the forever sparks of divinity existing in all individualizations of immortal-Man flicker without love, warmth, or recognition. Purgatorial-Man's divinity is now self-consciously rejected and eternally unreachable.

Here, there is no chastisement for wrongdoing because expressions of evil and sin are non-existent. There are no tears because these godless souls have found their non-divine eternal resting frozen, eternal igloo of self-consciousness. Now, they are only capable of following and obeying a self-chosen lifeless and godless destiny of godless fulfillment.

Now, their self-conscious reality has no divine purpose or significance. The treasures of experiencing living reality are now buried, in the aimlessly shifting sands of their barren godless wanderings. They wander haplessly and purposelessly in the sands of godlessness eternally self-realized, leaving only their footprints of godlessness in the sands.

Their inner strength once relied upon remains impotent. An eternity of self-chosen godless existence is one thing, but forever godless reality would most assuredly be an unbearable Hell. Luckily, this present form of godless reality only lasts for a single eternity. Continuous and infinite self-conscious existence without God is not possible. The end times of an eternity become the beginning times of a new eternity.

Fortunately, these spiritually hopeless-hapless beings remain forever individualizations of their infinite and indestructible-Man identities. They are eternally lost but never lost beyond the terminus of any eternity. It is divinely fortunate that they will eventually return to their formless realm of their eternal transbeingness.

In the formless realm, everyone is given a new opportunity to discover and live a spiritually-derived existence, rather than a spiritually deprived reality, in the wondrous self-actuating process of self-consciously experiencing life. A new experience of life as existence is ultimate reality's forgiveness for their self-conscious choices to reject God.

Both Heaven of the spiritual realm and Hell of the physical purgatorial realm are the outcomes for our self-conscious realizing or non-realizing of our spirituality in objective reality after we experience our lives. Who knows where these godless divine family members may end up in the next transbeingness of their self-realizing of eternal existence, Heaven or Hell?

Spiritual World

The spiritual world is the spiritual realm God would know if He had a Self-actuating self-conscious awareness and was capable of experiencing His existence. Each spiritual world is born at the same moment as each physical world is born. The spiritual world contains the spiritually earned heavenly realm for the spiritual deserving to be experienced and enjoyed

The primary difference between the spiritual world and the physical world is the manner in which ideas are incorporated into the realm of experience and made manifest. In the spiritual world, there are seven spiritually earned destinations and each of these deserved heavenly destinations has its individual relationship with the idea realm.

The spiritual realm is the unfolding of an eternity undefiled by the godless influences of unpredictability. Once we enter the spiritual realm, experiences of beauty, joy, harmony, and the continuing realization of God are profoundly beyond anything encountered in the objective physical realm.

No divine family member gains entry into the spiritual realm by performing good deeds even good deeds grounded in the universal applicability of kindness. However, continuing expressions of goodness most assuredly put individuals on the spiritual path towards God.

Our divine salvation, our divine purpose, and our divine destiny are not to be self-acquired in the spiritual realm. However, in the physical realm, the practicing goodness and kindness uplifts God's family, and when combined with the self-acceptance and self-love of God, the spiritual realm is decidedly attainable.

Thus, the spiritual realm is reserved for divine family members who not only self-consciously express kindly good, but also combine their purposeful expressions of kindliness, with love and acceptance of God. Each of us is divinity in infinity, but we cannot realize our forever divine destiny if we deny or reject our divine heritage.

Our infinite self-aware existence must have a purpose, and that purpose must be comprehensible. In core reality, we exist without challenges, without suffering, without focused purpose, and without earned spiritual rewards. In core reality, we have no self-aware input into the knowingness of our forever existence. If the objective realm did not exist, we would infinitely realize an unearned and unasked-for core reality awareness, which would eventually result in infinite self-aware boringness.

However, since objective reality exists and it exists for each of us to experience, we must spiritually earn our entrance into the spiritual realm, which eventually allows us to return to core reality. There is no escape from this truth: our forever existence in objective reality, to be spiritually and meaningfully realized must be divinely understood, and include an awareness and acceptance of God.

Everything we do in the objective realm, we do for a reward of some kind, spiritual or non-spiritual. Rewards may be physical or non-physical, but all of our self-choices are grounded in expectations of rewards. As infinite spiritual beings, our timeless design mandates that we experience objective reality and realize it divinely, to receive the rewards given to those who spiritually evolve, to self-consciously inhabit the spiritual realm. Still, we are forever free to choose the rewards of our ungodly desires.

Thus, our self-conscious experiencing of existence is an infinite continuum of rewards spiritually and not spiritually realized. The problem for each of us is the things we interpret as rewards. Our downfall is to seek non-God desired rewards that blaspheme our forever existence as divinity individualized. Our successfully lived spiritual lives are our rewards because we have self-identified with the purpose for our infinite existence.

Each of us is divinely divine, but the dark and misty gallows of ungodliness forever torment us, with his or her parading distorted illusions of a false sense of reality, prodding us to self-deny our forever divinity. Why does our infinite objective existence involve so much ongoing self-tormenting suffering? Why are we so often lost in the loneliness of experiencing our infinite existence?

The reason is that each one of us possesses the self-powerful of understanding combined with an unbridled free will, a free-will oblivious to its use. The use of our free will without the spiritual understanding of God and God's nature often produces self-binding torments of suffering. Without a self-conscious acceptance of the nature of God, our existence may or may not be one of continuous suffering. However, with a self-conscious acceptance of the nature of God, any form of suffering torment is quickly dispatched into its palace of non-reality.

In the spiritual realm, all spiritual rewards have been objectively earned. These rewards are freely given, without struggles, challenges, or any required divineness of effort, except for the necessary efforts of our divine desiring. Rewards experienced in the spiritual realm result from our physical realm urges to find, accept, and obey God, and live up to our forever self-aware divinity, encasing our divinely desired destiny.

Thus, the combination of doing kindly goodness, finding God, accepting God and loving God is the fulfilling of our objective divine destiny. Without the love and acceptance of God, we have no divine destiny to fulfill or validate. There is only the fortune of an infinite unchosen existence without the realizing of the spiritual guardrails of our divinity. Thus, if we deny God's existence, our divine objective destiny is realized as the non-fulfilling of spiritual happiness.

True love of God extends beyond all ologies, creeds, and isms. How each of us understands God is determined by our continuing self-developing receptivity to things spiritual. Therefore, the spiritual realm exists solely for those who have found and accepted the God of their understanding. The God of everyone's understanding is tolerant, loving, and forever available. That God is forever and always the one true God.

In the spiritual realm, precise, independent, and limiting understandings of God are unimportant, as long as those understandings instill within true God-believers, a desire to find, accept, and self-consciously obey God with a gentle, harmless kindness, combined with love and tolerance for all things experiencing life. No one who disrespects the expressions of any aspect of life will ever realize a pure understanding of God. Godness is the goodness of life in all of its forms, as interpreted by each of us.

It is foolish to believe that anyone's lovingness of God is more spiritually authentic than another's. As infinite divine travelers, we are forever stopping and resting in endless inns of spiritual knowledge. These eternal rest stops where we find homes of comforting spiritual experience represent the ongoing evolving of our spiritual understandings, which express our infinite graspings of our infinitely divine existence.

Thus, how we uniquely manifest our love for God is our spiritual destiny in forever evolving divine realizations. Spiritual rewards must be based on our love of God because our genuine and sincere love of God determines the amount of our spiritual receptivity to infinity's immense outpourings of spiritual rewards.

Every member of God's perfect family is self-consciously equal in potential, to the accepting of God's callings; but, how each of us experiences our divine receptivity varies individually. Our understandings of God, forever determine our divine receptivity to His callings, but the experiencing of God's callings forever vary from individual to individual.

Our desire to understand and accept God is the only thing of true spiritual value. Thus, each of us forever expands our self-understanding of God. Therefore, our receptivity to God's Infinite Beingness may be in quantities that fill thimbles, fill buckets, fill tubs, or fill oceans vast. Whether or not our receptivity to God nature fills thimbles or oceans, we are all equal because each of us is forever spanning the same spectrum of our divinity.

Infinity exists infinitely. We exist infinitely. Our destiny is infinite. We comprehend and fulfill our receptivity to God infinitely. How we individually infinitely and finitely realize and experience our receptivity to all the divinely uncontaminated things of God is our divine destiny in realization.

Our free will determines the paths to the realizing of our ultimate divine fate. Thus, our relationship to God is infinitely evolving and expanding in divine receptivity to all things spiritual. There is no judgment ever placed upon our receptivity to God's forever callings. Still, spiritual rewards are only bestowed upon the divinely worthy.

Ideas which come into our self-awareness, in the physical realm, are most often based on our ongoing interaction with the anomalies of chance, opportunity, randomness, and general unpredictability. These ideas, as with all ideas, have within their nature a woven process of orderly development. For example, in the physical realm, the idea of a particular type of tree evolves from its seed to become a tree full blossomed.

However, in the spiritual realm, there is only the manifestation of a fully blossomed tree. Here, there is no evolvement, development, or evolution of any kind. Here, all ideas are expressed in their final evolved state of perfection, harmony, and indestructibility. Thus, the spiritual realm consists of the organized externalization of ideas, in the fulfillment of their innately expressing identities.

In the spiritual realm, external disharmonies or unexpected demanding influences of any type have no homes to occupy. Those previous unexpected influences that seemingly shaped our physical realm destiny are now no longer meaningful or relevant. Now, we are divinely enwrapped and rapt in a holy environment of harmony, peace, joy, and ever expanding happiness.

Thus, our eternal existence in the spiritual realm is unblemished by the physical realm's bumpings and poundings of chance, opportunity, randomness, and general unpredictability which continuously bombarded our self-consciousness with false proclamations of godless unreality. In the spiritual realm, there is only the wholiness of divinity self-known and self-experienced.

In the spiritual realm, there is no sickness, pain, heartache, or sorrow. There is no need for laws because the commission of crimes is not possible. There is no envy because everyone is seen and accepted as spiritual coequals. The governing authority is a divinely shared self-conscious consensus of spirituality, abiding within the self-awareness of all heavenly citizens.

The beauty of perfection encompassing the spiritual realm is beyond our present physical realm ability to see, describe, comprehend, or experience. In the spiritual realm, perfection and harmony are a thousand times more exquisite than anything presently experienced. Here, the loveliest music ever to harmonize emanates from all things, including trees, flowers, grass, clouds, et cetera.

As inhabitants of the spiritual realm, we understand our self-conscious connection with God and this understanding is divinely inviolate. Here, divine truth is self-consciously understood and accepted without the limiting scar-laced adhesions of non-reality, infringing upon our evolving spiritual awareness.

Here, each of us is free to experience the spiritual realm as we desire, within the limits of the self-acceptance of our divinity. Here, there are no restrictions placed upon us, other than by the extent of our imagination, the depth of our spiritual understanding and evolvement, and our continuing commitment to the realizing of God's love, in all of our heavenly experiences.

In the spiritual realm, there are seven designed and designated holy destinations. Henceforth, I will refer to these celestial terminals as Heavens. All seven divinely mandated Heavens have the same spiritual environment. However, each one is a separate spiritually earned divine destination.

Thus, the only difference between the seven Heavens is determined by the commonly shared spiritual evolvement, of all those who've earned their heavenly sanctuary in each of the seven designated Heavens. Each Heaven has its access to its designed and assigned section of the idea realm, and thus its own spiritually received rewards.

Thus, spiritual rewards are uniquely experienced in each Heaven. The depth of one's developed spirituality, self-consciously understood and accepted, establishes the range of spiritual rewards available in each Heaven. Thus, when it comes to the distributing of spiritual gifts, all depths of evolved spiritually are not receptively equal. Even within each of the seven Heavens, there are degrees of individual spiritual depthness and thus differing capabilities of experiencing spiritual rewards.

In the spiritual realm, we experience only that which we are capable of experiencing. Spiritual rewards are designed to correspond to our ever increasing capability to experience the foreverness of our Godness, which gives ever-increasing accessibility to our God-based desires. We experience our earned spiritual rewards by tapping into the portion of the idea realm, allocated and designed for each of the seven Heavens.

Thus, the seven Heavens represent the progressions of our individual spiritual evolvement, from the sincerest lowest to the most faithful highest, of our forever developing self-awareness, of our self-divinity.

The method for attaining of all spirituality is equal, but the attaining of advanced spiritual understanding requires intense mentally divine effort and discipline.

As we spiritual progress through the seven Heavens from eternity to eternity, our self-identifying thoughts become progressively inseparable from our divine nature. Thus, through each spiritually attained Heaven, we self-spiritually advance to become the unyielding self-consciousness of God, knowing and seeing divinity in all things.

The depths of our spiritual acquiring of things divine are infinite. Thus, in all things spiritual, there are no limiting depths to our individual divine self-revealment. Our self-spiritual understandings always develop through our self-conscious discovering and acquiring of spirituality understood and accepted.

Our self-attained spiritual evolvement automatically relegates us to the earned Heaven of our spiritual understanding Thus; the seven spiritually deserved Heavens correspond to our ever ongoing amassing of divinely grasped certitudes and spiritually clenched understandings, as we continue to experience our objective physical realm existence, based on our spiritual understandings.

Thus, our divinely assigned consignments to one of these seven Heavens of divine reward become the spiritual gifts, for our free will fidelity to seek, find, accept, and obey the God of our understanding. In the Heaven of our spiritual deserving, we associate with divine family members of similar spiritual proclivities, spiritual development, and spiritual understanding.

All divine instructions and learnings occur in the objective realm of experiencing our existence. Thus, in the Heavens of our divinity self-realized, there is no spiritual knowledge to be acquired or learned. Each Heaven is self-consciously experienced, through the desires of our imagination, rather than the self-conscious creating of experiences; thus, there is no spiritual knowledge acquired, required, or learned.

In the spiritual realm, the purpose of experiencing existence is self-consciously intertwined, understood, and self-realized. In the seven Heavens, the experiencing of divine reality is progressively perceived, as an ever ascending heavenly crescendo of harmony, joyfulness, and beauty self-consciously interpreted.

In our spiritually rewarded Heavens, we re-know and re-experience the indescribable sense of peace, vibrating triumphantly within each one of us. Here, we self-consciously experience the spiritual harmonies we divinely earned, in the objective realm. These divine harmonies are similar to the self-known divinities we self-realize, in core reality, without any necessity of divinely driven effort.

First Heaven

This designed Heaven is where the vast majority of the divine family members find their eternal spiritual abode. Here is the spiritual realm of the fundamentally spiritually evolved individuals who believe in, understand, and self-accept a God of goodness, but have done woefully little to enhance their spiritual understandings, as they followed their fledgling spiritual paths.

This Heaven represents the minimal amount of spiritual self-development of any individual required to progress into this lowest expression of the spiritual realm. Still, even self-consciously existing in the lowest of the spiritual realms, is an existence of joy realized, which is incomprehensible to any of us now abiding in the physical realm.

For the most part, the experiencing of existence in the objective physical realm, for these divine inhabitants, has been caring, loving, giving, and law abiding. They self-identified themselves as sinners, but not as doers of things evil. After receiving their deserved punishment for their sins, they repented and accepted God, as the controlling authority, in their self-conscious, existence.

Thus, here these divine inhabitants self-consciously experienced their physical existence by their corresponding spiritual evolvement, development, and understanding. In the purgatorial realm while reviewing possible lives lived, they truly repented for their sinfulness and recognized and accepted their need to seek, find, and self-consciously abide in an ever-active self-awareness of the presence of God.

In this spiritual Heaven, they are at both the end and the beginning of their ongoing successful divine migration, into the continuing realizing of their eternal and infinite spiritual destiny. They are at the end because this first Heaven is their divine reward, for spiritually experiencing their self-conscious existence successfully.

They are at the beginning of their eternal and infinite divine migration because there are six more spiritual Heavens to achieve before they are spiritually capable of returning to core reality. Each progressing Heaven represents advancing spiritual understanding, depth, and an evolving and deepening commitment to the God identity of their forever beingness.

They have experienced all deserved punishment for their sins, forgave themselves, and thus realized their salvation. Most importantly, they chose to continue experiencing existence, combined with an ever increasing self-conscious desire to be in self-accord with their interdependence with God.

Second Heaven

The second Heaven is for the genuinely spiritually orientated individuals who, in their experiencing of life, consistently chose to accept God, and possessed a continuing desire for thoughts divine. When presented with spiritual opportunities, they accepted those opportunities to grow spiritually.

Thus, they found their divine paths of spiritual ascension, understanding, and an awareness of God that appealed to their spiritual understanding and uplifted their divine self-conscious existence, to an ever-increasing self-awareness of their divinity in God. Thus, they continually and consistently made divinely orientated decisions to progress spiritually.

Most often, in the physical realm, these heavenly inhabitants attempted to self-experience existence self-consciously while accepting God and expressing kindly good. They endeavored to exhibit loving-kindness in their thoughts and actions. They sincerely tried to treat all members of God's family equally, fairly, lovingly, and divinely.

When spiritual opportunities presented themselves, they assisted their fellow divine family members with love, kindness, and compassion. They strove to be good; to do good, and they consistently attempted to obey the God of their understanding, according to their spiritually evolving understood destiny.

Third Heaven

This third divine Heaven is the heavenly reward for the spiritual leaders, guides, practitioners, and teachers. These are the individuals who self-lovingly devoted much of their lives to the teaching and sharing, of the spiritual truths of their understanding. They thought of the spiritual welfare of others more often than the spiritual well-being of themselves.

Thus, they were spiritually supportive to all of God's divine family members and encouraged everyone to seek, find, understand, accept, and obey the God of their understanding. They lived to share their ever encouraging reliance on God. It is the desire to be self-actively God-centered, which permits entry into this wondrous Heaven. Specific understandings of God are never relevant to the receiving of spiritual rewards.

Their faith in God and their love for all members of God's family provided them with the self-conscious spiritual meaning and purpose for their physical lives. Thus, they continually devoted themselves to the spiritual upliftment of God's family, by maintaining a desire that everyone experience the presence of God in his or her lives.

They unequivocally understood that the only thing of lasting spiritual value is the willingness to find God, and to live in an ongoing acceptance, interpretation, and understanding of His forever infinite presence. They all believed that their understanding of God was the accurate and true understanding of God, and each one was correct.

Fourth Heaven

The fourth divine Heaven is for individuals who consistently taught their self-developing spirituality by example. These are the heavenly-minded among us who ministered to the sick, the poor, the downtrodden, and the imprisoned. They did not teach so much by words; rather, they taught by the visibility of their spiritually-based lives.

These divinely advancing souls enthroned kindness and compassion into their self-consciousness, and they loved everyone unconditionally. In the physical realm, they saw the presence of God in everywhere. To them, all members of God's family were to be unconditionally loved. For them, their self-sacrificing loving of others fulfilled their evolving spiritual needs.

In the experiencing of existence, they were non-judgmental and were divinely motivated for the purpose of comforting the lonely, needy, downtrodden, and suffering members of God's family. From the divine perspective, these are the saints of God walking among us. They continually put the welfare of God's family above and beyond their own.

Here also is the spiritual home for those who love God and unselfishly sacrificed their lives to save the lives of others. These individuals are the real spiritual heroes of self-conscious physical existence. They demonstrated their commitment to preserving the sacredness of life, by their willingness to lay down their lives, so others might continue to experience the gift of self-aware physical existence.

Their sacrifice in the giving up their lives to protect the lives of others is the demonstration of pure selfless spirituality in Godly expression. They showed, by their selfless example, what is the second most import thing in the self-conscious experiencing of life, the protection and preservation of all life.

The most important aspect of self-consciously experiencing existence as physical life is to understand, accept, and obey the God of our understanding, with a heart filled with loving-kindness. Anything we do in life is meaningless to our infinite existence if not done, with God as the ever-present self-aware substance of our forever self-awareness.

Fifth Heaven

This fifth Heaven is where spiritual understanding reigns divinely supreme. These heavenly dwellers are the Godly minded members of God's family, who were consistently and self-consciously spiritually triumphant victors, in their experiencing of physical existence, from one eternity to the next.

They always remained unaffected by the challenging influences of chance, opportunity, randomness, and general unpredictability. Their spiritual understanding and confidence remained steadfastly unshakeable. They did all the things required for entry into the previous four Heavens, but now they did those things with unwavering and consistent spiritual courage, commitment, and steadfastness.

The ongoing source of their strength and identity was their consistent and permanent reliance upon the nature of God, forever abiding divinely triumphant within them. All their physical realm actions were as if the presence of God was to walk shoeless in the midst of ever-pressing godlessness.

They revealed their spiritual evolvement by demonstrating their unswerving allegiance to be forever faithful to their spiritual understandings. They continuously and self-consciously lived in the presence of God. Their understanding and experiencing of their self-divinity were no longer a self-aware stinging challenge. They interpreted and saw the presence of God in the appearing reality of all things.

They consistently banished all self-awareness of fear, doubt, and sin from having any authority, substance, influence, claim, or sway upon their free will choices, during the experiencing of their physical existence. Thus, they experienced unfettered joyfulness while they experienced their physical lives. For them, the physical realm became the spiritual realm of victorious divine understanding.

Thus, they demonstrated a consistent and fearless knowledge of their divine selves, as they experienced their lives in eternity following eternity. For them, the experiencing of existence, in the ongoingness of eternities, became an ever decreasing requirement of divinely expended effort.

Sixth Heaven

This sixth Heaven is the Heaven of divine sacrifice. Here, the joys of the spiritual realm are forfeited to minister to the spiritual floundering members of God's family. After completing their brief stay in the purgatorial realm, these highly evolved spiritual beings are now rewarded, with this Heaven. However, when they arrived here, they choose to obey a higher understanding sense of their self-divinity.

Here they understood the spiritual joy of self-consciously contributing to the divine unfoldment of God's spiritually broken family members buffeted about by their physical realm self-conscious choices. Thus, these holy inhabitants of Heaven six dedicated themselves to the spiritual upliftment of the entirety of God's earthbound family.

Thus, they willingly gave up their earned spiritual rewards to spiritually uplift and administer to God's physical family, by spiritually encouraging divine family members, to find their wholiness, wholeness, and completeness in God. They understood the often non-controllable perils of physical life, and they especially choose to minister to the eternally lost, with an unshakeable faith in their self-realizing of divine truth.

Thus, they reentered the object physical realm to encourage spiritual regenerative opportunities for the divine evolving of others. As they spiritually helped wayward divine family members to find God, the entirety of God's family is spiritually benefited. From the perspective of the physical realm, these divine spiritual beings are the guardian angels among us.

They continue experiencing their existence, in this sacred manner, through eternity after eternity until they self-choose to move on spiritually. At times, they come to the spiritual realization that some divine family members are incapable of spiritual regeneration, until the timelessness of time bends them to their knees, through the towering pains of existence, godlessly self-willed.

They eternally vanquished from their self-consciousness, the infinite reality of perpetual unreality. Thus, for these divinely evolved members of God's family unreality no longer exists. Therefore, instead of returning to the formless realm, at the end of the eternity, these divinely exalted beings choose to move on spiritually and enter into the seventh divine Heaven.

Seventh Heaven

This seventh Heaven is the final, complete, and divine objective self-knowingness, in their finite-infinite sojourn through objective reality's ongoing progression of eternities. Here is the last spiritual nesting-resting place for all who have passed through eternities continuous, and have progressed through the previous six heavenly Heavens, of the ever-evolving self-understanding of their infinite divinity.

Here, the highest spiritually evolved of God's family have met and overcome all spiritual challenges, through the power of their spiritual understandings, which objective existence had to offer. They have progressed through countless eternities to arrive successfully at this final divine heavenly realm of ultimate self-conscious objective beingness. In the experiencing of eternities following eternities, they attained their highest spiritual understanding power of themselves, as individualized expressions of God.

They achieved their ultimate spiritual victory, not only for themselves, but for all members of God's family to acknowledge, aspire to, and follow. They are the self-consciousness of their divinity in pure and contiguous self-realizing understanding. They are the spiritual presence of pure divinity in the objective realm.

It is the objective realm destiny for every member of God's family to gain admittance, into this seventh divine Heaven. However, from our current spiritual perspective, it will require each of us seemingly eternities endless, until we spiritually progress to this final divinely earned and deserved Heaven.

Still, it will happen, for each of us, due to the foreverness of our existence. It is possible to deny who and what we are for eternities endless, but it is not conceivable to eternally and infinitely deny the trueness of our forever divine identity. Unbelievable as it is, the unending realizing of our spiritual identity requires the infinity of self-conscious experience.

Since we infinitely exist to understand our existence; the understanding of our existence is infinite. Thus, the foreverness of our divinity and the seeming foreverness of our non-divinity, is in our non-chosen infinite self-aware reality? Therefore, self-conscious existence, in this sojourn into objective reality, seems as though it could be endlessly lost, in the smokiness of perpetual unreality.

In the endlessness of eternities, the spiritually successful realizing of our divine objective existence is but an eyeblink, a grain of sand on the forever beach of time, or a twinkling dot of light in the foreverness of infinity. From our individual perspectives, our lives seem monumental. However, to infinity, nothing is seen as monumental.

To the infinity of ultimate reality, our understanding of our infinite spirituality is not evolving because each of us infinitely coexists with God, and our evolving spiritual understanding only manifests in the infinite realm of the unreal. We objectively exist to bring meaning into our infinite existence, which is meaningless if not experienced.

Imagine how much of our infinite spiritual existence is to be objectively experienced, based on our present spiritual evolvement? We know that we eternally exist now, but how many eternities have we experienced, after being pressed into objective existence. Based on the bountifulness of evil's seeming reality surrounding us, as the collective-We, it does not seem reasonable that we have experienced many eternities. It could be hundreds or thousands, but probably not more than that.

Still, we can attain infinite ongoing harmonious spiritual happiness because we are ever capable of experiencing infinite objective existence, as the self-evolving purity of divinity, eternally beginning to understand and demonstrate the power of behind the divine truth of our infinite existence through the spiritually evolving power of our self-understanding.

Here, in this seventh Heaven, self-spirituality has been earned and is now purely known without any opposition. Here, the capability of returning to core reality has been spiritually achieved. These final spiritual victors have spiritually evolved from their unequitable self-understanding of God to their unequitable self-knowingness of God. Thus, they have objectively developed to a self-aware understanding-knowingness of their existence in core reality.

Here, their final incremental divine unchallenged grasping of spiritual understanding in their present trek, through objective reality is the uncompromising acceptance and realization that the entirety of their real objective real self-beingness is God. This final objective knowingness and self-comprehensible cognizance of their forever divine existence provide them with the understanding capability to return to core reality.

Thus, their ultimate objective destiny to finitely-infinitely self-know the wholiness of God with God and to finitely-infinitely understand the wholeness of God with God, outside of God's reality, has been spiritually reached in the totality of their divine objectively evolved understanding.

Thus, their infinite self-aware existence has now become their uncompromising divine self-conscious knowingness of their objectively realized selves. Now they are prepared to relinquish the all-powerfulness of understanding to become once again powerless in their infinite self-aware union with God.

Their infinite divine voyages into objective reality have forever brought them ceaseless understandings of their relationship to God, with God, as God self-individualized. When they return to core reality, all memories of past treks through objective reality vanish into the complete knowingness of their self-identity in God.

Returning to core reality is their final spiritual reward for experiencing their physical existence. Thus, as these spiritually advanced triumphant victors have totally made non-existent, the objective realm claims of unreality, they have become once again Godly qualified, and Godly entitled to return to core reality.

In this seventh divine Heaven, these souls triumphant eventually choose to move on into a realm where they no longer self-consciously think, self-consciously understand, or self-consciously experience their indestructible self-beingness. Rather, they spiritually opt to entirely and self-consciously unite themselves with the presence of God; thus, they automatically ascend to core reality, to continue their infinite self-aware existence, self-consciously embedded within the all-presence of God. Returning to core reality is a process of self-driven rapture, and it occurs infinitely.

CHAPTER VI

Evil and Sin

Evil exists to glorify the good. Evil is a negative good. It is a relative term. Evil can be transmuted into good.

Mencius

At the time of birth, we are all born divinely equal. However, the propensity of past recent evildoers, to become present doers of things evil persists, due to their continuing lack of spiritual progression and spiritual self-identity. Thus, the false vaporous essence of evilness seemingly magnetizes itself, from one eternity to the next, through the ongoing self-conscious rejection of God. Thus, evil's persistence of seeming real existence appears to be ongoing and continuous.

Thus, we allow ourselves to become mesmerized by the illusionary sins and evils we experience. However, evil has no infinite independent life of its own anywhere, anytime, or in any place. Still, looking about and observing our created experiences, in the realm of appearance, it certainly appears as though evil self-evidently exists.

It is through our self-created experiences that we reason, assert, and reassert evil's seeming presence. However, as I reiterate throughout this work, all self-consciously created physical realm experiences have no real reality attached to them. Therefore, our experiences of so-called evil have no real validity in ultimate reality.

Still, why does evil seemingly persist in its appearance? Buried deep within every consistent doer of things evil and harmful are deep-seated resentments of God, life, and self-aware existence of themselves. Evildoers have no desire to harness their godless free will to understand themselves as infinitely divine. The good news is that when evildoers atone for their wrongfulness, they become once again divine self-conscious unblemished co-members of God's family.

We, as the Godly designed knowers of infinity, can use our individualized power to create an evildoers' reality, or, we can use our individualized power to self-consciously uncover and create a reality to reveal our self-divinity to ourselves. Thus, we forever have a free will choice to validate or condemn our infinite self-aware existence: we each have the forever choice to be ungodly. Evildoers become godlessly lost in their attempts to create their profane interpretations of existence. They desire to control their destiny rather than strive to realize the forever nature, of their forever purpose, for their forever self-aware existence.

Benefiting spiritually from the gift of an infinitely imposed divine existence requires obeying the forever instilled rules for the right to possess everlasting self-aware beingness. Thus, even though not one of us ever asked to exist, the realizing of our infinite destiny demands that we realize and accept infinity's rules for our spiritual survival. Evil's lasting survival results from the unwillingness, of so many members of God's family, to obey infinity's soul-branded rules for infinite self-aware existence.

Evildoers self-consciously determined appearances of evil self-knowingly imprisons them and prevents their ability to divinely self-interpret their self-awareness. Agents of evil are trapped in their self-conscious rebellion, to control their non-controllable divine destiny, rather than understand that which is non-controllable and then seek to self-realize and accept their forever divinity.

Often, questions arise, such as: If evil exists, how or where did it originate? If God is all-powerful, why does He not choose to destroy evil? How can we protect ourselves from evil's influence? Why do evil and bad things happen to good people? Thus, to our individual self-awareness, the existence of evil most assuredly seems viable and real.

To accept the reality of evil's existence darkens our self-awareness to the point of hopelessness, before its professed self-pounding awesomeness, strength, and persistence. Thus far, in the evolution of humanity's collective mind thought, all explanations for the existence of evil have proven unsatisfactory. Simply stated, how can good and evil infinitely coexist?

Evildoers do not cherish a gentle, harmless, and all-encompassing love of self-aware existence. Instead, they cherish all forms of godless pleasures, devoid of the spiritual influx of divine understanding. Evildoers self-use their power of understanding to abuse the gift of their forever existence.

Evildoers care nothing about the consequences of their godless acts. They care only to experience their non-spiritual and unbridled desires with no remorse. For them, their ability to experience their self-acceptance of evilness is their opportunity to experience their existence devoid of the self-conscious awareness of the presence of God.

For evildoers, self-conscious existence without God is preferable. Their self-awareness has lost all self-contact with their self-divinity. They forge an ongoing existence for the purpose of experiencing life, without partaking in the spiritual gifts that the experiencing of life offers. Thus, their eternal lives become a reality of spiritual depravity leading to their self-aware existence, incapable of spiritual interpretation.

Their individualized self-consciousness has turned its back on God, and they flounder about in their self-professed wickedness. As they self-consciously choose to experience their wrongdoings, they continue to blaspheme their infinite divine existence. Unfortunately, the doers of things evil appear to be lost forever in the foreverness of eternities endless.

Reasons for evil's seeming existence vary from the ridiculous to the thoughtful. However, what makes the discussion of evil's existence difficult is that within the framework of discussing its existence, its existence seems to be accepted as a reality. Thus, to address the godless unreality of evil seems to presuppose that it possesses real existence.

Evil is the assertion of the reality of shadows without causal substance, existence, or light. As we look outwards towards the universe evil is unseen. Thus, in the heavens above us, we see only the entrails of harmony. Even where there appear to be remnants of chaos; still, the expression of chaos is harmonious chaos. For evil to have a claim for existence, it must be self-conscious experienced by the individualized-Us.

I side with the thoughtful pioneers on this subject, who opined on evil's existence, and declared that its self-professed existence, in and of itself, is devoid of any infinite reality, infinite substance, or any absolute identity of its own. Thus, evil has no real existence, in any aspect of ultimate reality.

Within our infinite innate divine nature which includes our objective reality, we have the forever capability of understanding all things spiritual or non-spiritual. This everlasting ability for the understanding of all things represents our ongoing powerfulness to make our individual lives, in the experiencing of objective existence, a blessing or a non-blessing.

Thus, our infinite existence is a self-conscious possibility of unlimited choices. What we choose to make ourselves become is how we choose to self-identify ourselves. We seem to exist infinitely in a dichotomy of our divinity. First, we infinitely exist as the forever divine self-aware indestructible part of God. Second, we exist as the infinite self-awareness of our interpretation of ourselves.

Thus, for our self-existence to be a self-controllably meaningful blessing, we must understand and accept the things that are true, and then know and deny, out of seeming existence, the things claiming to be true. If we understand and accept ourselves as expositors of things evil, our infinite individual existence becomes a self-accepted curse.

Thus, our understanding of the seeming existence of evil is an integral component of our infinite spiritual process of unfoldment. The apparent existence of evil encapsulates the forever obstacles we must infinitely encounter, endure, and overcome in the ongoingness of our spiritual quests to understand the depths of our forever divinity.

The more we dethrone the false-thumping claims of evil's seeming existence, the more we understand the strength of our inner divinity. The power which forever permeates our self-conscious spiritual understandings of ourselves and ultimate reality infinitely validates the wholiness of our infinite existence. Our self-spiritually understood life is our forever divine destiny fulfilling itself.

The appearances of evil manifest to us as godless struggles in a godless non-real reality. Without evil's so-called protrusions into our objective experiencing of existence, we would be unable to acknowledge and demonstrate our true divine nature. We validate our infinite existence by controlling the factors of our beingness, including the false claims of evilness.

Thus, our infinite divinely innate nature could never be understood, learned, interpreted, empowered, or experienced as divine truth in physical expression, without evil's false claims. Therefore, the seeming forever claims of evil provide us with infinite opportunities, to reveal our infinite non-evil nature, to our forever questioning selves.

So-called evil continually dances and prances into the non-real realm of experience, to be accepted and nourished by our self-consciousness willingness to be entranced by its sparkling acidic-droplets of unreality. Just look about and see how many of the countless lost among us embrace the shimmering spiritual weaknesses within themselves. The doers of things evil are ongoing embarrassments to the realizing of their self-divinity.

Anything ungodly having a seeming identity of its own is our lack of spiritual understanding, reflecting an unreality for our self-acceptance. If our self-consciousness is tied securely to our inner and divine identity, all receptivity to the apparitions of godlessness is self-willfully denied and rejected.

Thus, whenever God is not self-consciously absorbed, evil continuously vies to take godless control over our spiritual reins. Evildoers most often realize that their evil acts are ungodly, but for them, ungodliness identifies with their self-awareness of existence. Unbelievable as it seems, some doers of evil think that their evil actions are actions of genuine good

However, the evildoers' defiance and rejection of their divine nature will not prevent them from experiencing harsh sufferings for their evil wrongdoings, whether or not they self-interpret their actions as evil. Evildoers are punished harshly because of the harmfulness they cause directly to others, and the washing effects down of evil's harmfulness caused to others. Of course, I have no way of knowing this for a fact, but I think that Hitler is the most self-punished person in this eternity. He was the living embodiment of evil and surprisingly he believed that he was doing good.

The free will self-conscious acceptance of ungodly evil establishes the need for spiritual salvation. Thus, the individual destiny of everyone, in the experiencing of existence is to accept their forever incorruptible divinity and thereby banish the nothingness of the godlessness of evil from their self-awareness.

The corrupt things we do not accept about ourselves serve as the basis for understanding the strength of our divinity. Our innate spiritual capability for understanding ourselves is our infinite source of salvation. Our everlasting salvation is our infinite self-aware non-acceptance of whispering tones of godless unreality.

Thus, we infinitely save our real incorruptible selves from our endlessly unreal corruptible selves. Thus is the divine paradox of our infinite existence; we forever are forever experiencing evil in real reality, as we forever self-consciously exist in the objective imaginary realm of self-created experiences.

If the horribleness of evil's existence was real, meaning real in the sense that it had a forever identity and substance of its own, the doers of things evil could deny responsibility for their evil actions because they would be merely expressing an aspect of ultimate reality.

What would be the purpose of any infinite real presence, such as the assumed infinite existence of evil, having the capability of willfully causing harm? If it is true that evil infinitely exists and exists to cause harm, infinite reality would be grounded in crushing everlasting cruelty. Who would desire to live self-consciously in such a reality? Still, evil is required to exist as unreality.

Also, if evil was real, no one could ever be saved from its ongoing influences. If evil had an independent reality, our self-conscious existence would remain in a forever state of helplessness, hopelessness, and despair because evil would have an independent power outside of our self-awareness, to continually pound away at our free will choices, with the self-validity of real existence.

Our salvation from evil's continuing influence can only be realized by our self-conscious non-acceptance of its claims to exist as reality, through the elevated spiritual ascensions, of our billowing understandings of our divine destiny. If evil had a reality, it would infinitely vie for our self-conscious recognition and acceptance with the credibility of infinite real existence. In a sense it does.

I believe that we all agree upon the truth that God exists and that He has existed infinitely and that He will exist infinitely. Also, for this discussion, I will accept the belief that God is all-power, all-knowing, and all-present, and that He is capable of self-conscious thought, even though I reject those interpretations.

Based on the above assumptions of God's nature, the questions become: Does evil exist or more precisely stated: Does evil have an identifiable existence of its own, within ultimate reality? Thus, assuming God is the source of ultimate reality and assuming evil exists, does evil independently exist within ultimate reality?

Let's say for a moment our earth houses the only environment, in all of the reality of ultimate reality, capable of containing and sustaining independent and individualized self-conscious existence, separate from God's Self-conscious existence. In other words, excluding God, Earth provides the only self-conscious awareness throughout all of the infinity of ultimate reality.

Now, let us suppose a meteor crashes into the Earth, pushing it into the Sun; thereby, destroying our planet and thus eliminating the existence, of all individualized self-conscious awareness throughout infinite objective reality. Under such a disastrous situation only God would continue to exist self-consciously throughout all of the infinite cosmos, as we now understand it.

If all self-aware life, were eliminated from the universe, through Earth's destruction, would evil still exist? If so, would it produce random chaos in the heavens, where such chaos would not be self-consciously noticed or interpreted, by any individualized self-consciously aware existence? If so what would be the purpose of such evil activity?

Thus, the question persists: Without the objective existence of individualized-Man self-consciousness, does evil retain a reality of its own, as a function in ultimate physical reality? Thus, does evil have an infinite independent power to impress and express itself separate from individualized-Man? If it does, then to deny the existence of evil would be to deny the existence of ultimate objective reality, itself.

However, if God ultimately exists, and evil is also maintained to possess a reality of its own; evil must have an infinite identity, separate from God's Infinite Self-identity. Therefore, evil must have an independent existence, and an independent power to express itself. If evil is assumed to have an independent existence, then the question remains: If, by definition God is all-powerful, why does He not destroy evil? If evil ultimately exists and God chooses not to destroy it, then either God is not omnipotent, or He allows the existence of evil to coincide with His forever infinite Self-existence.

Still, if God is assumed to be all-powerful and He allowed evil to co-exist infinitely with Him that would presuppose that He would have an awareness of evil. I categorically reject the idea that an infinite Self-aware all-knowing God, all powerful God knows anything concerning the reality of evil, or that He even has an awareness of evil's assumed, presumed, or seeming reality.

An all-knowing, all-powerful, all-present infinite Self-aware God could only know things ultimately and infinitely real. Logically, if an all-knowing God understood the false claims of godless unreality as the existence of evil, those false claims would be real because those false claims are forever retained in His infinite mind. Hence, if God was aware of the false claims of evil's existence; evil would have an actual reality in the forever existence of God.

If evil coexisted with God, it would have to have an independent power to express itself separate from God. Even if evil had a separate objective existence of its own from God, it could have no influence on God because, by definition, God is infinitely all-powerful, infinitely unchanging, and infinitely indestructible.

Still, assuming evil has an unlimited independent authority and existence of its own, what purpose would its separate and independent existence serve, if there was no individualized self-conscious awareness to understand and interpret it into seeming reality? For the claims of evilness to have a meaningful presence, those claims must be self-consciously understood and accepted.

True, each one of us as individualized-Man self-consciously explains and interprets evil's false claims, but we only do this in the non-real realm of experiencing objective existence. Unreality has no infinite real presence; however, it has the claiming potential for having a seemingly real presence in reality.

Thus, the claims of unreality can be self-consciously understood, interpreted, and realized, by each one of us as individualized-Man, into a seemingly consistent appearance of existence. Anything unreal claiming a reality it does not possess, needs a form of receptivity to admit its claims. Hence, each one of us is that source of receptivity for the false claims of evil, which arise from within our self-conscious interpretations of reality.

Again, our individualized self-conscious understanding is the only power in ultimate reality capable of being purposefully directed. Without the efforts of our self-conscious understandings, the false claims of evil would forever remain powerless and mute. Through the efforts of our self-conscious understanding, we have the capability of creating the appearance of evilness and powering those appearances into the experiencing of existence.

If evil infinitely exists, evil must be part of God's nature. Unfortunately, that statement is true. The seeming infinite existence of evil is part of God's nature because each one of us is part of God, and the potential for the realizing evil's claims trumpeting their non-real existence is part of our infinitely divine God identity.

We, alone, create the conditions for our self-experiencing of our self-existence. In the ongoing understanding and experiencing of our lives, as part of God, we are the only component in all reality, capable of interpreting reality's baseless appearances of presumed evil, into an existence-experience of our making and design.

Thus, evil is part of God because we are part of God. The infinite potentiality for creating and experiencing sins and iniquities reside forever within each one of us. Thus God, in His foreverness, which includes each one of us, is the endless source of the possibility of unreality experienced as the incessant false appearances of evil.

However, if evil were truly an independent part of God's Self-aware nature, then God would exist as both simultaneously good and non-good. Also, if evil was a real and actual component of God's infinite nature: Why should anyone ever be punished for committing evil deeds, if evil's existence is real and actively rests forever in God.

If a Self-aware God is all-knowing; He would know all the evils, sins, and tragedies that have ever occurred, are occurring now, or will ever occur? Thus, within an all-knowing God's Self-awareness would be an infinite repository, for all manners of evil's awfulness. Goodness and godlessness would infinitely and simultaneously comingle within God's Self-knowingness. Thus, the purity of God would forever coexist along with the non-purity of evil's infinite existence.

However, it is the members of God's spiritual family who create the manifold expressions of evil, in their self-aware experiencing of existence. All things self-consciously created as experience, in the realm of objective existence, are non-real illusions; hence, evil cannot be identified as having any existence in absolute reality, including God, except through our self-conscious creations as individualized-Man.

God is infinitely good, and there is no absolute opposite to infinite good. God's divine nature is the infinite unfolding of the purity of harmony, purity, and wholiness. Each one of us is capable of interpreting evil into a presumed existence, but such interpretations remain forever unknown, within God's Self-awareness of Himself.

One of the major thrusts of this book is to reconcile the concepts of God, Man, and free will, with the existence and persistence of evil's non-real appearing existence, for determining any meaningful interpretations of infinite our self-conscious beingness. It seems self-evident that the concept of evil, having any real ultimate permanence of its own, cannot be valid in the absolute sense of ultimate reality.

If evil truly had infinite real existence, our infinite self-aware reality would be a reality of ceaseless and unrelenting torment. If that were the case, our unasked-for infinite beingness would truly be horrid.

However, evilness has no real existence. We self-determine our destinies, we self-experience the joys of our divinity, and we self-infinitely coexist with God.

Further, if the traditional concept of God, as all-powerful, all-knowing, and all-present is accepted; it is unimaginable that the infinite God of trust, support, and reliability could ever allow the horrors of evilness to evolve into any form of tangible existence? If He could prevent evil's existence and does not, He is the author of all the evil's horrors.

A personal God, who would create infinite self-conscious beings possessing a free will capacity to do evil, is a God far beyond my understanding and far beyond my desire for knowingness. A personal all-knowing, all-powerful God, if such a God exists, could have performed a much preferred creative process to bring an individualized free will exercising man into the reality of self-aware existence.

For God to be responsible for a creative process which brought infinite evil into existence is spiritually mystifying and incomprehensible. In essence, an all-knowing, all-powerful God created man; He created many individualizations of man to suffer infinitely. God created man to suffer because He pre-knew the forever outcomes of all of His creations. Would you bring a child into this world, if you pre-knew that child would suffer infinitely?

It seems self-evident that an all-powerful God would Self-consciously terminate the existence of any form of so-called evil. Do we not, as individualized God-Man seek to banish all vestiges of evilness from our environments? Is not our forever individualized spiritual will, the will of God individualized?

The paradoxical problem concerning our infinite existence is that so-called evil must have an infinite presumed existence, for each one of us to understand the infinite divine nature and identity, of our infinite existence. Thus, we have infinity to experience who and what we are, and that realization is infinite.

Evil seems to exist as a result of our free will capability of misinterpreting the harmony within idea realm ideas. Thus, our ability to misinterpret ideas, combined with the rejection of God, is the origin for all of evil's unreal accepted manifestations. God does not and cannot create evil because He does not possess an infinite free will, the ability to understand or the capability to interpret ultimate reality.

The appearance of seeming evil thrives in a thinking atmospheric aroma of non-spirituality. Choosing to accept evil is choosing to allow a godless corrupted form of a false sense of right over genuine goodness, forever sewn into the fabric of our infinitely unique divine beingness. The composition of our infinite self-aware existence is the forever goodness of Godness.

Experiencing existence is always a choice between accepting the goodness or the non-goodness of things. Evil results from our godless interpretations of non-goodness. If we make spiritually correct decisions, in our accepting and understanding of God, all the other choices we make, become our divinity in self-expression.

Thus, our physical, spiritual destiny is to accept reality in a self-consciously correct manner. The potentiality of evil forever endures as we interpret godless unreality into reality, without a self-understanding acceptance of God. Thus, evil is forever persisting as a self-chiming claim of God's absence. Whenever we are not allowing our self-consciousness of God to lead and guide us, the enticing nudging of evil beckons to us through the ethers of its unreality.

We alone give the existence of seeming evil the God-power of our self-evolving understanding. Imagine: evil's seeming power to exist and persist is part of the divine nature of God, expressing through each one of us. We as individualizations of God create the appearances of evil. In the fullness of our forever divinity, we alone do those things. Truly, that is a disheartening self-realization.

Our misinterpretations of objective reality create all appearances of evil. Thus, through our self-awareness, evil has a permanent, eternal and infinite sense of existence, in the self-conscious awareness of all those who knowingly reject God. Although evil does not exist in any reality, its identity persists in various forms through its continuing false appearances that we choose to self-inject into our experiences of existence.

The degree of our individual separation from God is directly proportional to the self-power we give ourselves for the accepting, of so-called evil's reality. As we interpret objective existence, our free will nature enables us to see or not see the Godliness in all things. In the objective realm, Godliness is the visibility of harmony understood and accepted.

We create our individual realms of experience, where seeming evil has a potentiality to reign unchallenged, making its presumed existence a persistent throne of non-reality. Thus, the sticky interweaving assumed forces of godless unreality bind us to the dominion of evil, where our self-existence becomes an existence of meaningless meandering sorrow.

The significance of whether or not God infinitely exists, to the experiencing of our present life, is meaningless if we self-consciously reject Him from our self-awareness. Our continuing attracting of things godless to ourselves is the quicksand of our spirituality, hopelessly and haplessly descending into the abyss of divine darkness, where God no longer is self-consciously known.

The only salvation given to our infinite unasked-for existence is our ability to self-understand the pillars of truth; on which reality forever rests. When we come to the spiritually correct understanding of our relationship to God, our salvation becomes self-actualized, into the experiencing of our existence.

Thus, the realization of our forever divinity delivers us from godless unreality, forever being perceived, in the realm of the real, we are willfully and woefully experiencing. Thus, without a self-reliant commitment to identify our nature as God's nature individualized, the dominating influences of chance, opportunity, randomness, and general unpredictability determine our objective destiny.

When we encourage ourselves to seek God, we are impelled to discover our spiritual inheritance, forever delivering us from evil's appearances of godless unreality. Thus, as we willfully seek, follow, and obey God, we are the infinite self-conscious source of our forever self-individualized salvation.

Thus, our forever personal savior remains the forever self-choices of our free will. We realize our salvation, as we choose to obey our desire to understand and accept our forever incorruptible divinity. It is the imperative of our infinite existence that we hold fast to the self-realizing understanding of God's foreverness of expression in and through us, as the incorruptible divinity of our beingness.

Wherever our active self-conscious acceptance of God is present, evil withers and slithers away into its commanding realm of nothingness, through the understanding power of our free will, divinely and rightly directed. The exercising of our self-willed power to harmoniously control the direction of our destiny is directly proportional to our understanding and self-identification with God.

The cherished secret of our infinite power of self-conscious understanding is that we have the potential to use our infinitely available self-power, at all times, in all places, and in all circumstances to vanquish the callings of unreality. The sad reality concerning our infinite existence is that each of us is all-powerful; but, presently we are not capable of realizing that understanding.

The doers of evil commit harm, but the only spiritually-stalling harm evildoers ever commit, is within the confines of their understanding of their forever existence. Only when evildoers relinquish their godless based desires, through the cleansing power of their individualized free will choices do they banish the shadowy iron shackles, of evil's influence.

Evildoers affect the lives of non-evildoers, based on the spiritual depth of understanding of the non-evildoers. In other words, a self-consciousness buttressed in the wholiness of God is impervious to the venomous bites of evil's unreality. Most evildoers persist in their self-conscious and godless atmosphere of ignorance and non-spiritual free will choices.

There are ongoing evildoers, and there are continuing recipients of evildoers' evil doings. These receivers of the purveyors of evil's doings remain hapless sufferers to the hypnotic whisperings of unreality, as long as they self-yield to the seeming claiming powerfulness of unreality, inside their self-conscious free will.

The evilness of evil is overcome through the self-translating of evil's appearance, into ongoing spiritual stepping-stones, to an ever incremental understanding and acceptance of their forever divinity in

God. There is nothing that doers of evilness possess; that has any power to affect anything that is infinitely indestructible, such as ourselves.

The only power seeming evil ever has upon anyone self-consciously committed to God, is their ungodly willingness to accept idea-thoughts asserting a pretended existence to manifest themselves, into the realm of appearance. To the Godly-committed, the corrosive-laced shadows of evil always dissolve to reveal the trueness of reality.

Our self-understanding and our self-accepting of our divine nature is the basis for our divinely and successful experiencing of life. In the ongoing process of spiritual evolution, whether being self-understood or not self-understood, all members of God's family, even the corrupted and corrupt doers of things evil eventually find their spiritual wholeness, in their self-accepting of their divinity.

However, the consistent doers of things evil seem forever frozen in their wickedness and non-acceptance of God. At times, they return to an understanding of their divine identity, only to quickly reject it once again. Still, the infinity of our existence assures a divinity of knowledge for everyone.

Our infinite choice is to recognize the forever power residing in us as the faithfully real, or to accept false offerings of power forever asserting themselves, as the forever unfaithfully unreal. When we encircle our self-awareness with the presence of God evil is relegated to the underworld of non-existence. Still, the underworld of nothingness remains the infinite realm of non-real existence.

Whenever we accept the light of goodness to shine brightly within our self-awareness, the fragmented shadows of non-reality become lifeless and powerless to command our attention. Thus, evil is rejected and not realized in the self-experiencing of our existence. Still, it is this overcoming of evil that gives us the divine status for self-consciously asserting that we are the triumphant indestructible Sons of God.

Sin

There is a significant difference between sinners and doers of things evil. Evildoers continuously and persistently self-consciously choose to reject God. However, sinners only temporarily forget their identity in God. Thus, the primary difference between sinners and evildoers is the strength of their determination, to self-consciously turn from God. Sinners temporarily lose sight of their divinity; evildoers persistently reject their divinity

Thus, the rejection of God by evildoers is long-term lasting. The rejection of God by sinners is short-term lasting. Thus, the long-term rejection of God is ongoingly infinite. The short-term rejection of God is finite-infinite. Sometimes, sinners briefly become complex evildoers, and sometimes evildoers revert to simple sinners.

Sin's cause for existence in the living of life is similar to evil's cause for existence. All sins and evils result from the misinterpretations of idea realm ideas, combined with varying self-misleading realizations and understandings of God-awareness. Evil doers self-willfully reject a loving God. Sinners who are not as doers of things evil, usually do not self-willfully reject God.

In a sense, even the misunderstandings of God represent some sense of God-awareness evolving. Incorrect interpretations of ideas determine everyone's life-altering responses to their evolving God-awareness or unawareness, within the self-realizations of their experiencing of existence. Even in non-spiritual actions, everyone spiritually evolves because everyone is self-consciously evolving. Whenever physical-Man is self-consciously evolving, he has the opportunity to learn spiritually, from the circumstances impacting his living of life.

Spiritual truth realized divinely evaporates sinful misconceptions of reality, into their non-existence of non-existence. Often divine family members allow the sin buoyed clouds of unreality to cover over their spiritual self-awareness, until the light of their sacred wholiness is seen beaming out from their self-divinity, dispersing the cloudy mists of non-reality billowy puffs of harmless self-conscious recognitions.

Although all sinfulness results from the misunderstanding of the ideas of life, sinners, including debauched sinners, generally value life. How these evolving sinners succumb to the dewy-fingers of godless unreality determines the stranglehold strength their acceptance of non-reality has upon their self-aware divine beingness.

Evildoers do not value life. Evildoers self-willfully misinterpret life as godless existence. Sinners may temporarily reject God and at the same time do evil things, but the doers of things evilly harmful consistently and finite-permanently reject God. Thus, their self-conscious rejection of God makes their experiencing of God spiritually and eternally hopeless in expression.

The understanding of sin is interestingly and challenging subject because sin, as well as evil, have no basis in reality, to claim an independent existence of their own. Thus, sin and evil lack any real substance for their ever daunting unreal claims to a permanent presence in reality. So much of the self-conscious experiencing existence involves weeding out the sources of unreality to see reality's actual and forever roots of purposefulness. Ultimate reality, excluding the infinite existence of God, is not divine.

The denial of sin and evil as having any real validity seems to abuse our rationality because evil and sin appear so authentic and everlasting, to the forever misleading interpretations of our senses. The great understanding concerning our infinite existence is that each of us infinitely possesses the self-aware power to reject and destroy all the godless claims of unreality. Thus, we have the forever power to destroy, but the things we destroy have no real existence. We destroy the false claims of unreality.

When we self-willingly experience sin, it is always a choice. As sinners, it is somewhat comforting to realize and understand that we are only finitely and temporarily adrift, in our expressions of the non-spirituality of our existence. Thus, as we recognize and accept ourselves to be sinners, we are preparing ourselves to be self-conscious recipients of God's wholiness.

From the ever-present vantage perspective of infinity, we are forever moving spiritually onward undaunted by temporary lapses, in the self-acknowledging of our divine overarching authority of harmonious foreverness. As sinners, we realize an unworthiness to assert our divinity, and we redeem ourselves through suffering the torturous pangs of disappointing ourselves. Evildoers remain unredeemed because they suffer no such self-torture. Salvation for the sinner is nigh at hand who says to himself each day: "My solemn desire is to be a better person today, than the person I was yesterday."

Evildoers use their infinite powerfulness of ungodly understandings to create an existence where they become self-active shadow-gods, and then they attempt to engulf and destroy divinity's everlasting Plan of Goodness realized and experienced. Evildoers interpret their lives and degrade the worthiness of their lives. Sinners interpret their lives to enhance the spiritual worthiness of their self-aware existence.

To accept and experience sin is to take and experience a version of godless unreality. To receive the correct understanding of ourselves is to accept what is real and everlastingly true. To be aware of sin, yet choose not to self-consciously accept sin begins the fulfilling of divine salvation self-derived. To be able to do what is right while enveloped in an aura of sin is the self-conscious removal of the dustings of unreality.

There is no punishment for the recognition of sin that is not self-consciously empowered by way of self-conscious acceptance. However, to become spiritual victors in this objective reality we must evolve, to the self-realized place where we never accept even a self-conscious awareness of sin.

The divine salvation of evildoers is lost eternally, as they embrace their self-acceptance of evilness. Sinners sin their way to salvation. Evildoers damn their way to salvation. The divinity in life is always available for finding, but the amount of suffering, in its finding, varies from the squeezing of sins to the poundings of evils. The living of life is suffered less by sinners, more by evildoers.

As we endeavor to realize our spiritual destiny, sin disappears, into the unreal murky-filled expanses of non-reality. It remains forever and always true that our free will delivers us from the sense-binding clutches of nothingness, continually affirming itself as reality's somethingness.

Our ongoing sinfulness always remains directly proportional to our ever self-evolving understanding of our experiencing of life. Our sins and evils are always visible, to our self-awareness; however, our sins are always self-consciously spiritually malleable. As long as evildoers reject God, their evilness will not bend to the power of divinity as they self-actively express their godlessness.

Our sins fall away from our self-conscious attachments to wrongdoing, as we rejoice in the holy atmosphere of our self-acceptance of God. Through our self-acceptance of God, we sinners will continually evolve out of our sinful ways. As our self-knowingness of God increases in our self-consciousness, our sinfulness becomes overwhelmingly unbearable. This unbearable sense of sin than delivers us into the self-knowingness of our unshakeable identified self-divinity.

As sinners, our forever self-aware destiny is to realize God's nature as our only authority, in the ever-arching rainbows that forever hover above us, as we forever experience our divine existence. Thus, our destiny is to unmovingly realize, true ultimate reality forever resting behind the perpetual false finite-infinite appearances of non-reality.

As sinners, the chime sounding clangs of godless unreality continually fade as our evolving self-consciousness finds its spiritual way. When our desire for the self-realizing of divinely golden truths encourages us to be expressions of kindness, love, and respecters of all things living, our sacred pathway has been self-consciously blessed, revealed, and divinely validated, to the understandings of our self-awareness.

This understanding of divine purpose separates sinners from the doers of things evil who choose, to continually remain spiritually hardened in their hearts, thoughts, and desires in the rejection of their self-divinity. Evildoers live a hopeless existence because they self-consciously deny their infinitely divine identity. They eternally attempt to identify with evil by doing things evil; but, in truth, they can never permanently deny their true reality which is the infinity of divinity.

These hard-hearted filled doers of evilness eventually find his or her spiritual redemption, but the cost in sorrow suffered is monumental. When each evildoer achieves his or her divine redemption, no one knows, but their redemption is an ever-present eternal certainty. In the infinite transbeingness of Man, individualized-Man has eternally *eviled*.

However, look at our infinite selves, we see evildoers who continue gleefully to destroy their lives and the lives of others. How can our infinitely shared existence include such continuing spiritual abuse? It appears that the collective infinite wielding of the all-powerfulness of self-conscious understanding remains eternally and divinely uncontrollable, unfathomable, and ungodly. Evildoers continue to be eternal prisoners of their non-spiritual desires which continually shape the direction of their evolving divine destiny.

Thus, it appears that some members of God's family who continually lack identifying with their spiritual identity are consistently unable to understand themselves to be the progeny of God, in their forever experiencing of their existence. When individualized-Man's self-aware desires persistently hang on the claims of unreality, the desire to seek God is skewered by the claims of the ungodly.

As long as we continue to find and know the ever enlightening power of truth, our perceptions of truth's shadows continue to dim, in their godless reflections of reality. Thus, the evolving of our collective self-aware existence demands overcoming sinful-evilness which is eternally hiding in the self-created darkness of our self-divinity. Thus, sinful-evilness is eternally hiding in the *darkenings* of our soul to be divinely understood out of its professed existence.

If we cannot find and identify with the light of our inner divinity, we are eternally lost, and seemingly infinitely lost. The question remains: If each of us, as objective individualized-Man has existed forever, why has there not been greater spiritual progress, in the understanding of our infinite self-divinity?

The answer is that each of our excursions from core reality into objective reality seems to each of us, as our first ever self-conscious contact with the physical material realm. However, in the truth of our infinite beingness, each one of us has made endless excursions into objective reality, and we will continue to do so infinitely. Thus, this is forever destiny ingrained in our never-asked-for infinite self-aware existence.

Every time we enter into the objective realm from core reality, we must self-consciously find our forever divinity, anew. Thus, in each new material realm existence, we must learn who and what we are, as if this was our first time into objective reality. This infinite continuing process guarantees that no will ever totally understand ultimate reality in unbroken self-knowingness. Also, the depth of our individual understanding of ultimate reality varies in each physical incarnation, eternally and infinitely

As we learn that we are infinitely divine, we eventually spiritually evolve to the divinely supreme place for self-exercising the all-powerfulness of our evolved spiritual understanding. At that time, all the secrets of infinity are ours to know, except the secret of our infinite existence. Each one of us exists infinitely to understanding ultimate reality infinitely, through the infinite individualized understandings of ourselves. In other words, ultimate reality is infinitely and uniquely understood and interpreted by each one of us.

The responsibility for all sinners who are not the consistent doers of things evil is to understand sin and evil's godless unreality to protect themselves, from losing their self-attaining spirituality. Sinners are further along the spiritual path than evildoers because, in the range of sinfulness, all sinners understand their need for divine redemption. Evildoers have not reached that self-aware realization.

Evildoers must promote themselves to sinners before they can seek self-conscious redemption, for their wrongdoings. The way an evildoer elevates himself to become a sindoer is to develop a desire to self-acknowledge God as part of reality to be understood. Without an understanding and acceptance of God, there is no divine redemption.

Evildoers seek no redemption until compelled to do so, through the infiniteness of their divine existence. No evildoer can sustain infinite suffering, without finally seeking divine redemption. It is a truism of our infinite existence; that perpetual misery is only perpetual if the reality suffering is a forever self-chosen desire. Thus, self-suffering can be made to last infinitely, but that is spiritually unlikely.

Most evildoers, as well as sinners, begin to realize their divine redemption as they are painfully self-driven to discover the purpose for their lives forever implanted into their eternal and infinite nature. It is their infinite existence that commands, demands, and eventually delivers the infinite way, for their spiritual salvation.

It is through the processes of infinity that spiritual understanding becomes sought by all, understood by all, interpreted by all, and experienced by all. Thus, is the fulfillment of the infinite cycle of self-aware existence? Imagine each one of us has existed infinitely with our same self-consciousness, interpreting itself and interpreting ultimate reality?

As forever individualized-Man, the only thing infinitely new is the choices we make in our experiencing of infinity. The immortal experiencing of life is our continuing self-conscious destiny, a forever realization never to be altered or aborted. We exist infinitely, but we experience existence finitely-infinitely.

As sinners, we sometimes do evil things, but we quickly and sincerely repent when our sinful, evil actions become self-revealed. As sinners, our inner developed awareness of spirituality quickly uprights itself, and we return to the understanding of ourselves as penitent sinners, not consistent doers of things evil. As sinners, we become saddened by our sinful ways. Evildoers self-rejoice in their evil ways.

As sinners, things spiritual are easier realized and accepted when they had been cultivated and desired in the quiet chambers of our self-thought. Even when random influences involved in the experiencing of existence, momentarily overshadow our divine self-identity, we continue to harbor a desire to find a divinely comforting understanding of God, and a divine comforting understanding of ourselves in God.

Sometimes as sinners, we become temporary evildoers. Most often this happens when we allow life's unpredictable occurrences to override our free will. However, thankfully as ongoing sinners, we are repulsed by any self-sustained exhibitions of evilness. We quickly turn to God and self-consciously re-grab onto our self-identity, and we save ourselves from the type of torment evildoers eternally perpetrate upon themselves.

Sometimes this divine turnabout is instantaneous as we see the light of goodness, repudiate our wrongful actions, and we re-dedicate ourselves to follow and obey God's will of their understanding. The vast majority of us sinners receive our salvation because we understand that we are sinners, and we understand the need to self-identify ourselves with God. Evildoers do not have the evolving spiritual understandings of sinners.

The one thing that separates consistent doers of things evil from temporary evildoers is the self-willed amount of time each chooses to remain in their spiritually-locked opaqueness. To most sinners, his or her self-divinity is revealed to them, in proportion to their desire to understand things spiritual. To the consistent doers of things evil, their self-understanding of their divinity has no spiritual rooting-sod to know themselves divinely.

Most sinners are spiritually teachable, as opposed to evildoers, who are not spiritually teachable. To the teachable sinners, all needed divine instructors will appear to them, in their experiencing of existence, to encourage the understanding that their forever self-aware existence is a divinely supreme gift, and that all salvation from the perils of living self-aware lives is forever within their self-knowingness.

Thus, sinners, who are self-consciously advancing spiritually, are predisposed to be teachable. The doers of things evil who do not self-consciously improve spiritually are not disposed to be spiritually teachable. To be spiritually teachable means to maintain a humble and welcoming attitude to receive enhanced spiritual understandings, of God and reality.

A willingness to be spiritually teachable provides ways for our sinning self-conscious awareness, to accept new avenues of divine truth's appearing. To be spiritually teachable requires a readiness to understand the tumults of our self-aware existence, to allow God to guide our thoughts, and to realize that God exists within each of us, at all times, as we are forever self-consciously experiencing life.

Thus, the realizing of our divine destiny encompasses the understanding that all things are surrounded by the love-exuding goodness of God, through the ever-presence of our objective self-active thoughts. Whatever we understand, God understands, wherever we are, God is, whatever we think, God thinks, and whatever ever we are doing, God is doing. We are the self-conscious self-active self-beingness of God interpreting ourselves and reality.

Therefore, to be divinely teachable is to use our free will to seek ever increasing understandings of God, to make our infinite existence spiritually meaningful, to ourselves God, and ultimate reality. My understanding of the infiniteness of all reality makes the God, of my understanding, all-powerful, all-knowing, and all-present, through the self-consciousness of each one of us.

Thus, to be spiritually teachable is our self-desiring endeavor to understand, interpret, and self-consciously secure our infinite divine place in existence. Because each one of us has the potential capability of being all-powerful in the infinite self-understanding of our infinite existence, we are the only ones, in all ultimate reality, capable of making our infinite existence desirable and meaningful.

If each of us did not possess the realization that we have the potentiality of being all-powerful, we could never be successful in the long-term controlling our infinite divine destiny. Therefore, due to our collectively myopic spiritual understandings of God, ourselves, and ultimate reality, we can only realize our divine destiny in short arcs divinity, self-understood and accepted.

Thus, if we were not all-powerful, we would be incapable of eternally subjugating the reality of unreality. It is though the progressive revealing of our potential all-powerfulness that we can self-consciously embrace the eternally infinite fulfilling of our divine destiny, and thus we can become infinitely grateful for our infinite self-aware existence.

However, in our continuing existence, because we so often lack the desire for spiritual evolvement, we seem unable to prevent the godless unreal from driving our free will choices. Thus, it is difficult to be thankful for such an unasked-for infinite existence. In fact, who would ever self-choose an infinite existence in which the claiming-clamoring of the infinite unreal, incessantly bang away at our self-consciousness, pushing for our self-recognition and acceptance?

Paradoxically, even though each of us has the unlimited capability of determining and controlling our lives, we will never finally determine, control, or complete the purpose for our forever infinite existence.

However, each of us does fulfill our eternally infinite objective destiny. The continuous eternal fulfilling of our divine destiny is the purpose of our divine destiny. Thus, the ultimate fulfillment of our divine destiny is not a destiny ever to be fully realized, strange as it seems.

Our infinite existence would be forever sorrow-filled and worthless if we were not capable of infinitely filling the mold of our divinity with the self-conscious awareness of our divinity combined with the power of our understanding rightfully and spiritually directed. We forever have the authority to know, understand and experience the harmony of our divinity. However, the continuing lack of spiritual progress dims our ability to comprehend the all-powerfulness of our self-divinity.

Still, we are what we think ourselves to be, and each of us has the all-powerfulness to make it so. We self-consciously exist to understand the meaning of our self-aware forever existence. Thus, it is the infinite understanding of our infinite existence that gives meaning to our infinite divine selves. We have the forever choice to give meaning to our infinite self-aware lives as evildoers, *sindoers*, or God-doers.

This world of we inhabit spews forth all breeds of unbridled sin. All the sinful perversions enveloping our self-aware lives are devoid of any identifying objective real substance. Even so, the pains resulting from sinfulness are as real to us, as if they had a real infinite substance of their own.

All experiences of sin and pain seem real because our self-aware senses make no distinctions between the concepts of real or unreal sin and pain. However, all experiences interpreted as pain are unreal because the experience of pain has no real identity or reality of its own. Unfortunately, it is too easy to become lost, in our self-aware living of life, where we accept as real the godless claims of sin and pain.

The question to be reasonably asked is: What difference does it make to our infinite self-aware existences, if the sins and pains we suffer from are real or non-real; after all, suffering is suffering is it not? The difference is that each of us is a self-consciousness interpreter of all things infinite. We have the interpreted power of understanding to eliminate sin and evil and return them to their home in unreality. If sin and evil possessed infinite reality, that would not be possible. In short, we determine our interpretations of reality, and we have the power to destroy the unreal claiming authority over us.

Thus, the reality we understand and accept is the reality we experience. It is the overcoming of sin pain through spiritual understanding that fulfills the meaning of our divine existence, which is to rely upon the infinite understanding of our forever divinity, to eliminate life's challenges to our divine self-knowingness. We exist to understand the wholeness of our infinite existence forever knowing and interpreting true reality into the realm of experience.

Our sinful misinterpretations of things unreal, manifesting in the experiencing of our existence, produces the experiences of pain. Thus, our non-real interpretations of life give testimony, to the non-reality of pain. In truth, the reality of harmony is behind all appearances of sin and pain.

As we interpret our existence, we interpret our understanding of the reality of life. Our free will determines the experiencing of our existence. Thus, each of us forever decides the realizing of our forever destiny, in the realm of experience. Thus, we alone and individually are responsible for creating all experiences of our sin, pain, and suffering.

Also, we alone are responsible for not creating self-harming experiences, by holding fast to the forever faithful, forever unchanging, and forever consistent. If experiences were infinitely real, sin, evil, and pain would be part of ongoing reality, and whatever exists in ultimate reality cannot be altered, influenced, or eliminated by our self-conscious thoughts.

For God to be helpful to us, in the experiencing of life, we must elevate our spiritual understandings to be receptive to the outpourings of His nature. All of the foreverness of ultimate reality is harmonious and non-alterable. The only thing that ever changes is our interpretations of ultimate reality. It is only through our correct understandings of God's infinite perfection that we can heal our misconceptions of ultimate reality as unreality.

To ultimate reality, we are sinless. To ourselves, each one of us is an infinite sinner overcoming infinite sinfulness. The greater our evolving understanding of God, the greater is our renouncement of the sinful unreal. If we had no personal interpretations of sinfulness to overcome, objective existence would not be meaningful to us.

If we were non-evolving sinless beings experiencing the objective realm, we would never be making any wrongful interpretations of reality. Our living of life would be meaningless because we would no longer have a need or requirement to understand ourselves, through our knowingness of God. Again, it is the overcoming of our false interpretations of reality that enables us to understand, interpret, and live up to the forever self-reality of our divinity.

Since our understanding of our divinity is infinite, the overcoming of our misinterpretations of our forever existence is infinite. When we are no longer sinfully prompted to understand our divine infinite divineness in God, we are close to our return to core reality. If there were no challenges in our objective realm experiences, we could experience the objective, but we could never understand ourselves, God, or ultimate reality.

Thus, as we advance spiritually, the so-called appendages of sin lose their continuing unreal-real influences to affect the understandings of our divinity. Thus, through the power of our directed free will, the illusions of unreality are transmuted into their true native nothingness. These transmutations to nothingness seemingly coexist with objective reality, as long as we accept the non-reality of godlessness. Throughout this process, we are continuingly progressing in spiritually understanding ourselves.

We are responsible for our deliverance from things unreal, through divine truth sought, accepted, and obeyed. Our salvation is always from false reality proclaiming itself to be true reality. Salvation results from our thought-active desires to rely upon our understandings of God when facing the armies of godlessness. Nothing gives us more self-conscious power than our spiritually earned understandings of God.

It is only through our spiritually-guided free will that salvation, from the pains of throbbing sinful unreality, is earned, deserved, and attained. Our individual free will determines our responses, to the mesmerizing allurements of godless illusions. There will come a time, in the earning of our self-aware spirituality, when we only us our free will to self-consciously align ourselves with God's nature. At that time, we have earned the spiritual possession of all-powerfulness.

There is never need to petition a capricious personal God, for divine salvation in the overcoming of our sins because God is the forever source of all of our forever deliverance, from all things non-real. However, our deliverance or salvation from our sin-filled actions never comes from a Self-conscious God, rather, salvation results from the understanding the spiritual light of God's nature self-consciously embraced and accepted by each of us.

Our objective destiny is the continual renouncing of our self-propelling sinful and evil misinterpretations of reality. Still, as sinners, our infinite future remains finite-infinite, in the forever unfolding of our existence. As evolving divine beings, we must always understand ourselves as infinite, and also as finitely-infinite.

The spiritual illumination we all seek and accept is an endless beacon forever guiding us through the troubling, muddling, burdening, gurgling waters of our wave-making real realm experiences. Thus, our understanding of our self-beingness is our forever guide. In this continuing realization of our infinite divinity unfolding, within the self-realizing of ourselves, we are the divine trumpeters self-proclaiming of God's infinity divinity within us.

We forever realize our destiny, as we forever conquer the sinful non-real and the sinfully non-spiritual. Our ongoing self-realization is to know that a sin filled godless unreality is ever-present, as an illusionary shadow of the divine. We understand our real lives through experiencing the illusions of our non-real lives. The lives each one of live is an enigma, and cannot be successfully spiritually lived without a self-awareness and self-acceptance of God.

Thus, as our continuing understanding is infinite, our victories are infinite, our apprehensions are infinite, and our failures are limitless. All the things we do are infinite except we forever do them finite-infinitely. We exist to understand our choices in the living of our lives and to understand that the living of our self-conscious lives is infinite.

It is somewhat puzzling to realize that we infinitely exist to apprehend our real beingness, and to understand our interpretations of our non-real beingness. Thus, spiritually cemented into our never asked-for infinite self-conscious lives is the forever encountering of genuine and non-genuine reality.

As long as we interpret the experiencing of our existence the false contentions of sinful, godless unreality continually begs us to be experienced. Look at our present spiritual state of beingness, and again realize that we have infinitely existed! If the spirituality of our eternal beingness is our evolved up to date self-attained spirituality in expression, we certainly are pathetic spiritual creatures unworthy of self-consciously experiencing existence.

The understanding of this seeming conundrum of existence is that in core reality, the infinite expression of our spiritually requires no effort. In core reality, we are the self-knowingness of spiritual incorruptibility without any infinite opposition. In objective reality, our forever realizing expression of spirituality requires continuous spiritual and non-spiritual effort. Thus, our destiny of self-conscious experience is to understand ourselves as if we were in core reality, through the exertion of spiritual effort in our objectively lived reality.

Self-conscious objective awareness without God wrenches the divinity from our self-understood selves. As we spiritually evolve and devolve to the highs and lows of our sinfulness demonstrated, we reveal to ourselves the amount of veering from the divine, in our self-conscious awareness of the presence of God.

The only difference between each of us, as sinners, is the extent we have self-consciously removed ourselves from our self-active awareness of God's forever divine presence. Life without goodness is sinfulness. Life without God is pounding sinfulness. Life willfully rejecting the expression of kindness and the acceptance of God is evilness, clapping, dancing, and rejoicing in its divine rebellion.

As each of us sins God sins. God is forever with us, as us. We are forever with God, as God's physical Self. We are forever one with God; however, we alone choose to separate ourselves from Him; still, this self-voluntary separation is an illusion only. In the foreverness of ultimate reality, when we feel separated from God, we are the only ones doing the separating.

We experience and interpret objective existence, even though our interpretations often entail our self-conscious denial of God. We can deny the God within us, but we cannot expel God from within us. Thus, we are forever God in our self-expression. However, even though we infinitely understand ourselves God-sinners, God has no infinite Self-awareness of our sinfulness.

Our objective destiny is to exist infinitely and to experience our understanding of happiness endlessly as existence. Thus, to experience genuine happiness, we must continually seek to follow our divine paths and boldly reject the forever untrue, by holding steadfast to the certitudes of divine truth.

If we allow ourselves be bounced about by the illusionary influences of sinfulness, the result is a hazy developing sense of spirituality. These hazy, foggy fragmentations become a breeding hatchery, for all the modus operandi of all the false illusions, crying out for our obedience. Only our spiritual understanding brings divine happiness and joy, into the programming experiencing of our infinite existence.

Our infinite objective existence demands spiritual courage. Without spiritual courage, we become divinely weakened through lack of a firm reliance, on the power of our self-conscious unity with God. Because each of us is capable of understanding the nature of God, our infinite power of understanding has no opposition.

Spiritual courage is our unflinching adherence to the forever divine, while others bow, scrape, shuffle, and stumble about the throne of ungodliness. Divine Courage is the resolved conviction to reject all godless unreality, by relying solely upon the wholiness of God. Thus, our divine destiny is to experience the self-knowing wholiness of God when confronted with the Hydras of unreality.

CHAPTER VII

Life

Challenges are what make life interesting and overcoming them is what makes life meaningful.

Joshua J. Marine

The commonality for all life is the experiencing of existence. The experiencing of existence as life includes the following: each one of us as individualized-Man, animals, and all the multi-varied forms of vegetation, insects, and microorganisms? As individualized-Man, we are the only component of ultimate reality, to self-consciously experience our infinite existence as life.

All other manifestations of life have no self-conscious awareness of their individual enduring existence. All life not having the capability of self-conscious awareness is a finite-infinite and forever real functional component of objective reality. These forms of life are infinite, and all aspects of their expressions exist in the wholeness of ultimate reality.

It is the objective physical reality that provides a means for all of life to express their meaningful purpose, and functional for existence. The purpose of all life is to act, react, and experience existence harmoniously within the confines of their environments. Ultimate reality interprets forever harmony into its infinite real components. Each one of us, as individualized-Man interprets spiritual balance, into ultimate reality as non-real experiences.

As individualized-Man, we did not create our infinite selves, but we forever do create the expressions of our infinite selves, through our self-conscious creations in our experiencing of our infinite existence. We exist endlessly to understand and express ourselves infinitely. However, we forever know ourselves at the spiritual level of our spiritual evolving.

Each one of us is a permanent inexhaustible well of divinity. Thus, there are wondrous infinities within us all, to be revealed, understood, and expressed into objective reality. Our infinite divine nature is forever whole in ultimate reality, and forever expanding in objective reality.

Therefore, we are infinitely interpreting the understanding of our forever completeness. Even in darkness, we seek the empowering light of knowledge; thus, even in darkness, we are fulfilling our destiny. Our objective divine purpose is to discover and experience our true divine selves.

However, this infinite ingrained design also allows for the misinterpreting and experiencing of our divine selves. In the final analysis, our finite expression of existence is our infinite expression of life, finitely expressed. At all times, in the objective realm, we are the understanding of ourselves, realizing or not realizing the divinity of our destiny.

As individualized-Man, each of us is self-consciously, subconsciously, or non-self-consciously self-determining the objective experiencing of our forever existence. No other life form in ultimate reality is capable of any self-directed self-determining means of self-conscious expression.

Thus, as individualized-Man, each one of us is forever in control of the expression of our objective existence which includes the realizing our divine destiny. We are forever objectively compelled to follow the ingrained design of our foreverness. Each one of us is the self-conscious fulfilling of our designed purpose for existence.

We are without an infinite choice in the realizing of our infinite divine destiny, spiritual or non-spiritual. What we are infinitely being and what we forever understand about our infinite beingness is our objective divine destiny, in progressive infinite self-conscious realization. With the self-conscious power of understanding, we can only attempt to interpret an understanding of our infinite beingness because our infinite beingness is beyond understanding in its entirety.

Still, our individualized infinite existence is forever traced by our understandings of ourselves, but our true infinite selves are never touched upon, scratched upon, engraved upon, inscribed upon, impressed upon, or etched upon, in any way. Thus, each one of us is the forever self-conscious, forever evolving purity of infinite self-conscious existence observing the kingdoms of infinity's unlimited domains.

Non-self-conscious aware forms of life are real, eternal, and infinite components of ultimate reality. Non-self-aware life expressions are characterized, by an innately designed non-self-aware intelligence which enables their experiencing of life to adapt successfully to their environments with unpredictable changeableness and creativity.

Objective reality is harmoniously whole. Non-self-aware ongoing manifestations of life are segmented expressions of the wholeness of objective reality. Also, objective reality is composed of lifeless infinitely whole harmonious segments, complete portions, and entire arcs of unbroken reality. We understand objective reality by interpreting the segmented arcs of its wholeness, not by the wholeness of its wholeness.

The varying forms of segmented expression occurring within objective reality represent and determine the evolving totality, of its changing-changeless timelessness. In other words, there is no purposefully self-aware directing governing power influencing objective reality. There is only the continuing expression of the infinite randomness in wholeness.

It is each one of us that gives meaning to objective reality's random arcs of experience. Without each of us, the ultimate reality of things would consist of the expressions of infinite physical manifestations, without the power of our understanding to give their appearances meaning and purpose.

In the commonality of experiencing existence, all of life is immersed as one. Real infinite actions are comprised of the forever functionings, within objective reality, manifesting in arrays of infinite innate organized randomness of purpose. The purpose of randomness is for non-self-aware life expressions to give opportunities to adapt and readapt to their environments.

Our objective understanding of ourselves is our segmented expression, of absolute reality. All experiences, self-aware and non-self-aware are segments, of the infinite whole. From our individualized perspective, all real experiences are finite-infinite and exist for our understanding, utilization, and experience. We, alone and individually, interpret the togetherness of our individual and shared existence.

Our self-consciously experiencing of life is our thought-desires manifesting objectively. Our self-conscious existence understood and valued prepares our self-evolving self-conscious awareness, for the realizing of our divine destiny. Spiritually speaking, the experiencing of life is the spiritual evolvement of our self-conscious understandings objectively manifesting, in the realm of experience. In our forever self-conscious existence, the only thing of infinite importance is our desire to understand all things spiritually.

Thus, our continuing spiritual evolvement necessitates our experiencing of life as existence, as we interpret our true selves to ourselves, understand God, interpret our relationship with God, and understand our relationship with all objectively expressing as life. Our understanding of life as existence is our interpretation of life as existence. Thus, we alone have the power to define the experience and describe life.

Objectively, we are always in the process of expressing and experiencing life: also, we are continually revitalized and stimulated by the sheer process of experiencing life as existence. However, objective reality continues ever onward, unawares of our individualized understandings, interpretations, and expectations.

In the objective physical realm, we interpret all things as having beginnings and endings. However, through spiritual understanding, we continually awaken to the divine realization that anything self-consciously created has within its manifestation, a designed start, and a designated ending, and thus self-consciously created experiences are wrinkleless wrinkles, in the physical fabric of a seamless objective infinity.

Even without the presence of individualized-Man, the objective realm consists of endless streams of real things having seeming beginnings and endings. Still, nothing in objective reality changes, nothing is influenced, and nothing ceases to exist, as a result of our self-realized efforts. Anything that seemingly changes in objective reality is nothing but a new understanding of its infinite reality.

The influencing powers of chance, opportunity, randomness, and general unpredictability are engraved in the functionings of objective reality, meaning any apparent occurrences of beginning-ending cycle changes are part of objective reality's infinite changing changelessness. Thus, planted into the design of physical objective infinity is the changelessness of unpredictability.

There is no answer to the following question. Whom or what placed a design into infinite objective reality? God did not put a divine design into us: God is powerless to accomplish anything. Man, God's expression, did not design himself because Man is part of objectively reality's forever design. Also, as omnipotent as we are as individualized immortal-Man, we are not capable of altering objective reality's inherent design or even understanding the 'why' of our forever existence, including our forever design.

Infinity's expression of its design is inherently part of its infinite existence. There is no explanation or answer as to the existence of the totalness of ultimate reality. Moreover, remarkably, all the components of ultimate reality are interconnected. The existence of any aspect of ultimate reality is a forever never-to-be-understood enigma.

All things real are composed of incorruptible identities, varying in their expressions, but finite-infinite and changeless. Their real beginnings and endings consist of the mechanical functionings forever incorporated into objective reality. These functions are infinitely perpetual, endlessly predictably unpredictable, and infinitely uniquely designed, as forever components of the infinite whole.

For example, a blowing sandstorm, objectively appearing in reality, is a real experience having a real beginning and a real ending. Still, the sandstorm is a finite-infinite experience of the whole of the sandstorm's intertwined existence within objective reality. All real experiences represent the wholeness of objective reality expressing finitely-infinitely.

We, alone and collectively, interpret identity existence into the wholeness of objective reality.

Our self-created experiences operate within the laws governing objective existence. However, we alone and individually interpret and make meaningful those laws. Our interpretations of objective reality make objective reality meaningfully useful to us. Thus, there is a nexus between the real created experiences of objective reality and our non-real designed experiences.

Each one of us individually gives self-conscious meaning and interpretation to our nexus with objective reality, which seemingly interlaces reality with non-reality. To the actuality of non-reality, the objectiveness of reality remains forever indifferent. Thus, we create seeming realities that are real to us but are forever unreal to objective reality.

Real identities are infinitely changing-changeless expressions within the objective realm. The unpredictability within objective reality never alters its forever designed nature, purpose, or laws. It is interesting to note that objective reality never disobeys its physical laws of existence. However, each one of us, as immortal-Man, has the potentiality to experience an overruling of the physical laws of ultimate reality.

The pattern of actual objective existence is encased in its infinite and purposeful reality, relegating all non-self-aware life to a forever randomly active and reactive determined existence. Still, all life is sacred because it is the experiencing of life by life gives meaning and purpose to all life. From the perspective of absolute reality, what could be more important than life experiencing existence?

All self-conscious or non-self-conscious life shares the commonality of infinite existence. All non-self-aware life is a gift, for our self-aware identities to discover, rediscover, experience, and re-experience, as we forever interpret the progression of our individual and collective divine destiny. Ideally, recognizing the commonality of all life instills, within each of us, an understanding of all life's sacredness.

Understanding and experiencing all aspects of infinite life is our unalterable and indisputable objective future. If we misinterpret life, we misinterpret the purpose of existence. It is our divine destiny to understand our objective existence as a continuance of life as an extension of our understanding of life. Thus, we are to understand ourselves, as the forever inhabitants of infinities, infinities of life-expressing and experiencing self-beingness.

We are forever capable of comprehending our infinite existence. How we choose to experience life is a forever option in the interpreting of our objective divine destiny. In the realizing of our divinity in infinity, we contain the potential of experiencing our infinite understandings of ourselves, in life-producing objective reality.

Thus, our infinite existence gives each of us the opportunity to experience an understanding of our real selves, and an endless opportunity to experience our non-real suppositional selves. If that is not true, our infinite self-aware objective existence will lead to a similar type of boredom that we self-consciously encounter in core reality.

Therefore, objective reality would become a self-aware boringness ensuing from an infinite designed restrictions placed upon the experiencing of our self-understanding of existence, similar to core reality becoming a boringness of unrestricted divine knowingness.

In experiencing life, we create the experiences of our evolving or devolving understandings of ourselves. Since we are the only aspect of objective existence capable of creating self-directed experiences, our ability to create experiences is our most cherished self-aware activity. If we experience our lives unselfishly and kindly, we are embracing our divinity in self-conscious expression.

When the strengths of our thoughts, fully realized or not fully realized manifest or mirror themselves in the realm of experience, we are continuing to interpret, reinterpret, or misinterpret ourselves forever anew. We are forever objectively interpreting the design of our self-aware existence. Each of us possesses the forever gift of understanding our created experiences. Sometimes we allow things into our self-conscious awareness we do not understand.

Each one of us, whether or not we realize it, is a forever growing seed of spirituality. We are ordained by infinity to forever reveal our real selves to ourselves, through the process of interpreting into experience, our non-real selves. Thus, if we were self-consciously unable to interpret our understandings of ourselves into experiences in physical reality, we would never be able to discover, rediscover, reveal, or re-reveal our true self-identity to our forever selves. Thus is why we experience life.

Objective reality provides the means for us to self-consciously experience the understandings of ourselves. All non-self-aware life and all of the realities within objective reality exist for our individual understanding, experiencing, interpretation, and enjoyment. Each of us rules over our interpretation of objective reality through the power of our self-conscious understandings.

Objective reality has no ability or means for any self-conscious interpretation of itself. However, the real functionings within objective reality may be understood as its non-self-conscious interpretation of its infinite existence. However, we can understand and interpret the truths within the objective realm; we are infinitely able to interpret our infinite selves, in relationship to all things infinitely real.

In the objective realm, we experience life as endless finite-finalities in our continuing apprehensions of our forever objectiveness in reality. Each new divine excursion into objective reality results in a new eternal understanding of our forever selves, and thus results in the experiencing of a new physical realm finality, in the forever infinity of finalities through the endless process of self-experiencing our existence.

In the experiencing of life, we always have a choice in the interpreting of our lives, based on things real, or things non-real. All things we perceive as non-real are the out picturing assumptions of our evolving self-awareness. All perceived unreality results from our self-aware realm interpretations of objective reality.

In the foreverness of objectively experienced time, we are what we self-consciously think ourselves to be. One of the interesting aspects concerning our physical lives is that our lives are always objectively verifiable. By that I mean, what we self-mentally construct ourselves to be, we express, attract, and experience in the non-real realm of experiences. Take away our self-interpretations of our lives lived in and by the constraints of time; we are self-knowingly indestructible forever divine beings.

This process governing our physical lives is non-judgmental, and only reflects back to us our state of our self-aware understandings of ourselves. Thus, in the objective realm, we are the image of the self-understanding of ourselves, being viewed by ourselves. If we become unable to see and experience the forever divinity within us, we have become the expression of godless unreality claiming a right to self-existence.

When we accept ourselves as non-divine beings, we lose the power of understanding to save ourselves from the ebbs and flows of unpredictability. Thus, we become objectively lost in the running waters of self-realized aimless drifting. Still, it is this process of imaging ourselves to ourselves that leads to our finite-infinite salvation.

No matter what we perceive in the objective realm the imaging of ourselves, the inner spark of our forever divinity is never capable of being self-consciously extinguished. In other words, we are always and forever divine, and our divineness is forever available to be self-discovered, self-understood, and self-experienced by each one of us. Even when we find and accept the foreverness of our divineness, we will forever understand little of our infinite beingness. Thus is the destiny for the understanding of our forever infinite self-aware existence.

This process of revealing our evolving lives is multifaceted and complicated. It is complicated because our physical lives are experienced, as an infinitely combined mixture, of goodness interspersed with non-goodness. For example, an individual may provide food and aid to the poor and needy while at the same time embrace bigotry and intolerance as self-aware desires.

Thus, our objective physical existence always fluxes in our self-understanding until only the forever gravity of goodness of God shines self-consciously bright within us. Each one of us is forever destined to be the Goodliness of God in self-expression. If that is not true, the existence of God could never be spiritually validated or spiritually understood by us.

Also, our physical lives are eternally influenced by the ever-present rolling thunders of chance, opportunity, randomness, and general unpredictability. Even though these factors are unpredictable, we often attract them to ourselves in the crowded density of our self-accepted convictions.

The ever evolving of our spiritualized individuality dispatches into nothingness the seeming limitations within the self-aware acceptance of ourselves. At times, these unpredictable factors that bombard us seem overwhelming but by of the forever evolving of our understandings, they are destined to become transmuted by us into higher vibrations of harmonious truth.

If we truly, consistently, and unswervingly understood ourselves to be the outward manifestation of the power of God, the experiencing of existence as life would be effortless and without challenges because we would know, choose, and express the spiritually correct option in all situations. In fact, this is our destiny which guides us to our return to core reality.

Thus, we objectively exist to experience our return to core reality. This process of understanding eventually occurs in the infinite objective eternities we experience. In this divine wholeness and wholiness of thought, our self-awareness must always have an objective formless beginning and a spiritually triumphant ending. Then, after our return to core reality, we non-self-conscious wait for our next physical excursion into the experiencing of existence.

It is troublesome to me, to think that we may be experiencing our first individual and collective excursion into objective reality from core reality. If that is true, our experiencing of objective reality is virtually infinite. However, it is more likely that we have experienced objective reality untold numbers of time.

Our infinite individualized self-aware lives consist of scaling the mountains of objective reality through our spiritually evolving God-understanding of ourselves. Our divine understanding ourselves is our non-escapable forever divine destiny. We forever exist to realize our God-divinity.

Although we are infinite individualized spiritual beings, the expression of our objectively lived lives is not judged from any infinite perspective. In other words, the progression of our physical lives is determined by our non-spiritual free will. There is no goodness or

Godness attached to our infinite free will until the free will choices we make are consistently and divinely inspired and understood.

The things we spiritually and self-consciously desire and cherish, in our forever free will decision makings, liberates us from the godless constraints of the never-was, never-is, and never-shall-be. We individually and alone forever determine the spiritual worthiness of self-aware existence.

We exist to understand our infinite spirituality in forever God and forever existence, but why? Each one of us is a designed mystification simultaneously complete and simultaneously incomplete. As we comprehend our objective reality, our infinitely evolving ability to understand reality forever attempts to complete and the mystery of our experiencing of self-aware beingness. Why are we infinitely consigned to experience ourselves as part of God?

Our infinite existence, in core reality, is the completeness of our designed beingness self-consciously known, but not understood. In core reality, we are truly God individualized. In core reality, our existence is never self-realized or self-embraced. Here, we only exist to forever self-know the divinity of our infinite co-God existence, but again why?

We are always self-consciously destined to discover our true selves. The misunderstandings of our forever individualized beingness are infinitely delaying the spiritual completing of the forever true self-realization of ourselves, as we evolve in our understandings of ultimate reality. We have an infinite identity, an identity which is forever untouchable. We are the infinite self-conscious existence of immortal-Man. However, as immortal-Man, we forever identify ourselves as evolving-Man, in the objective realm and core-Man in the core realm.

In this regard, infinity is both our friend and our foe. The difficulty with experiencing our objective existence is that there is never a final finality; there are only infinitely ongoing finite-infinite finalities. In other words, the experiencing objective reality is infinitely and inherently designed into our forever self-aware nature.

Our infinite experiencing of objective reality makes our infinite individual existence questionable. When we enter objective reality, from core reality, we begin self-consciously existing in an objective realm in which we seemingly experience endless eternities before returning to core reality. Our spiritually successful excursion into objective reality is infinitely forgotten, with our return to core reality.

Thus, it appears that we self-consciously exist in infinite individual infinities and having no lasting memory of any of them.

Each eternity seems like infinity. Also, our entire sojourn, through objective reality, seems like a vast infinity of its own. Therefore, each one of us is forever living an infinitely unique and individual understanding of ultimate reality. Our infinite experiencing of eternities, in the objective realm, is our forever infinite destiny; there is no escape. We exist in a forever objective dream where nothing ever occurs except in our individualized self-aware minds.

Thus, when we first enter objective reality from core reality, we have no remembrance of any other self-aware existence, in any of our other infinite excursions into the objective realm. Therefore, the reality that we self-consciously experience may as well be the one and only infinite reality there is to know because that is the only reality that will be presently self-consciously meaningful to us.

Therefore, we begin anew our forever self-aware thinking existence each time we enter objective reality. This infinite process creates a limit to our ability to self-consciously evolve spiritually because we are always starting with an infinite clean slate. The spiritual progress each of us makes, entitling us to return to core reality from objective reality, is the most comprehensive spiritual progress any of us will ever infinitely experience, although this successful spiritual development still varies in spiritual depth, from individual to individual.

Thus, the foreverness of our infinite objective existence answers the disturbing question: If each of us has existed with God in the perpetuity of timeless time, why have we not individually and collectively evolved, into a higher developed sense of spiritual understanding? The answer is that each of our journeys through objective reality represents just one infinite self-understood excursion, among infinite journeys through infinite infinities. Our self-conscious existence as we begin our experience of a new object reality has no self-conscious understanding or knowledge. We begin each new experience of the objective realm on the same basis of having no self-conscious understanding or knowledge of anything,

Regardless of how objective reality is presently defined, interpreted, or understood, it cannot be denied our collective self-aware existence is at a primitive stage, of spiritual awakening. The lack of depth of our collective spirituality is readily determined by the omnipresent appearances of sin and evil and by noting that as a world society, the spiritual worth of life is discarded, devalued, and shredded at all levels, of our collective self-conscious awareness.

Thus, in our present objective realm existence, we are in a group state of spiritual stagnation. Only when the sanctity of all life, is enthroned in our shared self-consciousness, will it be possible to progress to new spiritual horizons. The continuing abasement of life devalues our collective sense of divinity and our collective purpose for existence.

Our self-awareness of existence is meaningless if not expressed. All life is awareness of existence in expression. The awareness of existence, by lower forms of life, is easily seen in their interactions with their environments. All life is sacred. Thus, it is not spiritually achievable to self-consciously advance in our increasing realization of our collective divinity, while simultaneously disparaging the gift of all life, at all levels of our collective self-knowingness.

Humanity's present self-conscious experience of objective reality seems long enough to realize, acquire, and successfully demonstrate a genuine and definite understanding of our divine destiny. Therefore, if we have not thus far significantly advanced spiritually, we most likely never will, based upon humanity's presently active disparaging of all life.

We are hopeless bystanders experiencing a spiritual destiny not understood, not realized, and seemingly not desired. The self-conscious evolving of our spirituality determines all successes, in the realizing of our divinity. We are divine, and we must continually understand ourselves as divine.

It is only through experiencing our existence that we are capable of understanding and realizing our divine nature. Thus, the experiencing of life as existence mandates that the experiencing of all the facets, of the foreverness of objective reality be confined within our self-awareness, which is eternally infinitely interpreting itself.

It is our individualized free will that determines the density of our divinity understood or not understood. The depth of our divinity self-known is infinite in our experiencing of existence. Presently, it seems that the depth of our divinity self-known is but a shadow dent in the infinitude of our divine wholeness.

The present primitive state of our infinite individual and collective divine existence is a sad and pathetic realization. Even though none of us ever asked for infinity's blessing, we are all still spiritually wretched breathing creatures. Each of us contains the forever potential self-power to reign supreme spiritually, over our individual interpretations of objective reality. Instead, we chose to lose ourselves self-consciously in the godlessness of spiritually crumbling unrealities.

However, we will, at some seemingly infinite future time, finally and successfully achieve a conclusive spiritual victory to our present objective reality existence, and we will return to our infinite and blissful beingness in core reality. Eventually, our forever blissfulness will stir within us, once again, a self-aware sense of divine boredom. Then, as always, we will be unceremoniously propelled out of core reality, to experience another objective reality existence; and so it seems to go forever and forever.

If we were not capable of experiencing existence, our presence in core reality would continue to be infinite boring blissfulness without purpose. Thus, there is never a final finality to the objective experiencing of our existence; there are only endless forays into the objective realm of finite-finalities. Thus, it seems now and in foreseeable future eternities; we are the self-realizing hapless and loathsome inhabitants of infinity.

We exist to understand our existence. Our beingness is infinite, and the understanding of our beingness is infinite. As we experience our forever existence as life, our perceptions of our reality infinitely expand. At present, we are a spiritual component of ultimate reality understanding ourselves eternally and infinitely at a forlorn spiritual pace.

The power of our ability to understand breeds both ongoing restriction and continuing freedom. The mistake we make in wielding the power of our understanding is not stopping to reflect upon the things we do not understand. The things we do not understand usurp the strength of our evolving knowledge. Thus, we tend to remain spiritually sluggish in the understanding of our existence.

In this eternity, as in all eternities, our common spiritual destiny is individually and uniquely being realized. Imagine that there are endless eternities for each one of us to discover, interpret, understand, and experience? Each one of us is forever God-individualized eternally attempting to realize our infinite individualized Godness.

I ask again: Is the experiencing of objective reality an infinite blessing or an infinite non-blessing? My understanding is that existence itself is not a blessing; unless we individually choose to make it so. Our self-conscious understandings of our relationship to life-existence itself are somewhat comforting. However, as we waste our lives, self-trapped in the jinglings, janglings, and jugglings of unreality, we continue to self-willingly deny our existence as a forever blessing.

All individualizations of Man comprise God's family. Each of us is responsible for our individual spiritual evolvement. Thus, the number of our objectively experienced eternities varies significantly, as to the manner in which each of us, understands and interprets God, understands and interprets objective reality, and understands and interprets our individual and shared destiny of divinity.

Only our individual consistent and persistent interpretations of divine truth eventually transport us out of objective reality, to return temporarily once again to core reality. Thus is the forever cycling between our experiencing of objective reality and our non-objective non-experiencing of core reality.

We are infinitely designed to understand all aspects of objective reality. As we know objective selves, the forever to-be-realized parameters of the objective realm infinitely increase. Our treks through self-realizing objective existence are infinite, our victories are infinite, our failures are infinite, our punishments are infinite, and our rewards are infinitely immense and immeasurable.

I have said it before, but it deserves repeating. As we increase in our objective understanding, our awareness of infinite realities to be understood also increase. Thus, our relationship to ultimate reality forever remains unchanged. Our forever self-awareness consists of our infinite understanding of infinity, infinitely expanding. Thus, each one of us represents infinity, infinitely understanding itself.

Each new eternity we experience represents a spiritually challenging journey, of spiritual victories and spiritual failures. In experiencing existence, we experience new Heavens in new eternities, as we self-consciously understand, renew, and enshrine God into our forever self-spiritual awakenings, to accept our forever divine self-divinity.

Unfortunately, in each new eternity that God's family experiences, many are those who choose to endure an eternity of eternal hell, due to their self-conscious departure, from an awareness and acceptance of the ever-presence of God. In the eternal infinity of our self-aware existence, each of us is destined to do evil and deny God. We are co-equal in God's family, and we are co-equal in our infinite realizations of godless depravity.

For those who love God, eternal Hell is tortuous punishment. For those who consistently choose to reject God, eternal Hell is their self-aware existence without God. Self-aware existence without a self-awareness of God is lifeless self-beingness. Existing in eternal Hell is a denial of the blessing of life, and thus a rejection of our infinite self-conscious beingness.

Experiencing existence is our forever evolving self-understanding, of our forever selves, in finite-infinite realizations. In the experiencing of our existence as life, we become finite-infinite interpreters of objective reality, rather than the infinite knowers of ultimate reality that we are, in core reality.

Our self-aware existence in objective reality continually stimulates and re-stimulates our thought producing self-awareness. Without the stimulation for self-conscious thought, we would have no divine destiny to be incrementally fulfilled. In a sense, we self-think ourselves into infinite self-aware existence.

To self-consciously acknowledge our existence as infinite is to understand our existence self-consciously as finite-infinite. Our common united destiny forever elevates within each of us and delivers us from all things ungodly. We infinitely exist as part of God; therefore, a portion of each one of us is infinitely divine. Thus, we can deny our divinity, but we can never change our endlessly unbroken sacred identity.

Eventually, our experiencing of existence is understood to be the self-conscious externalization of our divinity, probing itself incessantly into the objective realm of experience. Whenever we self-consciously experience our divinity, we are praising the God, constituting the forever divineness, of our forever beingness.

Just as we are infinite, the blessings of experiencing life are infinite. The wonder of it all is shown by the foreverness of the blessings, bestowed upon us. Imagine each of us resides in the all-encompassing of objective reality, where the unveiling and spreading forth of infinity's marvels are infinitely eternal, infinitely unique, and infinitely provided to the self-chosen ones of God, who are the ones who love the truth of their divinity reverberating throughout their forever beingness.

The wonders in infinity are infinite. Our experiences of infinity's wonders are infinite. That realization is most assuredly a blessing, but it is only a blessing if we so desire it to be, by commanding our inner self-conscious free will to be divinely receptive to the foreverness of seraphic truth. In the inner sanctuary of our self-knowingness, the divinity of God is who we are, what we are, and what we choose ourselves to be.

We exist to understand our true selves as we dismember into nothingness the non-spiritual pleas of our untrue selves. By accepting the understanding of our true selves, we become the spiritual victors our infinite existence intends us to be. Our free will determines our destiny, our sufferings, and our blessings. If our free will choices are not securely affixed, to the true God of our self-awareness, our infinite existence loses desirability to be self-known.

The nature of God realized and understood by each of us, gives objective reality its spiritual meaning and purpose. Through each of us, God experiences objective reality. Our awareness of God enables us to be His divine representatives to all things real, all things we interpret, and all things we experience, in the environs of the real and non-real.

Experiencing life is our self-awareness of our existence expressing self-consciously through the objective realm of experience. Our experiences of life manifest as the ability to act, react, and interact, within all the enclosures of self-actualized realized existence. Each one of us is the deity of our understanding. There is no God, whom Self-consciously chooses to guide, comfort, protect, or love us. As we choose to love the divinity within us, the divinity within us fills our self-awareness with love.

We have eternities endless to repair the forever false and fragmented self-accepted understandings of ourselves. However, the perpetual gifts to our self-conscious lives are only bestowed upon the consistently God-minded, who willfully obey their inner edicts of divine truth. Our divinely pure self-existence is infinitely real and forever harmonious. Each of us possesses a self-existence that cannot be clogged, by anything objectively existing as reality. Our true identities are indestructible pillars of infinity.

Unreality seems to be part of actual existence, but unreality does not have any forever identity in the expanses of infinity. The appearances of unreality are the experiences of objective reality correctly and incorrectly interpreted. Our individual self-consciousness is eternally corrupted by the ungodly things in which we love to regale ourselves. All the horrible things we perceive in and about us result from our diminished spiritual perceptions being reflected back to us as experiences.

Thus, the appearances of unreality arise from our erroneous and self-conscious interpretations of the ideas of existence. When we become the self-conscious Goodness of God in expression, all the buoyed horrors of awfulness drift portless, in the mental non-real subterranean waters of experience.

Godless unreality is never part of existing reality. The awfulness of evil and sin's depravity, in their self-chiming horrific forms, are never a real part of the divine-Us, God, or objective reality. All presentations of horribleness are chiseled, by our ungodly interpretations of reality, into the depthless chasms of unreality, forever seeking a real existence without any true identities.

Godless unreality is in darkness surrounded by the unnoticed and unwanted presence of light. The false claims of unreality infinitely exist to be infinitely exterminated, by the understanding of our infinite existence in the wholeness and wholiness of God. Thus, as we return unreality into its non-accepted un-realness, we infinitely enhance our self-understanding of our forever identity in and with God.

Horrific tragedies occur making the living of life seem intolerable. In these moments of utter despair, the question is often asked: If God is all-powerful, how could He allow such horribleness, and other assorted forms of the godless ungodliness to occur, in all its forms of utter depravity?

All expressions of our human sufferings result from our free will interpretations of a reality of a self-aware existence forever unknown to God. God's unknowingness of our sufferings provides us the self-realization that we alone are responsible for all the horrid appearances of non-reality, in their multi-colored garbs of suffering, pain, and heartache.

Thus, we alone are responsible for overcoming of suffering. We are the ships of our infinity, infinitely steaming onward, with each one of us being the forever Captain of our forever self-evolving destiny. Our divine goal as the captains of our divinity is to navigate through the troubled waters of experiencing existence, to experience the calm, peaceful, and restful waters of the eternally divine in expression.

Tragedies and evilness often make their trashing appearances when our collective experiencing of existence is misdirected, by belief systems which combine the goodness of good with the wrongness of wrong. Whenever we mix evil with good, the goodness of good is diluted into watery shades of goodness.

Thus, we are forever chained to the beguilements of unreality, as long as we self-consciously conjoin the brightness of good with the darkness of evil. Objectively, each of us possesses a combination of goodness and evil until evil becomes unhinged from our self-awareness. Our infinite existence enables us to dislodge evil from our self-conscious forever beingness, but the Goodness of God forever permeates us and is forever inseparable from our forever beingness.

Wherever the self-conscious presence of God is self-activated, understood, and accepted, the appearances of tragedies dissolve into the harmony of goodness realized, as our self-acknowledgement of the ever-presence of divinity is self-accepted. Through the understanding of our everlasting divinity, unreality relinquishes its claim to a self-existence of its own. Thus, unreality no longer poses a pretended existence for our self-awareness to accept.

The lack of our collective ability to harmoniously determine the outcome of experiences is indicative of the spiritual poverty of our collective spiritual evolvement. Tragedies often result from chance, opportunity, randomness, and general unpredictability which overshadow our receptivity to things divine. Thus, in this manner, random misfortunes reflect back to us the progress of our spiritual understanding, self-acknowledging itself. The way in which we self-deliberately deal with tragedies is collectively attained spirituality unfolding, at the level of our collective self-conscious realization of our God-identity within us.

When we use our spiritual understanding to destroy the nothingness of unreality, we are the power of God in self-active triumphant expression. Only when all tragedies become transmuted into truth realized is our ongoing final objective victories won, as we spiritually surf our way through objective reality. At that time, sinfulness and evilness cease enticing our self-awareness for acceptance.

We can spiritually progress individually, but we are also constantly influenced, by the spiritual progress of the entirety of God's spiritual family. Unfortunately, in our present collective divine family spiritual progress, the divine light forever brightening our overall destiny towards truth realized, understood, and accepted, flickers distantly, within the foreverness of our universal soul.

All spiritual successes result from the self-conscious rejection of all things untrue. In the advancing of our spiritual understandings, the interpreting of our spiritual journeys become revealed, as spiritual defeats transformed into spiritual victories. As spiritual truth is self-consciously accepted, by each of us, spiritual triumph is displayed in its finite-infinite increments of divinity self-realized.

As we understand our true divine place in absolute reality, God is experiencing His existence through each of us. As long as it is required for each of us to use our free will, to repeal the ungodly unreal, we will remain spiritually and objectively yoked and locked in place. Only when the negative imagination of things is self-consciously and consistently unrecognized is our finite-infinite victories secured.

Until we understand and accept our divinity, in the realm of our directed Godly expressions, our self-aware happiness is never achieved. We reveal ourselves to ourselves, through our self-conscious understanding of ourselves forever torching forth, and emblazing all aspects and dimensions of objective reality, with our forever divinity secured in our forever awareness of our God-identity.

Our ultimate existence is interrelated with infinite joy, manifesting in the realms of experience. Our destiny is to experience joy forever, in the realizing of our perpetual individual identities. If joy were not a real component of actively demonstrating our existence, we would be soulless, and our self-conscious awareness would lack the thrill of forever realizing its divinity.

The successful experiencing of our self-aware lives leads to expressions of joy. However, who's to say that non-self-aware life is not also capable of experiencing joy? For example, does a rose experience some sensation of joy-awareness, as it stretches earnestly towards the warmth of the sun?

For the infinite existence of consciousness, either self-aware or non-self-aware, joy must be the central aspect in the experiencing of life. It is my opinion that all manifestations of non-self-aware, organic life forms sense-experience some sense of joy, at the levels of their growth-evolved receptivity.

For our self-aware existence to be meaningful, we must self-conscious experience joy. However, our self-conscious experience of joy must be spiritually earned. Thus, none of us is ever given an automatic sense of everlasting joy. For non-self-aware existence, experiencing joy is infinitely effortless and unearned. The experiencing of effortless joy, in objective reality, is objective reality blessing its infinite existence, in the infinite experiencing of itself.

Joy is the soul-substance of all life. Thus, I maintain that non-self-aware life is forever experiencing joy. Thus, joy is perpetually experienced by all non-self-aware life forms because all non-self-aware forms of life ceaselessly experience their existence. Thus, all non-self-aware life expressions are continuously and forever experiencing the joy, which each of us as individualized-Man, yearns to experience self-consciously.

It is only us, as immortal-Man, who has the capability of non-joyfully interpreting our existence. Our misinterpretations of non-joy have no finality for impacting the forever realness of non-self-aware life. Our misunderstandings of objective life reality only damage the spiritual understanding of ourselves.

The foreverness of joy, infusing all life's real non-self-aware experiences of existence, remains forever untouched by our ignorant destructions of their joyful expressions. We can destroy the experiences of joyfulness, for non-self-aware life from our perspective, but from their infinite perspective, their experiencing of joy never changes.

All things real are understood and interpreted in our individualized self-conscious mind. Non-self-aware life possesses infinite unscratchable existence. We alone abuse non-self-aware life by the godlessness of our spiritually deprived thoughts and actions. Our self-conscious abuses of non-self-aware life continually contribute to the experiencing of our tear-drenched and battered lives. The things that we ignorantly do to all of life, we are only doing to ourselves.

We, as individualized-Man, are the only portion of ultimate reality impacted by the spiritual substance, or non-substance of our self-conscious thoughts. How unbelievably foolish we have been, are now, and seemingly will forever be. We interpret outer reality from our inner reality. We are the infinite creators of our countless expressions of non-spiritual understandings when it comes to the non-self-aware form of life. We are the self-conscious stupidity of forever existence.

However, our infinite destiny is forever secure in our infinite existence. The realizing of our destiny is spiritual, as we self-exist spiritually. Our destiny is not spiritual as we do not self-consciously exist spiritually. We are infinitely capable of being ignorant; thus, we are infinitely capable of choosing not to understand our divinity. Our self-conscious capability of choosing to be self-ignorant is the forever bane upon our infinite objective existence.

We realize the presence of joy, in two ways. First, we know joy through our infinite existence in core reality. Second, we experience joy through our self-continuous evolving, as we spiritually jungle through eternity following eternity. Thus, we infinitely seek an objective realm realization of the joy we knew in core reality.

In core reality, we are only aware of non-experienced joy. In core reality, the knowingness of joy is the knowingness of uncontaminated, incorruptible ultimate beingness infinitely and divinely self-realized in its pure divine beingness. In the objective realm of experience, the realizing of joy results when our self-awareness, of non-desired unreality, is devoid of any spiritually crippling influences.

In objective reality, we only experience genuine joy intermittently. Our knowingness of worldly-based joy is forever incomplete because we are forever incomplete, in our self-evolving self-conscious integrating and combining of the inner realm of our divinity, with the outer realm of our self-consciously determined experiences.

As divine beings, the experiencing of objective realm joy results from the realization of true divine love, permeating the self-experiencing of our self-aware existence. Thus, experiences of joy are forever experienced and are forever awaiting our spiritual apprehensions. Thus, in the objective realm, the experiencing of joy is interwoven with our increasing spiritual understandings.

Our self-conscious self-actuating existence without the ability to experience-create joy would be infinitely torturous and unbearable. The worthwhileness of objective existence must include the experiencing of a joy-filled reality. In this understanding, joy is all about us waiting for receptivity by our spiritualized self-awareness.

Our objective realizing of joy is the murmuring heartbeat of God throbbing divinely within each of us, throughout the unending vibrating eternities, we forever walk upon, as divine beings wielding the power of spiritual understanding. The self-awareness of pure joy is our infinite birthright, but it is only welcomed into our self-consciousness through a love of God self-grounded in kindness, tolerance, forgiveness, and respect for all life.

Experiencing pure joy provides the meaning for our self-existence to be self-realized. Within the realizations of pure joy, there is no harm, no fear, no heartache, and no sadness. Experiencing joy results from our self-conscious existence understood divinely. Thus, experiencing life is sacred because it provides the only reliable means, for each of us to individually and infinitely identify ourselves with the purity of joy.

What is preferable: To infinitely self-know the non-self-experienced pure joy we are infinitely self-aware of in core reality, or to increasingly self-consciously experience our spiritually earned joy, in objective reality? Our infinite self-existence provides for both possibilities. Our self-experiencing of objective, pure joy is forever incremental. In core reality, the forever self-knowingness of pure joy is forever stretching infinitely, into the far-reaching realms of our infinite existence in God.

We experience joy and death forever. Within us is the forever understanding that our self-consciousness of existence never ceases awareness of itself. Thus, so-called death is not the absence or destruction of our self-conscious existence as life. What we identify as death is but a finite-infinite process of evolving self-realization. As immortal-Man, the only time we self-consciously experience so-called death is when we exit the physical realm to enter the purgatorial realm.

What appears as death is not the beginning, the interruption, or the ending of any real life. Physical death is just the end of one of our infinite objective interpretations of life self-realized as experience. Experiencing death is infinitely experienced just as experiencing joy, is infinitely realized.

To our forever existence, death is unknown and only has significance in the objective realm of the changing-changeless. What passes for self-aware life ceasing its existence evolves into a new awareness of life understood and experienced. Thus, what we term as the self-realization of death is but the doorway to a new understanding of our ever-evolving self-beingness.

Even as we choose to eternally self-exist in the shadows of our spiritual ignorance, there is never any cessation to our divine beingness. The concept of death is a misinterpretation of the idea of life. All real existence is absolute and infinite. There is no idea for the cessation of anything possessing real existence, which includes each one of us as infinite, immortal beings.

Death is an assumed ending to a life realized existence. The idea of death is nothing but the acceptance of non-real truth asserting its spiritually deprived deception. If we accept death as the finality of self-conscious existence, we accept the finality of life occurring in a forever changeless infinite reality. What we identify as death is nothing more than an imposed change in our understanding.

We are the designers of our infinite irreversible destiny. Physical life begins and ends in our self-conscious interpretations of existence as life. However, all seeming beginnings and endings are but the finite understandings, of our ever evolving finite-infinite self-awareness. In actuality, our physical death results in the renewal of our physical life.

If physical death was indeed real, our self-aware objective existence could not perpetuate itself. What then would be the purpose of our self-aware existence, if our self-aware existence could cease to be self-consciously revealed, due to the irrevocability of a permanent self-existent death? The appearance of death is a natural part of our infinite objective existence; it should never engender fear. Our self-existence is infinite, indestructible, and divine, what is there to fear?

The experiencing of existence is the meaning of life. Appearing death is the denial of the sacredness of life. For me, it is unquestionably understood that everything experiencing life has the capability of acting, reacting, and interacting with its environment and is sacred. Thus, all of life including each of us, animals, and the myriad forms of life, in the living environments are sacred and infinitely deathless.

There is a divine imperative mandating that all things experiencing existence as life be divinely understood and safeguarded. Without the recognition of the sanctity of all life, our common spiritual heritage languishes in the valleys, of our non-self-consciously evolving spirituality.

Thus, our collective divine family destiny goes unrealized for eternity upon eternity.

The self-conscious sharing of our divinity strengthens our spiritual self-revealing love of God. Our self-evolving spiritual progress requires maintaining divine concern for the welfare of all God's family members. Thus, through the re-experiencing of our existence, we are given countless opportunities to influence the spiritual well-being of all divine family members.

How our spiritually motivated concern for others manifests, reflects the spiritual depth of our divinity self-acknowledged. Although our spiritual evolvement remains forever individual, without a spiritual concern for the welfare of others, the realizing of our divine destiny remains in the valleys of the peaks and valleys, of our never-ending spiritual ascension.

The successful self-realizing experiencing of existence as life is not possible without progress, occurring in all fields of human endeavor. We forever exist to understand our existence and the existence of ultimate reality. It is through our infinite ongoing understanding of all reality that our moral understanding of living life evolves.

If our moral understanding of our expression of existence is divinely motivated, it then becomes the spiritual morality of our self-realization of life as our lives expressing. Without a sense of divine moral goodness, with or with a self-acceptance of God, our infinite existence would be a self-aware existence of infinite uncontrollable chaos. Indeed, that seems to be the present situation in the collective expression of our spirituality. We exist as infinitely divine but not as the trueness of our divinity in expression.

We must never lose sight of the divine realization that our experiences of life are not realities because they are not attached to anything possessing real existence. Our true divine selves never change, but experiencing our infinite interpretations of our divine beingness forever changes.

The unreal realm of experience enables us to understand, express, and experience ourselves as the self-consciousness of God, or the self-consciousness of objective reality if we choose not to self-accept God.

Ultimate reality is godless in the sense that it does not need the Self-consciousness of God to support or validate its existence.

We are the forever children of the infinite stamping out our impressions of life-existence, onto infinity's forever veneer, but this is only from our perspective. As we trudge the depths of our spiritual depravity, we realize our universal divine destiny. Our spiritual progress may be delayed, due to our ungodly eruptions of our non-evolved spirituality, but we are never ceasing our evolving heavenward.

All of ultimate reality is within the mind of each one of us patiently waiting for our forever infinite realizations. Through all of our self-awareness of existence, infinity understands us unconditionally. We imprint godless unrealities onto infinity's self-unknown surface, and we wash them off with the revitalizations of our forever ongoing spiritual revelations. We interpret the infinity of ultimate reality in our individualized God-minds.

Our common destiny must be understood, followed, and obeyed or our self-conscious awareness becomes one of idolized hopelessness. It is each one of us, in the expressing of our infinite beingness that makes self-aware existence itself meaningful. We are all divinely equal in all aspects; however, it is our individual self-conscious awareness that brings about seeming appearances of unfairness to infinite existence.

Thus is the forever disparity in our objective self-aware existence because each of us makes life meaningful to ourselves, through our individually desired talents, abilities, proclivities, and uniqueness. Thus, in the successful expression of the things we cherish, we make it appear that some individualizations of Man are more blessed than others.

There will come a time in the experiencing of objective existence, when each of us will spiritually cherish and enshrine, within our spiritually evolving self-awareness, the sanctity of all life. At that time, the finite-infinite achievement of our objective destiny will be in divine sight.

Thus, we realize that everything involved in the preserving of all life is spiritual. We become the ongoing self-conscious understanding of our forever divine identity as we embrace, protect, and divinely love the preciousness within all life. There is no ultimate salvation for anyone if we allow the abuse of life into our self-conscious acceptance, of our understanding of life.

Soon, from infinity's viewpoint, our often tear-scorched and drenched journey through this objective realm of reality will end. We did not ask, desire, or choose to self-trek through objective reality, but all of us will eventually become its spiritual conquerors. However, as we measure our joys in the eternal branding-burning tracks of our tears, we ask ourselves anew: Is our sojourn through objective reality worth the price of our self-aware eternally infinite indestructible and immortal divine existence?

If a spiritual truth is not practically understood and demonstrated, it remains, non-understood, non-expressed, and without purpose. Following are a few examples for the understanding the experiencing of life, from the perspective of our transbeingness, as individualized immortal-Man.

For each of us, our self-conscious recognition of the sanctity of life is a significant turning point in our spiritual progression. Self-conscious reverence for all manifestations of life, and a desire to protect all of life is the ubiquitous and forever required unyielding prerequisite, for our spiritual enhancement, advancement, and divine entrancement as God's infinite and perfect family members.

Human abortion is horrid and awful. It represents a spiritual callousness towards the living of life which promotes the de-spiritualizing of our individual and infinitely shared divine identity. Even kind and sincere non-spiritually minded members of God's family must recoil at the idea of willfully terminating an unborn baby-fetal life, through the cold, callous, and mechanical means of abortion.

To the evolving spiritually minded abortion is self-evidently wrong, evil in its intent, and is an abomination to our infinite self-knowingness of existence. In the devaluation of life through abortion, the genuine purpose for life fades into insignificance. Abortion is the perpetuation of a rejected spirituality that hardens the heart, numbs the soul, and restrains God's perfect family's individual and collective spiritual understanding of itself.

Abortions should always be avoided, except for the narrowest of reasons; saving the mother's life is certainly one of those narrow reasons. Still, even that is a concession to our collective and primitive spiritual non-evolvement. If all life, especially the unborn, were truly cherished, the physical means for saving and protecting all of life would always be made available.

Abortions performed merely for the purpose of convenience or due to some baby-fetal abnormality are total, complete, unequivocal, and non-excusable abominations, to our experiencing of existence as life. The willfulness to take any life is the destruction of our divinity, in the ever spiritually creating of our self-conscious awareness.

For God's family to allow such an abhorrence to occur demonstrates beyond all cavil, our collective spiritual deprivation in the conscious realizing, of our collective divine heritage. Abortion is a godless act denoting a preference to terminate life, rather than to unite in efforts to save, protect, preserve, and enhance life.

Spiritually misunderstanding the purpose of life establishes the wrongness of abortion. An unborn baby is preparing itself to become an individualized physical-Man for the purpose of experiencing actual physical experience. Thus, abortion is a deliberative attempt to deny physical existence to an individual immortal-Man.

The act of abortion is the negation of life itself. Abortion is deliberate divine blasphemy by trying to destroy the indestructible. However, abortion only delays an individualized immortal-Man's entrance into the physical realm. Individualized immortal-Man is never permanently prevented from experiencing objective physical existence.

Abortion for the purpose of ending a life is a spiritually void delusion. Abortion is a willful and demonstrable attempt to deny immortal-Man's gift of self-aware physical existence, although that is eternally impossible Abortion is a spiritually debilitating lie that challenges our understanding of existence as life. Life is sacred. Any willful attempt to destroy the sanctity of life is spiritual darkness, darkening in its evil intensity.

From the perspective of absolute reality, no individualization of immortal-Man is ever ultimately denied objective physical existence.

We enter the physical realm, from the formless realm, as we take our first breath. Up to that moment, the embryonic development of any baby-fetus has no divine self-identity, and therefore has not yet become an individualization of infinite, immortal Man, but still, any unborn baby-fetal life is the expression of life, nonetheless.

An abortion made before a baby's first breath only temporarily delays immortal-Man's physical entry into the objective realm of reality. Thus, no individualization of immortal-Man has ever been affected, impacted, or touched by any act of abortion. However, that realization in no way takes away from the depraved awfulness of attempting to destroy life, especially the unborn life of God.

As long as the need for spirituality is self-consciously denied, spiritual progress cannot occur. Anyone who self-willingly chooses to have an abortion or anyone who self-abets in the process of abortion is in a sad spiritual state. To deny the expression of life is to deny the purpose of life. Abortion is the self-conscious and unequivocal rejection of progressive spiritual understanding.

For those who have had an abortion and regret that decision, they should not continue to beat themselves up. For the purveyors of abortion, their self-torment will abate with the realization that no individualization of immortal-Man has ever been denied the opportunity, to experience existence as a physical life lived.

However, to callously terminate a baby-fetal life is a serious spiritual matter. Attempting to destroy the non-destructible severely limits an individual's receptivity to things divine. As long as the desire to commit abortions continues, all of God's family is mired in spiritual ignorance.

Thus, in its entirety, God's family cannot progress spiritually beyond that of individual divine realizations, until all of self-aware life recognizes that abortion is self-evidently wrong, as well as the aborting of any form of life. Our infinite existence demands the expression of life; life is sacred. If the entirety of reality existed, without the expression of any life, what meaning or value could the existence on non-life have?

The desire to understand, accept, and experience divine truth forever saves. For individuals who have chosen to renounce their decision to have an abortion, in order to resurrect themselves spiritually, they must make a divine commitment to protect and safeguard all life, especially God's potential physical realm members. In so doing, they will self-consciously erase the evil awfulness of abortion from their self-awareness. Then, their experience of abortion is transmuted into divine truth, spiritually realized and embraced.

As spiritually debilitating as the act of abortion, capital punishment is coequally and woefully abhorrent. The taking of anyone's life is always wrong even when buttressed by seemingly valid rationalities. Our primordial collective spiritual myopia justifies the taking of life, particularly when capital punishment is concerned.

The spiritual destiny of God's family demands the recognition that all life is sacred. In this present spiritual reality, some individuals are justifiably killed in wars. Some justifiably killed to save others. Some justifiably killed to prevent crimes. The justifications for taking human life seems to have a non-God based sacredness of its own.

Thus, our present collective spiritual evolvement condones the taking of human life, under so-called morally proper and correct circumstances. However, our divine objective destiny demands that we inculcate into our collective spiritual consciousness the realization that there is never a spiritually or morally justifiable excuse for attempting to destroy any life, especially self-aware infinite life. As a society, we are not spiritually close to that spiritual recognition; however, that is where we should all spiritually strive to be.

One of the positives of the self-conscious experiencing of life is that life is always providing a means for its spiritual interpretation and understanding. Thus, we have advanced divine family members serving God's family as teacher-guides, combined with the teachers of unpredictability continuously providing spiritual learning opportunities, to all members of God's family, to discover the spirituality forever dwelling in their self-awareness.

Our collective divine salvation demands all members of God's family understand themselves to be Godly self-divine. All members of God family have the exact identical amount of God's divine presence within them. Thus, all of God's family universally shares in God's collective sacred identity; but, the self-interpretations of our inner divineness will vary, but the total content of our inner divineness never varies.

Thus, every member of God's family is coequal to every other member. The difference between divine family members is how each of us chooses to understand our divinity, in the experiencing of our existence As long as we self-consciously experience life; we have the capability of self-understanding our forever divine destiny. With the taking of a physical life, the sacredness of divinity dies in the collective spiritual understanding of ourselves.

In this present physical realm, acts are committed that are so awful, so vile, and so evil-filled, that only capital punishment can mitigate against the horribleness of such depravity. However, capital punishment is pure revenge, and revenge is not indicative of our divinely shared self-evolving of spirituality.

Our collective and individual destiny demands that the realization for the taking of any life is forever and always wrong. What about the taking of lives to save lives? That is a necessary concession to our present group-primitive spiritual evolvement. Nonetheless, the self-willingness to take anyone's life is forever wrong.

Evolving spiritual understanding eliminates all unfairness to our self-realized existence making the willful taking of any life spiritually impossible. Thus, the time will come, in a far distant eternity, when the spiritual knowledge of all of God's family members, will prevent the taking of any life, for any reason.

In the correct understanding of our spiritual reality, the taking of any life would never be considered an option in the process of experiencing life. It should be presently understood; life is sacred even for the most despicable among us. Understanding the nature of objective reality assists us in understanding the spiritual non-need for capital punishment. The taking of any life is the expression of spiritually in non-evolved limitation. In the correct understanding of our spiritual reality, the taking of any life would never be considered an option.

In the ultimate truth of immortal-Man's existence, the experiences of abuse, suffering, and death are unknown. Still, everyone is thoroughly punished for all self-created sinful-evil wrongdoings, manifesting as created experiences. All self-conscious life is to be valued because the living of life promotes the understanding of life and the perceptions of life enable us to understand the purpose of life.

Let it be fully recognized and understood that there is no escape from all deserved punishment. The punishment for evildoers is exceedingly harsh due to their willful abuse of life which devalues life's meaning, making the living of life seem worthless. We punish ourselves far beyond any punishment received in the objective physical realm, including the punishment of capital punishment.

The non-divine density of evil and sin is realized by each of us individually. Thus, the overcoming of unacceptable godless unreality should be encouraged, through the sanctioning of everyone's experiences of life. The understanding of life leads to the spiritually successful self-conscious demonstration of life.

The spiritually evolving experiences of life lift the entirety of God's divine family's realization of divine goodness. The spirituality of understanding, self-realized and accepted, by any wrongdoer experiencing life, makes all of their past sins and evils no longer self-tortuous.

Nothing complements the living of life more than the acquiring of spiritual knowledge. It is far better for God's family to encourage the attaining of spiritual knowledge, then to prevent the acquiring of spiritual knowledge through enforced physical death, as imposed by capital punishment.

In the physical realm, capital punishment is a temporary expediency, to our present non-understanding of things spiritual. I repeat the taking of anyone's life is always wrong, even with seeming justifiable reasons. The taking of any life highlights the realization that so much of our present collective existence revolves around our group-lack of spiritual understanding.

It is the lack of our evolving spirituality that is forever on trial, in the objective realm of experiencing life. In other words, we, as group-common divine-Man, have not evolved to the understanding that the willful taking of any life, for any reason is abhorrent to our infinite self-conscious existence.

Also, I repeat, all punishments received in the physical realm, for evil and sinful wrongdoing are insignificant compared to the earned punishing penalties, all of us eventually impose upon ourselves, in the purgatorial realm. There is not a hint of wrongdoing, a drop of sin, or a splash evil that goes unpunished. In this realization alone, capital punishment is shown to be spiritually degrading and divinely unnecessary.

From our divine perspective, there is never a discontinuation of life. Thus, in that understanding of life, capital punishment is the demonstration of spiritual ignorance by the non-recognition of the indestructibility of life and the spiritual ramifications of infinite self-realized experiencing of existence. The only thing accomplished by capital punishment is to deny an individual's existence the opportunity for physical realm spiritual self-regeneration. How foolish is that?

Denying anyone's potentiality for spiritual self-regeneration delays the spiritual progression for the entirety of God's family. Thus, in capital punishment, society in general and the lethally condemned, in particular, share in the same common non-spiritual darkness. The experiencing of life should be recognized and cherished as experiences of beginnings only, never endings.

Our free will ability of self-choice determines the realizing of our destiny. Through the practice of capital punishment, we as the persecutors of self-aware existence lose sight of our spiritual receptivity to things divine. At present, in our everyday myopically feeble eternal migrations, we enable the hammer-poundings of chance, opportunity, randomness, and general unpredictability to shape the direction of our collective divine destiny.

Always and evermore, we chose to become the image of the things we self-consciously idolize and allow to validate our self-awareness of self-existence. Thus, as we cast our human eyes upon a saint or evildoer, we are looking at the possible spiritual or non-spiritual assumptions of ourselves. We cannot rise above the realizing of our perceived destiny if we box ourselves into self-evidently wrong choices of godlessness.

Presently, our self-consciously-willed disrespect for human life continues to manifest when it comes to the lives of animals. Animals experience life in their self-identifiable ways, just as much as we experience our lives in our self-identifiable ways. Although animals are not self-consciously aware of themselves, they are still consciously experiencing their existence.

Animals exist to experience existence, as do all forms of non-self-aware reactive life living their reality. To abuse life, at any level of life's expression, is self-evidently wrong, immoral, and non-spiritual. Our self-conscious abuse of life, especially animals, is our self-conscious awareness rejecting our divinity because the sacredness of all life is a divine imperative we all must accept.

Animals are consciously aware of experiencing life, but they are not self-consciously aware that they are experiencing life. Animals exist in a perpetual state of 'nowness' regardless of the intervals between their physical realm appearances. Thus, all of non-self-aware life and all self-aware life are infinitely and continually aware of their surroundings, in the self-living of their reality, and thus aware of life itself.

The killing of animals is totally and spiritually offensive and divinely revolting because animals are forever and always the living innocents of infinity. It is a sad spiritual commentary, in our present human condition with all of its incredible technological advancements that we cannot provide humanity's nutritional needs, without the barbarity of killing animals.

Moreover, the killing of animals for any reason including for food is a total abuse and a spiritual abomination, regardless of any rationale for so doing. Destroying animal life to promote human life is an anathema, and it only serves to prolong our collective non-spiritually advancing stay in our embryonic spiritual cloudings of self-divine obscurity.

Abusing and killing animals hardens the soul of the entire divine family. Wherever and whenever life is not cherished, the God of supreme divine genuineness cannot be self-consciously discovered. It is eternally self-obvious that the infinite expression of life, whether self-consciously experienced or consciously experienced is sacred?

For God to be God, His divine nature requires the exercising power of our infinite and our growing spiritual understanding. Thus, our God-based evolving self-identity is to sanctify the essence of God by respecting all life as sacred. As we bless our self-awareness of God into our self-conscious understanding, our infinite divine destiny must automatically include being the self-recognized protectors of all life, including and especially animals.

Cruelty to animals, including the hunting and killing of animals for the fun of the sport, the greed of profit, or the believed need for food is spiritually unconscionable. Humanity's callousness to animal cruelty is a powerful recognition of human kind's non-developed spirituality. Can anyone watch the clubbing to death of an innocent baby seal, without that self-evident awfulness eliciting a tear?

To take pleasure in the death of anything is to disparage the gift of life itself. The self-willful pleasure in abusing and killing animals is the tragic misunderstanding of the experiencing of life. As long as any form of life, especially innocent animal life is devalued, harmed, abused, and destroyed, our individual and collective divine destiny will eternally wait for our spiritual appearance.

The existence of all life shares the experiencing of life together. Due to our ability to think spiritually, it is our responsibility to protect all of life. To destroy life is to destroy the infinite blessing of life. I understand that here are many good, decent, and spiritually upright individuals who hunting and fishing. They take pleasure from the killing of so-called non-evolved animal life. However, is it not patently self-evident that the slaughter and killing of animals is never spiritually justified unless it is done to preserve life? If not, I am repulsed that I exist in such a world.

To interpret the killing of animals, as a joyful experience cripples our spiritual understanding that life is a blessing. The willful killing of animals, for any reason, spiritually harms all of God's family through the loss of our self-conscious advancement of our spirituality. Thus, when we, as God's family, do things that are obviously divinely debilitating, our collective spiritual progress suffers eternally.

Thankfully, ultimate reality never abandons infinite life especially the lives of animals. When animals are about to die and leave this physical realm, ultimate blesses them with a sense of calmness. Thus, animals are given the understanding feeling that they infinitely exist and that there is nothing for them to fear. To infinity, animals are sacredly loved, cherished, blessed, and protected by the realization that they exist infinitely.

We have a divine mandate to safeguard the expression of all life. Each individualized representation of life is sacred. Is it not self-evident that because we are self-comprehensible of existence itself, we must safeguard all of life that is not self-comprehensibleness of its existence?

A butterfly, as a child of life, experiences its reality of existence but has no self-awareness of being a butterfly. However, from the viewpoint of experiencing life, is the life-awareness of a butterfly less desirable than any other life-awareness? If a butterfly could think, would not it think that its experiencing of life was the most extraordinary, the most beautiful, and the most desired?

More importantly: Does a butterfly ever abuse its existence, or harm the life of any other living creature? If in the life of a butterfly, it causes no harm or injury to other expressions of life, it is experiencing its living presence far more successfully than any of us, because not one of us can make that same claim. Imagine, a butterfly lives a more spiritually based life than any of us? A butterfly does not understand its spirituality; it is spirituality in expression, and the expression of spirituality is the sacredness of life in expression.

Also, the living environment deserves our spiritual respect. Life is continuously presenting itself in never-ending displays and arrays of wonderment. Compliance with all life also includes the livingness of nature. We have no understanding of how vegetation experiences life. Still, we have no divine authority to harm any form of life in an irrelevant and non-caring manner.

If we self-consciously and spiritually disrespect the living natural environment, with all of its multifaceted bewilderments, we are continuing in our disrespect and rejection of the gifts of life, the blessings of life, and life itself. We, as part of God, spiritually bridge our forever existence, to include being part of all life. Thus, God is also part of life; thus, life is forever sacred.

Sexual orientation is another topic to be understood from the perspective of our transbeingness, as physical-Man. However, before the discussing this subject, let me emphasize that there is no such thing as any assigned sexual identity or orientation that is forever mandated, infinite, or non-changing.

Wherever we are expressing our forever self-aware existence, we are immortal-Man devoid of any sexual identification. Thus, when we self-consciously exist in core reality, we have no sexual identity or orientation. Sexual identity is only relevant to our objective appearance in the physical realm of our forever existence.

In objective reality there is no such thing as an eternally infinite unchanging male or female nature; there is only our infinitely individualized divine nature individually understood. To each of us, as objective individualized formless-Man and individual subjective core-Man, there is no such thing as sexual identity.

However, due to the variables of the objective realms physical influences of chance, opportunity, randomness, and general unpredictability upon the expression of life, sexual orientation occurs as we enter into the objective physical realm. Thus, in the objective environmental world, the experiencing of life as existence allows for many possibilities and potentialities for our individual sex-based expressions.

Thus, in the present experiencing of life, we may experience life we all may vary in our sexual orientation depending upon the unpredictableness, of chance, opportunity, randomness, and general unpredictability. The sexual preference in the expression of life is never self-determined until we self-consciously rule over chance, opportunity, randomness, and general unpredictability.

Thus, our physical realm sexuality is a by-product of physical realm unpredictability. Unless the truth of our divine beingness is unshakably cherished, in our self-awareness, chance, opportunity, randomness, and general unpredictability shape the parameters of our self-living of life, including our sexual orientations. Thus, no one has an infinite individual sexual self-identity. Therefore, it is not possible for any of us as immortal-Man, in the experiencing of our existence, to forever maintain the same sexual orientation, because experiencing life is infinite, and thus infinite life combines with endless possibilities and potentialities.

We divinely embrace the realizing of our designed destiny when we become the final victors over chance opportunity, randomness, and general unpredictability, in our present sojourn through objective reality. Until that time comes, all of our self-conscious experiencing of life is continually impacted by situations and circumstances unforeseen.

Even so, sexual orientation of any type only has relevance in our ongoing stays, in the physical and purgatorial realms of our objective world existence. There is no relevance to sexual orientations in the formless or spiritual realms. Since no one chooses their sexual orientation, sexual identity assuredly varies from eternity to eternity.

However, in the spiritual realm, we retain the sex orientation we had in the physical realm, but only to maintain a sense of continuity, for our spiritual realm understanding of existence. In the formless and spiritual realms, the concepts of sexual identity are meaningless to the experiencing of physical objective reality.

Our ultimate existence is far beyond any of our evolving self-accepted individualized understanding of our objective realm physicality. The spiritual destination for any self-aware sexual identity is the same as the spiritual destination for everyone. No one's individual expression of spirituality is limited in any manner by his or her sexual orientation.

In divine truth, the only thing of lasting spiritual value, applying to all members of God's family, is for everyone to continue practicing kindness, respect for all life, combined with love and obedience to the God of his or her understanding and acceptance. In this way, God forever encourages His divine family to be the self-conscious expressions of His infinite divinity.

Only when our self-conscious love of God extends beyond the realms of understanding and interpretation are things divinely accepted. In truth, we are all divine beings unblemished by the vagaries of experiencing existence. Our divinity is universal and non-changing. What we are as one, we are as all. Sexual orientation is merely one finite-infinite experience, in the foreverness of our experiencing self-aware existence.

Now, I will move from the subject of sexual orientation to the subject of racism. In the physical realm, the contrails of racism repeatedly appear in the news. This subject once again highlights the spiritual privation and progression of the family of God. Racism represents the most non-spiritual self-conscious understanding of ourselves that is possible to accept, in our experiencing of our objective existence.

Anyone who embraces racist thoughts is devoid of the universal understanding of colorless self-conscious divinity. We are immortal divine beings, and we are all infinitely equal, in the dispersing of spirituality. There are no colors of divine beingness enveloping our forever self-knowingness divinity. The forever collective divine-Us shares equally in the presence of God.

Anything that exalts one individual over another, whether it is racism, ethnicism or religionism is a perversion to our infinite existence. We are all individual members of God's family. Each one of us has the exact identical amount of spirituality dripping into our forever soul-beingness. Each one of us is divine, and divinity is not separately dispensed or measured.

Of course, the concept of racism is unknown in core reality. In core reality, we all equally realize our relationship with God. Racism only occurs in the physical and purgatorial realms. In these realms, racism exists due to the non-spiritual accepted influences of chance, opportunity, randomness, and general unpredictability. It is our collective lack of spiritual understanding that gives receptivity to racist impulses of collective man.

The concept of racism presupposes unequalness in the allotment of our infinite divinity. How could there ever be such a thing as the unequal distribution of divinity? If such a thing were possible, infinite self-aware existence would be grounded in an infinite reality of divine unfairness. Thus, all self-aware existence would be forever impaled on a spear of non-changeable ignorance.

It is not possible to divinely understand the workings of ultimate reality and hold racist thoughts. We possess the infinite potential power of understanding to self-determine the forever and infinite self-expression of our forever beingness. There is no discrimination in our self-conscious access to the forever knowledge power of our infinite self-conscious beingness.

Our individual ability to interpret things divine gives each one of us a unique spiritual understanding of reality. To erase all forms of superiorness of divinity, from our individualized self-awareness, is to recognize that our divine identity is common to us all, as we uniquely and infinite experience our existence as one.

A relatively new topic occurred in the news: human genetic modification. In England, a baby was recently created with DNA from three separate individuals. A gene modification was performed to eliminate, from the evolving baby-fetus, an inherited life-threatening condition.

Here are the concerns: Is there anything morally wrong in the practicing of such technological achievements and advancements? In the practice of genetic modification, are we playing God? In the application of genetic medication, are we in any way interfering with the inherent design of our infinite physical reality beingness?

My answer to the above questions is "No." I maintain all technological progress including new medical advancements constitutes a continuing blessing to the entirety of God's family. All scientific achievements and advancements, along with our spiritual growth, may be delayed, but never permanently stopped.

The individualized-Man of God or immortal-Man forever exists perfectly. A genetically modified baby-fetus is not created with a soul, having self-awareness of its own. Self-conscious awareness only appears as a baby takes its first breath. Therefore, nothing in the physical realm or any other realm has any finite-infinite impact, on any of individualized-Man's forever appearances into objective reality.

All identities of immortal-Man infinitely and presently self-consciously exist in some realm of infinity. It is not possible to create infinite individual self-consciousness. All genetically modified babies and I will add cloned babies will always appear as forever identities, of immortal individualized-Man.

Before continuing to the last chapter, I now give the following summations, of the important thoughts discussed in this work. The final chapter is the most important section because it explains how these new ideas are used to increase our spiritual receptivity to things divine, through prayer or what I prefer to describe as our self-directed desire to unify with divine truth, for the achieving of specific object realm results

- Ultimate reality consists of God; Man; Core Reality; the Idea Realm; the infinite progression of Physical, Purgatorial, Spiritual Worlds; Infinite Void, and the Formless Realm. Although God is infinite, He is not all-powerful, not all-knowing, and not all-present. God exists as an independent co-component of ultimate reality.

- Objective reality enables each of us to experience our infinite existence physically. Objective reality is the portion of ultimate reality containing all its aspects except God and Core Reality. New universes and new worlds are created infinitely. Each newly created universe with a newly world especially for us represents one eternity.

- The purpose of our forever beingness is to experience our self-aware existence as the living of life. We experience life to understand ourselves as infinite divine beings, forever following our divine destiny. Our destiny is to experience our divinity in the self-awareness of infinite joy and harmony and including the wonderments of infinitely understanding and interpreting our forever self-aware existence.

- Experiencing life involves possessing an innate free will. Our free will gives us the ability to interpret and understand all aspects of ultimate reality. Unfortunately, interpreting our existence means interpreting the living of our self-aware existence as experience as pain, heartache, sorrow, unhappiness, et cetera. Still, these unpleasant experiences continually prompt us to realize the real purpose and direction, of our ongoing, infinite self-conscious reality.

- God and Man are forever interconnected, yet forever separate. God is forever and only Self-aware of His unfolding divine nature of infinite completeness. As individualized core-Man, we are infinitely self-consciously aware of ourselves as total self-conscious unity with God. As the transbeingness of Man, in the objective realm, we are eternally cognizant of our capability of interacting with all aspects of ultimate reality.

- God's forever destiny is to infinitely Self-perceive His unfolding divine nature within Himself. Our inner nature as individualized-Man does not unfold; it is to be infinitely known infinitely understood, and infinitely experienced. Our soul is our self-conscious identity with our infinite inner divinity, in God. Our infinite destiny as individualized-Man is to discover self-consciously and experience our inner divine nature while traversing through the realms of objective reality. Thus, our individual physical destiny is to seek, understand, interpret, accept, and experience, and obey the divine dictates of our forever divine existence.

- Our individualized trek through objective reality has a beginning in what I have described as core reality. In core reality, we are self-consciously at one with God. However, we are not God per se because our purpose for the realizing of our self-forever existence and God's purpose for realizing His Self-forever existence is infinitely separate.

- Core reality is Self-known by God in the fullness of His Beingness and self-known by each one of us individually. We do not self-consciously experience core reality. In core reality, we exist in an environment of total and infinite blissfulness, self-consciously known. However, it seems that infinite self-aware blissfulness eventually becomes a self-aware existence of spiritual boredom for individualized immortal-Man; hence, the divine requirement that we each must eventually experience objective reality. Thus, we are compelled into objective reality, consisting of infinitely created eternities for each of us to discover, understand, interpret, experience without infinite self-conscious boredom.

- The transbeingness of Man is our individualized objective-Man presence in objective reality's infinite eternities, as formless-Man, physical-Man, purgatorial-Man and spiritual-Man. Thus, the four phases of our transbeingness as individualized objective-Man represents our adaptability to the objective realm. Each one of us progresses in the above order of our transbeingness through each physically created world until each universe ceases its eternal existence. Then, the collective-We return to the formless realm to await once again, a new transbeing existence, into a new objective world.

- Although God and each of us coexist infinitely; God has no recognition of our individualized-Man existence. Therefore, God does not Self-consciously comfort, guide, bless, protect, sustain, or love us. However, God is the forever source of our infinite self-divine identity. Further, we are the only component of ultimate reality, with the capability of knowing, seeking, understanding, accepting or rejecting God.

- The idea realm is a separate independent component of ultimate and objective reality. I did not originate the concept of the idea realm, but I believe that my description of it and how it functions in relationship to our infinite objective is original. All ideas concerning all the aspects of infinite existence come from the idea realm.

- Without ideas, the purpose for our self-conscious lives, and the design of ultimate reality could never be understood. Our self-awareness, as individualized-Man, combined with idea realm ideas, gives each of us the ability to think self-consciously. Thus, our self-conscious thought requires constant self-conscious interaction with idea realm ideas. God's Self-knowingness has no relationship, connection, or interaction with the idea realm; therefore, God does not have the capacity to think thought self-consciously. The collective-We is the only aspect of ultimate reality having the capacity for self-conscious idea thoughts

- The godless unreality of evil and sin certainly is not original with me. Many individuals throughout history have postulated on their non-existence. What is original is my understanding of how evil and sin manifest in the objective, with their seeming demanding-to-be-known identities. All appearance of evil and sin result from the misinterpretations of idea realm ideas, in relationship to our understandings or non-understandings of God. When our self-conscious thoughts combine with a confused understanding of God, sin results. When our self-conscious thoughts combine with a decisive self-conscious rejection of God, evil results.

- Any of us is capable of experiencing existence while self-consciously denying God's presence; yet, remain a sinner instead a doer of things evil. Godless minded evildoers self-willfully demonstrate their disdain for God, by the godlessly driven evilness of their actions. Evildoers attempt to control the actions of others, through the godlessness force of their godless powered will power. Even if evildoers professed a belief in God, their harm-filled hateful actions prove that they have no understanding of God's true Divine Beingness.

- As each of us belongs to the collective divine-Us, we are forever punished for all the evils and sins we commit in all the lives we self-consciously live. All punishment is self-imposed and consists of self-consciously experiencing the pain, harm, and heartache we have caused ourselves and others. Thus, we are punished eternally and infinitely for all of our purposeful, non-purposeful wrongdoings we have caused to ourselves and others. All deserved punishment occurs after our physical death, and it only takes place in the non-physical section of the purgatorial realm. All deserved punishment lasts until God is consistently, self-consciously, and unequivocally accepted or rejected. Either way, there is an eventual end to our eternal punishment.

- We experience objective reality in two ways: both as real and non-real experiences. Real experiences result from the infinite mechanical functionings, within objective reality. These practices lack any self-consciously driven force and represent objective reality infinitely evolving and devolving within itself.

- The second type of experience is experience created by each of us, as self-conscious self-actuating individualized-Man. The experiences that each of us creates is the outer imaging of our self-conscious desires. Our self-created experiences require an infinitely functioning free will to be forever made manifest. All self-consciously created experiences have no real objective reality of their own. Therefore, they have no actual infinite intact forever existence. All self-consciously designed experiences consist of correct and incorrect interpretations of idea realm ideas. Also, all self-consciously created experiences have designated beginnings and designed endings. Infinite real experiences have no beginnings or endings. Objective reality expresses itself only through real experiences, and it is not capable of interpreting itself. We understand ourselves as we interpret the objectiveness of forever existence, through our self-created experiences. Our self-conscious ability to understand and explain our forever lives enables us to separate real objective reality from objective unreal reality.

- Experiencing existence is the expression of our existence as the living of life. Our lives are sacred because experiencing life provides the only true meaning to our infinite existence. Our forever divine destiny is to spiritually self-understand our true infinite and indestructible selves. Experiencing our existence does not in any way change or impacts our infinite divine nature. Without our ability to experience existence as life, each one of us would lack the impetus or ability, to seek the spiritual understanding of ourselves. We are infinitely and forever divine, and we are infinitely and ceaselessly part of God.

- Awaiting each one of us is the infinite experiencing of spiritual Heavens, and infinitude of possibly experiencing godless-filled Hells. Holy Heavens become the experiencing of our divinely rewarded and awarded to us when our self-acceptance of God has become cherished and finite-infinitely irrevocable, in our experiencing of self-conscious objective reality. Hell is not the punishment for harm perpetrated at any time, at any place, or to anyone. Hell is experiencing godless objective reality combined with a self-conscious rejection of God. Spiritual Heavens are the rewards for the unequivocal God-minded, who have prepared themselves and made themselves spiritually worthy.

- Hell is the reward for the spiritually unworthy. Thus, Hell is the destination for the self-aware ungodly who remain defiant, in their desire not to seek, understand, or accept God. For the God-minded, Hell would be unbearable torment. However, for the eternally ungodly minded Hell is not punishment, Hell is their self-chosen destiny forever devoid of the self-conscious presence of God. In Hell there is no self-conscious self-actuating experiencing of existence, there is only self-awareness excluding God-awareness and life awareness. Hell is an earned place of eternal joylessness. In Hell, purgatorial-Man retains his power of understanding, but in Hell, there is nothing to understand, there is only the self-awareness of godlessness.

- I maintain each one of us is our personal and infinite Savior, from the wrongdoings of our self-interpreting existence. I mention individual salvation because it represents a significant understanding of this work. There is no need for any salvation that is beyond our inner selves. There is a requirement for salvation that I believe that everyone would agree upon regardless of anyone's understanding of God. For the salvation needed for self-consciously abusing existence as life, there must be some self-conscious effort made to acknowledge and receive the answer for desired salvation. In other words, individual salvation must be self-consciously desired before it can be acquired. Thus, our own self-conscious effort to obtain salvation becomes the motivating source, for the realizing of our salvation. Therefore, our individual salvation results from our divine desire to understand, interpret, and practice divine truth. Our infinite understanding of divine truth is our infinite savior. Thus, my definition of salvation is the process whereby our spiritually correct self-conscious understanding and acceptance of the forever divinely true replaces our divinely incorrect self-conscious acceptance of our thought-corrupted interpretations of reality. Then, our salvation is the result of our identifying with and accepting our inner divine nature. Salvation remains a never-ending objective process. Understanding the true beingness in God always remains the source of our salvation, but only from our individual perspectives. Thus, each of us is our forever infinite Savior, infinitely saving, and resaving our self-accepted understandings of ourselves.

- Our individualized self-conscious thought-based understanding provides the only power, in infinity, which is self-consciously controllable, and self-consciously directed. Thus, our self-conscious power of knowledge gives us the ability to create, in the realm of physical experience, the understanding of our infinite existence. Nothing else in ultimate reality has that capability. Our self-conscious power of knowledge results from the interaction of our self-awareness with the idea realm ideas. Thus, each of us has the infinite power to demonstrate the forever understanding of our infinite existence throughout infinity. Thus, we are infinitely choosing to experience our forever evolving infinite understanding of ourselves. The endless experiencing of the understanding of ourselves only occurs in the objective realm. In core reality, we have no finite or infinite understanding of ourselves, God, or anything else. In core reality, we just exist in the infinite self-awareness of harmony, perfection, and wholeness, and never self-consciously separated from the presence of God. In core reality, each one of us is completely and totally powerless.

- All the powers infinitely expressing in objective reality result from the countless functionings within objective reality, and they have no identifiable purpose without our power of interpretation to understand and explain. The countless inner-powers of objective reality functionally manifest through their infinite subjugation to the uncontrollable and unpredictable elements of chance, opportunity, randomness, and general unpredictability. Thus, the objective realm consists, in part, of immense powers creation, destruction, and erosion expressing infinitely. The individualizations of Man possess the only power authority in ultimate reality, capable of subduing and controlling objective realm's unpredictability of the expressions of power.

Thus, as individualized-Man, infinity is forever subservient to each one of us, as individual and infinite immortal-Man.

- Each objective life we self-consciously live is responsible for countless self-consciously lived potential lives. Potential lives are self-chosen or imposed upon us by the forces of unpredictably. A potential life is a life we would have lived and is dependent upon varying circumstances. Suppose a child is accidentally killed. If the child had not died young, the child would have lived a life. That potential life exists somewhere as an unknown aspect of infinite reality. However, that potential life is self-consciously lived and self-consciously punished. Also, that potential life can all result in additional potential lives. The possibilities are endless. The only thing of supreme infinite importance is our infinite self-awareness and our infinite free will choices. No matter what life we are living or potentially living, it is always each one of us that is self-consciously making decisions. We are the self-consciousness of existence infinitely understanding existence in infinite ways.

Chapter VIII

Accepting the Forever True

Know thyself.

Socrates

God forever exists; however, there is never any Self-conscious God for us to pray to because there is no God in the foreverness of existence which is capable of hearing our prayers. Thus, there is no God, whom Self-consciously loves us, comforts us, encourages us, guides us, blesses us or disappoints us. God is the substance of our soul, but each of us is forever self-alone in the divine content of God's forever Beingness. All healing takes place in the divine atmosphere of pure thought.

Our destiny is to know God; however, we alone and individually determine our knowingness of God. From our individualized perspective, God is the Provider for every aspect of our self-aware beingness. In the self-awareness of our infinitude, God is always facing us, but we cannot see Him if we do not know Him. Thus, God never turns to us; we must turn to Him. As individualizations of God, there is nothing we cannot divine accomplish when powered by a self-realizing self-acceptance of God.

Each of us forever exists as an equal portion of God. All that God Forever Is is our divine destiny to discover, uncover, and recover. Our infinite divine beingness demands to be infinitely self-known. We can only know our God-divinity, as God's self-conscious understanding of

Himself. Therefore, in the objective realm, to know the divinity of our God-identity, we must understand the divinity of our God-identity. Our divinely sincere desire to understand the Beingness of God brings the Beingness of God into self-aware expressions. All divine healing results from our understandings of God combined with an unflinching self-conscious allegiance to our understandings of God, and the purity of kindness in our self-expressions buttressing our desires to manifest God's healing presence, in our objectively appearing world.

Thus, progressive spiritual unfoldment is the realization and demonstration of God, in the non-real accepted realm of physical experience. Divine truth self-consciously experienced, contains the forever divine authority to transmute the illusions of error into the acceptance of truth self-realized. Thus, the driving purpose of our objective existence is to bring the healing truths of God, into our evolving objective world as harmony in our self-conscious self-accepting expression.

In this chapter, my intention is to show the practical application of the self-awareness of truth manifesting in the realm of physical experience. I define the accepting of the things forever true, as our self-conscious identification with the infinite divine source of our forever Beingness, God.

All consequences in the experiencing of existence, whether God-based or non-God-based, are thought-based. Our successfully directed acceptance of the forever divinely pure is the result of our spiritual understanding, forever ascending the ladder of spiritual truth made visible. In the realm of objective reality, we experience the mental digestion of our self-consciously accepted thoughts.

In our self-humble acceptance of truth, God is never petitioned. My definition of divine petitioning is our self-conscious acceptance and affirmation of the only things which are divinely authentic. In other words, through the acceptance of the forever real qualities of God, we petition ourselves to accept ideas of God's forever and divinely unopposed nature, in their undefiled and unpolluted states of harmonious perfection.

Spiritual truths always exist to be understood, accepted, and realized; that are far greater than the circumstances we non-harmoniously choose to experience. Our salvation, from experiencing our free will acceptance of self-determined errors of existence, is forever assured because our experiencing of life as existence is the greatness of truth ever to be finitely and infinitely realized, and each of us has infinity to realize that truth.

Thus, our successful acceptance of the wholeness of truth-ideas results in the overcoming our deserved consequences for our actions, through truth self-understood, truth self-embraced, and truth self-displayed. Throughout the infinite increasing of the understanding our forever expanding divinity, nothing in our experiencing of life, cannot be seen from our point of view of God's wholiness, which then becomes wholeness in our realm of expression.

The only things that we self-consciously experience that are real are the purity of happiness and joy self-realized, in the experiencing of our objective existence, by self-consciously identifying ourselves with the God-source of our foreverness. Without self-identifying our forever beingness in God, our perceptions of objective reality become aimless and meaningless.

Without the awareness of God surrounding our self-identity, we will continue to manifest our forever existence through the unrestrained force of our self-will moldings of godless unreality, into self-created experiences to be identified as objective godless happiness. True divine objective happiness is only known and experienced through a self-understanding and love of God.

When it comes to the subject of petitioning God, this question may be reasonably asked: How is it possible to prayerfully petition or plea to a non-personal God? In other words, how is it possible for a God who knows nothing of our trials and tribulations, to be spiritually pleaded to or beseeched to by us?

There is no such thing as prayerful requests or pleas to a non-personal God. In truth, to ask God for anything is to misunderstand the nature of God. In this book, the healing of non-real experienced disharmony resulting from misinterpretation of infinite truth emerges from the affirming and accepting the foreverness of divine truth. For the divine truth of healing to take place, it is not self-consciously necessary to deny the untrue unreal; it is only necessary to affirm the substance of the forever divinely real.

The results to all of our affirmations and declarations of spiritual truth reside within us waiting to be revealed, for our self-conscious affirmation and acceptance. Our forever realizing of the foreverness of God's presence, as the substance of our self-beingness, is the basis for all successful outcomes of divine truth self-realized and made visible in the realm of appearance.

Our infinite identity is forever divinely God-based and nothing in infinite objective reality has the capability of altering that truth. Thus, our acceptance of the everlasting divinely true is based on our realization of God, as the only source and substance of our forever self-beingness. Our acceptance of idea realm ideas in their wholeness demonstrates our understanding that God never Self-actively heals anyone or anything.

All divinely-sought healing results from the forever wholeness of truth-ideas understood, accepted, and self-consciously enthroned in our self-conscious awareness. To experience true divine healing, we declare, avow, and affirm the truth and substance of our forever divinely evolving self-realized infinite existence. We are the infinite indestructibility of God, forever self-consciously completing the wholiness of the wholeness of God in our forever lives.

The concept of unreal existence is only relevant to our spiritual evolving self-consciousness. Without the power we surrender and cede to false beliefs, godless unreality has no real existing authority to declare any unlimited non-real authority over us. All the power unreality ever seems to exhibit is the reflection of the divinely infinite power residing within each of us.

We forever understand our forever real selves by rejecting our forever non-real selves. As divine truth is forever self-realized, the reality of non-reality is continually diminished into its native nothingness. Our infinite ongoing understanding of forever reality infinitely demands that we each overcome the claims of non-reality.

Thus, our knowledge of divine truth does not eliminate godless unreality; godless unreality is only eternally transmuted, into harmony self-receptively realized and accepted. Therefore, anything asserting pretended existence can be spiritually removed from our experience, but can never be eliminated as a claim, as we forever experience objective reality. I repeat, as each one of us experiences life, we are forever divinely evolving or non-divinely devolving, in the realizing of our divine destiny.

However, as divine truth is accepted, by our self-conscious awareness, divine truth forever replaces our previous self-accepted misconceptions of reality. The seeming presence of unreality forever objectively exists because it is the forever eternal byproduct of the self-evolving self-understanding. Still, it remains forever true that experiences have no reality-based authority for their assumed existence.

Within each one of us, our objective experiences are self-consciously determined. Limitations to our successful acceptance of the forever real seem to endlessly, encircle the depths our spiritual certainties. Eventually, our spiritual progression of divine certitude moves us from mechanical means of healing to the non-mechanical God-based healings through our spiritually chosen acceptance of truth-filled ideas.

In the forever self-conscious spiritual progress of anyone, the answer to all spiritual petitions to God, regardless of how God is understood, must be spiritually earned. The divinely unworthy are never recipients of the saving delivering grace of divine truth. It is our birthless birthright to make ourselves self-consciously worthy to determine our divine destiny as forever individualized expressions of God.

Affirmations for healing deliverances of any kind, devoid of any significant individual spiritual evolved development are only answered, by the unpredictable godlessness of chance, opportunity, randomness, and general unpredictability. Thus, the degree and depth of our self-evolving spirituality must correspond to our understanding and commitment to the divinity of truth self-known and self-cherished.

Our infinite existence is inescapably divine. The self-accepting of truth is the process of spiritualizing our self-conscious thinking. The purpose of accepting the forever real is to elevate our spiritual awareness to receive ideas in their wholeness, with the clarity of divinely supreme self-confidence. Thus, our divine destiny is to become self-consciously that which we infinitely are forever, the self-knowingness of God.

The more we identify ourselves with God, as the source of our infinite beingness, the more perceptive and receptive is our self-consciousness, to the divine wholeness and wholiness of ideas. Accepting the wholeness and wholiness of ideas is accepting the wholeness of truth made manifest in the experiencing of our self-understandings.

In this present physical realm of our transbeingness God heals no one and the attributes of God, in and of themselves, heal no one. All true healing results from our correct acknowledgment, interpretation, and understanding of idea realm ideas, in consonance with our self-acceptance of God's indwelling presence.

The degree we have steadfastly accepted the falsely unreal into our self-consciousness determines the healing success, in our demonstration of the eternally and infinitely real. In other words, our self-conscious receptivity to harmful unreality is directly proportional to the strength-density of our God-awareness and God-acceptance.

In truth, the only knowledge of healing ever needed is to reject the false idea that there ever was, ever is, or ever will be anything requiring the need of healing. However, the mere rejection of a falsely assumed reality has no power to heal. Healing is the result of our self-conscious rejection of non-reality by replacing it with our divinely thickening understanding of forever truth.

There are automatic forms of healing which occur as mechanical bodily functions. These forms of healing result from following and obeying so-called physical laws of existence. Also, it is possible for misinterpretations of truth to heal. Thus, in our present fledgling current state of spiritual discernment, these forms of healing often combine truth with untruth.

Thus, all forms of non-spiritually based healing have their place in our physical realm existence. Our evolving understanding of spirituality guides each of us to the type of healing, corresponding to our developed spiritual or non-developed spiritual receptivity. The headache of the evilest person that ever lived is assuaged, by the healing quality of aspirin. Thus, all healing results from our growing spiritual understanding reflecting back to us, as the layers of our infinite divinity self-understood.

All forms of healing contribute to the evolving of our spirituality because they appear at the accepted level of our divine awareness being self-realized; thus, many forms of healing are available to everyone, whether they do or do not seek God. In our present collective state of spiritual progression, all healing seen as comforting should be considered a divine blessing.

Non-divine based healing is another example of infinity providing us with comfort, as we self-consciously exist, in an infinite existence in which we had no say of participation. Thus, it remains forever objectively valid, that all stages or realizations of healing are divinely inspired, because all healing, to one degree or another, is a rejection of non-reality.

Presently, healing is understood both spiritually and non-spiritually. There are many forms and types of healing void of any understanding or reliance upon God. Often, non-God based healings result from the godless balms of evolving technologies. These worldly technological truths continually tug at us for our acceptance, instead of encouraging us to rely upon our divine understanding of God. Thus, for the spiritually unawares, technological advancements often replace the need to understand the divinely wholistic healing nature of God.

The self-rejection of God is always an infinite free will choice; thus, divine healing is always an infinite free will choice. Interestingly, assuming that we are collectively and infinitely divinely based God-expressing beings, which we are, and then not to be punished for self-consciously rejecting God seems counterintuitive. However, infinity places no judgments upon our individualized self-conscious thoughts; we are only punished, for our destructive self-conscious actions. We have infinite self-freedom to deny the reality of our divine beingness.

However, the rejection of God results in automatic and unlimited limitations, which manifest as a seeming form of punishment. For example, the self-conscious rejection of God prevents experiencing the power of divine healing. Thus, spiritually interpretations of objective reality, by our self-attracting of the wholeness and wholiness of idea real ideas cannot be made.

Thus, if the existence of God, which includes His infinite divine nature, is rejected, God-based healing idea-thoughts are not available for self-conscious acceptance. Thus, a self-conscious living reality, devoid of the self-awareness of divine self-conscious substance cannot access idea realm ideas for the realization of divine healing.

Ideally, healing should not require any self-conscious efforts to elevate our spiritual understanding to the atmosphere of the purity of divinity. Rather, our self-consciousness of divine truth revealed and accepted should float effortlessly the ocean of our self-consciously understood divinity forever buoying the stumbling, wavering, shilly-shally progressions of our spiritually faltering understandings.

Real spiritual healing occurs as we self-consciously align our ascending spiritual thought-reception of harmonious ideas with our active awareness of the presence of God. Thus, whenever God is understood, accepted, and cherished, without the snags of non-spiritual truths; healing is self-actualized as the presence of divinity, in the non-real realm of experience.

Unfortunately, this form of healing awareness is rarely seen in our ever now experiencing of existence. Our understanding of truth can only appear to us in direct proportion to the depth, of our spiritually derived knowledge. Thus, our evolving spiritual need to understand things divine gives us the earned divinely based effort to experience the wholeness and wholiness of truth, self-consciously as healing.

Except for individuals, whose expressions of spirituality, are far beyond our present collective spiritual understandings, we are now at a common place where the need for genuine spiritual understanding is recognized. Still, we can never attain spiritual knowledge until we collectively understand and embrace its divinely required need.

Presently, spiritual understanding is achieved in self-conscious advancing increments of truth, understood and accepted; therefore, clear unpolluted divine healing only occurs in the advancing stages of our spiritual evolvement. At that place, we are self-consciously able to rid from our self-evolved consciousness, all the inharmonious claims that eternally badger our self-awareness.

Thus, there will come a time, in the spiritual evolving of each one of us, when our spiritual understanding spontaneously heals any perceived display of the non-harmony of existence. At that time, we will, without any crippling of doubt, self-consciously understand the holy and evolved divine certainty mandating our divine realization that nothing ever experiencing the existence of life requires healing.

God-based healing validates our spiritual self-awareness through our self-conscious desire to objectify our divinity. God-based healing is most desirable because it is grounded in the self-acknowledging of our ever present evolving spirituality. God-based healing replaces the falsely accepted assumptions of our existence with the understanding of things which are forever and divinely true.

In our evolving spiritual progress, just as spiritual understanding requires effort; spiritual healing requires effort. However, when true final objective realm spirituality is achieved and experienced, healing results from divine self-knowingness without any healing effort. However, that divine realization in the physical domain of our spiritual evolvement is to be a far distant spiritual attainment.

Continuous and divinely fruitful God-based healing is our final stepping-stone to the objective realization of the understanding of our forever lasting divinity, in our present odyssey through the objective realm. All self-consciously directed healing is the expression of divine truth self-willfully understood, earned, and accepted, and made self-consciously manifested in the realm of appearance.

Thus, all of our self-conscious healings result from our understanding of God's infinite inwardness within us, in our present capacity to understand the foreverness of God, which divinely comprises our infinite divine nature. Self-consciously desired divine healings result from accepting the wholeness and wholiness of idea-truths combined with the recognizing and acceptance of the wholiness of God.

Even in our attempts to be spiritually concentrated, we still allow untruths into our self-awareness, which means that we are merely treading water spiritually. Until our faith in God becomes our self-conscious all-powerful wielding rod of divine understanding, the continuous shredding of non-reality into its forever-based nothingness is never to be fully realized, in the objective realm.

Instantaneous healings resulting from our understanding of God is the unmistakable proof of our self-conscious acceptance of our forever divinity. At present, that expression of healing is rarely seen, understood, or accomplished, and certainly not consistently accomplished. Our current inability to repeatedly and consistently perform divine healings highlights the dearth of our individual and collective spiritual evolvement.

Instantaneous healings resulting from our understanding of God are the unmistakable proofs of our advancing self-developing spirituality, in self-conscious expression. At present, that expression of healing is rarely seen, understood, or accomplished, and certainly not consistently accomplished. Our current inability to repeatedly perform divine healings highlights the dearth of our individual and collective spiritual revealment

Real divine healing is the result of our God-understanding, God-acceptance, God-identity, and God-endowment, self-actuated without the impediments of doubtful uncertainties. In our present healing desires, we should never totally rely upon our spiritually primitive evolving understandings of God; unless or until we are unconditionally convinced that our desired divine healings will appear in the realm of appearance.

Presently, the seeming realities of non-reality diminish God from our collective spiritual awareness. As we currently look about us, all that we see, we see through spiritually pathetic weak eyes. Thus, at our present collective state of spiritual progression, it would be foolish for anyone to rely totally upon the God of their understanding.

In the current moment of time, we are divinely lost in a world, where our collective God-awareness, is buried in the godless frozen grounds of our self-grabbing depravity. As I write these words, I am filled with pitifulness and wretchedness of our present collective spiritually deprived existence. Sure, there are isolated lights of God divine realizations, but woefully sad is collective-Man's non-seeking of God.

The fact that we are presently experiencing the loathsomeness of our thoughts and actions is undeniable proof that we will eternally encounter the wretchedness of our self-desired living of godless lives. Our inner divinity eventually wins out, but the penalty we pay is the self-conscious experiencing of the eternal torments of suffering.

Again I ask: Why were we given an infinite unsolicited self-aware existence, when we so often experience the living of life, in a lonely non-God loathsome existence? We are all infinitely trapped in an endlessly recurring objective existence, in which we can never rise higher, in our spiritual evolvement, than that is required to return to core reality.

However, what happens if we chose never to return to core reality? I do not know. However, that is an interesting speculation. If we were spiritually advanced enough to go back to core reality but opted to stay in objective reality, we would exist in a reality that held no more challenges to provide the means for us to advance spiritually. Would we still progress in acquiring spiritual knowledge? Regardless, we would be the self-conscious divine emperors over all of objective reality.

However, our present concern is to acquire the supreme self-confidence that powers our spiritual understanding and assures the success of our desired healings. Even though we are far-far from any consistency in total reliance upon the God of our understanding for our healings, the total divine commitment to consistently rely upon God is forever designed into our objective divine destiny.

The evolving of our spiritual understanding gives meaning to our objective existence. Our need for healing represents our continuing misinterpretations of objection reality. We often misinterpret things we do not understand. Thus, our self-conscious need for healing is the recognition of our spiritual ignorance and impotence. Our physical destiny is to be the divine warriors who never accept the godless unrealities of forever non-existence.

Thus, as long as there is a continuing belief in the need for healing, our self-evolving understanding of things spiritual is restricted and constricted. We become spiritually victorious as we continuously and unequivocally understand, accept, and obey the wholiness of divine truth without exceptions.

To fully understand our infinite indestructibility is never to seek the forever need of healing, or even self-consciously consider the thought of healing. Thus, our forever inwardly engraved destiny is to embrace divine truth, cherish divine truth, and share divine truth with all of life. It is our acceptance of pure divine understanding that vanquishes all self-conscious acknowledging nods for the need of healing.

In our experiencing of existence, physical healing results in the experience of joy. Joy is our infinite soul reflecting back to us the essence for our true beingness. All facets for the realization of joy-filled happiness are structured divinely into our beingness. If we self-consciously deny our divine identity, we reject the experiencing of joyfulness from our infinite experiencing of objective living of life.

The experiencing of joy is the continuing consummation of our infinite existence. If we never experienced joy, we would have no ongoing desire to experience life as reality. Would an infinite life-existence where joyfulness, is never self-consciously realized, be a desirable infinite reality for our self-conscious habitation?

The acceptance and awareness of the harmony of ideas displace the disharmony of things unreal, producing experiences of equilibrium and wholeness. In short, affirmations of the divinely real truths are our self-acceptance of divine truth replacing our evolving self-awareness of non-reality, as spiritually primitive as that may seem.

In our self-awareness, true and the untrue contend for our self-acknowledgement and acceptance. In the declaring and accepting of affirmations of divine wholeness, we spiritually cleanse our self-consciousness so that only the perfection of ideas in their wholeness is self-accepted.

We are the objective expressions of the things we cherish ourselves to be. The successful or non-successful outcome of our declarations of truth is determined by the depth of our commitment, to realizing the divinity of our understanding. In all perceptions of reality, we acknowledge and accept the ideas of truth we cherish most. Spiritual healing is often difficult because, for many of us, it is difficult to give up cherished accumulations of self-accepted unrealities.

Our continuing understandings of God are the reasons and purpose for our infinite existence. God is the healing substance for all of our successful proclamations of divine truth. Each of us is solely responsible for our evolving self-conscious divine revelations. Thus, all favorable answers to affirmations of truth are self-determined and individual. Our spiritual understandings are always God's answer divinely interpreted and accepted by each of us.

Since our understandings of God are the source of our spiritual power, the answers to all of our pure divine petitions forever reside within us. Through our perceptions of spiritual and divine truth, God is our comforter, our healer, our guide, and our genuine source of transmuting love. Gentleness and kindness are part of God's infinitely ongoing nature occurring in the evolving of our objective existence. Any so-called spiritual self-awareness not girded in kindness and gentleness lacks the capability for progressive spiritual evolvement, progression, and expression.

How we see ourselves in expression is how we know or not know the reality of objective ourselves. Gentleness is the sister of kindness. Gentle kindness is the understanding of God's nature touching our collective and individualized self-consciousness. The successful affirmations of truth resulting in truth demonstrated, requires a prepared self-consciousness grounded and rooted in the countenance of gentleness and kindness.

God possesses no Self-understanding of His divine nature and possesses no Self-directed divine will. God never responds to our petitions for His intervention. God is only aware of Himself and His infinite unfolding divinity. In short, there is no God, who is Self-aware of our existence or has the Self-conscious capability to create, de-create, impact, or influence our infinite existence in any manner. We determine who we are in the infinity of our self-expressions.

The realization that each one of us, individually, is solely responsible for our infinite divine destiny should be a forever self-liberating thought. All that there ever is to rely upon is our individual self-conscious understanding of ourselves. We are not responsible for the infinite reality of our self-aware existence, but we are forever responsible for the mental content forever filling our self-awareness.

We pray to accept the divinely correct realizations of ourselves. The self-knowing of our true selves is our infinite salvation from the curse of an infinity of self-awareness. Our forever self-awareness is a curse when it is not divinely self-understood and a blessing when it is divinely self-understood. Our infinite destiny is not controllable; we only control the realizing of our infinitely evolving divine fate. Spiritually understood self-prayer is the fulfilling and completing of our infinite destiny.

The reality of understanding, correctly interpreted, exalts our infinite existence. Thus, from our perspective, there is no meaningful understanding of God separate from our evolving self-understanding self-awareness. Our true self-conscious at-oneness with God provides the mental framework for our spiritually correct interpretations of idea realm ideas.

When our self-conscious interpretations of idea realm ideas, are self-consciously surrounded by our self-knowingness of God's nature, our understanding of ultimate reality is glorified, within the confines of our self-understood divinity. At that time, our control over the jagged-gnarly ogre-shaped shadows of godless unreality is supreme.

We are self-knowingly divine whenever we self-knowingly reveal the divine truth, to ourselves. Now, there is no opposition to our understandings of truth; there is no opposition to the revealment of our divine nature, and there is no opposition to the incorruptibility of our forever divinity expressing in the realm of our self-conscious understanding.

Our acceptance of truth does not rely on the whims of a personal God. Our desire to understand divine truth is our divine destiny self-consciously realized. Fidelity to real truth is the only means required for the favorable outcome of our self-spiritualized petitions, unveiled to our self-awareness.

We forever become divine as we surrender to God's divinity within us. Our self-conscious demonstration of things real is our self-conscious realization of truth held fast, cherished, desired, accepted, and glorified. If we self-think ourselves divine, we realize ourselves as divine. If we self-think ourselves non-divine, we realize ourselves as non-divine. We forever self-realize ourselves to be that which we forever self-think to ourselves to be.

Still, our mere desire to demonstrate things forever real denotes spiritual weakness, in the evolving of our divine understanding. To desire anything spiritually, presuppose a lack of the spiritual knowledge of divine truth. In the wholeness of our true divinity, all things forever real reside in the forever-Us, because each one of us possesses the all-powerfulness of the self-conscious understanding of existence.

For all of the self-acknowledgment of our infinite divinity, we remain forever as self-evolving spiritual beings. Thus, in our ongoing acceptance of divine truth, we seek deliverance forever from the invited and uninvited unreal that we have falsely and erroneously interpreted themselves into our self-aware appearing reality.

The realizing that our advancing individual and collective spiritual understandings and evolvement is difficult to attain spiritually highlights the primitiveness of our combined eternal progression. At present, the seeking of spiritual deliverance is hard because our free will is constantly assailed and enticed by the legions of doom's holy uncertainties.

The demonstration of true spirituality is the experiencing of our existence through the directing power of our free will choices, to attain and maintain, an unwavering and unbroken allegiance to the forever God of our self-identity. We are spiritually weak because we have little divine control over the infinite expressing power of our free will.

The process of healing results from the self-certain understanding of our divine selves. Our free will choices, whatever they may be, sets out the self-knowingness of our divine destiny. Our divine destiny is realized divinely as we free-willingly accept ourselves as infinitely divine and indestructible supreme beings. Thus, as we self-understand ourselves as infinite, immortal divine beings, no healing of any type is ever necessary.

The divinely perfect answer to all of our affirmations of existence is the recognition of our forever divinity self-understood and held fast. The success of our divine statements of beingness mandates the understanding of our true divine nature as God's nature individualized.

We lose the all-powerfulness of our divinely interpreted knowledge if we choose to seek healings, in the self-consciousness atmosphere of the godless non-dependable and faithless unreal.

God's forever nature and God's unknown divine purpose for each of us is always understood and interpreted from our individualized personal perspectives. Thus, all answers to the realizing of divine truths always correspond to our ongoing interpreted-understandings of our God-individualized selves. Thus, all our self-declared apprehensions of God involve and evolve the realization of our harmonious self-divinity, in the realm of experience.

The only divine truths we are ever capable of successfully demonstrating are those truths we cherish, accept, and understand above all things. Through our self-conscious self-cherishing of sacred truths, we exalt our never-ending divine existence to the place in our self-consciousness, where we are truly grateful for the infinite existence of our beingness.

Our self-determining assertions of truth are understood, received and realized by God, through each of us. Each of us is God's understanding of Himself. Our acceptance of reality brings the knowledge of divine revelation into the realm of our experiences. The etchings of truth we experience, in our self-aware knowingness of objective reality, are the corresponding answers to our inwardly driven divine desires.

Divinely successful prayer-type acceptance of the forever real requires our self-conscious effort to replace our misinterpreted wrongly-based thinking with spiritually correctly right-based thinking. The forgiving of ourselves, for not heeding things forever divine, is mandatory to facilitate our increasing receptivity to divine truth. Thus, all of our wrongdoings must be self-consciously recognized, uncovered, replaced and forgiven by us.

The only forgiveness ever required by our self-conscious awareness is the forgiveness of ourselves. The purpose of expressing divine understanding is to experience existence spiritually, through the realization of divine truth in its outward manifestation. Thus, self-forgiveness is a ready replacement of our God-void self-acceptance, with the seeking of divine self-awareness.

Taking sacred responsibility for our wrongdoings is the beginning, middle, and ending of our ever ongoing spiritual evolvement. Sometimes we forgive others for their wrongdoings against us. However, that type of forgiveness is never spiritually mandated. It is the self-forgiveness of ourselves which results in our personal and individual spiritual salvation. Therefore, we must first and foremost forgive ourselves for our divine lapses, both great and small.

Everything that ever happens to us happens in the perimeters of our individualized self-awareness. Our self-forgiveness is the outcome of our sinfulness and evilness self-realized and repented. Therefore, understanding the necessity of forgiving ourselves is most important to our self-realizing success, in the demonstrating of divine healing.

In the self-forgiveness of ourselves, we accept a new self-realization and understanding of ourselves. Our self-forgiveness is two-part. First, we forgive ourselves for self-consciously recognizing the corrupted contraband of unreality. Second, we forgive ourselves for allowing those corrupted unreal brandings of sin and evil entry into our self-conscious awareness.

If we do not or cannot self-consciously forgive ourselves, our sinful and evil wrongdoings continue to remain self-known in our self-aware conscious, and we continue to wander spiritually aimless and lost, in the objective realm of our self-torturing of our eternal existence. Any unwillingness to self-realize the expressions of our sinful-evilness denote a total self-willingness to understand ourselves from the perspective of self-judging our self-evolving divinity.

We cannot accept the divine truth about our forever beingness as long as we self-consciously embrace the untruths of our forever existence. Thus, when we unwillingly refuse to give up the lies we have self-accepted about ourselves to ourselves, we become infamy's liars testifying to a false-forever divine self-identity that repudiates our infinite divinity.

Attempts made by others to spiritually harm us, darken the spiritual paths of the harm-makers and impact the harm-receivers to the extent that they self-willingly allow hurtfulness to befall them. However, all harmful acts directed at us, can, if we choose to-make-it-so, provide us with divine opportunities to become the blessed receivers of the golden truths of our forever divinity. Thus, in expressions of sin and evil, divine truth is forever available for our self-conscious knowingness and acceptance. To understand that all of godless unreality is a lie makes us the spiritually based self-acknowledged rulers over our forever infinite divinity.

Wrongdoings are eternal and infinite burdens to be divinely removed, by the increasing understanding and acceptance of spiritual truths. If we choose to forgive the harm-makers, it is to aid them in the recognizing and understanding of their inability to demonstrate their seeming inability to know themselves spiritually as divine children of the forever infinite. Thus, we forgive others by seeing them as the perfect spiritual offspring of infinite goodness and thus see know as divinely blessed.

We are infinitely good with the potential to do infinite evil; we are not infinitely evil with the potential to do infinite good. Misguided harm-doers experience their non-spiritual enslavement to godless unreality until the inevitable time comes when their need for true spiritual repentance dawns upon their self-awareness.

Any understanding of God purporting to encompass divine love cannot coexist, with displays of unlovingness, towards any member of God's family. The successful realizing of the forever faithfully true and pure into the realm of experience is not possible, if there is so much as a tinge of self-tarnished unlovingness, darkening our self-aware acceptance of the divinely forever real.

In the divine evolving of our eternal lives progresses, we all must bear the suffering for the self-realizing of our infinite forever divine beingness. Forgiveness of ourselves is especially necessary to turn divine challenges into spiritual victories. By forgiving ourselves, we self-consciously acknowledge our evolving spirituality taking place in our self-awareness. Thus, harmful acts made against us, both delay and abet the self-realizing of our divine destiny.

In objective reality, we are born to learn our true identity as infinite indestructible divine beings. Our individualized free will forever and always is the director for all things allowed entry into our self-consciousness. As we forgive ourselves in our acceptance of truth, we renew ourselves spiritually. All affirmations of self-accepted truths we make become the divine source for freeing-up of our self-imposed non-spiritually accepted ignorances, from our self-chosen cherished ungodly based thoughts.

When we understand ourselves as divine, we are self-consciously accepting our infinite existence. Spiritual affirmations devoid of self-understood spiritual evolvement simply become our self-conscious desires lacking the power of divine truth to be made manifest.

Successful outcomes for spiritually manifesting the pure divinity of truth become the spiritual rewards, for our fidelity and divine mindfulness to our God-based reality, in the seeking and receptivity to the things everlastingly true and real.

We can self-willingly manifest the experience of harmony into the realizations of our lives; as we self-realize and self-accept the wholeness and wholiness of perfection. A clear understanding of our relationship with God promotes within us a clear perception of the wholeness of ideas needed for successful objective-realm healing answers, to manifest in the realm of appearance

Too often, we act as spiritual bumpkins to stupid to desire, seek, and cherish the foreverness of our divinity. If our affirmations of divine truth go unclaimed, our spiritual progress requires self-evaluation. Our inability to manifest divine truth in the realm of experience denotes the shallowness of our objective spiritual evolvement. We should always be divinely truthful to ourselves.

As we allow all circumstances which forever affect our spiritual journeys, to promote within us, a developing spiritual sense of unfoldment, the forgiving of others for their non-spiritual actions becomes unnecessary. In the reality of self-consciously experiencing existence, all things are spiritual. Thus, the plagues of godless unreality become spirituality understood and serve as divine stepping-stones, to the self-aware evolving of infinite self-consciousness of our forever beingness.

Eventually, in the experiencing of objective existence, there comes a time when self-forgiveness is no longer required. Self-forgiveness is unnecessary when we have self-consciously and spiritually evolved, in the objective realm, to the place when all of our actions become our self-aware expressions of the will of God, as we ever dynamically grow in our understanding of the will of God.

Thus, when we reach that ultimate realization in the expressing of our infinite existence that forgiveness of any kind is never required, we are revitalized into a new spiritual reawakening. We become empowered with the self-conscious understanding of the everlastingness of infinite truth, and we understand that all real existence is divine.

Now, everything becomes sacred to us because everything becomes evolvingly self-known, in its spiritual purity of harmonious perfection. Thus, the wholiness and wholeness of our forever God-beingness are revealed to us as the forever divinely enthroned presence of God, radiating forth from our individualized self-awareness.

As we self-consciously realize our infinite divinity, our objective destiny is fulfilled with our self-realization of golden divine truths. Now we are evolving into the understanding-knowingness of the Self-consciousness of God in forever continuing self-realization. Our divine objective realm destiny is to be, in the visible domain, our self-acceptance of God in the inner sanctuary of our thoughts. Thus, the purpose of our infinite existence is affirmed, and both God and infinity smile to themselves.

What we understand of infinite selves is the realization of our infinite divinity. It is infinitely within each one of us to be self-understood and self-experienced. We infinitely exist to understand and explain all of forever existence, as the divine rulers over the infinity of our personal perceived reality, in the endless discovery and rediscovery of ourselves.

Thus, our forever destiny is to be the creators of our understandings of existence. How marvelous and fantastic is that! Each one of us exists to experience our infinitely shared and infinitely individual destinies. Thus, we are forever destined to know the infinity of God's family, and the infinity that belongs to each God, family member.

Our infinite existence necessitates that the experiencing of our infinite existence be uniquely unique. Also, this means that our infinite experiencing of God's nature be infinitely unique. The one forever God is known infinitely and individually. Thus, the God of God's divine family is separately, differently, and uniquely understood.

Therefore, each of one of us is destined to know God individually, and each one of us is destined to experience infinite existence individually, and each one of us is forever destined to furnish our eternal and infinite self-conscious homes, individually and uniquely with divine truth self-realized. For each one of us to understand the forever infinity of our self-aware existence is our divinely gifted-destiny.

Our greatest spiritual gift to others is to affirm spiritual truth for others. As we choose to see only the divine goodness in others, we are purifying the collective divine family's mind-consciousness of its godless acquired claims of the forever untrue. Thus, in our self-conscious expression of our divinity, we choose to see others enveloped in the incorruptibleness of their infinite individually designed destiny of wholeness and wholiness forever self-realized.

Spiritually understood, all declarations of truth are the expressions of divine forgiveness. By understanding and accepting the actual reality of things, we forgive ourselves for having adopted the godless reality claims of the untrue. In the understanding of our forever divinity, we are choosing to forget the alluring raspings of forever non-divinity.

The successful manifesting of actual healing reality is the outcome of our effortless understandings of the eternally divine. When we entrap ourselves in godless pursuits devoid of divinity, the realizing of truth becomes blurred to our senses. For example, how much error-prone opaqueness in our self-consciousness is due to our inability to relinquish and surrender unkindliness in our thoughts?

Our destiny is to understand our self-divinity as God in expression. More simply put: What are we willing to give up or forsake to rely self-consciously upon the understanding power of our self-divinity? Too often, the forever ripening density of our self-aware non-spirituality engulfs the light of divine truth, making the forever authentic seem impotent and worthless.

Divine truth cannot be self-realized when its opposite is self-idolized. It is the corrupt things we cherish in our thoughts that sap our divine strength, from asserting and accepting our real existence. Our infinite beingness is a continuously waging war between the certainties of reality vying against the claiming certainties of non-reality.

We are the forever battling soldiers in an infinite understanding of our self-aware existence. Thus, we are all in a never-ending battle, an endless battle in which not one of us self-consciously enlisted. Still, we are the forever victors, and we are the forever vanquished. We forever inflict suffering upon ourselves and others, and we forever receive pain and misery. We forever understand and forever do not understand our infinite divinity.

Each of us sits individually on infinity's throne as a king infinitely surveying his kingdom. We are the divine rulers because we are infinitely spiritual beings. We are all-knowing because we everlastingly possess a forever growing knowingness of reality. We are all-powerful because we forever create experiences. We are all-present because we infinitely exist with an individual self-awareness that sees, knows, understands, and interprets all aspects of ultimate reality.

Our self-understood divinity is our infinite armor against all things untrue. Our existence demands consequences or our beingness itself would lack motivation for divine guidance. Without divine guidance, our destiny would infinitely bound and rebound about as finite-infinite experiences without any divine substance, as we would continually conjure up the godless unreal and bring it into the realm of experience.

Our self-conscious spiritual self-awareness projects from the understanding of divine truth to the self-acceptance of divine truth. Our successful realization of the forever valid and true results from divine truth incrementally desired, accepted, understood, and focused on the harmonious expression of goodness, self-absorbed and self-realized.

I repeat an essential understanding of this work: the self-realization that all things ever occurring to us happen within our circumscribed individualized self-conscious awareness. Therefore, it is always desirable to accept the spiritual truth for others and to reveal and unveil the truth within ourselves, for ourselves and others. In our individualized self-aware divinity, we should desire to see everyone as joyful and harmonious expressions of life.

Our self-acceptance of the divinely authentic encourages and blesses the entirety of God's family. Although the self-realization of spiritual truth may be self-accepted for others, the accountability for their spiritual progress, spiritual illumination, and the wholiness of their free will choices always remains their individual responsibility.

For the better or non-better, each of us individually and forever determines the direction of our divine destiny as individualizations of infinity's knowingness, as individualizations of God, and as individualizations of God's spiritual family. Also, for better or non-better what we cherish in our forever desire to understand our objective existence determines the experiencing of our forever destiny.

When each of us becomes a self-aware spiritual blessing to God's family, our collective divine destiny is spiritually blessed. We all share one divine mind. Thus, truth understood, by any member of God's family, makes truth increasingly available to all members of God's family. The spiritual understanding of any one of us impacts the spiritual understanding of the united-Us.

As I have iterated numerous times, our divine destiny is never fully realized because our infinite objective realm existence is forever divinely cyclical. Thus, as the infinite-We, we together and individually determine and fulfill our divine destiny. Thus, we are forever realizing our divine destiny finite-infinitely.

If we ever were to fulfill our divine destiny, we would no longer self-consciously have a divine destiny to experience. Then, our purpose for self-aware existence would no longer be etched into our foreverness of timeless time. Although we are forever self-consciously fulfilling our divine destiny, we are also infinitely self-consciously fulfilling our divine destiny unawares.

All things occurring in experiencing existence become blessings when our understandings our objective reality are spiritually based. Spiritual understanding demands that we maintain a humble attitude of gratefulness for life's blessings, self-consciously received. If we are not grateful for the infinitely outpouring gifts to our forever existence; we are not grateful for our infinite self-aware existence. The truth is that some members of God's family are not grateful for their infinite existence.

What makes our forever reality so intricate and exciting is in the contemplation of our infinitely infused design. The infinitely designed plan for our self-aware existence is forever and divinely embedded, in our self-awareness. Our infinite design is infinite perfection and provides for all of our requirements for our experiencing our endless self-aware purposeful living of life. Thus, the ever-increasing rewards forever bestowed upon us by infinity ameliorate, to some extent, our infinite unasked-for self-aware beingness.

Our ever increasing spiritual understanding enables us to see the blessings in all things, is our God self-awareness actively expressing in its divineness. All affirmations recognizing the sanctity of life fortify and strengthen our individualized spiritual paths. As we understand ourselves as infinite and divinely perfect, we are justifying our infinite existence to ourselves.

Regardless of the circumstances befalling us, in the forever divine process of self-consciously experiencing life, there are always attached blessings to all things spiritually understood and accepted. To realize all the happenings in the experiencing of our lives are spiritual benefits for us to understand the inner workings of our forever divinity.

We are forever part of God, and forever not part of God. Therefore, it is our forever objective destiny to see all the happenings in objective reality as God would see them, through each one of us. Thus, if the God of my understanding observed all my objective realm expressions, He would only see the wholeness and wholiness of my infinite harmony in divine appearance.

To self-consciously seek, discover, and learn from the different happenstances of life, demonstrates our ever evolving spiritual reawakening. When all happenings in the eternities, of objective reality, are understood as blessings, our eternally infinite experiencing of our physical existence nears its terminus.

All blessings, in the answering of our self-accepting prayers, are the reflections of our spiritually evolving progress, our spiritual understanding, our spiritual development, our spiritual unfoldment, and the implanting within our self-knowingness, of our divinely pure sacredness. As we forever understand our self-expressing divinity, there are no petitions for the revealing of divine truth unsatisfactorily or unknowingly answered.

Our developed self-consciousness of goodness enhanced by the teaching assistance of others establishes the basis for our divinely strong affirmations of divine truth, in which we declare the forever real to be divinely true. It is an infinite imperative that each one of us understands ourselves, as an unfolding blessing to our forever evolving self-awareness, and to all of God's family, as each one of us is infinity's blessing to itself.

In our evolving spiritual self-consciousness, we are forever self-participating, in the experiencing of things unquestionably divinely authentic. Our self-understanding and acceptance of truth is our self-conscious declaration of truth desired, understood, and manifested, in the realm of our self-conscious awareness.

Acceptance of the forever divinely real gives us spiritual control over the godlessness of chance, opportunity, randomness, and general unpredictability. Through the power of our divine understanding, all the uncertainties of unpredictability become blessings to be self-discovered and self-revealed to our forever evolving understanding of our forever self-divinity. Thus, each one of us is to understand the reality of existence as an infinite fount of divinely inspired blessings.

Let it be forever known to ourselves; we can never hide from the understandings of ourselves. Thus, the desire for truth realized and the expression of truth realized is not the same. All things which forever impact us represent our ongoing self-interpretations of ourselves, as we express through the realm of experience.

We are the self-visibility of the understanding of our forever beingness in infinite expression. What we infinitely are in our real, self-aware existence is our infinite beingness understood finitely. In divine truth, we are forever the self-accepters of our forever self-understandings. Only divine truth self-consciously sought, understood, and accepted brings the divinity of our existence into our conscious self-awareness.

Our destiny in the expressing of our existence is to know God and our God-selves, through our forever continuing experiencing of our existence. Experiencing reality gives us the ability to understand our evolving divinity in expression. All appearances of divine truth provide the impetus for our continuing self-conscious reawakening to the realizing of our inner divine divinity and destiny.

Here is the secret for the spiritual obtaining of divine truth. First, we prepare our self-conscious awareness to receive the wholeness and wholiness of the harmony of divine truth by exalting, affirming, accepting, and relying only upon the goodliness and Godliness of our forever self-aware existence.

Second, we choose to welcome into our self-consciousness only specifically desired harmony-filled ideas which disperse displays of disharmony, by bringing the visibility of harmony into the situations or circumstances requiring the manifestation of truth self-realized. Thus, it is the forever affirming of our self-conscious divinity that replaces the self-conscious understanding of unreality, with our divinely humble acceptance of genuine truth in appearance.

Healing is the result of the replacing of falsely interpreted reality, with the acceptance of the wholiness and wholiness of ideas. We attract the things we treasure most. If we treasure expressions of truth and harmony, the self-acceptance of divinely whole ideas carries forth, truth realized. Understanding how the process of healing occurs is not necessary because there is nothing ever requiring or needing healing. To try to understand how healing occurs is to try to understand the workings of non-reality.

In the purity our understanding of divine truth, we affirm our infinite beingness, our infinite divinity, and our forever indestructibility. We realize, without any self-imposed restrictions, that whatever appears before us, in the realm of experience is the reality of truth made visible. Our self-accepting of the reality of the forever real is an infinite process in our infinite self-realization.

The actions of others should always be interpreted as spiritual lessons, seeking our spiritual realization to be acknowledged spiritually, challenged and understood spiritually, and seen as blessings bringing gifts, for our ever-evolving understanding. What greater gift can there be, than the gift of experience prompting us to ever greater divine understandings of ourselves.

Our spiritually directed healing outcomes denote our self-conscious self-willingness to understand and affirm the forever authentic and real. Thus, in so doing, we should always be grateful for all life lessons, prompting us to move, towards the eternally divine realization of ourselves. The more divinity we gather in our spiritual understandings of ourselves, the greater is the power we have in realizing the trueness of our forever divine destiny.

We are not objectively destined to be kind or to be unkind; to be good or evil; to be happy or unhappy; to be spiritual or non-spiritual; to know or not know God. However, we are forever justly intended to experience the understandings of our infinite existence. Each of us possesses the infinite capability to experience the infinite understanding of ourselves. Why is that so? That answer is never to be known.

Thus, each one of us has the infinite choice as to how we experience the infinite purpose of our infinite objective existence. Each one of us is king and servant to our individually self-realized world. Presently, each one of us is ruling over our world with pathetic minuscule and paltry spiritual understandings. The forever divinity imbued into each of us is not deserving of our recognition unless we fight for its existence, in the confines of our self-realizations of our forever self-divinity.

We eternally demonstrate the accurate understanding of ourselves in the real-unreal realm of experience. No matter how we direct our forgiveness, either towards ourselves or others, it should always rest on our self-awareness of God. It is our forever understanding of God's nature that divinely restructures unreality into divine truth self-realized by us.

Simply put, forgiveness results from spiritual understanding self-consciously acknowledged and accepted. Forgiveness devoid of any humble acceptance of God becomes our evolving divinity anchorless in the drifting seas of uncertainties. The expression of goodness, without the self-awareness of God is a forever choice, but a divinely foolish one.

Presently, our accepting of godless unreality seems to reign supreme. Thus, at this stage of our collective spiritual progress, our confidence in spiritual truth is self-realized feebly. Therefore, our individual spiritual healing efforts are feeble in their demonstrations. For the spiritually minded, their highly directed spiritual understandings overcome the false assertions of the never-was-to-be, never-is-to-be, or the never shall-to-be.

By affirming and accepting the forever real, we are mandating our collective self-conscious allegiance to our identity in God. To understand ourselves divinely gives us the capability of denying the strangling vines of godless unreality. Our self-awareness of unreality is representative of our limited spiritual evolving because we are still interpreting unreality as a self-generating power of existence to overcome.

Our spiritual understandings must be self-experienced, or our strength and confidence in the revealing of our divine identity are never ongoingly realized or understood. We must understand ourselves as infinitely spiritual before we can become the visibility of our divineness to ourselves.

God is the source for all the answers to the continuing challenging of the understanding of our divinity. Presently, all things describing our self-aware existence are eternally manifested at the level of our self-aware God-understanding. Our infinite unchosen destiny is forever upheld, by our never-to-be extinguished divinity.

Thus, we can never change reality; we can only infinitely transform our understandings and interpretations of reality. In the foreverness of our existence, we are the divinity of ourselves, understanding ourselves, and expressing ourselves. We are the Self-conscious thoughts knowing and demonstrating the infinitude of God's nature.

Our ever evolving spiritual understanding of things divinely real provides for all of our self-conscious demonstrations of spiritual healing. In our present stage of our collective spiritual evolvement, the healing emollients of truth must be self-consciously declared, avowed, and averred in the spiritual clarity of our understandings, for us to realize the wholiness and wholeness of truth made visible.

Our divine destiny is eternally realized, through the accepting of divine truth. Whatever appears to require healing is an illusion. However, there is no such thing as healing an illusion. Spiritual healing is the self-consciousness of truth made manifest, in the realm of experience, by replacing the claiming-to-be genuine with the real and genuinely true.

Our collective and individual ability to sustain the seeking of truth rests upon a quagmire of uncertainties. The godless unrealities of this world wage a constant assault upon our efforts for self-conscious spiritual enlightenment. We can never adequately repel the attacks of godless unreality until we understand ourselves to be divinely indestructible.

At present, we are only capable of temporarily raising our spiritual awareness to accept the forever pure, forever whole, and forever harmonious to experience the power of divine healing, as a result of the self-realizing of divinity interred into our forever beingness. However, in the ever awareness of divine truth, the only thing ever requiring healing is the self-conscious elimination of our self-conscious accepting of spiritual ignorance.

Our spiritual ignorance highlights again how we as individual members of God's family are in a spiritually primitive state, in our collective eternal enslavement to the godless claims clamoring to exist in this world. Our only escape from our self-accepted assertions of godless unreality is the divinity of truth understood, held firm, interpreted, and self-consciously practiced at the forever level of our self-spiritual unfoldment.

Since our progression of spiritual knowledge is infinite, our progressions in the spiritual realizations of truth are infinite Thus, from our contemporary individual perspective; our experiencing of existence requires the seeming need for healing. Healing results from our understandings of the wholeness and wholiness of God's divine nature empowered by our spiritual understanding and then replacing our self-misinterpretations of the forever real.

Presently, our individual and combined knowledge of divine truth are increasingly incremental. Our present perceptions of reality are rooted in our past understandings of truth. There comes a time in our eternal self-evolving when the power of our unwavering understandings of truth heals instantaneously, by our self-realizing and self-accepting of the forever divinely true.

The spiritually successful outcome of truth declared requires no thankfulness to God. It would be foolish to thank God who knows nothing of the paralyzing vapors of our objectively transpiring existence. God is indifferent to each one of us, as indifferent as the sun is to the heavenward stretchings of roses seeking the warmth of life.

From our perspective, the affirming actions of our spiritual understandings are spiritual bridges to our God-identity. However, no spiritual bridges ever directly coming from God to us. No God watches over us. No God comforts us. No God cares for us. No God heals us. No God loves us. We are each divinely self-consciously alone to discover our divinity, realize our destiny, and to forever understand our forever beingness.

To feel the urge to be thankful to God is interesting because we are individually and collectively part of God. None of us ever asked to exist in the context of being an infinite part of God. Thus, to be thankful to God is to be grateful for our infinite existence. Thus, the question remains as to whether or not our infinite existence in God is something for which we should be thankful.

Still, it is always spiritually beneficial to be grateful, for our existence, and grateful for our ability to understand the foreverness of God's nature, forever blessing us with the truth of His divine beingness. Our understanding of God's nature enables us to spiritually quench all of our so-called needs of objective existence, including the need for healing.

Our existence would be one of experiencing an infinite reality of chaos if our forever reality was not God's reality. Without the self-awareness of our forever God-identity, we would be incapable of interpreting the trueness of ideas. We would be incapable of understanding actual reality and non-real reality. Actual reality and non-real reality would then combine uncontrollably, as the infinite total expression of reality.

Divine healing is a result of truth self-consciously directed, understood, accepted, and obeyed. All self-consciously created experiences are unreal, in the physical environments of our present objective existence. Thus, only our self-conscious misinterpretations of our experiences require healing through divine truth understood and accepted.

Our desire for healing is, in fact, our willingness to overcome our spiritually limiting perspectives. We need only know that our indestructible divinity, keeps us forever safe from all the false avowals of unreality's godless claims drumming incessantly for our attention.

Authentic divine healing is the result of our self-aware acceptance of idea realm ideas, in their spiritual wholeness and wholiness of their forever purity. Then, these spiritually whole ideas manifest in our lives as truth understood, realized, and accepted replacing accumulated false perceptions, with divine truth made visible. All divine truth-based healings result from the self-realization of our forever indestructible divinity.

Following is a review of the key concepts for the successful demonstration of the process of self-consciously understanding the forever divinely true and reliable, as acceptance, understanding, petition, or whatever terminology is preferable. We heal as we self-acknowledge and accept our divinity; we heal as we understand our divinity; we heal as we self-consciously put divine claim to our divinity, and we heal as we demonstrate our divinity.

The appearance of healing results from self-allowing the reality of divine truth to replace the non-reality of self-accepted falseness. Non-reality is an illusion. Divine truth does not heal anything, real or non-real. Healing is not a function of our forever existence. The appearance of healing results from our self-conscious spiritual evolvement which allows the acceptance of divine truth into our self-awareness.

Our true identity is spiritual. Our forever self-beingness is the expression of God. Our mind is the mind of God individualized. Our existence is indestructible, eternal, and everlastingly infinite. We are the divine champions of God forever banishing the testimonies of non-reality into their identifiable self-nothingness.

Our real divine identities rest securely in the objective reality of time-filled timelessness. As spiritual beings, we have always existed, exist now, and always shall exist in ultimate perfection, undisturbed by any false illusions attracted to our spiritually unwashed thoughts.

The purpose for our existence in objective reality is to discover our divine selves, understand our divine selves, and experience our divine selves so that we may accept the spiritual wonders objective reality joyfully offers. We are rewarded for our genuine spiritual understanding of infinity. We exist to demonstrate our infinite existence as the spirituality of divine wholeness.

Every eternity in objective reality is our eternal home for the realizing of experiences. Whatever seemingly appears as the experience of disharmony in any form is the falseness of reality trying mightily to darken the forever process, of our spiritual awakenings and reawakenings. By self-accepting the claims of godless non-reality, we allow the understanding of our forever divinity to be corrupted and distorted into perverted shadows of the divine.

However, throughout eternities everlasting, no one has ever been harmed, lost, died, or separated from God. In other words, the intactness of our infinitely divine existence has never been touched by anything claiming a godless reality of its own. Our individualized beingness is the indestructibility of infinitely real divine permanence. We are the divine truth of ourselves forever denying the ungodly untruths of ourselves.

Whatever manifests as disharmony is our false interpretation of reality given power, by our non-spiritualized interpretations of ideas. False understandings or beliefs manifest as self-created experiences; but again, self-created experiences are not real. Our self-created experiences represent our interpreting of reality and non-reality into objective existence.

Dangers of every variety are always an eternal and ever-present possibility due to chance, opportunity, randomness, and general unpredictability. To spiritually conquer objective reality requires making these unpredictable influences powerless, as we spiritually evolve in the understanding power, of our self-directed self-awareness. Every unforeseen danger is a spiritual opportunity to praise our infinite existence with divine truth self-acknowledged, understood, and demonstrated.

Final spiritual victory is to experience objective reality, without the withering hammerings of doubtfulness. We only doubt things we do not understand. When doubts circumscribe our self-awareness, we are ceding the power of our self-conscious existence to the seemingly non-understandable.

Our forever increasing spiritual awareness is our opportunity to bring the wholiness of conviction into our self-conscious understandings and thus, remove the imprints of hesitation, uncertainty, and confusion. The divinity of truth is never confusing. We interpret the confusion of complexity into our acceptance of divine truth because our understanding of our self-aware objective existence is a confusion of ideas understood incrementally.

We are forever the only authors of confusion; ultimate reality and God are never confused. Self-conscious existence is confusing because we forever interpret our reality as we forever understand the reality of our forever beingness. There are spiritually unknown aspects of our forever identity that we have not spiritually evolved to the point of understanding. Infinity is the author of surprises.

God is Self-aware of Himself but knows nothing beyond His Self-realized identity. For God, there is nothing to know, understand, experience, or to be, other than Himself. He forever is and for Him, nothing else evermore exists. His Isness regarding each of us is His infinite forever divine nature unmovingly grounded within us.

To successfully dispel the false illusions of reality, we must embrace a self-conscious awareness of God, embrace a self-conscious identity with God, and embrace a self-conscious desire to remain obedient, to God's indwelling divine presence, forever active within us. It is God's presence within each of us that drives our infinite desire to understand our infinite divinity.

God is Self-consciously impersonal and knows nothing of our existence or our transbeingness. God knows nothing of the tribulations we experience, as we self-consciously choose to separate ourselves from His divine presence. We may self-consciously choose to separate ourselves from God, but our infinite divine interweaving with God is never broken or abridged.

Our experiences always reflect the self-conscious spiritual substance of our thoughts. As sincere and honest seekers of truth, we recognize and understand that the realizing of our destiny is tied irrefutably to the things we cherish and cultivate in our thought-thoughts. Our infinite ability to understand reality gives us the power to express the things we self-consciously adore.

Thus, our picturing forth of self-accepted understandings of our interpretation of existence, in the realm of experience is the reflection of things we self-consciously love, desire, covet, cherish, accept and adore as the defining of who and what we are. Thus, our objective existence consists of defining, redefining, and *undefining* ourselves.

All things occurring to us happen within the confines and limits of our individualized self-awareness. More precisely, whatever happens to us is interpreted into an accepted form of understanding, by our individualized self-conscious mind, and the results manifests, in the experiencing of our existence.

Our interpretations of objective reality become the objective reality we accept, and thereby becomes our finite-infinite fate, realized as ongoing spiritual stepping-stones, to our forever self-discover stomping out our divinity, through eternity following eternity. Each eternity traveled provides the substance, we self-thinking shape to discover and understand the expressions of our forever divinity.

We have no choice in the matter when it comes to the process of understanding ourselves, in our experiencing of existence. In other words, in our infinite non-self-asked-for self-existence, we have no choice but to follow our infinite existence forever and ceaselessly.

Unfortunately or fortunately, our unlimited ability to understand reality has the forever capability of being infinitely self-corrupted, by the siren calls of non-reality. Our self-acceptance of unreality's false interpretation of reality is the source of all of our infinite sorrow. However, it is the overcoming of unreality's claims for existence that enables each of us to understand the power of our divinity.

Our spiritually defined destiny is our individual and shared destiny. This destiny is only achieved in one eternity at a time. Our forever spiritual destiny is to understand or not understand our infinite divinity until the time comes when the deity of truth is the only truth; we are capable of accepting, interpreting, and understanding. When this occurs, it is still a forever finite-infinite process.

The greater our self-conscious separation from our self-identity to God, the greater becomes our misinterpretations of idea realm ideas. Thus, all our misrepresentations of ideas are the root-cause of all disharmonies that so often break in upon us, and godlessly corrupt our experiencing of life, weakening our self-will and resolve to evolve spiritually.

Our ability to misinterpret ideas results from our lack of self-motivation to have the purity of divine desire to interpret and understand ourselves as divinely perfect, infinite, and indestructible. Our self-limiting and unlimited ability to misunderstand ourselves prevents us from being able to separate the goodness in reality from the non-goodness of a godless self-claiming reality.

Thus, each one of us is forever determining the reality of understanding we chose to live. Still, no matter how we decide to experience the living of life, ultimate reality continues to shower us with the blessings of reality's wonderments. Whatever we self-choose to experience in the living of life is a blessing because, in the self-experiencing of our lives, we are forever interpreting ourselves to ourselves, in bewitching environments of forever enchantment.

In the foreverness of ultimate reality, we are infinitely discovering our true divine selves. Thus, infinity forever gives us that which we self-choose to accept. When the interpretations of ourselves are spiritually based and correct, we know ourselves divinely. When the interpretations of ourselves are spiritually false and incorrect, we understand ourselves non-divinely. Either way, we are cognizant of our forever self-identity.

Each of us self-consciously exists as a process of spiritual understanding, unfoldment, and progression. God's existence is infinite, but our existence is both finite-infinite and infinite because we self-consciously experience life as existence. Our self-awareness of reality means that we can realize the totality of God's wholiness, as it corresponds to our divine progression. Ultimate reality is for each of us to discover, understand, and experience individually, uniquely, and forever. Thus, infinity's gift to us is the forever well of infinite knowledge. We self-consciously exist to infinity understand infinite existence which can only be understood finite-infinite. To each of us, finiteness is infinite.

How marvelous is that? Waiting for each of us is objective reality consisting of infinite eternities to explore, understand, interpret, experience, and enjoy. Thus, there is a forever ongoing progression of wonders unimaginable, to our present stage of our seeming spiritual enslavement and ineptitude. Still, consider that we have infinitely existed, and this is our present collective state of our infinite evolving spirituality! We are pathetic spiritual creatures, unworthy of infinite self-aware existence. As we presently exist, we are, without exception, blaspheming our forever divinity.

Exploring the foreverness of infinity is our endless and continuous destiny. Thus, our forever divinely designed fate for our infinite self-aware existence is unchanging, but it can be and forever is misconstrued, and thus our divine fate becomes subjectively changed. Our real and non-real selves comprise our knowingness of infinite reality. Thus, we are forever knowing and forever unknowing our forever selves. We are infinitely divine, and we have our place in infinity to reject our divinity.

Our spiritual impetus should always be, to dedicate and rededicate ourselves to be kind in our actions, forgiving in self-realization of truth, and unswerving in our desire to seek our self-conscious unity with God. When we choose to self-consciously deny our divine bonding heritage to God, our experiences of existence become nagging burdens, resulting from our willful shredding, shattering, and tattering of divine truth, rather than the blessings of divinity self-realized and embraced as our divine destiny.

Forever enthroned in the unopened chambers of our self-awareness is the reality of our true divine identity waiting infinitely for our self-recognition. Our spiritual desire for happiness, joy, and progress must self-*wantingly* permeate forever, the channeling of our divine self-awareness. For the successful declarations of divine truth, our wrongful and self-destructive acts must cease, by the manifesting authority of our self-divinity.

Otherwise, our self-consciousness becomes uncontrollably jostled, tickled, scratched, bounced, plummeted, and badgered about by the godless whims of chance, opportunity, randomness, and general unpredictability. None of us ever asked to exist forever in this never-ending war for dominance for the self-realizing control over our experiencing of existence. Still, our only hope for finite-infinite salvation is to understand, accept, and self-consciously obey our forever divinity in God, abiding forever within us.

To our present state of our spiritual unfoldment, we are what we choose to be in experience. Divine prayer-like petitions to ourselves become our acceptance of divine truth in dynamic self-expression, through us. The realizing of our forever destiny is to see divinity in all things, accept divinity in all things, and experience the divinity of all things.

Through the process of self-experiencing existence, we are continually reinforcing our accepted beliefs about ourselves. Thus, our destiny as we trek through eternity after eternity is to uncover our true divine selves, when our false selves emerge from the realms of our experiences, to captivate and enslave our self-awareness to accept an unreal understanding of ourselves.

The highest truth in our experiencing of life is to brand into our self-awareness, the realization that our spiritually oppressed self-willed desires control and determine the fulfilling of our divine destiny. Thus, our spiritually oppressed desires drive the understandings and interpretations of our divinity in expression. Our spiritual non-oppressed freedom forever and always chooses to understand our self-divinity in God.

In our affirmations of divine knowingness, we must speak the truth, affirm the truth, accept the truth and obey the truth or our self-divinity remains unexpressed. Our successful acceptance of things forever pure and divine depends on the spiritual certainties and depth of our spiritual understandings. We cannot instantaneously create a spiritually-grafted certainty of divine existence because spiritualized certainty is the outcome of our desires. We should begin now and always to choose self-consciously to live self-consciously in the presence of God.

Without self-cherishing the qualities inherent in our divinity, we cannot experience those qualities. In our realizing of the divinity of truth with unshakeable conviction, there is no opposing power having real self-existence. The degree of our spiritual depth perception always coincides with our self-conscious desire to be kind, forgiving, truthful, tolerant, and obedient to the evolving of our self-divinity.

The infinite presence of God within us is our collective soul. In the unity of our thoughts, we as members of God's family, have the same divine soul-mind, abiding equally within each one of us. Our existence mandates our earnest dedication to the spiritual unfoldment and uplifting of all members of God's forever perfect family. The universal unity we have with God is the permanent bond of our thought-infinite existence.

Through our expressions of the forever true, real happiness results from self-consciously self-experiencing our true selves, rather than desiring the self-experiencing of our false selves. Our destiny is to discover who and what we are, as we are forever confronted by the false assertions of ourselves.

Self-consciously accepting the divinity of truth for the same desired result can be repeated as often as desired. There is no such a thing as an overabundance in the practice and application of divine truth self-realized. It is through the practice of consistently affirming the forever divinely faithful and true, that our self-awareness is uplifted to witness our divinity in expression.

Spiritual affirmations of divine truth embody the demonstrating power of our spiritualized thoughts. Each accepted statement of the everlasting real empowers our spiritual upliftment. Self-consciously affirming the eternal and infinite divinity of reality is always and continuously our evolving spirituality forever manifesting, at the level of our divine understanding, no more, no less.

Our divine affirmations grounded in truth, are unfailingly answered because the answers to our forever affirmations, always correspond to the spiritual depth-density of our divine understanding. Any seeming non-answers to our divinely desired supplications are due to the lack of our self-conscious spiritual receptivity, determined by the strength of our self-conscious commitment to the forever knowingness of our divine identity.

The manifesting of spiritual truth always corresponds, to the degree of our spiritual uncertainties self-consciously subjugated. Sheer will power cannot force spirituality into objective compliance. Only through spirituality desired, embraced, understood, and cherished, is our self-realizing of divine truth earned, in outward appearances.

We subject ourselves to our unevolved spiritual understandings, as we seek to experience the wholiness of our spiritual wholeness. The first step in the realizing of our spiritual power is the recognition of our spiritual impotence. We cannot self-willfully see through our self-imposed blindfolds of unreality and acknowledge the divinity of truth. The power of divine truth, understood, accepted, and self-declared is the final and only divine authority, for the demonstration of divine truth, in the realm of appearance.

All falsely interpreted situations, conditions, or understandings are healed, improved upon, or eliminated through our ever increasing spiritual knowledge, combined with sincere and continuous acts of kindness, expressing as love emblazoned with the Kundalini fire of divine self-assurance. The successful realizing of the forever spiritual valid results from the understanding of what we understand to be forever true.

We must always be grateful for the realization of spiritual truth in action, for it encircles each and every member of God's family with blessings, resulting from our understanding acceptance of God. Our self-realizing of divine revelation brings us to the God of our understanding which enables us to demonstrate our spiritual mastery of things divine, in the realms of our self-expression.

This world about us is awash with heart-numbing tragedies where the experiencing of our self-aware existence often drives us to our knees, not in prayer but total despair. Realizing and accepting the truth for those who are suffering is a spiritual blessing, which enriches ourselves, and enriches all members of God's forever family. Our self-conscious expression of divine truth should always be a giving and a received blessing. The self-acknowledging of our divinity is a blessing we forever give to ourselves.

Without an enduring-caring love for all members of God's family, our spiritual progress becomes nullified, by our inability to inner-reach the love triumphant, forever abiding within the alcove of our God-soul. Thus, we should always endeavor, while meditating on the divinity of truth, to accept divine healing for the hurting, pained, and suffering members of God's family. The divine truth self-known in our self-consciousness is the only truth there is for us to demonstrate. Thus, what we individually spiritually understand can change any experience if we self-consciously possessed the irrevocable power of focused and directed divinity in expression.

The answers to all sincere affirmations of truth are blessings self-deservingly received. Also, even unanswered declarations of truth are blessings because they reveal to our evolving self-conscious awareness, our mind-buried needs to realize our spiritual salvation, from the eternal bumps and thumps of self-accepted errors.

Thus, our recognition of divine truths not understood quickens our spiritual desires to understand and express the forever truly divine. We are infinite divine spiritual beings with an infinitely divine nature. Does it not make sense that each of us should have a self-controlling self-determining understanding of our forever real selves before we embark upon self-accepting realities concerning the understandings of infinite beingness?

Affirming and reaffirming the eternally pure is the expression of our individualized-universal self-consciousness of God's goodness in action. We are grateful for all answers or non-answers resulting from our affirming avowals of the forever real, because, through the process of divine affirmations, we are self-realizing our forever evolving spiritual understandings.

We all suffer through the pains of experiencing our infinite existence. We accept all answers to our directed affirmations as the present divine level of self-unfolding self-awareness of divinity reflected. In the trueness of our forever existence, we are forever in the divine process of understanding ourselves. Let us always spiritually understand ourselves as the self-conscious infinity of our divinity expressing divinely and eternally forever!

By our active self-awareness of the presence of God, we demonstrate our love for one another. We are together and forever the infinitely bonded expression of the one true God, finding our way eternally home. Our eternal and forever home is the understanding of our true self-divine unbroken identity with God, as we self-consciously experience our existence.

Following is an example of accepting and declaring the forever real, for the realizing of divine truth manifesting in the realm of appearance. No two divine affirmations of truth are exactly alike because truth is infinitely understood and eternally and infinitely expressed uniquely. For each one of us, our self-aware relationship with God is the only self-aware relationship there is to God, in all of the infinity of ultimate reality. In the self-realizing of our forever individualized divine mind, we each possess all-powerfulness in infinity. No one has any greater healing power of understanding than another. The only thing that separates two individuals is the depth of divine spiritual self-knowingness.

For the organization and applicability of divine truth, this form of affirming the forever divinely true and real has three primary components. First; we must raise our self-conscious spiritual self-awareness to understand and accept only the infinitely true and real. Second, we claim for ourselves the forever power of truth self-realized. Third, we must be grateful for our ability to bring the forever reality of divinity, into the realm of experiencing life, as existence. If we are not thankful for our understanding of divine truth, we have not spiritually earned an understanding of the divinity in truth.

Affirming the Forever True

I am a unique individualized and indestructible expression of God, forever divinely unfolding throughout the infinite arrays of self-creating universes. I am one with God in all manners of my spiritual expressions. My infinite destiny is to increase forever, in my self-conscious awareness and self-acceptance, of the presence of God. In the objective realm, I am the expression of God's goodness forever touching all reality, with the harmony of divine wholeness.

My present purpose is to experience each new eternity in harmony, joy, wonderment, and ever increasing happiness. The wholeness of God is the wholeness of my self-divinity in current and forever expression. I affirm the divine essence of God is forever internalized within me, as an ever-streaming outward flowing of golden divine spiritual truths, interlacing my self-conscious divinity with my self-conscious identity, which is the divine source of my forever beingness.

I affirm that whatever God is, I am. I understand and accept the realization, that God and I are united in infinite indestructibility and wholeness. We exist together in the oneness of reality. God and I exist forever in eternal, perpetual perfection, harmony, joy, and the love of self-conscious existence. I am now and always the forever heir to the allness of God's nature.

God forever dwells peacefully within the depths of my self-beingness, as the essence and substance of my ceaselessly-existing soul. I am the forever the self-evolving self-awareness of God individualized. I accept the foreverness of my understanding of self-aware existence as an infinite blessing. My eyes are the individualized eyes of God seeing only divinity in expression.

My infinite never-ending desire is to explore, discover, express, and experience the continuing progression of the true divine essence of my self-conscious beingness. I am an individualized expression of God existing in the full glory and light of divine truth. My soul is God's light shining forever brightly, into the far-reaching corners of my forever existence.

Nothing unlike the reality of God is part of my genuine and real identity which is my infinite self-divinity proclaiming the purity of God's forever-presence, within me. I am the individualized self-consciousness of God, loving and embracing all that I see, all that I understand, all that I interpret, and all that I am.

I now bring my self-consciousness into harmony with the presence of God's Beingness and essence. I am the self-actualization of God's existence permeating all the realms I forever inhabit. These words consist of my understanding of divine truth, and the understanding of my wholly oneness in and with God. I affirm my spiritual understanding forever returns to me, at the spiritual level of my divine receptivity to all things true, real and forever.

Accepting the Forever True

For my beloved wife, I accept these divine truths. For my wife, I affirm the perfect idea of a healthy and pain-free body. I declare that my wife is a forever divine member of God's family, and therefore she is divinely self-consciously entitled to accept the Godliness of good, the Godliness of wholeness, and the Godliness of wholiness as her self-divinity in expression. I affirm for her, the wholeness of the idea-concept of a healthy and energetic heart.

For my wife, I accept the whole and perfect ideas of tranquility and strength. I affirm that as my wife experiences life, she is surrounded by the divinity of love, blessed by the wholiness of vitality, sustained by an ever surrounding aura of divine peace, and vibrant in the joys of experiencing existence. I accept the wholeness of the health-filled idea of harmony and perfection coursing through every function of her physical body.

I affirm for my wife a sincere and forgiving heart combined with a continuing increasing desire to move ever closer, in her self-conscious understanding, to her ever unfolding awareness and acceptance of her divinity as the goodness of God in expression. Thus, I accept goodness and harmony as her true identity. Also, I accept for her, the self-conscious realization that she is the forever self-conscious recipient of divine truths. Her body is the perfection of God individualized.

I affirm that nothing unlike the nature of God is now, ever has been, or ever is attached to her. I accept the realization that her self-awareness is filled with the love of God, a love that eliminates all fears, and illumines her self-consciousness, to be receptive to the divinity of truth only. I affirm her spiritual understanding provides her with divine direction, for the forever unfolding of her infinite divinely ordained and defined destiny.

For my wife, I accept the knowledge that she is in this present world, as an individualized expression of the presence of God, as individualized-Man. I affirm for her that all existence, in the realms of experience, manifests for her understanding, acceptance, interpretation, and enjoyment. Her body is the fulfilling of harmony in expression.

Thus, where peace and balance are understood, the pincers of disharmony are bound in their false appearances to cast no shadows, as I accept for my beloved wife, the forever divinely pure, the divinely true, the divinely real, and the divine holy. I affirm with unchallenged authority that my beloved wife as the expression of God is eternally and infinitely perfect.

I affirm and reaffirm that my wife forever exists in infinite harmony and joy. I affirm there are no assertions of godless unreality having any authority to affect her. She is infinitely divine, and nothing non-divine is ever self-accepted into her forever self-identity. I accept and affirm that she is forever in the love and the presence of God and that she is forever receptive to all things divinely genuine, harmonious, pure, and whole.

Gratefulness for the Forever True

I gratefully realize my beloved wife is a forever divine individualization of God. I am grateful for the realization that all truth in God forever abides within her, as the foreverness of her evolving spiritual self-awareness. I am grateful for the understanding that her infinite existence is the glory of God in individualized expression.

I am grateful for the realization that my wife understands and accepts God, as the source of her infinitely divine beingness. I am grateful for the ability to understand truth and to be able to bring that understanding of truth, into a spiritually meaningful manifestation of divine truth's appearing, in the objective realm of appearance.

I am grateful for the realization that my beloved wife is in truth an unencumbered individualization of divine-Man. There has never been, nor shall there ever be, another self-conscious awareness exactly like that of my beloved wife. I am grateful for the realization that infinity awaits my wife's presence, and all infinity uniquely exists for her understanding, exploration, and experiencing. Thus, infinity is forever expecting my wife's self-aware presence.

I gratefully acknowledge each eternity in the endlessness of eternities, exists for her to explore, experience, and enjoy in her own divinely distinctive and unique manner. I am grateful for the realization she is part of permanent divine existence, forever expressing harmoniously. I am thankfully grateful she is the self-conscious love of God in active spiritual expression.

Thus, I am grateful for the truth she is a forever manifestation of God's love, joy, peace, and harmony in appearance. I am grateful for the truth of these realizations giving me the ability to understand the truth, know the truth, speak the truth, and bring the truth, into the realm of experience. I am forever grateful to know and direct truth for the forever spiritual upliftment of my beloved wife.

Finally, I am grateful for the divine understanding that my beloved wife is a representative of God, in the divinely continuing marvels; we accept and understand, as the experiencing life as existence. I am grateful that my beloved wife forever expresses the goodness of God, the love of God, the heart of God and the wholiness of God. I affirm that my wife is forever blessing the entirety of God's perfect family, with her self-styled love of God.

These self-conscious self-actualizing truths represent my understanding of my beloved wife's divinity in expression. In the realizing of these truths, I am eternally and forever grateful.

> A life is either all spiritual or not spiritual at all. No
> Man can serve two masters. Your life is shaped by
> The end you live for. You are made in the image of
> What you desire.
>
> Thomas Merton

Appendix

Questions

After completing this work, I made a google search to find questions concerning some of the concerns others have arising from the assumed existence of God. To those individuals, the nature of God and the circumstances concerning the living of life seem irreconcilable. My purpose is to answer those questions from the perspective of my understandings of God, Man, and ultimate reality contained in this work. My ideas in this section may be difficult to understand if this book has not been previously read.

Why does not God heal amputees?

First of all, God does not Self-consciously heal anything or anyone. God is entirely and completely impersonal to our infinite existence. Also, God is not capable of Self-conscious thought and therefore knows nothing of our existence, the existence of ultimate reality, or any need for healing or even any supposed need for healing, which may be self-desired by anyone. In the context of a self-knowing God, there is no such thing as divine healing, spiritual care, or divine intervention.

Without any understanding of God, all healing is based upon worldly understandings of healing, mechanical healing, and automatic healings performed by the functioning of the human body. There is no

God that interdicts Himself into our human affairs and heals anyone. Thus, when it comes to healing without any acknowledgment of God, the man of this world can only rely upon humankind's mechanical understandings of healing. Thus, undoubtedly through the evolving technological advances of humanity, someday amputees will be able to grow new limbs.

However, in my book, I describe divine healing in relationship to God. God is the source of all divine healing. Thus, God is the source of harmony, accord, completeness, wholeness, purity, perfection, et cetera. God healing requires our self-conscious interaction with the idea realm. Also, for successful God healing to take place, our interaction with the idea realm must include our self-conscious spiritual understanding and acceptance of God.

God-based divine healing operates by the following understandings. We are part of God, and all that God is indwells each of us. For God healing to take place, we self-consciously declare our relationship to and with God. We must affirm that the qualities of God also belong to each of us. Then, we self-consciously request the particular idea of healing from the idea realm and combine that idea with the self-conscious strength and conviction of our oneness with God. Thus, healing results from our spiritual understandings and our strength, confidence, and reliability on God alone.

Thus, God healing rests upon us individually and involves the depth and certainty of our divine trustworthiness to the divinity of our understanding. In this God healing, can amputees be restored to their pre-amputee state of physical beingness? The answer is "No" because the spiritual progression of humankind is presently pathetically primitive. Few, if any, God healings are taking place. However, in the future, the answer is "Yes" because there will come a spiritual time of divinity self-known when the healing of amputees will be as easy as smelling a rose.

Why are there so many starving people in the world?

Again, God knows nothing of our world, any world, the individuals in our world, or the conditions of our world. God's infinite awareness consists only of His Infinite Self-knowingness. In our primitive collective stage of spiritual evolvement, all things happening spiritually, in this world, are the result of the unpredictabilities of chance, opportunity, randomness, and general unpredictability.

Thus, the starving people of this world are humanity's problem, not God's. The terrible condition of so many of the world's improvised citizens seems to make self-existence itself undesirable and unfair. If each of us only had one life to experience as self-realized objective existence, the non-fairness of anyone's self-aware existence would be manifestly and completely unexplainable. However, we live untold numbers of lives, and we are infinitely impacted by the randomness, of chance, opportunity, randomness, and general unpredictability. In this book, I discuss this subject in full.

Starving aside, humanity's encounter with all forms of unpredictable unhappiness, results from the forever and always endless stages, of our collective and individual spiritual evolvements. All encounters with grief and sadness should be understood within the realization, that each one of us is an infinite indestructible being that has never been taken advantage of, never been harmed, and never died out of their infinite self-aware existence.

Why do bad things happen to good people?

We are all spiritual beings presently living spiritually deprived existences. The seemingly bad things eternally happening to good people is not by experiencing bad things. The cause of experiencing bad things results from our individual self-interpretations of the things that unpredictably befall us.

Throughout this book, I emphasize the point that all things that ever happen to each of us, occur within the confines of our self-understood awareness. There is an unreal-real outer world of experiences which becomes our objective home, but our interpretations of these unreal-real worlds of experiences are always within the inner realm of our self-aware understandings.

We self-determine our responses to the unpredictability of unfortunate happenings. Thus, it is the spiritual preparation that we each must make within our self-awareness that prevents the experiencing of bad things, by mentally replacing the spiritually untrue with the spiritually true and real. Thus, each of us has the spiritual ability to interpret happiness where seeming unhappiness exists. Bad things happen to good people due to a lack of spiritual diligence to know, embrace, accept, and self-determine the knowingness of our forever evolving spirituality.

If God created the universe, who is it, that created God?

God did not create the universe. Our present universe is the result of ultimate reality's never-ending process, of eternal creations of infinite universes, which also includes infinite physical, purgatorial spiritual worlds, combined with infinite formless realms. In my understanding, each physical universe, which always includes a world for us to inhabit is an eternity. Thus, ultimate reality consists, in part, of infinite ongoing eternities.

Who or what created God? The question should also include who or what created us? The answer to both questions is that God and each one of us have infinitely existed. However, we infinitely exist as part of God. God infinitely exists as a separate component of ultimate reality. Can God's forever existence and our forever existence be empirically proven? No, but it can be, in my opinion, logically inferred.

Each of us has self-aware existence. How or where did our self-awareness originate? Did our self-awareness evolve out of the infinite components of non-self-aware reality, or has our self-awareness infinitely existed? I prefer to believe that our self-awareness and God's

Self-awareness has existed infinitely, rather than to believe that we self-consciously evolved godless matter.

Because we have self-awareness, and we function in a reciprocal relationship with the idea realm, we are capable of self-conscious thought. Since we are capable of self-conscious thought, we are capable of understanding. Thus, through our self-acquired ability to self-consciously understand things, we have the infinite power of self-determination, through the exercise of our free will. Also, since we have the capacity to understand the infinity of all things, we know that God exists, and we know that each of us is part of God.

The purpose of our self-existence and God's Self-existence is answerable and is the subject of this book. However, the "why" of our forever existence and the purpose for our forever existence are two separate subjects. We understand the purpose for our infinite existence, but the "why" of our infinite existence is not knowable. We infinitely exist, but none of were created, and none of us ever chose to exist infinitely. Thus, to me, there is unfairness to an infinitely imposed existence, an infinite imposed existence, from which there is no escape.

Does God have Free Will?

The direct answer is "No." However, I discuss this subject in my chapter on God and reference it throughout this work. In short, God does not have a free will, and He does not eternally punish anyone. God does not create natural catastrophes nor does He permit them to happen or not happen. All catastrophes are the result of chance, opportunity, randomness, and general unpredictability, or planned evil.

How do we tell false religions from authentic religions?

Each of us is at his or her spiritual growth-point of divine understanding. Therefore, what is spiritually appealing to one person may not be spiritually appealing to another. What is of spiritual importance, in the considering of what religion to give self-conscious allegiance too, is in the determining of whether or not that religion is a catalyst for true spiritual growth.

Rituals and dogmas fulfill needs and have their place. However, it is primarily those spiritual things which promote the transformative spiritual demonstrations of divine truth, which are of divinely supreme importance. In other words, does a religious belief system encourage its followers to be the proponents of kindness, tolerance, love, and compassion?

Spiritual understanding without the demonstration of kindly goodness is comparable to unthawed ice. To spiritually know the divine course of action to be taken in experiencing the circumstances of life is one thing; but, to self-consciously take those actions is another. Spiritual understandings must be grounded in spiritual conviction. Even so, we are forever the spiritual or non-spiritual understanding of ourselves in expression.

Sincere followers of God recognize the depth or non-depth of their self-acquired spirituality. A true religion encourages its followers to understand who they are and helps them move divinely forward in their expressions of kindly goodness – which is the visible and tangible outpouring of God's love.

If God sometimes interferes in human events, why didn't He either prevent the Holocaust or arrange for it to end sooner?

God does not have the ability or capacity to interfere in the human events or affairs of man. God knows nothing of the evil doings of humanity and nothing of the eternal processions of physical worlds. Immortal Man always determines, in his expressions of eternal transbeingness, the evolving of his eternal destiny. All things good or bad, unexpectedly appearing in our physical world, are the result of chance, opportunity, randomness, and general unpredictability or dictated by proclivities of man. We are the cause and result of all things happening to us; God is divinely uncaring concerning all events happening in our infinite existence.

Also, most often physical-Man, due to his lack of spiritual desire or understanding, temporarily relinquishes his supreme ability to influence events to the collective group-think of humankind. It is physical-Man, alone, who guides and directs the power that spiritually leads and guides him onward throughout the timelessness of eternities. However, God is now and has always been the source-power of the divine understanding of himself.

If we pray for an answer to a question, how do we know God answers?

God does not have the ability to answer our prayers; thus, God answers none of our prayers. For God to answer prayers, would presuppose that God was aware of our self-conscious divine solicitations, much less Self-aware of our individual lives. God never Self-consciously knows us, watches over for us, guides us, comforts us, heals us, or loves us. God has no Self-awareness of our existence. Each of us is the sole determiner for the answers to our prayers.

Seeking any form of guidance, intervention, or comfort from God, outside of our individual self-conscious awareness is utterly futile. Still, God is our eternal and infinite source of all of that is divinely true and real. God is the infinite Provider for the fulfilling of our spiritual needs. Our spiritual needs are fulfilled from our individual perspective, that God always answers our needs.

All that we ever receive from God, we receive by self-consciously identifying ourselves with His ever-presence, within each one of us. Our individual relationship with God is such that we never ask Him for anything. In the understanding of our true spirituality, we fulfill our human and divine needs by raising our spiritual consciousness, to accept the wholeness of ideas which brings us the expression of God's nature, into the realm of appearance.

It is the inner nature of God, dwelling within each one of us which is our eternal guide, eternal comforter, eternal healer, and constant protector. The infinite nature of God's Beingness forever calls to us, forever talks to us, and forever guides but only as we are self-aware and self-accepting of His infinite divine presence. God's Isness is the only thing real to God, and God's Isness is our individual, eternal, and infinite destiny to understand.

If God told you to kill a child would you do it? If God told someone else to kill a child, would you interfere?

From my perspective, this question is beyond absurd. First, since God is not aware of our existence, He certainly does not overtly talk to us; thus, He could not ask us to do anything. Second, in my book, I emphasize the sanctity of all life. To take any life is spiritual darkness; such darkness is forever unknown to God.

God is the forever soul of each one of us and thus the forever source of our divine inspiration. Our true nature is forever divine, and we infinitely possess an inner divine compass guiding our self-identity to combine the infinite nature of God, in ever increasing evolvement and unfoldment. Thus, anyone who takes an innocent life does not understand divine himself, his divine destiny, or his God.

If God gave us intelligence, would not He want us to examine our beliefs with reason?

Of course, but God did not give us intelligence. We are the individualized self-conscious expression of God. Our self-consciousness combined with idea realm ideas produces our self-ability to think self-consciously. Through our ability to self-think, we develop intelligence. Our developing intelligence produces knowledge and knowledge coupled with our growing receptivity to and understanding of things spiritual eventually gives each one of us the infinite quality of all-powerfulness.

Thus, in the developing of our self-conscious understanding, we do, indeed, examine our beliefs with reason. In this self-aware mental process, we forever seek the everlastingly dependable and uproot the forever untrue. The process of self-consciously examining our beliefs is integral to our individual spiritual progression. The above thoughts are an abridged summary of my thoughts, on this subject expressed throughout this work.

What exactly is Hell?

I exhaustively describe what Hell in my chapter Physical, Purgatorial, Spiritual worlds, but I will express a few words on the subject now. Contrary to present assumptions about Hell; Hell is not a place for eternal or infinite punishment. I discuss punishment in full, in my non-physical purgatorial-Man section. Hell is the eternal abode for individuals who self-willfully reject God.

Thus, Hell is a locale where God is not present, is not sought, and cannot be found. Hell is a punishment free place. There is eternal punishment, but that punishment occurs in the mental realm of purgatory, where all punishment for all wrongdoings, is self-consciously imposed upon ourselves. Physical Hell would be punishment for believers in God, but it is not punishment for non-believers.

In physical Hell, there is no source of life, there is no experiencing of life, and most assuredly there is no love of life. This godless physical Hell is a place of eternal self-knowingness without God. Thus, Hell is self-awareness of godlessness, without the ability to change a constant self-aware knowingness of godlessness. Hell is self-existence without purpose, other than to eternally be godless in an environment of godlessness.

In this book, I describe the three essential qualities for the self-achieving of spirituality First: we should always try to express kindness. Second: We should always try to protect all life. Third: we should always try to seek, find, follow, and faithfully obey the God of our understanding. Would a loving God, cast any individual into a designed and designated infinite hellish place of everlasting punishment, if the only spiritual knowingness that individual ever practiced were the above three?

Which holidays may be celebrated together?

We should be happy for all persons who have found, followed, and obeyed the God of their understanding, if the God of their understanding encourages them to progress spiritually. There is no right or wrong understanding of God. There are only good and evil expressions in an individual's self-understanding of God. Either the manifestations in the experiencing of life are God-based or not God-based; simple as that.

We should celebrate with all those who have found their way spiritually, even if their spiritual way may not be the same as ours. Holidays represent individuals' enjoying their faith in the God of their understanding. We can all be grateful for everyone who has found their way to God, and we can if we so choose, share in the joyousness of their understanding of spirituality, accepted, and demonstrated.

If complex design requires a designer, who is it that designed God?

God cannot empirically be proven to exist or proven not to exist. This question involves the understanding of infinite existence itself. We know that we self-consciously live because we are self-consciously experiencing reality, which is the purpose of the self-conscious living of our lives. However, we will never understand why we exist to experience existence.

There is no convincing answer to the question: Why is there such a thing as reality itself, especially the reality of our self-awareness, and the reality of God's Self-awareness? The more interesting question is: If our self-aware existence is infinite, without any beginning or ending, is such an infinite self-aware existence something infinitely desirable?

I have discussed this issue throughout the writing of my book, and I have yet to come up with a definitive answer. However, I lean towards the understanding that our infinite self-aware existence is not such a desirable thing.

To ask questions presupposes there are answers. To answer questions presupposes the understanding of answers is possible. We know that we self-consciously exist. We are aware that we self-consciously think. We understand that there are things we do not understand. We are mindful of the fact that we possess the ability to attempt to explain the things we do not understand.

So, all that any of us can ever do is to seek understanding answers meaningful to ourselves. In this book, I describe the existence of God, the reality of Man, and the truth of ultimate reality, in a manner meaningful to me. If that understanding makes me a better self-aware individual, what difference does it make if my perceptions of reality are correct or not correct? If my perceptions of reality make sense to you, I say "Mazel Tov." If my perceptions of reality do not make sense to you, I say "Mazel Tov."

Therefore, what difference does it make how God is self-interpreted and self-understood if that understanding comforts and encourages individuals to live morally purposeful lives, either spiritually based or non-spiritually based? If there comes a Judgment Day, how could God punish anyone who's sincerely attained divine realizations, if those divine realizations made them better human beings, either morally and or spiritually?

Is there a crime that deserves punishment forever?

There is no sin, evil, or crime that deserves eternal or infinite punishment. First of all, there is no actual reality to the committing of any sin, evil, or crime. All things that ever happen to us happen as experiences and experiences are interpreted, in the confines of our individualized self-awareness, and are infinitely unreal.

Experiences are not real, in the sense that they have any infinite identity of their own, in ultimate reality. We eternally punish ourselves for our interpretations of our self-aware existence, as shown and revealed to us in the reflections of our self-interpretations of ourselves, in the non-real realm of appearance.

In this book, I thoroughly discuss the concept of punishment. In short, each one of us is punished eternally infinitely for our wrongful, sinful, and evil acts of godlessness. Also, we are eternally and infinitely rewarded for the goodness we have shown to ourselves and others. Thus, our infinite existence consists, in part, of endless punishment and endless rewards.

How can Heaven be a happy place and do we have a free will in Heaven?

Again, these are questions that I have discussed and answered throughout this work. Basically, how can anyone be happy in Heaven, if he or she knows their loved ones are suffering on earth? The answer to this question involves understanding the interwoven relationship between each one of us as individualized-Man, God, and ultimate reality.

Simply, our infinite, immortal, and individual existence is forever unharmed, untouched, and indestructible. Thus, the things we experience in this world have absolutely no impact on the forever and infinite individualized-Us. In fact, all things happening to us in the physical realms of appearance are spiritual learning opportunities. In Heaven, we know that our loved ones are experiencing their infinite self-existence, which is forever pure, whole, and indestructible, and they are forever held safe in the Palm of God.

Do we have a free will in Heaven? We are infinite beings; each one of us possesses an infinite free will. Thus, in Heaven, we have a free will. However, Heaven is a destination for those who have attained illumined spiritual understanding. Our self-attained illumined spiritual knowledge automatically prevents us from thinking or acting in any way contrary to our self-aware evolved spiritual realizations of ultimate reality. In Heaven, we have a free, but our self-attained spiritual understanding prevents us from doing anything ungodly, in Heaven.